Banking on Stability

Banking on Stability

Japan and the Cross-Pacific Dynamics of International Financial Crisis Management

Saori N. Katada

Ann Arbor

The University of Michigan Press

Published in the United States of America by
The University of Michigan Press
Manufactured in the United States of America
♾ Printed on acid-free paper

2004 2003 2002 2001 4 3 2 1

A CIP catalog record for this book is available from the British Library.

Library of Congress Cataloging-in-Publication Data

Katada, Saori N.
Banking on stability : Japan and the cross-Pacific dynamics of international financial crisis management / Saori N. Katada.
p. cm.
Includes bibliographical references and index.
ISBN 0-472-11211-2 (Cloth : alk. paper)
1. Japan—Foreign economic relations. 2. International finance. 3. Financial crises. I. Title.
HF1601 .K288 2001
337.52—dc21 2001001085

For my parents,
Toru and Hiroko Nakai

Contents

List of Figures ix
List of Tables xi
Acknowledgments xiii
List of Abbreviations xv

Introduction 1

Part 1. Theory, Background, and Data

1. The Motivation to Cooperate, Lead, and Follow 19
2. Japan's Economic Integration: Developing Regions and the United States 35
3. Quantitative Analysis: The Latin American Debt Crisis and Japan's Official Financial Flows 76

Part 2. Latin America

4. Introduction to the Comparative Case Study of Latin America 117
5. Japan and the Latin American Debt Crisis 123
6. Japan in the Mexican Peso Crisis and Its Repercussions 145

Part 3. Asia

7. Introduction to the Case Study of Asia 167
8. Japan and the United States in the Asian Financial Crisis Management 172

Conclusion: International Cooperation and Financial Crisis Management 209

Appendixes 221
Notes 231
Bibliography 265
Index 295

Figures

2.1 Regional distribution of Japan's total trade, 1973–98 37
2.2 Japan's trade balance with regions, 1973–98 40
2.3 Japan's foreign aid to various regions, 1970–98 43
2.4 Japan's other official flows (OOFs) to various regions, 1970–94 47
2.5 Composition of capital flows to developing countries in the 1990s 54
2.6 GDP growth of the United States and Japan, 1982–99 59
2.7 Real gross fixed capital formation, 1982–99 60
2.8 Share in world exports: The United States and Japan, 1973–98 61
2.9 US trade deficit with Japan and with the world, 1976–98 62
2.10 US total trade with Japan and with the world, 1976–98 63
2.11 Japan's long-term external asset: Stock and change, 1984–94 66
2.12 US long-term net liabilities to Japan and other foreign countries, 1969–97 68
2.13 Yen-dollar exchange rate fluctuation, 1971–2000 70
2.14 Real long-term interest rates of the United States and Japan, 1969–99 73
3.1 Net financial flows to Latin America from the United States and Japan, 1975–91 79
3.2 Japan's ODA and OOF to Latin America, 1976–91 82
3.3 Official flows and debt outstanding, average 1983–90 84
3.4 Official flows and total trade with Japan, average 1983–90 85
3.5 Official flows and GNP per capita, average 1983–90 86
5.1 Bank loans outstanding in Latin America, Japan, and the United States, 1980–88 134
8.1a The composition of foreign capital inflows into Asia, 1990–98 200
8.1b The composition of foreign capital inflows into Latin America, 1990–98 201
8.2 Country origin of bank debt in Thailand, Indonesia, and South Korea in 1997 202

Tables

2.1 Top Ten ODA Donors, 1980–1998 38

2.2 The Progress of JEXIM Bank Untied Loan Commitments by Region 47

2.3 Japan's Foreign Direct Investment by Region, 1965–1997 49

2.4 Samurai Bond Issuance, 1990–1998 55

2.5 World's Top Ten Banks in Terms of Their Capital 64

2.6 Composition and Geographical Distribution of Japan's Long-Term Net Capital Outflows, 1985–1991 67

3.1 Top Five Latin American Recipients of Japan's ODA and OOF, 1976–1991 83

3.2 Models, Variables, and Their Expected Signs from Time-Series Models (one-year, one-data-point variables) 90

3.3 Time-Series Regression with ODA as the Dependent Variable (Model 1) 93

3.4 Time-Series Regression with OOF as the Dependent Variable (Model 2) 95

3.5 Time-Series Regression with Private Capital Flows as the Dependent Variable (Model 3) 97

3.6 Models, Variables, and Their Expected Signs from Time-Series Cross-Section Models (one-year, *N*-data-point variables) 99

3.7 ODA Allocation within Latin America, 1975–1991 (Model 4) 104

3.8 OOF Allocation within Latin America, 1975–1991 (Model 5) 106

5.1 JEXIM Bank's Support to the Brady Plan with Signing Dates and Amounts 131

6.1 Comparison of Net Capital Flows to Seven Latin American Countries, 1982–1997 159

8.1 Japan's Bank Claims in Asia, Year-End 1996 through Year-End 1999 189

8.2 Japan's Foreign Direct Investment in Asia, FY 1995–FY 1998 190
8.3 Changes in US Total Trade with Different Regions, 1991–1997 193
8.4 Changes in Japan's Financial Asset Position in the United States by Investment Category, 1980–1995 194

Acknowledgments

This book would not be here without those who continuously supported me. I extend my utmost gratitude to two mentors of mine, Benjamin (Jerry) Cohen and Timothy J. McKeown. They patiently read and reread the manuscript and generously provided me with invaluable criticisms and suggestions. Their advice and encouragement was indispensable for the completion of my book. I am very grateful as a young scholar to have met these two academics with the greatest minds in their field and commitment to the highest standards in their scholarship. They have set for me a goal to aspire to throughout my professional career.

Generosity of many institutions and people there nurtured this project. Funding and fellowships from the Tinker Foundation, the Social Science Research Council (Japan Program), the University of North Carolina at Chapel Hill, and the College of Letters, Arts, and Sciences, the Center for International Studies, as well as the School of International Relations at the University of Southern California, helped me at critical times. The United Nations Development Programme (UNDP) office in Mexico and the World Bank provided me some independent research time while I was working for them full-time. Hitotsubashi University and its faculty greatly facilitated my fieldwork in Tokyo.

Many colleagues, teachers, and friends read the manuscript at its various stages. Three people in particular, Laurie Brand, John Odell, and T. J. Pempel, kindly read the entire manuscript and gave me valuable comments. I thank Karen Adams, Leslie Armijo, Chia-Shang James Chu, Eileen Crumm, Polly Diven, Kim Dietrich, Eileen Doherty, E. V. K. Fitzgerald, Benjamin Fordham, Jeffry Frieden, Michael Fry, Nora Hamilton, Jonathan Hartlyn, Himmat Kalsi, Peter Katzenstein, Jeffrey Knopf, Abraham Lowenthal, Mathias Moersch, Ramon Moreno, Thomas Oatley, Louis Pauly, David Rapkin, Lars Schoultz, Barbara Stallings, Jonathan Strand, James White, Meredith Woo-Cummings, and three anonymous reviewers for their comments. I am also grateful to those in Japan who guided me and helped me gather information and conduct interviews: Nobuhiro Ashida, Masako Ayakawa, Kotaro Horisaka, Mitsuhiro Kagami, Hidesuke Kotajima, Sayuri Kuwabara, Ryo Oshiba, Hideo Sato, Masaharu Shimizu, Toru Yanagihara, and Daizaburo Yui. Of course, I appreciate the generosity of those who kindly gave me their precious time for interviews while I visited Japan and Mexico, as well as various parts of the United States. The assistance of Sung Jun Jo, Yong Wook Lee, Wendy Lords, and Andrew Manning significantly facilitated my research while I was teaching. Editorial assistance by Leslie Wirpsa and helpful suggestions by the Senior Editor for Social Sciences of the University of Michigan Press, Ellen McCarthy, were invaluable.

Finally, I thank my family. This book is dedicated to my parents, Toru and Hiroko Nakai, who have had the misfortune of having such a rebellious daughter, but who have given her the maximum liberty to think and make decisions on her own. I am also very lucky to have another set of parents, James and Verdell Coleman. Ever since I was "adopted" by them as a foreign exchange student in high school, they and their four daughters have been so kind to make me and, later, my husband members of their family. Last but not least, Satoshi and Kay Katada deserve my deepest thanks. They have given me energy and confidence to go on. Satoshi has always been a patient listener and my best friend, and I thank Kay for being such a collaborative baby while I was managing this "double gestation." Without their love and support, completion of this book would not have been possible.

List of Abbreviations

ADB	Asian Development Bank
AGRI	Asia Growth and Recovery Initiative
AMF	Asian Monetary Fund
APEC	Asia Pacific Economic Cooperation
ASEAN	Association of Southeast Asian Nations
BAC	bank advisory committee
BIS	Bank for International Settlements
DAC	Development Assistance Committee
EFF	Extended Fund Facility
ESAF	Enhanced Structural Adjustment Facility
ESF	Exchange Stabilization Fund
FBIS	Foreign Broadcast Information System
FDI	foreign direct investment
FILP	Fiscal Investment and Loan Program
FTAA	Free Trade Area of the Americas
G-5	Group of Five (France, Germany, Japan, the United Kingdom, and the United States)
G-7	Group of Seven (G-5 plus Canada and Italy)
G-10	Group of Ten (G-7 plus Belgium, the Netherlands, Sweden, and Switzerland)
G-77	Group of Seventy-Seven
GAB	General Arrangements to Borrow
GAO	General Accounting Office (of the United States)
GDP	gross domestic product
GNP	gross national product
IBRD	International Bank for Reconstruction and Development
IDA	International Development Association
IDB	Inter-American Development Bank
IFC	International Finance Corporation
IFI	international financial institutions
IIMA	Institute for International Monetary Affairs
IMF	International Monetary Fund
JBIC	Japan Bank for International Cooperation
JCIF	Japan Center for International Finance
JEXIM Bank	Export-Import Bank of Japan
JICA	Japan International Cooperation Agency
LDP	Liberal Democratic Party

LIBOR	London Inter-Bank Offered Rate
LDC	less developed country
MITI	Ministry of International Trade and Industry
MOF	Ministry of Finance
MOFA	Ministry of Foreign Affairs
MOSS	Market-Oriented Sector Selective
NAB	New Arrangements to Borrow
NAFA	North American Framework Agreement
NAFTA	North American Free Trade Agreement
ODA	official development assistance
OECD	Organization for Economic Cooperation and Development
OECF	Overseas Economic Cooperation Fund
OMA	orderly marketing agreement
OOF	other official flows
OPEC	Organization of Petroleum Exporting Countries
PBL	policy-based lending
PCSE	panel-corrected standard errors
PKO	price-keeping operation
SAF	Structural Adjustment Facility
SAL	Structural Adjustment Loan
SECAL	Sector Adjustment Loan
SII	Structural Impediments Initiative
SRF	Supplemental Reserve Facility
TSCS	time-series cross-section
UN	United Nations
UNCTAD	United Nations Conference on Trade and Development
UNU	United Nations University
VER	voluntary export restraint
WIDER	World Institute for Development Economics Research

Introduction

As a series of international financial crises have shaken the world of swift capital mobility and growing financial interdependence in recent decades,[1] international economic leadership in the management of these financial crises becomes critical.[2] These crises have raised concerns over who, if anyone, will step in to rescue those economies in distress and contain the repercussions of these crises to protect the stability of the international financial system.[3] The issue is essential, because through timely and adequate crisis management efforts, the world can achieve international financial stability—a condition we can consider a kind of international public good[4]—after the onset of crises. The theoretical focus of this study is the provision of international public goods in the form of collective international financial crisis management among major creditor powers.

Analyses by economic historians and political scientists of international financial dynamics in the late 1920s into the 1930s demonstrate the devastating effects resulting from a lack of initiative in economic crisis management. In this historical case, the failure to adequately address financial crisis led to the emergence of exclusive bloc economies prior to World War II.[5] To prevent such disaster, private financial sectors and the governments of the countries that are home to the world's leading financial centers are definitely the best candidates to supply such goods, because of their high stake in the stability of global finance and their financial ability to react.

The widely discussed decline after the 1970s of the single leadership of the United States, the post–World War II hegemon, added urgency to the task of economic crisis management in the 1980s, particularly at the time of the Latin American debt crisis. The actions and roles of other major economic powers in association with the United States become a critical factor in maintaining a certain level of stability.[6] The rise of Japan as an economic power and its role as an international financier supporting the United States in the resolution of the Latin American debt crisis provide the case in point. The large financial contribution extended by the Japanese government led to the solution of the 1980s crisis under the U.S. debt initiatives. In the 1990s, however, the inability of the Japanese government to engage itself in crisis management actively and collaboratively has generated concerns in the international financial world and among policymakers. Despite the importance of nonhegemonic major powers like Japan, there appears to be a paucity in the scholarly endeavors to analyze, from a perspective of international political economy, the motivation of such countries to support (or not support) public goods provision in various issue areas. The analytical focus of this book, therefore, centers on the motivations of such a "number two" power or "supporting actor" to engage in collective management of international financial crises.

This study focuses on one such major nonhegemonic power: Japan.[7] Financial crisis management is understood to encompass policies that aim to provide stability in response to crisis in international financial markets. The cases studied include the financial crises in Latin America (1980s and 1994–95) and those in Asia (1997–98). At the time of a severe financial crisis, particularly among middle-income developing countries with sizable economies, financial rescue packages successfully assembled by the international financial institutions (IFIs) and the major creditor governments can lead to the stabilization of the situation and eventually to the recovery of the economies in trouble. Increased official financial resources, provided either through rescue packages or through foreign aid, constitute an essential component to enhance economic recovery and stability. When no single international actor is either capable or willing to fully shoulder the cost of supplying such a public good—especially as the crises become too large for the International Monetary Fund (IMF) alone to handle—collective action among major financial powers is needed. As is noted in the next section of this introduction, because neither the behavior of the Japanese government nor its level of commitment to various financial crises is uniform, an important empirical puzzle emerges. Why does Japan engage in management of some financial crises but not others? What factors lead the country to engage (or not engage) in such collective action with the United States and the IFIs?

The findings from this study indicate that most favorable conditions for coherent collective action by creditor governments in financial crisis management arise when there are substantial and coherent sets of private returns for a creditor government from its involvement. Strong and unified transnational linkages among the major powers, which augment pressure on the creditor governments to act collectively, also lead to solid collective action. Economic interdependence and the coalition of private sectors constitute these transnational linkages, and these forces can also transmit pressure domestically to their respective home governments for stronger collective action to manage crises.

Japan in Financial Crisis Management

Japan's actions in financial crisis management in the Pacific Rim vary across the cases, particularly in regard to its interaction with the United States. The Japanese government engaged quite actively, and in support of U.S. initiatives, in the Latin American debt crisis of the 1980s. In contrast, Japan was very reluctant to get involved during the 1994–95 Mexican peso crisis. In the Asian crisis, the Japanese government demonstrated an ambivalent position regarding its leadership and its collaboration with the United States. Before asking why Japan behaved differently in each of these three cases, definition of concepts and a brief history of Japan's involvement in the management of these crises are in order.

In this study, I define Japan as an exemplary supporting power, or "major nonhegemonic power," in the world of international finance.[8] A major nonhegemonic power possesses substantial enough resources, financial or other, to influence the dynamics in international relations but cannot on its own overwhelm the hegemonic power or change international structure.[9]

In the context of this study, the Japanese government's actions are operationally defined in the following manner. The Japanese government is "actively" involved in financial crisis management when the Japanese government either designs crisis management initiatives, collectively with the United States and IFIs or by itself, or commits large official financial contribution to the rescue packages. The Japanese government's "leadership" is considered high when the government proposes independent crisis management plans (i.e., not merely supporting the U.S. ideas) or when it does so before the U.S. government takes action, which is the case of the Miyazawa Plan during the Latin American debt crisis. Strong leadership by Japan does not automatically imply discord with the United States, although that is sometimes the case. Japan may commit a substantial amount of funds to a rescue package, but if these contributions follow the U.S. initiative, the Japanese government is "active" but not exhibiting "leadership." Finally, Japan's strong cooperation or collaboration with the United States in crisis management emerges when the Japanese government supports the U.S. crisis management preferences or initiatives by explicitly announcing its endorsement, adjusting its policies accordingly, coordinating its policies with the United States, and/or extending financial contributions.[10]

In the latter half of the 1980s, Japan emerged as a prime supplier of the additional financial resources necessary to assure the economic stability and growth of developing countries and to provide financial crisis management. During this period, the Japanese government gradually shifted its behavior away from that of a small isolated mercantilist country in Asia and began acting like a leading international economic power. This shift was evident when the Japanese government extended large official loans to the Latin American debtors hardest hit by the debt crisis since 1982. The Capital Recycling Program, first announced in 1986 and expanded between 1987 and 1989, provided a total of $65 billion in official financial flows to indebted developing countries, many of them in Latin America.

The 1988 Miyazawa Plan represented another Japanese government initiative to alleviate the debt crisis. The finance minister of Japan announced this new debt strategy that emphasized debt reduction. Although the plan was not immediately adopted by other creditor governments, the Brady Plan, announced by the United States half a year later, incorporated the core ideas of the Miyazawa Plan. Thanks to the Brady Plan—particularly to its debt conversion packages—the outstanding debt of major debtors signing on to the Brady deals decreased. Japanese public financial organizations, especially the Export-Import Bank of Japan (JEXIM Bank), significantly increased their financial commitment to support the operation throughout the course of the Brady Plan.

The picture changed in the early 1990s as the U.S. economy recovered and as Japan's economic presence decreased in Latin America and began concentrating in Asia. Prominent features of international financial crisis management during the 1994–95 Mexican peso crisis included a striking commitment by the U.S. administration to relief strategies and a reluctance by the Japanese to become actively involved. Although Japan was not totally absent from rescue efforts in Latin America during this period,[11] the modesty of the Japanese government's actions were noteworthy in comparison to its activist contributions during the resolution phase of the Latin American debt crisis only a few years earlier.

Japan's responses to the series of currency crises in Asia, two and half years after the Mexican peso crisis, represent an even more complex picture. On one hand, the Japanese government appeared to become actively engaged in the stabilization of financial crises during the Thai crisis, which began during the spring and summer of 1997; Japan assumed a leading role, along with the IMF, in assembling a $17.2 billion rescue package for Thailand in August. For the rescue packages for both Indonesia and South Korea (hereafter Korea), which faced acute financial crises between the fall and the winter of that year, the Japanese government consistently committed the largest bilateral financial contribution. In addition, it even attempted to launch a new regional financial mechanism—the so-called Asian Monetary Fund (AMF)—which aimed to provide an additional funding source for Asian countries facing currency and financial crises.

On the other hand, Japan's regional leadership in attempting to resolve the Asian financial crisis was at best ambivalent. From the beginning, the Japanese government insisted that Japan would not be able to provide any financial assistance to countries that had failed to negotiate with the IMF before turning to Japan. Particularly after the arrangement of the Thai rescue package without U.S. financial participation and after the unsuccessful bid to establish a regional financial mechanism (the AMF), Japan began to take a "secondary and financier" role in Asian crisis management. Japan adopted this subordinate role supporting U.S.-IMF initiatives.

The main feature of the difference in Japan's behavior in relation to the United States in the case of the Asian crisis, compared to the cases in Latin America, is the more prevalent level of conflict in the interaction between the two major creditor governments. Although in most cases, the Japanese government cooperated with the U.S.-IMF scheme of Asian crisis management without undermining creditor unity (except in the case of the AMF, which failed), there was visible tension between the two major powers. The United States persistently criticized Japan's lack of action to help solve the economic problems of these Asian countries, particularly by stimulating its own economy, while IMF-led financial crisis solutions have threatened the economic autonomy of Asian countries. Under such an environment, the Japanese government has revisited the idea of Asian regional solution to financial problems, once stillborn as the failed AMF proposal, in the form of the New Miyazawa Initiative (October 1998) and through the agreement on a regional financial arrangement (May 2000).[12]

Puzzles, Arguments, and Methodology

Puzzles and Questions

The solution to the economic problems of middle-income countries in Latin America and Asia can constitute an important factor of international financial stability due to the considerable economic repercussions that the financial crises in these countries have, particularly when contagion effects amplify the impact of financial crises. During the early years of the debt crisis of the 1980s, the U.S. government successfully argued that creditors should resolve Latin America's debt problems swiftly, lest the international financial system should be in danger. This same argument could also be made for Mexico in 1994–95 and for Asia in 1997–98. All these crises required urgent and active involvement of creditor governments to maintain international financial stability.[13] Assuming that all these crises have required collective action by major creditor governments to avoid worsening economic turmoil and that collective action is always difficult to attain (see chap. 1), Japan's uneven behavior as it faced different financial crises is certainly puzzling. The question regarding Japan's varying behavior begs a reliable explanation, because no conventional understanding regarding international cooperation or the nature of Japan's foreign policy behavior can satisfactorily account for the specific combination of Japan's action and inaction in different crises.

The first depiction of Japan's foreign policy behavior commonly associates Japan's international behaviors with its pursuit of selfish national economic interest. Japan has been perceived as an "economic animal," whose primary foreign policy objective is to succeed in its mercantilist quest of global market shares and natural resources. Moreover, the Japanese government has long been blamed for being a "free rider" in the international economic system, failing to shoulder enough of the burden of international public goods provision. This picture neither explains the variation in the behavior of Japanese actors in the different financial crises nor accounts for the Japanese government's substantial contribution as a major financier and provider of international public goods. It is particularly difficult to explain Japan's active commitment in the Latin American debt crisis, because Japan's economic interests in the region have been quite limited.

The second common profile depicts Japan as a reactive or passive state, particularly when it comes to foreign policy and in relations with the United States.[14] The Japanese government has, however, demonstrated active and occasionally independent initiatives, both in the Latin American debt crisis, in the form of the Miyazawa Plan, and throughout the Asian financial crisis, in the form of the AMF scheme and other regional solutions to the crisis.

The third image relates to the shifting economic power balance between Japan and the United States: Japan's overwhelming economic might in the latter half of the 1980s and its retreat in the 1990s. Japan looked very much like an emerging hegemon and a challenger to the U.S. economic supremacy by the mid-1980s. Meanwhile, Japan's economic weakness (especially in contrast to the U.S. economic rise) led to a major concern regarding the spread of recession from Japan to the rest of the world in the latter half of the 1990s. This shift seems to have influenced the Japanese government's financial capacity and Japan's self-image, as well as Japan's domestic conditions (see chaps. 6 and 8). Nevertheless, Japan's motivation to become or not to become involved in collective financial crisis management has often overcome such constraints, as is demonstrated by the Japanese government's active role at the time of the Thai crisis in the summer of 1997 and through the New Miyazawa Initiative in October 1998.

The fourth and final picture associated with Japan's foreign policy is its strong interest in Asia and lack thereof in other developing regions, including Latin America (with the possible exception of oil-producing regions). Asia is Japan's backyard, where the Japanese private sector has established significant economic interests through trade, investment, and financial activities, while Latin America is still a remote region for most Japanese firms (see chap. 2). Japan's political and social ties are wide and strong throughout Asia, weak and limited throughout Latin America (with the exception of a fairly large Japanese immigrant population in the region). Such perception of Japan's nonpresence in Latin America is one reason Japan's active involvement in the Latin American debt crisis is not more widely known and is puzzling. A good explanation is also required, then, as to why the Japanese government occasionally receded to a supporting position, following the U.S. lead, in some phases of Asian financial crisis management, despite Japan's prevailing stake to demonstrate leadership in the region.

Additionally, although not related to Japan's image itself, it is quite puzzling to find that the United States was sometimes opposed to Japan's active involvement in financial crisis management, even though the participation of Japan would mean increased financial contributions, lessening the burden on U.S. taxpayers or the U.S. economy. In the case of the Mexican peso crisis, for example, the Clinton administration designed a unilateral solution without explicitly resorting to Japan's support. The AMF scheme, furthermore, presented the United States with Japan's alternative solution in Asia (with a large financial contribution from Japan), but the U.S. government did not accept it.

As a nonhegemonic major power capable of significantly influencing the outcome of collective financial crisis management in the Pacific Rim, Japan's actions call for adequate explanations. Why has Japan engaged in collective action to manage some crises but not others? What factors determine the motivation of the Japanese government to become involved (or not) in financial crisis management, and which factors have led it to behave differently in different cases? As I discuss more extensively in chapter 1, existing theories cannot satisfactorily explain the variance in Japan's behavior.[15] Difficulty of collective action is prevalent. The hegemonic stability theory of formation of a "k-group," which attempts to explain how major powers supply public goods unilaterally or collectively, falls short in predicting the changes in Japanese behavior. Contemporary theories of regionalism cannot explain cases of Japan's active involvement in Latin America and its occasional passiveness in Asia. Finally, the "second image reversed" perspective provides an explanation of Japan's reactions to external pressure but cannot adequately address the variation in outcome when the pressure is similar. This study introduces a new perspective that can account for the empirical puzzle on the case of Japan and international financial crisis management.

The Argument

I pose two interrelated hypotheses to address the puzzle and to examine the question regarding Japan's uneven behavior in various financial crises. These hypotheses can be thought of as two sets of encompassing theoretical frameworks under which empirically specific factors are subsumed. These two sets of hypotheses are useful in defining systematically the impact of the specific factors and in outlining clearly my expectation regarding the impact of these factors on Japan's behavior. The first hypothesis deals with the nature of crisis management per se; the second emphasizes the importance of the influence of transnational linkages and domestic politics on the Japanese government's external behavior. These hypotheses also presume an asymmetry of power between the United States—not the dominant, but still the most powerful, financial actor in the world—and Japan and other major creditor countries, which must deal with U.S. dominance in international financial issues.

The first hypothesis focuses on the nature of international financial crisis management and claims that the motivation for managing international financial crisis strengthens as the private returns for a major creditor government from such management increases. These private returns emerge from the "joint product" nature of international financial crisis management, in which actions to manage financial crisis produce both public and private goods and thus facilitate cooperation among the participants. The term *private* here refers to exclusive benefits that do not have to be shared with others. Empirically from the cases of this study, private returns include such things as the creditor country's domestic financial stability, an improved relationship with the country's important trade and security partners, and the country's political and economic influence vis-à-vis other creditors and debtors. The term *public* here refers to benefits that are not exclusive and have to be shared with others regardless of their contribution.[16] The discussions among major creditor governments concerning financial crisis management emphasize the public nature of the benefits that such actions produce, such as international financial stability and faster economic recovery of the countries in crisis (and thus more certainty of economic well-being and a decreased security threat). However, creditor governments are usually motivated by greater payoffs to themselves and their citizens as they decide to commit themselves and their tax revenues (see chap. 1).

During the Latin American debt crisis, the high exposure and stake of Japan's financial sector in Latin America led the Japanese government to act to protect its financial sector, encouraging it to become actively engaged in the resolution of the crisis (see chaps. 3 and 5). In addition, as discussed under the second hypothesis, the Japanese government was also interested in supporting the U.S. initiatives because of its strong bilateral economic linkages. This raised Japan's stake in stabilizing the economic problems of Latin America, because such action can minimize the detrimental impact of these problems on the U.S. economy. The lack of these private returns helps explain Japan's limited association with the Mexican peso crisis of 1994–95 (see chap. 6). There was a lack of high exposure of the Japanese financial sector, which came from the "exit" of Japan's financial commitment from Mexico and other Latin American debtors after the conclusion of Brady deals and from the increasing concentration of Japan's economic and financial activities in Asia in the 1990s. Moreover, the strong economic health of the United States eliminated the Japanese government's important regional interests in the Western Hemisphere. Thus, active involvement in crisis management during the peso crisis did not appear to produce enough private benefits for Japan.

Finally, the Asian financial crisis embodied an interesting mix of the elements of high private and public returns and visibly constraining elements for the Japanese government's leadership (see chap. 8). Japan's interest in successfully managing the Asian crisis was extremely high in the region. Both the Japanese government and its private sector had high economic and political stakes in the well-being and stability of their Asian neighbors. Japan has had many more interactions and interests with these Asian countries than with the countries of Latin America (see chap. 2). Two elements of the mix of private returns that the Japanese government pursued in this crisis management, however, made it difficult for Japan to have a coherent leadership position. First, the interests of the Japanese domestic private sector were divided. Banks wanted an immediate solution to their loan exposures in these countries (particularly given domestic problems with bad loans), but Japan's manufacturing sector either wanted Japanese money to stay in these countries or welcomed the IMF solution as a means to pressure the Asian countries to further liberalize their economies. Second, under the asymmetry of power, the Japanese government's high commitment and its leadership in Asian crisis management created tensions with the United States. As observed in the case of Japan's AMF proposal (see chap. 8), Japan's independent initiative to provide an alternative response and to shoulder the costs of such an initiative as the regional power invited objections and criticisms from the United States. Moreover, although the U.S. position in the Asian crisis was similar to Japan's during the Latin American debt crisis,[17] Japan was not able to induce the same type of supportive collaboration from the United States. Rather, in most of the Asian cases, the United States took the initiative and Japan followed. After the slow start at the time of the Thai crisis, the U.S. administration began setting agendas and urging the Japanese government to support the U.S. lead.

In short, the critical factors directing the Japanese government's actions in international financial crisis management were the level, type, and coherence of the private returns that the Japanese government expected to gain from its active involvement in three sets of financial crisis management.

The second hypothesis, which is related to the first, asserts that transnational linkages and domestic politics in creditor countries translate private goods into active crisis management and cooperation among major creditor governments. Acknowledging fully the relevance of the perspective of "complex interdependence,"[18] I argue that the stronger the transnational linkages among creditor countries are, the greater will be a creditor country's efforts in collectively managing international financial crisis (see chap. 1). Two types of transnational linkages are relevant here. First are institutional linkages among private financial sectors—mainly commercial banks—that played a major role in influencing the formation of collective action among creditor governments. Second are general economic linkages that have arisen from economic interdependence among major creditor countries.

During the Latin American lending boom from the mid-1970s through 1982, commercial banks from major creditor countries formed a de facto linkage by participating in so-called syndicated loans. As many as several hundred banks participated in syndicated loan packages managed by a few leading banks and protected by cross-default clauses to create a single megaloan, which was usually extended to sovereign borrowers, such as the government of Mexico. The syndication mechanism was constructed to minimize the risk of a debtor defaulting on a loan, by creating circumstances under which, if a debtor defaulted on a loan, it would be totally cut off from sources of international finance. In response to the onset of the debt crisis in 1982, the same commercial banks—mostly the larger ones—formed bank advisory committees (BACs) for each debtor country, to create a uniform and united front in debt negotiations. The institutional linkages created through these processes functioned to transmit the preferences and priorities of commercial banks to each government (see chaps. 3 and 5).

Domestic dynamics between major Japanese actors involved in external financial flows—the financial sector and the government—have influenced financial activities in both Latin America and Asia. Without the Japanese government's ability to influence the banks and without Japan's involvement in development financing to Latin America during the late 1970s and early 1980s, Japan's initiative in resolution of the debt crisis after 1985 would have been quite different. The private financial sector in Japan is not, however, merely a passive actor. The financial sector has a voice that influences the government's foreign policies, particularly when it can play on the government's need to protect domestic financial stability. This influence is reinforced when the financial sector forms ties with supportive counterparts on the other side of the Pacific—American banks and financial institutions lobbying the U.S. government (see chap. 5).

During the 1994–95 Mexican peso crisis, Japan's private financial sector had a very limited interest in influencing the Japanese government to get involved in crisis management on its behalf. The financial sector was not greatly exposed to the crisis, and the new financing facilities for Mexico, mostly in the form of portfolio capital flows without interbank ties, inhibited the formation of institutional linkage among financial sectors (see chap. 6). Although the formation to some degree of a "united front" among international financial sectors did exist, its cohesion was not as strong then as during the Latin American debt crisis.

Within the series of Asian financial crises, the contrast between the case of Thailand and Korea provides solid support to the importance of the institutional linkages among transnational banks in establishing strong collective action among creditors (see chap. 8). Because loan exposure in Thailand was predominately concentrated in Japanese banks, other transnational banks did not have a high stake in resolution and thus were not interested in establishing the united front themselves or in influencing the creditor governments' policies. The high exposure of many European, American, and Japanese banks in Korea, however, made the formation of a coalition of banks inevitable.

Furthermore, by the mid-1990s, the domestic transmission channels from Japan's financial sector to the Japanese government, which had previously provided strong political power to Japan's financial sector, became weaker. Contributing to this weakening were such factors as intensified financial liberalization, financially and politically debilitated banks, various collusion and corruption charges between Ministry of Finance (MOF) officials and employees from major banks, the "loss" of the Bank of Tokyo (which merged with Mitsubishi Bank in 1996) as a leading foreign exchange bank and a coordinator of international financial affairs, and political instability in Japan. The Japanese government's reluctance or ambivalence as it became involved in the Mexican peso crisis and the Asian financial crisis was in part a reflection of Japan's domestic dynamics (see chaps. 6 and 8).

The second type of transnational linkages (economic linkages) establishes a link between Japan and the countries in economic crisis through another creditor country, such as the United States, in which Japan has a high economic and political stake. In the case of Japan's involvement in the Latin American debt crisis, an important factor influencing Japan's behavior was the intensification in the 1980s of U.S.-Japanese economic and financial integration. Obviously, the U.S.-Japanese bilateral relationship, including their security arrangement, has traditionally been very important for the formation of Japan's foreign policy, and the recent integration tied Japan's economic fate to that of the United States—through trade, investment, and exchange rate links—much more closely than before. Japanese banks held major vested interests in the economic well-being of the United States, and the Japanese government recognized the possible negative repercussions of increased economic problems in the United States. The Japanese government supported

U.S. initiatives to assist the economic recovery of Latin American debtors, thus behaving in a way that benefited the U.S. economy. Weakened in part by Latin America's economic problems, the United States counted on Japanese financial contributions when U.S. economic and budgetary problems kept the United States from acting on its own as a large financial supplier to the region.

These economic linkages corroborate the importance of the triangular relationship between the United States, Japan, and Latin America in the case of Japan's involvement in the Latin American debt crisis in the 1980s. Japan's interests in the health of the U.S. economy triggered Japan's involvement in Latin America, and this involvement, in turn, affected the form of the collective management of the crisis. A division-of-labor arrangement also took place in this triangle, as the United States provided more substantial support to certain Latin American countries in which it had a stronger security interest, while Japan provided support to those countries with higher economic ties to the United States (see chap. 3).

In the case of the Mexican peso crisis in the mid-1990s, although economic interdependence between the United States and Japan persisted, the robust U.S. economic recovery of the mid-1990s lowered the Japanese government's stake in supporting the United States. Concomitantly, Japan's economic downturn further limited the feasibility of Japan's supporting role, in the absence of its direct interest in the region in crisis (see chap. 6).

Finally, the Asian crisis management case allows us to analyze another triangle. In this case, Japan was suffering economically from financial crisis in neighboring countries, and the U.S. government needed to consider the added benefit that could come from Japan's recovery through successful Asian crisis management. As noted earlier, because of an asymmetry of power and different levels of dependence, the U.S. government's gestures of collaboration in managing the Asian crisis to support Japanese initiatives were limited, making it difficult for Japan to take leadership (see chap. 8).

In sum, the degree of private returns produced through collective action influences the motivations and efforts of creditor governments to actively engage in the collective management of financial crises. Private returns, however, do not appear merely in terms of a pursuit of narrow self-interest by a creditor government. Collective crisis management contributes to the production of international public goods, partly because of the strong economic interdependence among creditor countries, economic linkages that work to increase the economic and political stakes of crisis management even in regions where a creditor government does not have measurable direct interests. Furthermore, institutional linkages among private sectors influence the behavior of a creditor government. These linkages bind private financial sectors across borders and transmit common interests through domestic channels in respective home countries, thus influencing home governments.

Methodology

This study uses both the quantitative research method of inferential statistics (multivariate regressions) and comparative case studies of the Latin American debt crisis (1982–91) and the Mexican peso crisis (1994–95). Moreover, the study analyzes the Asian financial crisis (1997–98) to test in a different regional context the same hypotheses examined in the Latin American cases. The case of the Asian financial crisis enables us to draw a regional contrast and, at the same time, provides a test for a more robust and generalizable theory of a creditor government's behavior in financial crisis management. The variable to be explained is the varying behavior of the Japanese government in financial crisis management, particularly in collaboration with the United States, when these crises take place in a third country (i.e., neither in the United States nor in Japan). The factors that influence the outcome are disaggregated into (a) the production of both public and private returns from the collective action, (b) economic linkages that emerge from economic interdependence among creditor economies, (c) private sector interests in the solution of crises and their institutional ties, and (d) domestic political actions that transmit outside pressure on the Japanese government.[19]

The combination of quantitative and qualitative research has a certain advantage.[20] The formal quantitative analysis with multivariate regressions in chapter 3 has merit in establishing the microlevel dynamics regarding the various factors, with a clear specification of the model and of the relationship of the variables involved. The regressions allow for control of variables other than those of direct interest, and they in turn provide straightforward answers to the level of validity of the hypotheses with existing quantifiable information. But problems are always associated with the use of regressions. First, the operationalization and quantification of some variables are difficult, and data limitation can lead to a compromise as to the variables accurately captured by available information. Second, the results from the quantitative analysis have to be interpreted carefully, based on a qualitative understanding of the issue.[21]

The less formal qualitative analysis in the comparative case studies in chapters 5 and 6 serves not only to verify the results from the quantitative analysis but also to supplement them with historical information. The analysis of the stark contrast in Japan's involvement in two Latin American financial crises provides increased sophistication to the understanding of factors that led to Japan's actions and its cooperation with the United States. Although these qualitative analyses do not allow us to control for variables to the same extent as does the quantitative analysis, the comparison of the two Latin American financial crises provides a good basis for contrasting certain variables while keeping others constant.

The hypotheses examined through both quantitative and case study analyses of Japan's actions and its cooperation with the United States in the Latin American crisis are retested in the case of the Asian financial crisis (see chap. 8). By shifting the regional focus from Latin America to Asia, the case of the Asian crisis provides an excellent opportunity for generalizing these hypotheses. The regional contrast and its implications on collective financial crisis management are discussed in detail in the book's conclusion.

Book Structure

This book consists of eight chapters. The following two chapters lay out the theory and background of this study. Chapter 1 outlines the theoretical discussions that lead to the two major hypotheses noted earlier. These hypotheses aim to provide a framework to explain the variance in Japan's behavior and motivations during different cases of financial crisis management over the past two decades. The chapter also briefly evaluates possible alternative explanations for the behavior of creditor governments; these are discussed further in the book's conclusion. Chapter 2 provides a brief background of Japan's "rise to power" as a major financier and as a provider of capital and technology for the developing world. The discussion extends to an analysis of the dynamics between Japan and the United States, an interaction that has had a major impact on the character and intensity of collective crisis management. The point in this chapter is that with the rise of its economic power, Japan has become closely integrated with the United States as well as with Asia. The chapter also discusses the changes in Japan's relative economic power vis-à-vis the United States over the past two decades.

After the descriptive data analysis of chapter 2, chapter 3 examines quantitatively the two broad hypotheses stated in chapter 1, by operationalizing the concepts and analyzing how Japan's official flows were allocated in Latin America during the Latin American debt crisis. Japan's official flows (both concessional and nonconcessional) constituted a large part of Japan's contribution to the solution of the Latin American debt crisis, and the amount and timing of such financial disbursement captures the Japanese government's interests in engaging in the debt solution.

Chapter 4 provides an introduction to the comparative case study of Latin America. The following two qualitative chapters (chaps. 5 and 6) examine Japan's actions and collaboration with the United States in the Latin American debt crisis and the Mexican currency crisis, respectively. These two cases are contrasted in chapter 4.

Chapter 7 introduces the case study of Asia. Then, chapter 8 focuses on the dynamics of financial crisis management in Asia (Thailand, Indonesia, and Korea) since 1997.

Finally, the conclusion revisits the theoretical discussion of chapter 1, discusses the implications of the regional contrast, and lays out the future course of this type of study.

PART 1

Theory, Background, and Data

CHAPTER 1

The Motivation to Cooperate, Lead, and Follow

Financial crisis management comes in various forms, including emergency financial resources (rescue packages) and intervention of public institutions (the IMF or creditor governments) to influence the behavior of the market one way or another and restore international financial stability. Globally, such crisis management is important to avoid further repercussions and international financial disasters. It may thus be considered an international public good.[1] In the last two decades, the IMF has usually been in the forefront of international financial crisis management, but the IMF lacks coercive power, particularly against private creditors, and it fails to maintain sufficient funds to deal with crises on its own.[2] Thus, the active involvement of various financial actors, especially major creditor governments, becomes imperative. Several factors, however, make state actors reluctant to take up this role.

The first disincentive discouraging collective action in crisis management comes from the very nature of a public good and the problem of funding supply, considering that some entity or entities have to shoulder the costs of public goods. A public good is a good that cannot exclude noncontributors from enjoying the benefit of added funds. In these circumstances, the incentives to free ride are high; so are the disincentives to contribute. Although crisis containment aims to provide international financial stability at critical moments, the fungibility of added liquidity through bailout operations makes creditors reluctant to commit their funds.[3] In addition, uncertainty regarding the payoff from crisis management leads to noncontribution. Major creditor governments that want to stabilize debtor economies and improve their external balance might emphasize the global repercussions and systemic risks arising from a crisis. However, there is always the suspicion that a creditor government may be promoting the "public good" of international financial stability while actually trying to secure its own "private goods" in the forms of direct economic payoffs and political gains. This suspicion is even stronger when creditor governments are concerned about their relative gains vis-à-vis other governments, which discourages active involvement.[4]

The second factor that discourages state actors from becoming involved in active cooperative management are the uncertainties and criticisms associated with the impact of financial crisis management involving rescue packages. Some conservative critics of financial rescues argue that rescue operations by public institutions (creditor governments and the IFIs) create a typical moral hazard problem. Bailouts invite moral hazard problems for debtors as well as for lenders and investors.[5] Uneasiness and uncertainty also arise because of multiple perspectives on the desired modality of financial crisis management and crisis solutions.[6]

The third and quite obvious factor discouraging involvement is that government actions might invite taxpayer resistance. Financial rescue packages or extensions of loan repayments provided by governments require additional financial commitments to countries with financial problems. Rescue packages are provided either in the form of direct participation using the country's official funds (bilateral) or in the form of increased capital contributions to IFIs, such as the IMF and the World Bank (multilateral). In many countries, taxpayers in general object to financial bailout packages designed to help debtors, especially when taxpayers have no strong affinity or commitments to the debtors. They also object to assisting investors from their home country who, in the taxpayers' view, misjudged their investments. In turn, when asked to increase their financial commitment to problem debtors, private financial institutions wanting to exit promptly and with as little loss as possible from bad loans and risky investments also resist cooperating with creditor governments.

Finally, because of the tendency toward regional concentration of various economic activities, such as trade and foreign direct investment (FDI), the major regional power usually becomes the first candidate to take the lead in a rescue plan and to commit the largest amount of its own funds. But regional economic crises are usually closely connected to the economic conditions of the regional power, and those regional powers that are most motivated to take initiative might be in an economically weak position to proceed in this manner. This has commonly occurred when financial crises have originated in emerging market countries like Latin America and Asia. For example, the United States was constrained by its budget and trade deficits in the 1980s, when Latin America was in a desperate need for financial assistance. Japan, meanwhile, was criticized for not doing enough for Asia due to Japan's own economic problems at the time of the 1997–98 Asian crisis. As a regional crisis begins to affect global financial activities, the critical question becomes, who else—if anyone—will participate in the collective management of the crisis? Under these circumstances, tensions can occur between the regional power, which is more interested in its private returns, and other participants of the collective action, hindering successful crisis management.

Besides the production of international financial stability through the containment of panic and the provision of financial support to countries in crisis, collective action among creditors can be effective in urging "discipline" on debtors. Creditors, both public and private, have an ultimate interest in making debtors pay back what they owe. Creditors are at a disadvantage if they negotiate separately with various debtors, because that allows debtors to play one creditor against the other. This can create a typical case of a prisoner's dilemma among creditors. In a prisoner's dilemma situation, the creditors' best solution is to cooperate among themselves to impose stricter adjustment and payment conditions on a debtor, but creditors wanting to extract better repayment from the debtor might allow more lenient conditions without knowing what others are doing simultaneously. A simple bidding war might take place, thus enabling the debtor to extract favorable deals. Because they are concerned about international financial stability and with making the debtors follow the established rules of the game, creditor governments have every interest in preventing such a scenario.

One way of getting around the difficulties of establishing a unified front for collective action in financial crisis is through institutionalization. In the 1940s, having regretted that World War II resulted from a failure to adequately respond to the financial and economic crises after the Great Depression, the major economic powers, led by the United States, installed a new design of international cooperation for trade liberalization and balance-of-payments support under a fixed exchange rate regime. The latter was represented by the Bretton Woods system, which involved new international financial institutions, such as the IMF and the International Bank for Reconstruction and Development (IBRD), otherwise called the World Bank.[7] In addition, since the 1960s, countries with strong financial interests have established various forums for similar goals, including the Group of Seven (G-7), through which the political and financial leaders of the major powers can join together to discuss matters important to their economic growth and stability.[8] These institutions have helped establish in the global economy a certain level of consensus and a moral code, guiding the actors' behavior.

Although these institutional arrangements have facilitated crisis management on the international level, still state actors have to agree on the implementation of crisis management and on increased funding for countries in crisis. The importance of such agreements is obvious in the case of the G-7, but it is also critical for the IMF, where the members of the executive board—delegates from member countries who hold different shares of voting power generally based on the amount of a country's capital subscriptions to the institution—discuss and vote on important decisions. Furthermore, the commitments of major creditor governments vary significantly depending on the government's positions on respective financial crises. Because the institutions (especially the IMF and the World Bank) represent a disproportionately large influence of the U.S. government, the motivation of major supporting governments to follow (or not to follow) the U.S. lead becomes even more important. Scholars of international relations thus have to start with an analysis of the motivations that bring state actors to decide to cooperate (or not) in financial crisis management.

Various strands of explanation for states' cooperative behavior already exist, ranging from international systemic accounts to unit-level analysis. However, each cluster of explanation manifests some weakness logically and empirically as it tries to account for the behavior of nonhegemonic major powers, particularly Japan, in international financial crisis management. In the following sections of this chapter, I outline the challenges facing existing explanations and then pose the two core hypotheses in this study: the importance, in international financial crisis management, of the "joint product" nature of public goods and of transnational linkages motivating state actors. These hypotheses constitute encompassing categories under which various specific dynamics and factors are organized. They thus provide clues regarding the analysis of international public goods supply.

Existing Explanations

Regarding international cooperation and provision of international public goods, three types of arguments have been developed in the literature to explain the behavior of either nonhegemonic powers in general or Japan in particular. These include a systemic explanation; an explanation based on the power of regionalism; and an outside-in explanation of foreign policy formation, including Japan's "reactive state" thesis. These explanations, it appears, help account for the general tendency of these powers to act in some kind of concert. When it comes to the powers' variant behavior in financial crisis management, however, these explanations leave a theoretical gap.

The Systemic Explanation

A hegemon provides international public goods to help maintain world stability that benefits all states, including the hegemon.[9] The theory of hegemonic stability was empirically challenged when it became increasingly clear that despite the decline in the early 1970s of the dominant and unchallenged post–World War II hegemony of the United States, the world was not facing major economic collapse. On the contrary, a certain level of international economic stability persisted. Various scholars have explained this continuing relative stability by analyzing how the anarchic nature of international relations has been overcome or modified by collective action.[10]

The analysis of hegemonic behavior in the provision of public goods splits into two camps. On one hand, the "benevolent" version of hegemonic stability theory argues that there is usually an exploitation of a large player by small players, in which the hegemon contributes a disproportionately large share of public goods provision.[11] On the other hand, the larger country, which is assuming the leadership role, can become a "predatory" hegemon and manipulate or coerce the smaller countries to cooperate.[12] Intellectual neglect still exists in the analyses of why nonhegemonic countries sometimes support and other times do not support the hegemon.

Many scholars consider cooperation among major powers as a key explanation for the stability and maintenance of a certain level of public goods supply. It is clear that scholars' views on the world and on the fundamental logic of state actions largely determine their judgment of the origin of international cooperation.[13] Some scholars from a liberal tradition note that the reciprocal effects emerging from various transnational institutional linkages and issue linkages in the world under "complex interdependence" can provide grounds for international cooperation.[14] Such conditions as a small number of actors, long-term reciprocal relationships, and the existence of "epistemic communities"[15] increase these possibilities. Scholars from the realist and neorealist perspective claim that international cooperation of a liberal institutionalist style would be largely impeded even with the existence of international economic exchanges, because states desire to obtain "relative gains" in relation to other countries, particularly rivals. Grieco emphasizes that unless there is a balanced distribution of gains, states have a hard time achieving international cooperation.[16]

Scholars looking at the systemic structure of international relations emphasize the existence of international regimes or of a set of "implicit or explicit principles, norms, rules, and decision-making procedures around which actors' expectations converge in a given area."[17] However, despite efforts made in the past to set up arrangements to secure international financial crisis management, power relations and interests of creditor governments still dominate decision making, leading to case-by-case responses. Thus, the international regime argument falls somewhat short of explaining cooperation in the issue area of crisis management.[18]

Scholars focusing on the motivations of major powers emphasize the possibility of collective action among an intermediate group in the absence of a clearly dominant single hegemon. Snidal argues that if the size distribution among a few subhegemons (e.g., Japan and Germany) is arranged in such a way that these countries find it beneficial to collaborate with the declining but still most powerful hegemon (the United States), a "k-group" can form to provide the public goods needed in the world.[19] The question is, however, whether we can always count on these major powers to agree with each other when the real or expected benefits accrued through collaboration are either unclear or very one-sided. Moreover, how could one account for the variance in a "k-group" member's behavior when the costs arising from a systemic collapse would be the same?

Furthermore, the power relations within the "k-group" are not uniform. Asymmetry of power determines, in part, the willingness of major powers to cooperate in crisis management.[20] This power asymmetry in the world and the influence (or power) of each state are channeled through two somewhat distinctive conjunctures: the country's structural powers and its relational powers.[21] The advocates of this distinction define relational power as "the power of A to get B to do something they would not otherwise do," and they maintain that structural power "confers the power to decide how things shall be done, the power to shape frameworks within which states relate to each other, relate to people, and relate to corporate enterprises."[22] Consequently, asymmetry of power means not only that a superpower larger and more powerful than others can coerce smaller countries to do what it wants them to do but also that international structures and institutions in different issue areas can be set up in a way that significantly benefits the large and powerful. This point is relevant in discussing the dynamics in the IMF at times of international financial crisis. Moreover, the type of power that a state possesses could vary depending on issue areas or geographic regions.[23]

In sum, the systemic explanation of international cooperation falls short of satisfactorily explaining the collective action outcome and behavior of state actors involved. It is thus important to analyze specific cases of cooperation and noncooperation to determine which factors go into a state's logic and how they translate into its actions.

Regionalism

Regionally based financial crisis management, in which a regionally dominant power commits exclusively or most actively to the crisis solution, is an alternative to a global or a multilateral arrangement. It would increase the motivation of a creditor government in the region, as the government's interests in stabilizing the economy are often greater and better-defined in the regional economy than in the global one. Regional interests in the face of financial crisis may lead to an arrangement of less collaboration or to some kind of geographical division of labor among major powers seeking to secure financial stability.

From the 1960s until the 1980s, theories on regionalism were limited to empirical cases from Western Europe, but they expanded globally in the 1990s, as the cold war ended and various regional integration efforts began to materialize in regions beyond Europe (e.g., the North American Free Trade Agreement [NAFTA], the Asia Pacific Economic Cooperation [APEC], and Mercosur). Furthermore, the regionalism of the 1990s not only involved integrationist movements among the industrial countries but also the north-south linkage of three major economic areas—the United States with Latin America, Japan with Asia (particularly Northeast and Southeast Asia), and recently Western Europe with Central/Eastern Europe and Russia.[24] Scholars began to examine why it is arguably more desirable to arrange international economic matters (and security matters) on regional bases rather than on a global basis. These discussions might be relevant to the analysis of major powers' response to financial crises emerging in their respective backyards.[25]

Regionalism is considered a conflict-minimizing way to organize state relations, particularly in trade. Trade arrangements in the form of "minilateralism" (within a small group of countries, as in the case of the post-1985 European Community) should facilitate careful allocation of costs and benefits arising from trade and thus should benefit participating states more, particularly when a hegemon, the main supporter of multilateral trade, is experiencing decline.[26] Due to lower transaction costs derived from close distance and already existing economic, political, and social ties, regional grouping is the most appropriate structure for this minilateralism, in which cooperation is more likely to take place. Moreover, if public goods produced through regional arrangements are excludable (against extraregional countries), a regional hegemon can emerge to supply such regional public goods.[27]

The logic of regionalism does not, however, fit well when explaining international financial relations and thus does not seem to satisfactorily explain the behavior of creditor governments in financial crisis management. The relatively more global (rather than regional) nature of financial transactions compared to trade makes the argument of regionalism much less effective. Evidence from recent international financial crises arising in developing countries shows that formal and regionally based crisis management in the form of lender-of-last-resort arrangements are still incomplete.[28] The most advanced case of such an arrangement is the North American Framework Agreement (NAFA), signed (after the conclusion of NAFTA) among the United States, Canada, and Mexico and providing a $6 billion swap arrangement among the three countries.[29] Some relatively small financial crises might be contained within a region. However, any large crisis with potential extraregional contagion effects (as observed in many of those major financial crises in the past two decades) would require a global solution. Thus far, empirical evidence indicates that creditor governments have been involved in extraregional crisis management despite high transaction costs and limited economic, political, and social ties. Specific to this study, Japan's active involvement at the final stage of the Latin American debt crisis and its passive position vis-à-vis the U.S. active initiative during the second phase of the Asian financial crisis (the Indonesian and Korean crises) requires a more appropriate explanation than regionalism.

The Outside-In View of Foreign Policy Formation on the Unit Level

In examining motivations that lead governments to act in the international arena, analyses of domestic or unit-level factors are considered fundamental. However, Risse-Kappen correctly points out,

> Empirical research in comparative foreign policy has established that domestic politics accounts alone are as insufficient as international level explanations and that they have to be complemented by [the] "second image reversed" concept.[30]

International dynamics and transnational relations influence how respective governments respond to external shocks and demands from outside. Even as we focus on dynamics among major powers, which are not merely "policy takers" but also "policy setters," external influence becomes a critical component of their foreign policy formation. In their discussion on the impact of economic globalization, Milner and Keohane summarize that internationalization changes the policy preferences of domestic actors and that domestic institutions intervene to determine the domestic response of each country to the same external shocks.[31] The impact of and the response to international financial crises would be considered corollaries to this analysis. External shocks are transmitted through transnational channels and form policy preferences of important domestic actors, particularly in the financial sector, and then the domestic institutional arrangements and domestic politics create various layers of intervening variables, shaping the policy outcome. This perspective is thus quite pertinent.

Looking more specifically at Japan, however, the existing theory is quite limited. Japanese foreign policy behavior (and Japan as a country overall) is often labeled "unique" as a major power because Japanese foreign policy has been characterized by a readiness to cooperate with the United States, with the Japanese government frequently reacting favorably to U.S. demands. The theory of a "reactive state," as it is called, suggests that strong cooperation arises from a special U.S.-Japanese bilateral relationship that includes Japan's high dependence on the U.S. market and on America's diplomatic and military support, as well as Japan's unique and fragmented structure of foreign policy decision making.[32] The theme of reactive or passive Japanese foreign policymaking has dominated the theoretical understanding and perception of Japanese external behavior.[33] This theory fails, however, to account for the condition in which Japan's actions vary despite the same high level of U.S. pressure. Moreover, Japanese domestic institutions and domestic politics influence policy outcomes by aggregating and transmitting the policy preferences of major actors. When is the Japanese government more willing or less willing to support the United States in providing public goods in the international economic arena? How do Japan's domestic politics influence the outcome?

To answer these questions, both domestic- and international-level analyses are important. Schoppa, responding to the challenge by examining the effects of foreign pressure under the Structural Impediments Initiative (SII) negotiations between the United States and Japan, notes that the "key to understanding why *gaiatsu* (foreign pressure) succeeds in Japan in some cases but not others lies in an appreciation of how domestic and international politics interact during the course of international negotiations."[34] This interaction between domestic and international politics requires careful attention.

As is discussed later in this chapter, it was inevitable that external pressure would be brought to bear on the Japanese government's calculations, due to the rapid internationalization of Japanese private financial institutions in the 1980s and to their strong domestic ties with the Japanese government. These institutions created a solid channel for the transmission of external pressure on the Japanese government from abroad. A task of this study is to examine the impact of external forces on Japanese governmental decision making at the time when some strong domestic actors began playing "external pressure" and "exit option" cards as international linkages solidified. To clarify the links and dynamics between a country's domestic politics and international influences, it is important to analyze precisely how a "second image reversed" view becomes incorporated in a country's policy formation.

The Argument: Sources of Japan's Actions in International Financial Crisis Management

How can we account for the Japanese government's varying level of engagement in international financial crisis management since the 1980s? More generally, how can we explain the level to which a major (but nonhegemonic) state contributes to the provision of international public goods in cooperation with other major powers? Two interrelated arguments account for the important variation in creditor governments' behavior. Although this study specifies these two arguments as hypotheses for the sake of clarity, these arguments are rather encompassing categories, within which the empirically specific factors detailed hereafter are subsumed.

The first argument notes that cooperation occurs because successful crisis management not only produces a public good but simultaneously promises a significant amount of private goods to the contributors. Thus, a creditor government will naturally be more willing to engage in collective crisis management as private returns from its action increase. The public good in this case comes in the form of the stability of the international financial system, which benefits everyone without discriminating either against or in favor of a particular actor. Private returns, in contrast, manifest themselves in products that give direct and exclusive returns to a clearly defined beneficiary regardless of supply efforts by others. We can thus consider that collective action in international financial crisis management leads to a "joint product" that produces both public and private goods. Active involvement by a creditor government in collective financial crisis management is most probable when the government can expect to gain greater private returns.

The second argument, closely related to the first, arises from strong economic and financial linkages among creditor countries. The stronger such linkages are, the more active a creditor government becomes in financial crisis management. Transnational linkages are characterized in two ways in the context of this study. On one hand, linkages come in the form of formal and informal institutional ties among major private financial institutions from various creditor countries. These ties become channels through which the demands of financial sectors are transmitted from one creditor country to another and from private creditors to creditor governments. On the other hand, economic interdependence in general establishes transnational linkages among countries whose economic activities are closely associated with each other. These highly interdependent economies thrive on many transnational linkages created through trade, investment, and loans and through other macroeconomic ties, such as interest rates and exchange rates.[35] These linkages among creditor countries also generate a mutual dependence or symbiosis that has lasting effects on the behavior of respective governments. These transnational linkages also create a powerful domestic force that can transmit pressures from abroad and demands on its home government, increasing, in turn, the stake (private returns) that a government can acquire from financial crisis management.

Financial Crisis Management as a Joint Product

> Hypothesis: A creditor government's motivation and efforts in managing international financial crises increase as the private returns that it can reap from this effort increase.

Financial crisis management involving relatively large developing economies will lead to the production of "public goods" in the form of international financial stability. Such stability, which is enjoyed by each and all without depriving others, could, in the absence of adequate management, be disrupted by the external economic problems of the debtor countries. In most cases, financial crisis management includes a rescue package to calm the market and lead to financial stability.[36] This calls, first of all, for leading creditor governments to commit themselves to financial rescue packages—in addition to guiding their respective private financial sectors to slow amortizations and roll over existing debt—and/or to increase capital flows to the problem countries. However, even public agents may have a difficult time providing stability, due to collective action problems.[37] Nonetheless, historical evidence points to the fact that major debtors in the series of financial crises analyzed in this study received rescue packages within a reasonably short time, despite collective action problems. From analysis of the financial crises in the 1980s and the 1990s, it is also apparent that Japan was often willing to collaborate with the United States, either bilaterally or through the IFIs, to provide critical management. Where does the discrepancy between logic and reality emerge?

A better explanation of cooperative crisis management among creditor governments, particularly the supporting behavior of nonhegemonic major powers, emerges when such management is thought of as a "joint product." Sandler explains this notion as "collective activity yield[ing] multiple outputs that vary in their degree of publicness," adding, "Some output may be private, while others may be purely or impurely public."[38] Many seemingly "public goods" are produced because they include some elements of private returns for the suppliers.[39] In addition, private goods can be supplied most effectively as a joint product with the public goods, rather than separately.[40]

International financial crisis management demonstrates the nature of a joint product. In most cases when crisis management has been conducted with each creditor's private interests in mind, it has also provided public goods along the way. As the amount of private return increases, a creditor government begins to see that engaging actively in internationally collaborative crisis management efforts offers an attractive option. In general, major creditors want to protect their own financial institutions and investors exposed to outstanding loans to debtors. Because it is difficult for any major creditor government to solely bailout the private investors with public money, and because of the fungibility of such money provided to the economies in crisis, these governments prefer collaborative financial crisis management to unilateral actions. As a consequence, public goods are provided that minimize the negative repercussion of such crises and enhance financial stability on the international level.[41]

In the context of this study, the private returns that the Japanese government has expected from active involvement in financial crisis management have two dimensions: domestic and international. Within the domestic dimension, the Japanese government has sought to support its own financial sectors facing problems stemming from financial crises and to increase its domestic political support from specific domestic sectors as well as from the public. In the international dimension, Japan's relationship with the United States and with the regions in distress becomes critical. By contributing actively to financial crisis management, the Japanese government has improved and consolidated its bilateral relationship with the United States (in terms of both economics and security) and with the countries in crisis. The Japanese government has also demonstrated its leadership ability with some alternative ideas and initiatives regarding financial crisis management, both regionally and multilaterally. The Japanese government also tries to satisfy transnational demands transmitted to Japan through domestic actors. The following empirical chapters discuss how all these factors have influenced the Japanese government's behavior in three sets of international financial crises.

Transnational Linkages and Financial Crisis Management

> Hypothesis: The stronger the transnational linkages between a creditor country and other countries are, the greater the creditor government's effort in managing international financial crisis is.

An in-depth analysis of international financial crisis management renders support to arguments emphasizing political factors—the liberal economic order—and to complex interdependence perspectives. Economic interdependence among countries has created multiple channels through which influence is transmitted, raising the stakes in successful cooperation as negotiations take place among creditor governments. Influence and pressures passed on through transnational linkages can often become domestic pressures from private sectors to governments. While "borderlessness" in the world of finance is allegedly becoming more of a norm,[42] it does not mean that the relationship between private actors and governments is losing its importance. In this study, the term *transnational linkages* refers to two kinds of linkages, both resulting from increased economic interdependence. The stronger both linkages are, the hypothesis states, the greater their influence is in inducing creditor governments' involvement in collective actions in international financial crisis management.

The first type of transnational linkages, institutional linkages, arises among internationalized financial sectors from different countries, establishing cross-border institutional links. Strong transnational coalitions among financial sectors from different countries increase respective home governments' commitment to financial crisis management. Interaction among transnational financial sectors is a major component of institutional linkages that influence financial crisis management. In the deals involving sovereign lending and syndicated loans in the late 1970s, transnational coalitions among international banks from different creditor countries were strengthened in part by their financial activities and risk-hedging mechanisms.[43] Even after the onset of the debt crisis in 1982, the institutionalization of committees (e.g., the BACs) among the affected banks established moral and legal mechanisms to strengthen (sometimes voluntarily and other times coercively) ties within the coalition.[44] This process, put into motion to deal with major debtor countries, is described by Devlin.

> ... private banks had at their disposal the coordinating mechanism of an "advisory committee" with a track record of success in dealing with problem debtor countries. . . . in unregulated international markets there is unbridled communication. . . . Also facilitating communication and coordination among the banks are the legal incentives deriving from cross-default clauses that accompany almost all international loan agreements. . . . it can facilitate collusion and the formation of an effective cartel geared to skewing the distribution of the costs of a problem.[45]

The power of this kind of transnational coalition among different actors in the financial sector, particularly at the time of a crisis, establishes a strong cross-border link that transmits pressures and demands from one creditor country to another. Furthermore, such institutions as the London Club and the BACs provide international forums within which cross-national peer pressure is applied among transnational banks, making it more likely for banks themselves to act in concert.

The second type of transnational linkages, understood generally as economic linkages, increases as a country's economic stake in another country expands with an intensification of trade and investment activities by the former in the latter. As economic integration among major creditor countries deepens, their vested interest in each other's financial and economic health becomes a major focus of foreign financial institutions heavily invested in the countries. Furthermore, such economic linkages tend to be correlated with bilateral political and security ties that make one of the countries even more sensitive to the other's actions.

These economic linkages, in turn, bind two major economic powers when they deal with financial crises of third (i.e., not their own) countries, creating a triangular relation. The negative economic impact of a financial crisis in a distant region is transmitted to a creditor country not so much directly but through the negative economic consequences the crisis has on the economy of the major regional power, whose conditions influence other industrial countries via economic linkages.[46] Particularly relevant to this study are crises occurring in regions whose economic turmoil affects one major creditor country more severely than it affects another. In the case of the U.S.–Japan–Latin American debtor triangle in the 1980s, for example, the Japanese government considered both Japan's overall economic relationship with the United States and the restoration of U.S. economic health imperative at a time when intraregional economic ties in the Americas detrimentally affected the U.S. economy.

Strong transnational linkages therefore prompt creditor governments to become involved in financial crisis management. These dynamics provide good examples of the "second image reversed" analysis discussed earlier in this chapter.[47] Importantly, though, how such international forces influence the final decisions of a government depends on the nature of each state. Japan is commonly described as a typical developmental state in which the government plays a vital role in every area of economic activity, domestic and international.[48] Claims are made that Japan has been most successful in the area of controlling the external behavior of its private sectors.[49] Japanese banks have traditionally been willing to engage in international business in accordance with official state objectives because of a convergence of interests between Japanese banks and the government in the international sphere and because of the banks' deferential attitudes toward the home government.[50]

Although understanding the nature of the developmental state is important in correctly examining Japanese behavior, the country has gradually transformed itself into a more pluralist system with societal pressure influencing the government's behavior. This is increasingly true as Japan becomes exposed to international pressure. Some argue, correctly, that the nature of the autonomous Japanese state has changed since the mid-1970s.[51] There are two major reasons for this: (1) exposure to the international system has introduced various external pressures and uncertainties; and (2) the development of the private sector has undermined the power and autonomy of the government by changing the domestic power balance. Under conditions where deregulation and internationalization have enhanced the institutional linkages of Japan's financial sector, the sector has gained a stronger voice from its financial integration with the rest of the world as well as from its increased capital mobility. The power relationship between the two actors has shifted gradually in favor of the financial sector, particularly in the case of the sector's influence on the government's behavior in financial management abroad. These external factors and foreign pressures (*gaiatsu*), channeled through various paths, influence the government's foreign policy decision making. Japan's private sector has also severely undermined the state's power: "as private capital has become less dependent on the resources provided by the state, the state's relative dominance has diminished."[52]

As financial crises abroad accentuate tensions in the relationship between the Japanese government and its financial sector, Japan's banks have exerted significant pressure on the government to minimize losses, regardless of the government's positions. In exchange, they have collaborated with the government in financial crisis management.[53] The health of its own financial sector in the face of crisis and the likely repercussions that a financial sector problem might have on the economy concerns the Japanese government. These factors have thus motivated the government to accommodate the sector's demands as much as possible, increasing the likelihood that transnational linkage pressure would prevail in the Japanese government's decision-making process.

The domestic politics that translate greater economic linkages in general into the Japanese government's actions in financial crisis management are less straightforward. Of course, larger direct investment, higher trade dependence, and increasing trade tensions have prompted various agents in the internationalized Japanese private sector to push for greater accommodation of demands by the United States, so that Japan could support the U.S. economy and avoid its economic retaliation.[54] Furthermore, Japan's financial sector, which has a high stake in the U.S. economy as well as in the countries experiencing financial crisis, has added incentives to engage the Japanese government in crisis management.

In sum, the strength of transnational linkages matters to creditor governments involved in international crisis management. On one hand, the willingness of major powers to engage in collective action in financial crisis management lies in the degree to which institutional ties among transnational financial sectors can lead home governments to engage in financial crisis management on their behalf. Particularly in the case of Japan, where the government-bank relation is known to be symbiotic, the Japanese government's external behavior and the crisis solutions provided by the public sector are strongly influenced by the bargaining and quid pro quo between the financial sector and the government. On the other hand, economic interdependence among major creditor countries creates general economic linkages that urge increased collective action as one of these countries becomes greatly affected by a financial crisis in its region. These economic linkages induce increased private returns to a government engaging in financial crisis management via support to its closest economic partner. This study therefore places the impact of economic linkages on the behavior of creditor governments as an important component of joint product.

Finally, the outcome of this process presents itself in the international arena as the Japanese government's foreign policy behavior. In some cases, Japan cooperated fully and actively with the United States and helped solve crises; in other cases, it avoided deep involvement.

Summary

International financial stability is a public good that requires continual attention. The question of collaborative management in a world lacking a single dominant hegemon becomes critical when a financial crisis that has the potential to bring major international financial disaster occurs. The existing literature and theories on international cooperation in general or on Japanese foreign policy behavior in particular fall short in accounting for Japan's varying involvement in cases of international financial crisis management. Hence, we still need to seek pertinent explanations of the actions taken by the Japanese government that have shaped the solutions to some of the largest financial crises of recent years.

This chapter emphasizes the joint product nature of the process by which international crisis management aiming for financial stability brings about both private and public benefits to the creditor governments involved in the solution. In this context, joint products motivate a major creditor government, such as that of Japan, to actively engage in collective action among potentially adversarial governments that are otherwise reluctant to become involved. Related to this point, transnational linkages have, in the past, successfully transmitted influence from one creditor country to another, both through institutional channels and through the power of economic interdependence.

CHAPTER 2

Japan's Economic Integration

Developing Regions and the United States

Japan's politico-economic relations with the Pacific Rim countries, especially with the United States, have influenced the country's behavior in the management of financial crises in the 1980s and 1990s. On one hand, Japan has become a major provider of financial resources supporting the economic growth and recovery of developing countries in recent years. On the other hand, Japan's interaction with the United States influenced the behavior of Japanese actors as they engaged in financial crisis management. The shifting balance and intensity of Japan's economic integration with these countries over the past two decades corroborates the variance with which the Japanese actors reacted to different crises.

Japan's capital exporting status and initiatives for recycling current account surplus during the 1980s led developing countries with balance-of-payments problems to expect the Japanese government to act as one of their major sources of economic support. This was a vital way in which Japan contributed to the maintenance of international financial stability (considered an international public good) during financial crises as the Japanese financial sector and government engaged themselves in collective crisis management with other creditors. The financial contribution has become a significant component for the resolution of financial crises, because Japan, in general, has not been a generous importer of goods produced in developing countries, except for oil, certain natural resources, and agricultural products.[1] This is quite different from the U.S. case, where its import capacity has helped many Latin American and other middle-income developing countries improve their balance-of-payments positions.

U.S.-Japanese economic relations constitute the other important aspect of Japan's role in international financial crisis management. Throughout post-1945 history, the United States has been Japan's most important economic partner, with the United States acting as the structural power and Japan as its beneficiary. In the past two decades, moreover, there has been a further increase in the deep economic integration of the two countries, as well as a shift in the power balance.

This chapter does not examine Japan as a hegemonic power, though some scholars raised this discussion in the late 1980s.[2] The limited scope of this chapter precludes it from providing a comprehensive overview of Japan's economic relationship with the rest of the world. Data presented herein on the evolution of Japan's economic relations with developing countries and with the United States aim to illustrate the point that Japan's behavior toward Pacific Rim developing countries in financial turmoil derives from Japan's economic integration with developing countries as well as with the United States.

The first half of this chapter summarizes the history of the rise of Japan as a large economy after World War II and as a major source of global funding since the late 1970s, with reference to the changes in these trends in the 1990s. This half focuses particularly on Japan's economic relationship with Latin America and Asia. The second half focuses on the increasing economic integration and interdependence between the United States and Japan and on the tension associated with that changing relationship in the 1980s and 1990s. The organization of this chapter reflects how Japan's economic position represents a juncture between two different worlds, both of which Japan values significantly. On one hand, as the economic leader of the region, Japan has become a major investment and trade partner to developing countries in Asia. On the other hand, with its capital abundance and high technology, Japan is a member of the group of "rich countries," and it has relied and continues to rely heavily on its economic interdependence with the United States.

Japan as a Major Source of Development Finance

An important aspect of Japan's economic relations with developing countries in the past few decades is an increase in the flow of goods and money.[3] Fifty years have passed since Japan's failure of its imperial quest and since its devastating defeat in World War II, conditions that left Japan with very limited access to the developing world in the 1940s. Now more than half of Japan's trade is with developing countries (see fig. 2.1), and it has become the largest official aid donor to developing countries in absolute dollar amounts (see table 2.1). Japan has also become a major provider of private investment. Its role as a source of financial resources and technology has raised many expectations among developing countries.

The following data on trade and finance demonstrate the story of Japan's economic relations with developing countries: Japan's financial flows, both from public and private sources, have constituted an essential component of these relationships. With the major exception of Japan's ultimate reliance on

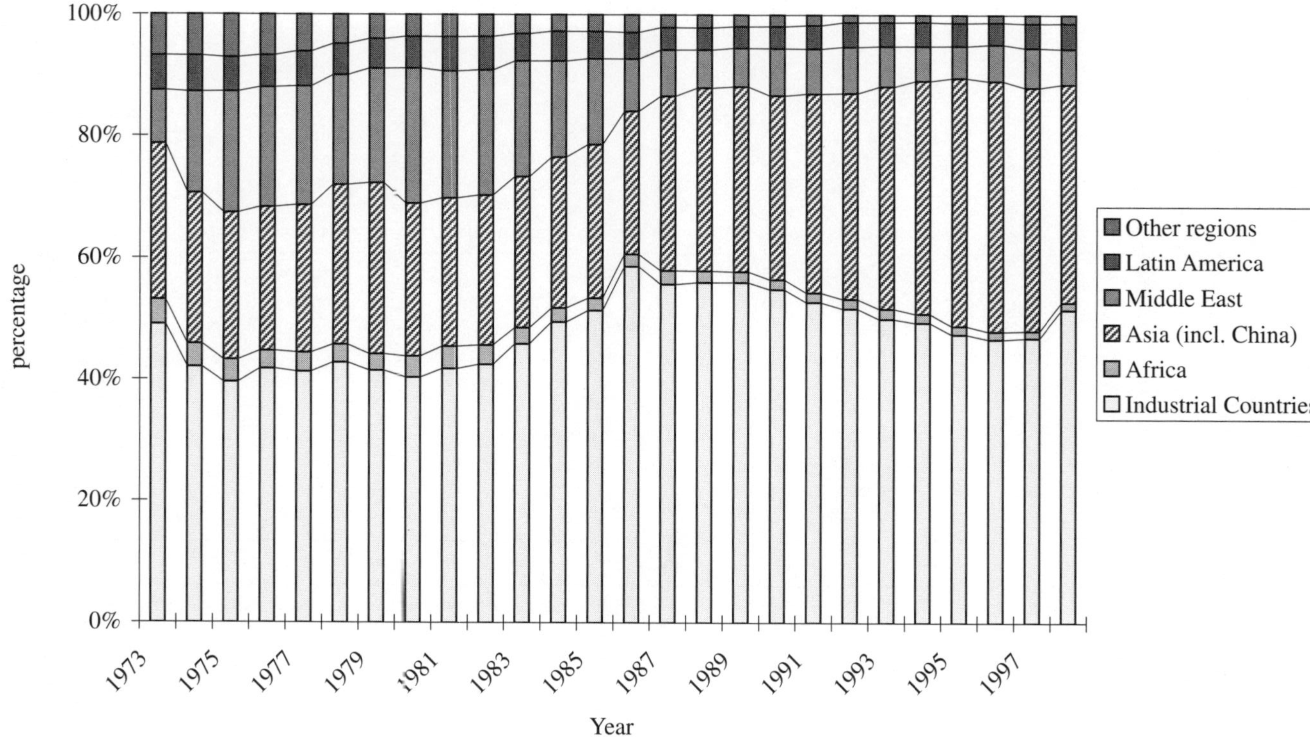

Fig. 2.1. Regional distribution of Japan's total trade, 1973–98. (From IMF, *Direction of Trade Statistics Yearbook.*)

TABLE 2.1. Top Ten ODA Donors, 1980–1998 (in millions of US dollars)

	1980		1985		1989		1990		1998	
1	US	7,138	US	**9,403**	**Japan**	**8,965**	US	11,394	**Japan**	**10,640**
2	Germany	3,567	**Japan**	**3,797**	US	7,677	**Japan**	**9,069**	US	8,786
3	**Japan**	**3,353**	France	3,134	France	5,802	France	7,163	France	5,742
4	France	2,8 89	Germany	2,942	Germany	4,948	Germany	6,320	Germany	5,581
5	UK	1,854	Canada	1,631	Italy	3,613	Italy	3,395	UK	3,864
6	Netherlands	1,630	UK	1,530	UK	2,587	UK	2,638	Netherlands	3,042
7	Canada	1,075	Netherlands	1,136	Canada	2,320	Netherlands	2,538	Italy	2,278
8	Sweden	962	Italy	1,098	Netherlands	2,094	Canada	2,470	Denmark	1,704
9	Italy	683	Sweden	840	Sweden	1,799	Sweden	2,007	Canada	1,691
10	Australia	667	Australia	749	Australia	1,020	Norway	1,205	Sweden	1,573

Source: OECD, *Development Report,* various issues; OECD Web site <http://www.oecd.org/dac/htm/dacstats.htm/> (July 5, 2000).

natural resource imports, particularly oil, it seems to have been difficult for developing countries to increase their exports to Japan. In compensation for the lack of imports from these countries, Japanese capital outflows have begun to constitute a major element of Japan's economic relationship, particularly since the mid-1980s.

Trade

Regional allocation of Japan's total trade indicates that about 50 percent of Japan's total trade (imports plus exports) has been conducted with developing countries over the past twenty years (see fig. 2.1). Two notable aspects of these trade patterns during this time are Japan's quest for natural resource imports and the expansion of its export market. The significant impact of the 1973 oil crisis, appearing on Japan's trade balance between 1974 and 1976, underlines the first feature. This event increased the value of Japan's imports from oil-producing countries, located mostly in the Middle East (plus Indonesia). The period between 1980 and 1982 reveals some of the same responses to the second oil shock of 1979–80, but this event was not as dramatic as the previous one.

The second feature of Japan's expanding trade relationship is the large increase in Japan's trade with industrial countries during the 1986–88 period, when the yen rapidly appreciated. One may interpret this increase as a very sticky J-curve effect (the volume of exports and imports responded slowly to the change in relative prices that the devaluation introduced). The period from 1990 through 1996 was characterized by the Asianization of Japanese trade relations, where the ratio of Japan-Asian trade against its total world trade increased from around 25 percent (in the mid-1980s) to above 35 percent. Both Africa and Latin America maintained their stable but declining shares of trade with Japan, with their shares falling from 4 to 2 percent and 6 to 3 percent, respectively.

Japan's trade balance (see fig. 2.2) shows that these increases in Japan's total trade with industrial countries (1986–88) and with Asia (1990–97) arose from increases in the amount of Japan's exports to these regions. The Japanese trade balance has been notoriously in surplus, causing criticism and retaliation by its industrial trading partners, including the United States, even before the 1973 oil crisis.[4] Asia is the only region with which Japan developed a significant and increasing trade surplus after the mid-1980s.[5] Japanese trade has been quite balanced with Africa and Latin America, and Japan consistently accrues trade deficits with the Middle East due to Japan's oil imports (see fig. 2.2). For the level of its economic development, Japan imports a relatively small amount of manufacturing goods from industrial countries and the

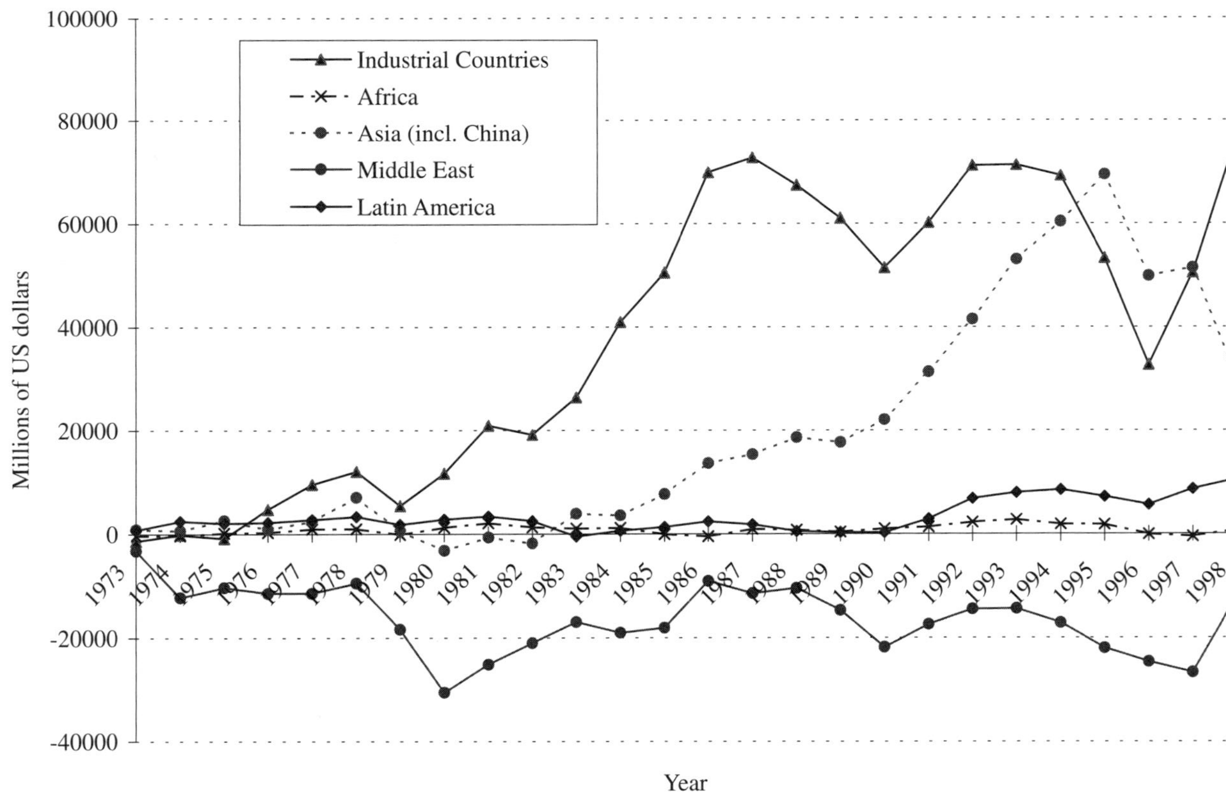

Fig. 2.2. Japan's trade balance with regions, 1973–98. (From IMF, *Direction of Trade Statistics Yearbook*.)

middle-income developing countries of Asia and Latin America, representing lack of intra-industrial trade (exports and imports of products falling within the same industry classification). The tensions arising from this trade practice are often cited as a bigger problem than the level of the imbalance itself.[6]

Easier access to Japan's domestic market for manufactured goods from developing countries is an important contribution that Japan could and should provide as a leading economic power. The stickiness of institutions and political arrangements created under what is labeled the "Yoshida Doctrine"[7] and the "catch-up process"[8] still exists in the Japanese economy. In addition, its need for heavy imports of natural resources has made the Japanese government quite cautious in opening Japan to a large amount of foreign imports that could drain its foreign exchange reserve. Finally, the nationalistic or mercantilist nature of Japan's economy has long hindered new or foreign entrants into the market. Whatever the motivation, long after the end of the Japanese economy's rapid growth period in the early 1970s, Japanese economic actors still promote exports and minimize "market-threatening" imports from abroad. The amount of primary goods Japan has imported from many developing countries has not apparently contributed much to the exporting countries' industrialization or to those countries' establishment of stable export income. Japan revisionists, who captured the spotlight in the late 1980s, have argued that Japan's unique domestic structure is maintained in such a way that it is difficult for foreign goods to penetrate and reach its consumers.[9]

This limitation of Japan's capacity to import from developing countries makes their alternative contributions to the stability and prosperity of developing countries even more important. Particularly with Japan's current account surplus (mostly against the United States and some other industrial countries) and its high savings rate, along with the strengthening yen since the early 1970s, investment and capital outflows from Japan became an essential component of the country's economic interaction with the developing world. Because such financial exchanges are conducted by private entities (e.g., foreign direct investment and bank lending) as well as by the government (official development assistance [ODA]), it is important to discuss them separately.

Financial Flows from Public Sources: Foreign Aid and Other Official Flows

Financial flows from public sources have been important components of Japan's economic relations with developing countries, particularly with countries where and during times when Japan's private sector was not ready to invest or had major reservations regarding country risk.[10] This foreign economic assistance has also constituted a major foreign policy instrument for the Japanese government as it increases ties with developing countries. During the financial crises of middle-income countries, the Japanese government employed these funds to facilitate crisis solution. Japan's ODA policy has attracted the interest of students of Japanese foreign policy due to a dramatic increase of its commitment in the 1980s and to its status as number one aid donor in the 1990s.[11]

Japan's foreign aid program started in the form of reparation agreements with independent developing countries in Asia in the aftermath of World War II, along with Japan's joining of the Colombo Plan.[12] Reparation agreements opened the doors for Japanese businesses to interact with developing countries in Asia.[13] This was particularly important for Japan in the 1950s, after the 1949 "loss of China" to communism. Although Japan continued to have economic relations with the People's Republic of China even after it severed diplomatic relations by recognizing Taiwan, a lack of stable economic ties with China led the Japanese government to turn to the rest of Asia and beyond for stable supplies of raw material imports and for export markets. The period between reparations and the 1973 oil crisis is characterized as the time when mercantilistic aid was used to promote Japan's economic development, in particular its exports. After joining the Organization for Economic Cooperation and Development (OECD) in 1964, Japan was expected to assume increasing global responsibilities as a member of this "rich countries' club." Japan, however, was not quite ready for the task. With the strong commercial orientation of the JEXIM Bank inherited by the Overseas Economic Cooperation Fund (OECF) in the form of heavily tied aid, Japanese aid policies appeared to have been solely for the purpose of export promotion.[14] As the voice of developing countries in the international arena rose through the collective power of the Group of Seventy-Seven (G-77)—the group of developing countries that constituted the UNCTAD (United Nations Conference on Trade and Development) in 1964—criticisms of Japan's foreign aid, in terms of both its strong commercial orientation and its high concentration in Asia, were repeated.[15] All through this early phase, Japanese foreign aid was very highly concentrated in Asia (see fig. 2.3). Even during the late years of this phase (1971–72), 99 percent of foreign aid was disbursed to Asian countries.

No doubt, 1973 was a defining year for the Japanese economy and for Japan's foreign relations with developing countries, when Japan's dire needs for natural resource imports played a large role. The quadrupling of oil prices and the increase in the developing world's power over resources represented a threat to Japan because it consistently imported over 90 percent of its energy supply. Japan then started to utilize its foreign aid to establish better relations with resource-rich countries, such as Indonesia, and with countries in the Middle East and Latin America. Some large-scale resource development proj-

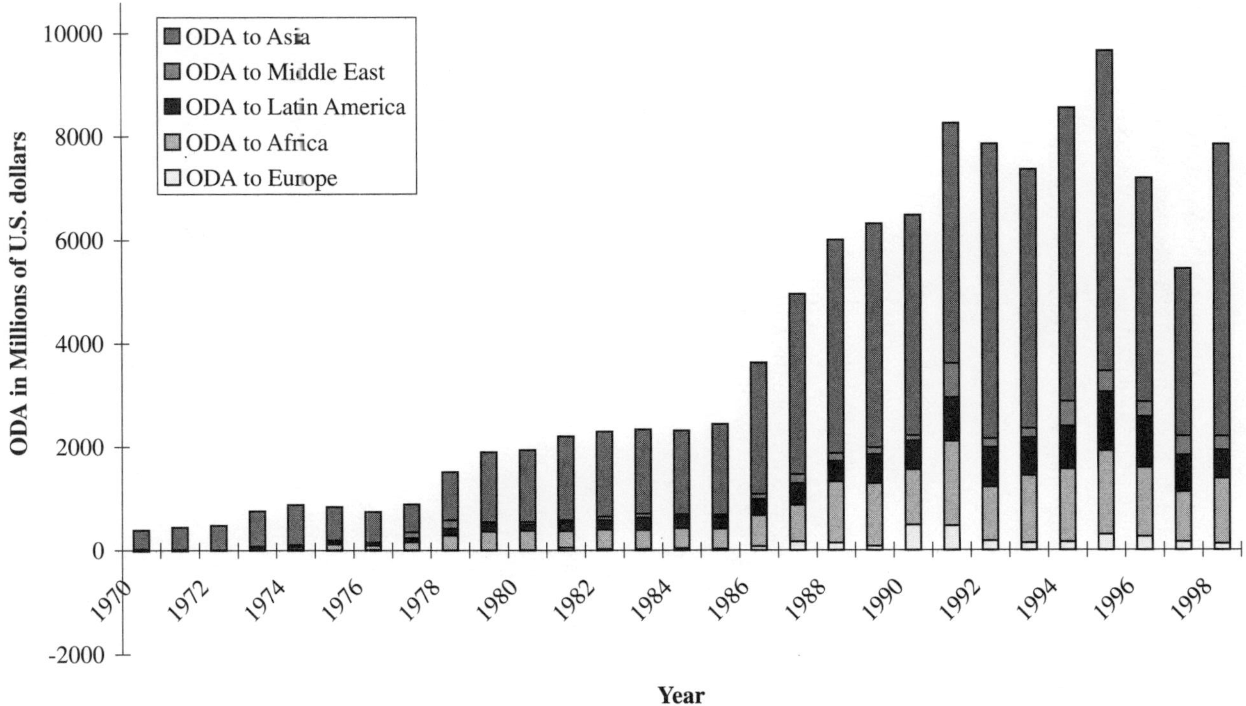

Fig. 2.3. Japan's foreign aid to various regions, 1970–98. (From OECD, *Geographical Distribution of Financial Flows to Developing Countries.*)

ects were financed by ODA.[16] During this phase, one observes some geographical diversification, out of necessity, of Japan's ODA. An average of 7 percent of ODA went to the Middle East during 1975–78, up from 0.1 percent in 1973, while aid to Asia declined from 90 percent (1973) to 70 percent (1975–78) (see fig. 2.3).

In the midst of this temporary regional reallocation of aid caused by the resource threat, the Japanese government launched a new phase of Japanese foreign aid policy by announcing, in May 1977, its first "Five-Year Aid-Doubling Plan." From this year on, various aid-doubling plans were implemented.[17] These plans, boosted by the rapid appreciation of the Japanese yen, made Japan the world's largest provider of ODA in 1989, for the first time in terms of absolute amounts.[18] Japan maintained its status as number one aid donor from 1992 to 1998 (see table 2.1). Accompanying the aid-doubling plans, aid pledges were made to increase the amount of foreign aid to certain countries or regions. Starting with Prime Minister Fukuda's visit to the countries of the Association of Southeast Asian Nations (ASEAN) in 1977, aid pledges promised many developing countries a boost in Japan's ODA disbursement.[19] Furthermore, since the signing of the Sino-Japanese Peace and Friendship Treaty with China in 1978, Japanese foreign aid to China has increased dramatically, particularly since 1982.

As the quantity of Japan's ODA increased, supporting Japan's economic integration with developing countries, there were also apparent improvements in the quality of Japan's foreign aid. At this time, the Japanese government began showing more sensitivity to humanitarian need, and it decreased the use of tied aid.[20] The publication *Keizai Kyoryku no Genjo to Mondaiten* (The current status and problems of Japanese Economic Cooperation) by the Ministry of International Trade and Industry (MITI) explains the rationale for this more active aid commitment on the part of the Japanese government since 1977.

> Due to the oil shock, the need for foreign aid by developing countries diversified rapidly, and at the same time "aid fatigue" of industrial democracies has become a prominent feature. . . . Under these circumstances, the expectation has risen that Japan would take a greater role in economic cooperation because of its current account surplus and strong yen.[21]

The Japanese government began to use a substantial amount of ODA to support Japan's emerging security agenda in the 1980s, and the agenda has related very closely to Japan's relationship with the United States. Playing an important role in the "comprehensive security" of Japan's foreign policy, Japan's foreign aid began to encompass "strategic as well as economic objectives."[22] The phrase *strategic aid* circulated in the Japanese media in the early 1980s. The programs so described aimed to strengthen Japan's assistance to "those areas which are important to the maintenance of peace and stability of the world."[23] Pakistan, Egypt, Sudan, and some Central American countries received increased amounts of Japan's foreign aid during this period. Inada argues that the phrase *strategic aid* largely meant that Japan's aid was "conducted in accordance with U.S. strategy."[24] This claim is empirically verified by the correlation between the recipients of U.S. Security Supporting Assistance and Japan's major aid recipients.[25]

In these contexts, the Japanese government began channeling its ODA in support of countries suffering from the consequences of the debt crisis triggered by the Mexican crisis in 1982. The Japanese government had increased its ODA steadily from the 1980s into the 1990s. In 1988, during the Toronto Summit, Prime Minister Takeshita of Japan announced a fourth medium-term ODA target (1988–92) of $50 billion. In addition to the increased quantities (of course, aided by a strong yen at the time), the characteristics of Japan's ODA transformed in various ways during the latter part of the 1980s. These changes appeared to have been designed to help not only debtor countries but also creditor countries in need of loan payments from those debtors.

First, the OECF began implementing policy-based lending (PBL) to some developing countries. PBL is a type of structural adjustment loan (not Japan's usual project loans) whose disbursement is based on the progress of the recipient country's economic adjustment. The Japanese government had traditionally avoided such loans. The shift was ostensibly prompted by the urgent need for quick loan disbursements to countries requiring new money for both economic growth and balance-of-payments purposes. Nevertheless, because of the increased fungibility of these funds, the recipient countries were able to channel funds to more politically important purposes, such as repaying the interest on their commercial loans. The second shift in Japanese ODA was a rapid decline in tied aid as a portion of Japan's concessional loans. According to an OECF report, the rate of aid tied to home country procurement dropped from almost 50 percent in 1986 to 9.6 percent in 1991.[26]

Japan has been one of the two largest aid donors since the late 1980s (see table 2.1).[27] Japan continued providing the most ODA to the developing world (directly and indirectly through international organizations) into the mid-1990s.[28] The United States, meanwhile, due to its budget austerity and the loss of the cold war rationale, retreated to a lower position, ranking as the second largest (1992–94 and 1996) or fourth largest (1995) aid donor. The increase in

Japan's aid donor status is reflected in the top donor profile of aid recipient countries. Japan provided more than 50 percent of the aid received by six countries in 1985–86 (averaged). However, in 1993–94, Japan was the majority aid provider to forty-six countries, including many non-Asian countries, such as Syria and Paraguay, although Japan's aid is still concentrated in Asia. The Japanese government, facing a highly strained central budget in the late 1990s, discussed a cutback in its ODA budget from fiscal year 1998. However, the onset of the Asian economic crisis in the latter half of 1997 and the dire need for increased funding to support Japan's initiatives in financial crisis management halted this process. Japan remained the largest ODA donor in 1998.

Other official flows (OOF) from Japan (see fig. 2.4) include overseas investment loans and untied direct loans implemented by the JEXIM Bank. Compared to ODA, with higher-than-market concessionality (a more than 25 percent grant element), OOF has lower concessionality and stronger commercial orientation. While the OECD governments are keen to advertise their contribution to economic development and concessional capital transfer through ODA, OOF is viewed as a financial instrument used by governments to promote their economic interests in both trade and investment.

In the case of Japan, OOF undertaken by the JEXIM Bank has two major purposes. The first, often stated purpose of JEXIM loans is to support and promote Japan's private industries in their expansion overseas. By the mid-1980s, the MITI reported that as much as 55 percent of Japan's foreign direct investment undertaken by small and medium-size firms was funded by public sources.[29] This is an indirect channel through which OOF enhances private flows. The official loans and guarantees provided by the JEXIM Bank to developing country projects have often contributed to increasing financial flows from Japan to the developing world.

OOF's second function is as a source of additional capital flow from Japan, which has been essential to developing countries, particularly since the mid-1980s. The OECF faced constraints when it tried to extend yen loans (ODA) to some middle-income Latin American debtor countries, for example, because the basic laws of the OECF did not allow any concessional yen loans to countries with a relatively high gross national product (GNP) per capita.[30] Under these constraints, the JEXIM Bank adopted an especially important function when it encouraged the extension of untied loans after the Japanese government announced its Capital Recycling Program in 1986 (further discussed in chap. 5). The JEXIM Bank disbursed a total of $23.7 billion by the end of June 1992.[31] The effort to recycle Japan's current account surplus through JEXIM Bank untied loans continued until the end of 1998 (see table 2.2), and it provided a total of $52.3 billion to developing regions in Asia/Oceania (48.4 percent) and Latin America (24.2 percent) and to IFIs (12.7 percent).

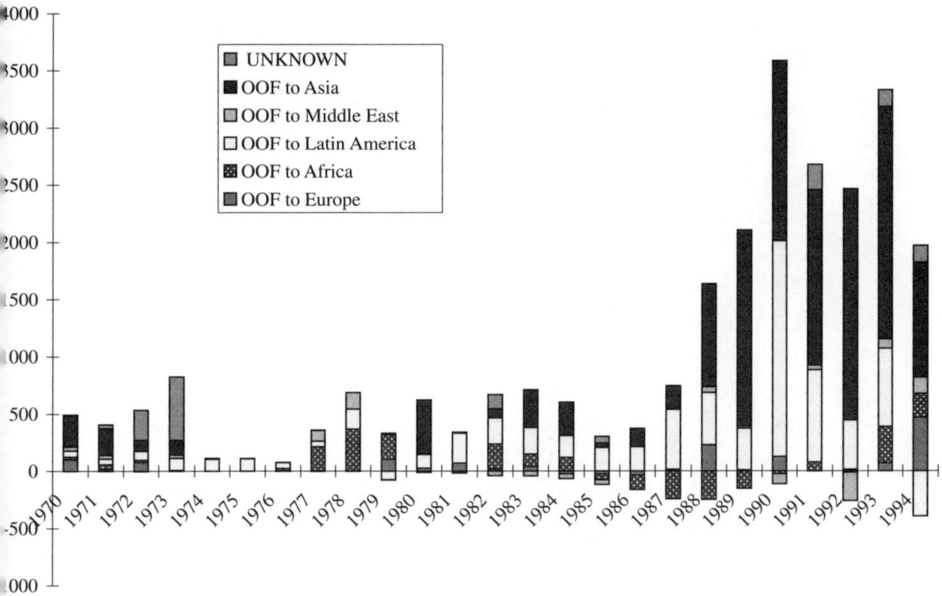

Fig. 2.4. Japan's other official flows (OOFs) to various regions, 1970–94. (From OECD, *Geographical Distribution of Financial Flows to Developing Countries.*)

Japan's financial flows from public sources, ODA and OOF, have established a strong quasi-economic link between Japan and developing countries. Japan's official financial flows have proven to be essential, particularly for middle-income emerging market countries in the 1980s and 1990s that faced financial crunch as they underwent financial crises.

TABLE 2.2. The Progress of JEXIM Bank Untied Loan Commitments by Region (as of December 4, 1998)

Region	Number of loans	Amount (millions of US dollars)	Percentage
Asia and Oceania	78	25,312	48.4
Europe, Africa, and the Middle East	63	7,642	14.6
Latin America and the Caribbean	64	12,665	24.2
IFIs	9	6,663	12.7
Total	214	52,282	100.0

Source: JEXIM Bank Web site <www.japanexim.go.jp/UntiedLoan/Index.html> (December 4, 1998).

Private Financial Activities: Foreign Direct Investment, Bank Lending, and Beyond

The Japanese private sector has been an important actor in Japan's economic integration with developing countries in the past three decades. Foreign direct investment (FDI) has constituted a substantial part of long-term financial flows, which have provided steady and productive sources of capital. Japanese bank loans, first prompted by the abundance of petrodollars in the mid-1970s, also provided long-term flows to creditworthy countries in the South. Finally, with the emergence of new avenues of investments in middle-income and rapidly industrializing developing countries (most of them otherwise called "emerging market countries"), portfolio capital flows into bonds and equities have surged since the first half of the 1990s. Although many consider these investment links largely market-driven or business-driven, Japan's domestic politico-economic structure makes these links an inevitable part of Japan's foreign (economic) policy.[32]

Examining the overall picture of Japan's FDI in the past few decades reveals a dramatic increase and changes in allocation. Until the 1980s, a relatively large portion of Japan's FDI went to developing countries in Asia and Latin America. Then, since the 1980s, as the overall amount of Japan's FDI drastically increased, the share of FDI to North America began to dominate, occupying more than 40 percent of Japan's FDI (discussed later in this chapter), until Asia made a substantial comeback in the mid-1990s (see table 2.3).[33] The sector disaggregation of Japan's FDI in developing regions demonstrates that the proportion of Japan's investment in the manufacturing sector decreased from 42.5 percent in 1980 to 23.1 percent between 1981 and 1985 and 22.8 percent between 1986 and 1990. The nonmanufacturing sector, dominated by natural resource extraction, which used to capture 52.8 percent, increased its share to over 75 percent in the 1980s.[34] Among developing regions, Asia and Latin America have been by far the largest recipients of Japanese FDI. While Asian countries began receiving more FDI in the manufacturing sector since the 1980s (30–40 percent), Japanese investment in Latin America went to nonmanufacturing sectors (80 to 90 percent), particularly in finance, insurance, and transportation.[35] Such a contrast suggests the clear differentiation of Japanese private sector activities in the two respective regions.

Japan's FDI in developing countries seems to be driven by three factors. First is securing the source of natural resources, which has been one of the most important and overreaching foreign policy objectives for Japan throughout its modern history. Accordingly, Japan's FDI behavior in resource-rich developing countries has long reflected this national preoccupation, particularly after the 1973 oil shock. In many resource-rich Latin American countries,

Japan's FDI then took part in so-called national projects. *National project* was the unofficial name for a development project defined by the following criteria: (1) the project was directly related to Japan's national interests, particularly in natural resources; (2) Japanese companies participated as a group in the project; and (3) government organizations supported the effort directly or indirectly. Support from the government came mostly in the form of public cofinancing for the Japanese private financial sector. The projects were usually developed by Japanese trading companies and discussed with the host governments, which requested financial support from the Japanese government. An arrangement to finance the project was then engineered between Japanese public financial organizations, such as the OECF or the JEXIM Bank, and Japanese commercial banks.[36]

The second factor driving FDI is a concern for Japan's economic competitiveness. Classic studies of Japanese FDI in the 1970s suggest economic rationales for Japan's investment in the manufacturing sector. Following the pre–World War II literature on FDI by Akamatsu,[37] Kojima argued in 1978 that Japanese FDI followed the principle of comparative advantage and that FDI supplemented Japan's trade. That is to say that Japanese manufacturing firms shifted their production overseas via FDI as they lost their comparative advantage in producing certain goods under Japan's factor endowments. In this case, most of Japan's FDI went to countries with cheap labor, to capture

ABLE 2.3. Japan's Foreign Direct Investment by Region, 1965–1997 in millions of current US dollars)

egion	FY 1965	FY 1970	FY 1975	FY 1980	FY 1985	FY 1990	FY 1995[a]	FY 1997[a]
orth America	44	192	905	1,596	5,495	27,192	23,221	21,694
percentage	27.7	21.2	27.6	34.0	45.0	47.8	45.2	39.6
urope	5	335	333	578	1,930	14,294	8,587	11,364
percentage	3.1	37.1	10.2	12.3	15.8	25.1	16.7	20.8
atin America	62	46	371	588	2,616	3,628	3,879	6,424
percentage	39.0	5.1	11.3	12.5	21.4	6.4	7.5	11.7
sia	35	167	1,101	1,186	1,435	7,054	12,361	12,355
percentage	22.0	18.5	33.6	25.3	11.7	12.4	24.0	22.6
iddle East	11	28	196	158	45	27	153	478
percentage	6.9	3.1	6.0	3.4	0.4	0.0	0.3	0.9
frica	2	14	192	139	172	551	381	336
percentage	1.3	1.5	5.9	3.0	1.4	1.0	0.7	0.6
ceania	0	123	182	448	525	4,166	2,816	2,087
percentage	0.0	13.6	5.5	9.5	4.3	7.3	5.5	3.8
Total	159	905	3,280	4,693	12,218	56,912	51,398	54,738

Source: MOF, *Kokusai Kinyukyoku Nenpo,* various issues. On notification basis.
Note: The Japanese fiscal year starts in April and ends in March.
[a]Beginning with FY 1995, Japan's FDI figures are published in yen rather than dollars. The average exchange ates used for converting yen figures into dollars are for FY 1995 ¥96.44 and for FY 1997 ¥120.99.

their comparative advantage. This characteristic of Japanese FDI has allegedly contributed to a "flying geese pattern" of industrialization within the Asian region, where "countries . . . follow one another in a developmental trajectory in which the latecomers replicate the developmental experience of the countries ahead of them in the formation."[38] In addition, Ozawa argued in the late 1970s that Japanese FDI supported the transformation of Japanese industries from low-technology and labor-intensive status to a high-technology position by enabling some companies to shift their production sites abroad.[39]

The strong need for Japan's manufacturing sector to export created a shift in Japanese FDI to developing countries as the Japanese government fully liberalized the majority of its capital controls in 1972. That was the year after the Japanese currency began to appreciate as the United States removed the dollar from its fixed rate to gold in 1971, a policy that ended the fixed exchange rate regime. To cope with a higher yen, Japanese manufacturing companies looked to invest and produce abroad. Thus, 1972 was considered the inaugural year for Japan's "real" FDI activities.[40] In the 1980s, Japan became more aggressive in using FDI to establish export platforms in developing countries with lower labor costs and more competitive exchange rates. This aggressive phase was further facilitated by the liberalization of Japanese finance from 1980 and was also forced by the rapid appreciation of the yen after 1985. In addition, facing strong import restrictions imposed by major industrial countries like the United States in the 1980s, Japanese exporters had to resort to overseas production to circumvent trade barriers.[41]

The third factor driving Japanese FDI in developing countries in the latter half of the 1980s was an increasing amount of investment in the financial and insurance sectors, particularly in Latin America. Aside from pursuit of tax-exempt status in some tax-haven countries in Latin America and the Caribbean, this development arose from Japanese manufacturing firms' reliance on foreign branches of Japanese banks for funding, a trend that forced the Japanese financial sector to follow the firms' rapid expansion overseas.[42] This leads us to the next major component of Japanese financial interaction with developing countries: bank lending.

Japan's bank lending to developing countries is a newer phenomenon compared to the history of Japan's FDI in developing countries. Although this phenomenon is less known (partly due to limited data), the presence of Japanese money became prominent in many developing countries by the second half of the 1970s.[43] Both the Japanese balance of payments recovered from the import shock of the 1973 oil crisis and the vast inflow of petrodollars into the country led to the relaxation of rules against capital outflow in the fall of 1976. Governmental restrictions on external lending activities by Japanese banks were lifted. A policy encouraging free outflows of capital followed during the next several years, with a temporary and short reversal after a second oil shock, in 1979–80. With limited investment opportunities in industrial countries due to the recession of the early 1980s, an increasing amount of Japanese capital was directed to developing countries. Many middle-income developing countries were undergoing "indebted industrialization" in the 1970s by taking advantage of the abundance of petrodollars floating throughout the international financial world.[44] Japan's MOF explained that such capital recycling contributed to an easing of balance-of-payments difficulties in the developing world.[45]

In a collection of his speeches from the late 1970s, an MOF senior official, Masao Fujioka, discussed the banks' important role in transferring funds from Japan to developing countries.

> Now Japan wishes to transfer incoming funds to the countries in distress and thereby to facilitate a proper international recycling of money. To this end, we are encouraging flotation of yen-dominated foreign bonds, and since last autumn [1976], we have resumed a *policy of encouraging the Japanese banks to provide medium- and long-term financing abroad.*[46]

The "policy of encouraging the banks" to lend abroad was comprised of various instruments to influence the Japanese private sector to allocate financial resources abroad. The instruments at the government's disposal included the JEXIM Bank's highly focused lending policies, the MITI's export insurance program, the ability to designate overseas "national projects," and the occasional provision of official foreign currency reserves to fund commercial transactions.[47] Semiprivatized or quasi-public "hybrid flows" were a form of surplus fund recycling employed by the Japanese government. These financial flows consisted of JEXIM Bank and OECF loans. These flows also served as inducements designed to redirect some of the profit-motivated private flows into a policy-guided, publicly desirable direction.[48] The political problems resulting from Japan's trade surplus with the United States had increased since the mid-1970s, leading the Japanese government to realize the important role of the major banks in offsetting external marcroeconomic pressures (e.g., rising yen) and political pressures (e.g., Japan bashing).

The outflow of Japanese long-term capital to developing countries was further facilitated by the gradual liberalization of the Japanese financial sector in the 1980s. In December 1980, a new Foreign Exchange and Trade Control Law was adopted, transforming foreign capital transactions from "closed in principle" to "free unless prohibited." In addition, the report by the Joint Japan-U.S. ad hoc Group on the Yen-Dollar Exchange Rate pushed for internationalization of the yen by opening up the Euroyen bond market between

April and December 1984. Many financial liberalization efforts followed in the latter half of the 1980s, increasing the importance of Japanese money in the world of finance by enabling outflows of Japan's net savings and current account surplus and by making its capital market accessible to foreigners.[49]

The use of the yen for Japanese financial operations abroad, however, never became significant, despite the internationalization efforts. The reliance of the Japanese financial sector on U.S. dollar-denominated transactions, along with the rapid fall of the U.S. dollar exchange rate in the second half of the 1980s (see fig. 2.13) accentuated the borrowing and lending behavior of the Japanese banks (i.e., borrowing short-term and lending long-term). Nakao writes:

> Although Japan had become the world's largest lender in the 1980s, the foreign exchange banks were heavy borrowers on another level. In contrast to the overwhelming accumulation of assets in the long-term capital account, therefore, there was an overwhelming accumulation of liabilities in the short-term account. As a nation, Japan was borrowing short-term and lending long-term.[50]

This behavior of the Japanese banks—borrowing short-term to cover outward long-term flows, otherwise called maturity transformation—has been quite invaluable for developing countries whose access to long-term capital is limited.[51]

Obviously, after the 1982 Mexican announcement of payment suspension on loan interests, and as many developing country debtors faced increased balance-of-payments problems in the early 1980s, long-term capital flows were allocated away from the heavy debtors, concentrated particularly in Latin America. Such capital then flowed into less risky borrowers, first and foremost to the United States, which had substantially high interest rates at the time (see fig. 2.14), and then to the developing countries of East Asia. Nevertheless, even during the height of the Third World debt crisis, outstanding Japanese loans (including capitalization of interests) to the developing world steadily increased until the Brady Plan reduced Japan's Mexican exposure in 1990. The same arrangement also reduced Japan's exposure to other countries, mostly Latin American ones, such as Argentina, Venezuela, the Philippines, and Costa Rica. In the second half of the 1980s, the nature of bank lending to developing countries also shifted away from syndicated loans and sovereign lending to project finance.[52]

In the early 1990s, as most middle-income developing countries reemerged from the debt crisis and privatized their government holdings in the process, they began to regain access to international capital markets, particularly through bonds and equities. The so-called emerging markets in Latin

America and Asia (and in other parts of the world, such as Turkey and Hungary) attracted capital from industrial countries during this period, when these industrial countries were experiencing very low interest rates under recession.[53] In these emerging market countries, country funds and regional funds set up to attract foreign investors to their stock markets also facilitated capital inflow to these regions, particularly in the first half of the 1990s (see fig. 2.5).

Developing countries from various regions have raised money in Japanese capital markets (see table 2.4),[54] and Japanese financial institutions, including institutional investors, have invested in these emerging markets. Japanese investors have shown a clear regional preference for Asian countries over Latin American ones. Financial institutions in Japan, especially major banks, have not yet gone through institutional rearrangements or a psychological destigmatization of the Latin American debt crisis, and economic difficulties at home and booming Asian markets nearby kept these institutions from venturing across the Pacific.[55]

Japan and the United States in the World Economy

I have thus far presented a historical evolution of Japanese economic interaction with developing countries in the period since the end of World War II, during which Japan has increasingly been integrated to these economies. I have also demonstrated how Japan has become a major contributor of financial resources to the developing world. Throughout this process, both the Japanese government and its private sector have been active and mutually dependent participants in their efforts to extend Japan's economic linkages with the developing world. This public-private interaction has influenced the level of Japan's presence in Asia and Latin America. Furthermore, Japanese economic expansion abroad has been closely linked to Japan's relationship and interaction with the United States.

For the past half a century at least, the economic relationship with the United States has been the most important dimension of Japan's economic exchanges with the outside world, and this relationship has also shaped, to varying degrees, Japanese foreign policy even toward other parts of the world. But while some Americans have emphasized the importance of the U.S.-Japanese relationship,[56] Japan is merely one of many important economic partners for the United States. Nevertheless, because the Japanese and U.S. economies are the two largest in the world, the economic and political dynamics between the United States and Japan and their respective economic interactions with the rest of the world constitute influential factors that shape the world economy.[57] Japanese actors, both governmental and private, have high stakes in their re-

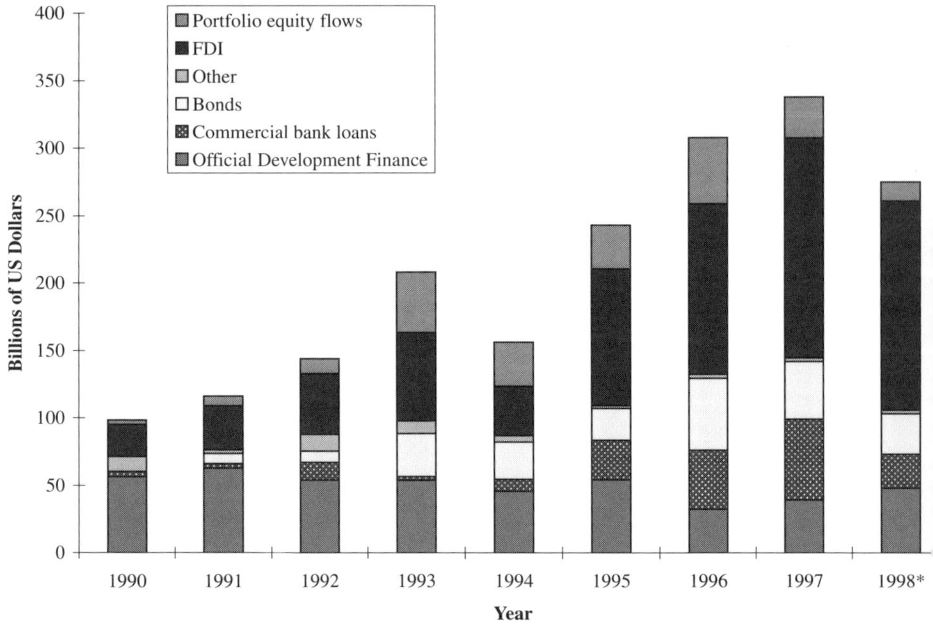

Fig. 2.5. Composition of capital flows to developing countries in the 1990s. (From World Bank, *Global Development Finance,* 1998 and 1999. *1998 World Bank staff estimate.)

lations with the United States, which makes their vested interests in the United States an influential factor as they interact with developing countries, particularly those in the Pacific Rim.

Appreciating the importance of U.S.-Japanese dynamics, scholars have exerted significant efforts to understand this relationship.[58] The U.S.-Japanese economic relationship endured and strengthened during the decade of the 1980s, when Japan began to compete with the United States in various aspects of economic life, including trade and technology. Despite political backlash in the United States against Japan's aggressive economic expansion, the economies of these two countries actually became increasingly interdependent during this period. The changes in U.S.-Japanese relations also have the potential to affect the well-being of other countries, particularly those dependent on both or either of these two powers for trade and sources of finance.[59] The interaction and interdependence of these two countries could potentially be the determining factor of economic stability in the world, which would benefit the economies of all interrelated countries. I therefore argue that Japan's role in maintaining international economic stability (considered an international public good) would be better examined by resorting to a trilateral perspective that takes into

TABLE 2.4. Samurai Bond Issuance, 1990–1998 (in billions of US dollars)

	1990	1991	1992	1993	1994	1995	1996	1997	1998[a]
Supranational body	1.9	0.7	2.0	0.6	0	1.4	1.7	0.7	0
US and Canada	0.7	0.3	0	0.6	0.8	1.7	6.8	3.4	0.1
Europe	4.6	2.6	4.5	8.7	5.1	6.5	14.3	6.0	1.0
East and Southeast Asia	0.3	0.9	1.2	2.2	3.4	4.1	4.8	2.4	0.1
Middle East	0	0	1.8	2.0	0.7	0	0.7	0.2	0
South Asia	0.2	0.2	0	0	0	0	0	0	0
Oceania	0.6	0.4	0	0.2	0.7	2.6	2.9	1.7	0
Latin America	0	0	0	0.5	0.4	0.1	3.5	1.5	0
Other	0	0	0	0	0.3	1.3	0.3	0.5	0
Total	**8.2**	**5.0**	**9.4**	**14.8**	**11.4**	**17.8**	**35.1**	**16.4**	**1.2**

Source: Euromoney and World Bank.
[a]Up to November 1998.

consideration Japan's bilateral relations with developing countries (particularly those of the Pacific Rim), Japan's relations with the United States, and U.S. relations with and U.S. interests in those developing countries, all of which influence each other.[60]

The main objective of this book is to analyze collective financial crisis management; it does not pretend to provide a fully developed or original analysis of the U.S.-Japan bilateral relationship. Nevertheless, it is worthwhile to highlight important aspects of U.S.-Japan dynamics that are essential to the analysis of the respective leadership roles of these two major powers in the world economy.[61] Both the changing relative power between the United States and Japan and their interdependence in the last two decades have affected the behavior of these respective superpowers, and these changes should have affected the shape of financial crisis management.

The Early Stage of U.S.-Japanese Relations: From 1945 to the 1970s

Japan and the United States started out from very different economic conditions in the aftermath of World War II. The United States, on one hand, was the victorious hegemon that dominated the world in all respects and that became, along with the Soviet Union, the major force shaping the postwar world, a period when many developing countries gradually became independent. Japan, on the other hand, was destroyed in the war physically, economically, and psychologically. It was also subjected to occupation by the United States for several years, and it experienced many institutional changes until formally regaining sovereignty in 1952. During the period of Japan's economic reconstruction and recovery, Japan lived under a long "free-riding" phase when economic self-interest allegedly drove Japan's external relations, with very little regard to its contribution to common international concerns, such as Third World development. From the 1950s through the 1970s, the country concentrated on its economic development particularly through upgrading its industry and expanding its overseas markets.[62]

Throughout this period, Japan enjoyed U.S. protection in the area of security as well as in external economic activities, such as access to foreign markets and long-term capital. The United States was quite generous to Japan's aggressive economic expansion. Cold war security concerns and Japan's important role in rebuilding the regional economy of Asia Pacific were perceived as important political priorities for the United States.[63] Japan, at that point, did not present a substantial economic threat. Japan ran a chronic trade deficit with the United States until 1965, and the U.S. administration at that time tried its best to increase Japanese exports to the United States. Nevertheless, there was some uneasiness regarding Japan's "free-rider problem" and its lack of burden sharing. The closed nature of Japan's market against imports (apart from raw materials and some primary goods) through restrictions and quotas, as well as Japan's limited financial contribution to developing countries via foreign aid and other preferential access channels, made it apparent that Japan was pursuing narrow, economic self-interests.

Somewhere between the late 1970s and the early 1980s, Japan shifted from acting as a complete free rider to being an active participant in the maintenance and structuring of international economic stability, along with the United States.[64] Beginning in the late 1960s, the Japanese economy experienced a strong boom due to favorable international economic conditions and to its successful industrial transformation. Japan's balance of payments turned to a surplus during this period, and with only a few temporary reversals at times of oil crises, this surplus has been maintained ever since. The trade balance with the United States registered a surplus for Japan in 1966, for the first time since its independence, and has never reversed since. In fact, this trend began to create political tensions between the two countries. Moreover, Japanese capital and technology became a source of admiration and envy for many developing countries.

In contrast, the decline of U.S. hegemony became the topic of debate during this period. According to Kindleberger,

> after about 1971, the United States has shrunk in economic might relative to the world as a whole, and more importantly, it has lost the appetite for providing international economic public goods—open markets in times of glut, supplies in times of acute shortage, steady flows of capital to developing countries, international money, coordination of macroeconomic policy and last-resort lending.[65]

Some scholars argue that the degree of American decline in the world varies from one issue area to another and that we cannot, on the basis of one case or sector, conclude that the American economy is in decline.[66] A great deal of macroeconomic data, however, indicate that during the 1980s, Japan caught up with the United States in terms of its economic capacity (though not necessarily in terms of its will) to be one of the leading powers in the world economy.[67]

Increased Competition and Integration between the United States and Japan: The 1980s

Assisted by the strong yen after the 1985 Plaza Accord, Japan's economic presence in the world seems to have expanded dramatically.[68] Japanese government publications from this period clearly demonstrate that by the second half of the 1980s, the Japanese government was well aware of the importance of Japan's role as a "contributing member of the international community."[69]

A few basic data, such as growth in gross domestic product (GDP) (see fig. 2.6), real gross fixed capital formation (see fig. 2.7), and world export shares (see fig. 2.8) indicate relative U.S. stagnation in the second half of the 1980s and dramatic growth of the Japanese economy during the same period. The figures in both GDP growth and fixed capital formation indicate that with an exception of 1983 and 1984—when the U.S. economy was boosted by the stimulus policies of the Reagan administration—Japan consistently outperformed the United States in the 1980s, until 1991. This picture changes dramatically after 1991, as I discuss in the next section.

The gradual closing of the gap between the United States and Japan in terms of world export shares in the 1980s (see fig. 2.8) indicates the dramatic increase in Japan's economic weight in the world. In 1973, Japan's export share in the world was less than half that of the United States, with more than a 7 percent difference between the two. However, by 1986, the gap narrowed to a mere 1.3 percent. This narrowing of the gap is even more impressive if one accounts for the fact that the size of the U.S. economy was about twice that of Japan's at the time.

More importantly, as Japan's trade power began to overwhelm the world trade system in the 1980s, the very lopsided trade balance in Japan's favor became the hot topic of discussion in the United States and elsewhere. Actually, throughout the fairly long history of the U.S.-Japanese trade imbalance, the United States has consistently complained about Japan's "unfair" trade practices. The dominant U.S. strategy for dealing with the Japanese threat in the earlier phase (1950s–1970s and somewhat in the 1980s) included measures to restrict imports into the U.S. market, such as voluntary export restraints (VERs) and orderly marketing agreements (OMAs) that covered products ranging from cotton textiles, steel, and color TVs to, in a well-known case, automobiles. During the 1980s, new pressures characterized the second phase of the U.S.-Japan trade conflict, with the United States pressuring Japan to open its closed market and for its selective concessions. Various market access measures were negotiated under the Market-Oriented Sector Selective (MOSS) talks, which targeted various products (e.g., electronic communication products, pharmaceuticals, medical equipment, electronics, and lumber), and the SII talks, which aimed to change the structure of Japan's market to increase its imports. Finally, from the late 1980s into the first half of the 1990s, empowered by the 301 provision of the 1988 Omnibus Trade and Competitiveness Act, the U.S. government began to put more retaliatory pressure on Japan than ever before, setting

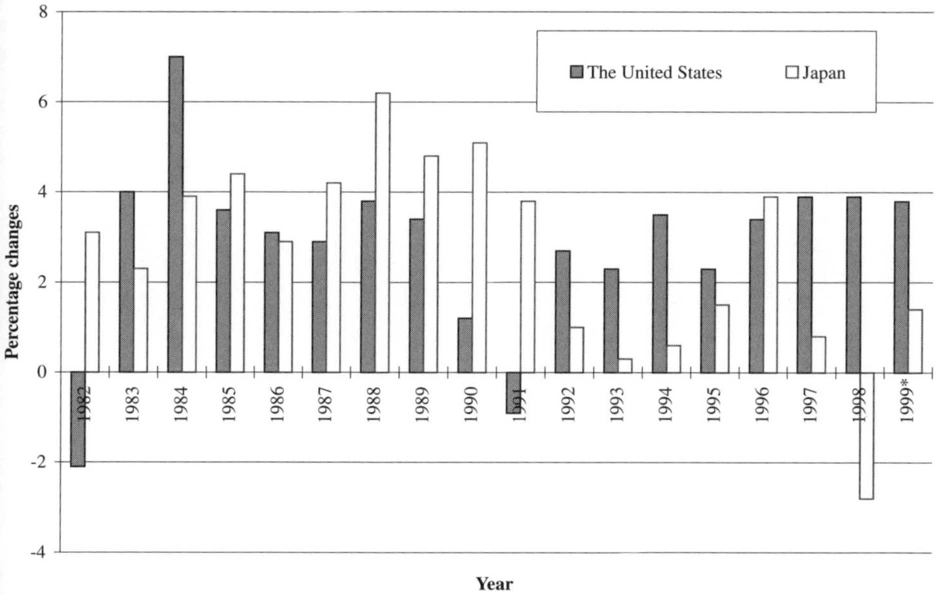

Fig. 2.6. GDP growth of the United States and Japan, 1982–99. (From OECD, *Economic Outlook*. *An estimate figure for 1999.)

"result-oriented" negotiations with quantifiable targets. The best example of this was the semiconductor negotiation of the late 1980s and the 1990s.[70]

The overall U.S. trade balance demonstrates the magnitude of the "Japan problem," which began to worsen in the early 1980s. The absolute level of the U.S. trade imbalance with Japan jumped from $21 billion in 1983 to almost $50 billion in 1986, and it has stayed that high ever since. The trade deficit with Japan has accounted for 30 to 40 percent of the overall U.S. trade deficit during this period. The deficit position of the U.S. trade balance has not improved in the 1990s. As the U.S. trade balance with the world improved due to the U.S. recession in 1992, the Japanese trade surplus captured 69 percent of the U.S. overall trade deficit (see fig. 2.9). Such data create an image of Japan as a free rider taking advantage of the American open market and of its security umbrella. In addition, the very limited intra-industrial trade between the two countries creates a bilateral trade panorama in which Japan exports high value-added and job-creating manufacturing products to the United States—a trend against which U.S. manufacturers have to compete—while the United States merely exports agricultural goods and raw materials to Japan.[71] These factors and the American perception of Japan's unfairness have angered the

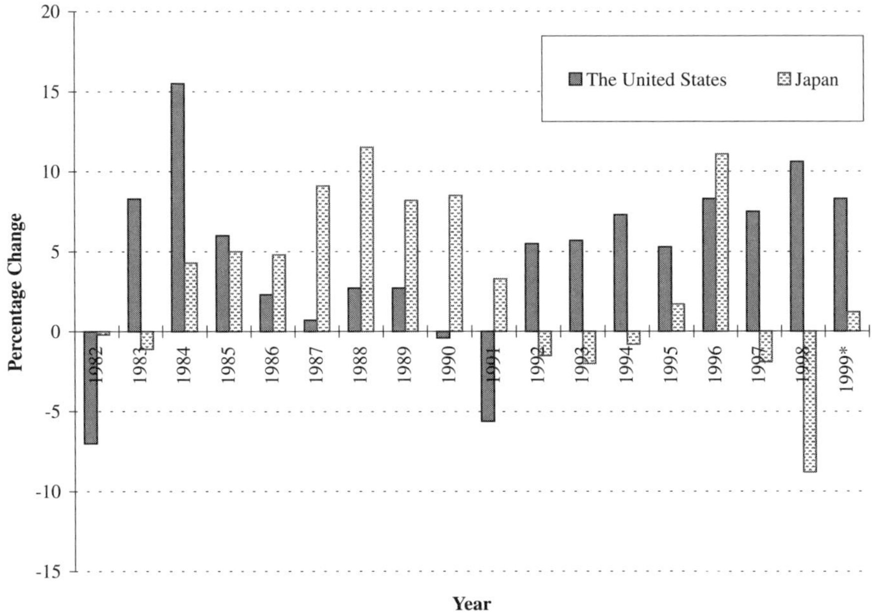

Fig. 2.7. Real gross fixed capital formation, 1982–99. (From OECD, *Economic Outlook.* *An estimate figure for 1999.)

American public and have led to increased protectionist sentiments and to discussions on strategic trade policies in the United States.[72]

Presentation of trade relations between the United States and Japan as dominated by competition and unfairness masked the increasing interdependence that characterized their trade and general economic relationships in the 1980s.[73] The weight of Japan's trade within total U.S. trade increased in the 1980s, peaking in 1986 when the Japanese trade share captured 19 percent (see fig. 2.10). The picture is the same and more impressive for Japan's trade relationship with the world. The share of trade with the United States soared to 29 percent of Japan's total trade with the world in 1984 and stayed at this level until 1989, after which it declined slightly. Around the mid-1980s, between 35 to 40 percent of Japanese exports ended up in the United States, thus accumulating the Japanese trade surplus vis-à-vis the United States.

Trade is not the only economic interaction that defines U.S.-Japanese relations. Japan's capital and financial power under the post-1985 strong yen was another critical factor in its relationship with the United States. Japanese banks occupied six of the top ten ranking positions of the world's largest (but not most profitable) banks in 1990 (see table 2.5).[74] Japan also acquired huge net

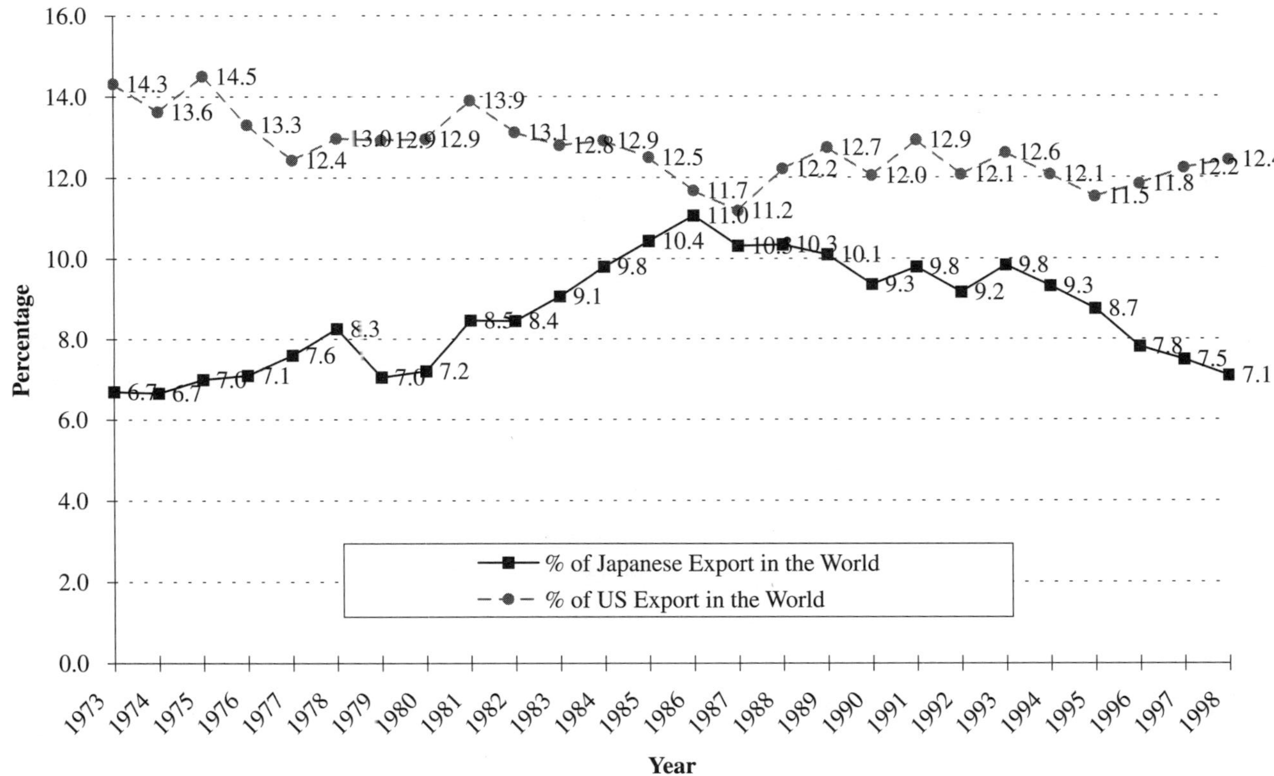

Fig. 2.8. Share in world exports: The United States and Japan, 1973–98. (From IMF, *Direction of Trade Statistics Yearbook.*)

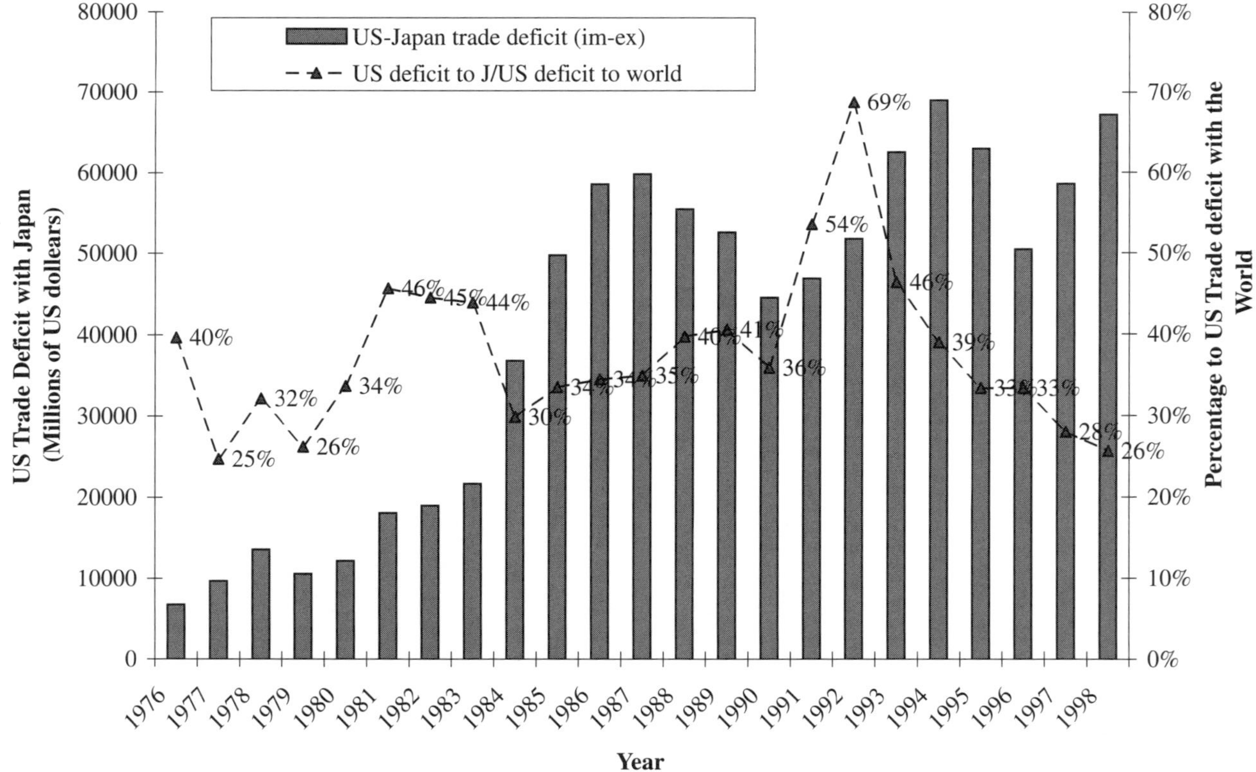

Fig. 2.9. US trade deficit with Japan and with the world, 1976–98. (From IMF, *Direction of Trade Statistics Yearbook.*)

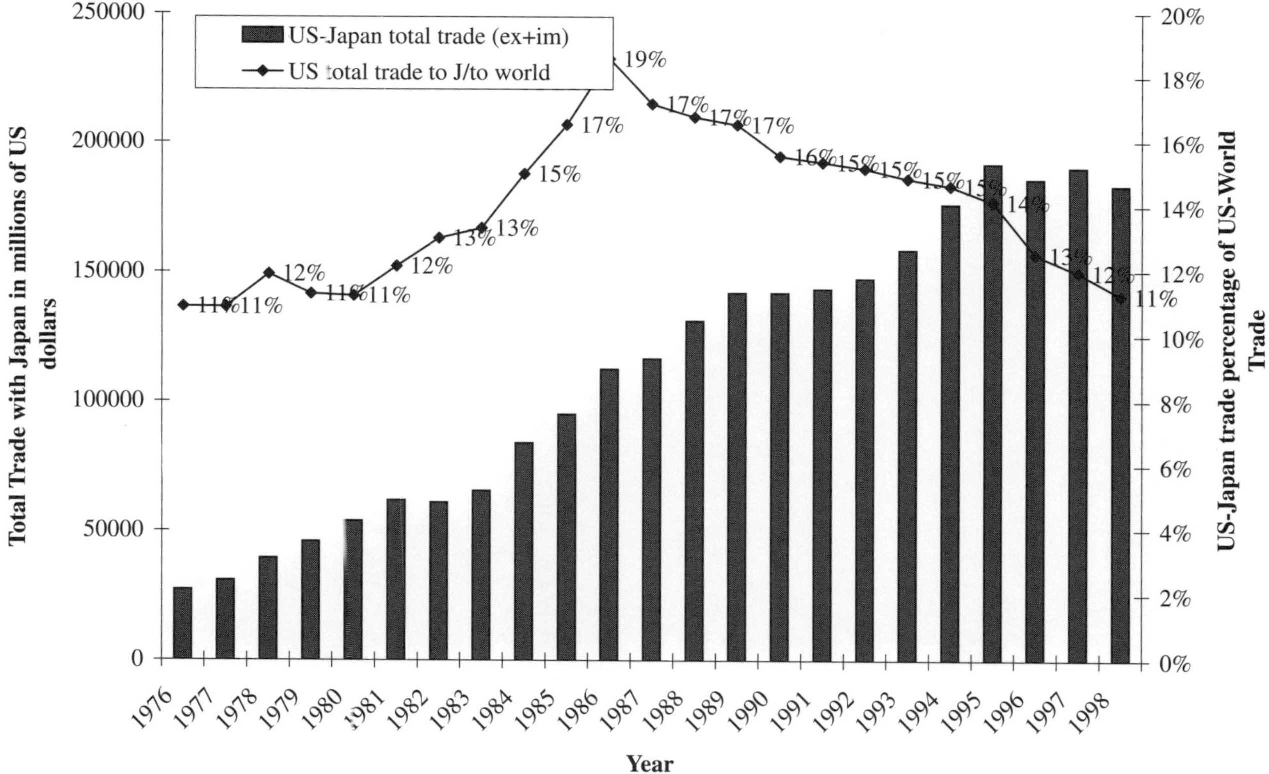

Fig. 2.10. US total trade with Japan and with the world, 1976–98. (From IMF, *Direction of Trade Statistics Yearbook.*)

TABLE 2.5. World's Top Ten Banks in Terms of Their Capital (measurement of strength)

	1984[a]	1986[a]	1988	1990	1992	1994	1996
1	Citicorp	Citicorp	National Westminster	**Sumitomo Bank**	**Sumitomo Bank**	**Sanwa Bank**	HSBC Holdings
2	Bank of America	National Westminster	Barclays Bank	**Dai-Ichi Kangyo Bank**	**Dai-Ichi Kangyo Bank**	**Dai-Ichi Kangyo Bank**	**Bank of Tokyo-Mitsubishi**
3	Chase Manhattan	Credit Agricole	Citicorp	**Fuji Bank**	**Sanwa Bank**	**Fuji Bank**	Credit Agricole
4	Banco do Brasil	**Fuji Bank**	**Fuji Bank**	**Sanwa Bank**	**Fuji Bank**	**Sumitomo Bank**	Chase Manhattan
5	Credit Agricole	**Mitsubishi Bank**	Credit Agricole	Union Bank of Switzerland	**Mitsubishi Bank**	**Sakura Bank**	Citicorp
6	J. P. Morgan	**Sumitomo Bank**	**Sumitomo Bank**	Credit Agricole	**Sakura Bank**	**Mitsubishi Bank**	Deutsche Bank
7	Manufacturers Hanover	**Dai-Ichi Kangyo Bank**	**Dai-Ichi Kangyo Bank**	**Mitsui Taiyo Kobe Bank**	Credit Agricole	HSBC Holdings	Bank of America Corp
8	**Fuji Bank**	Barclays Bank	**Mitsubishi Bank**	Barclays Bank	Union Bank of Switzerland	Credit Agricole	ABN AMRO Bank
9	**Mitsubishi Bank**	Banco do Brasil	**Industrial Bank of Japan**	**Mitsubishi Bank**	**Industrial Bank of Japan**	Citicorp	**Sumitomo Bank**
10	National Westminster	Union Bank of Switzerland	**Sanwa Bank**	National Westminster	HSBC Holdings	Union Bank of Switzerland	Union Bank of Switzerland

Source: The Banker, July issues.
Note: Starting with its 1999 issues (1998 numbers), *The Banker* stopped publishing the size of capital as the measurement of strength.
[a]Strength measured in terms of capital and reserve.

assets abroad, particularly in the United States (see fig. 2.11). In some cases, Japan's rapidly emerging financial power was considered a "hegemonistic threat."[75] Nakao writes,

> there was a danger of the Federal Reserve Board's losing its ability to influence events in a financial crisis and a risk of the U.S. national security as high-technology firms become increasingly reliant on foreign banks for loans.[76]

Indeed, Japan's financial power in the 1980s provides a key to understanding how the United States managed to accrue such a large trade deficit and still maintain an internationally acceptable balance of payments. The United States has managed to live under huge trade and federal budget deficits through substantial reliance on the inflow of capital. After suffering from high inflation and a stagnant domestic economy in the late 1970s, the Reagan administration resorted to an economic policy that has been labeled "Reaganomics." This policy consisted of tight monetary policy (high interest rates after 1979) and a lax fiscal policy (tax cuts and increased government expenditure, particularly on defense, since 1981). As a result, inflation stabilized (though the stabilization of inflation began during the last years of the Carter administration, when Paul Volcker was named as the Federal Reserve chairman), and the U.S. economy seemed to have slowly come back on track by the mid-1980s. However, this economic policy led to various unwanted, but expected, outcomes—namely, large current account and budget deficits.

The recovery of the U.S. economy and its expansion exacerbated the trade imbalance between Japan and the United States in Japan's favor, as I noted earlier; simultaneously, Japanese investors, under deregulation at home, were attracted by high U.S. interest rates. Japanese investors supported the expansion of the U.S. economy, in both the private and the public spheres. Possibly prematurely, Yamamura characterizes what happened in the United States throughout the 1980s as "the hegemon's last hurrah." He adds,

> by pursuing a tight monetary policy and financing absorption by debt instead of inflation, a necessary result was a rapid increase in borrowing from foreigners, especially from the Japanese, who found the high interest rates in the United States attractive.[77]

The rush of long-term capital outflows between 1986 and 1989 illustrates Japan's overseas investment boom. More than $130 billion in capital flowed out of Japan each year during these four years, and nearly half of this outflow was invested in the United States (see table 2.6). In addition to the FDI that set

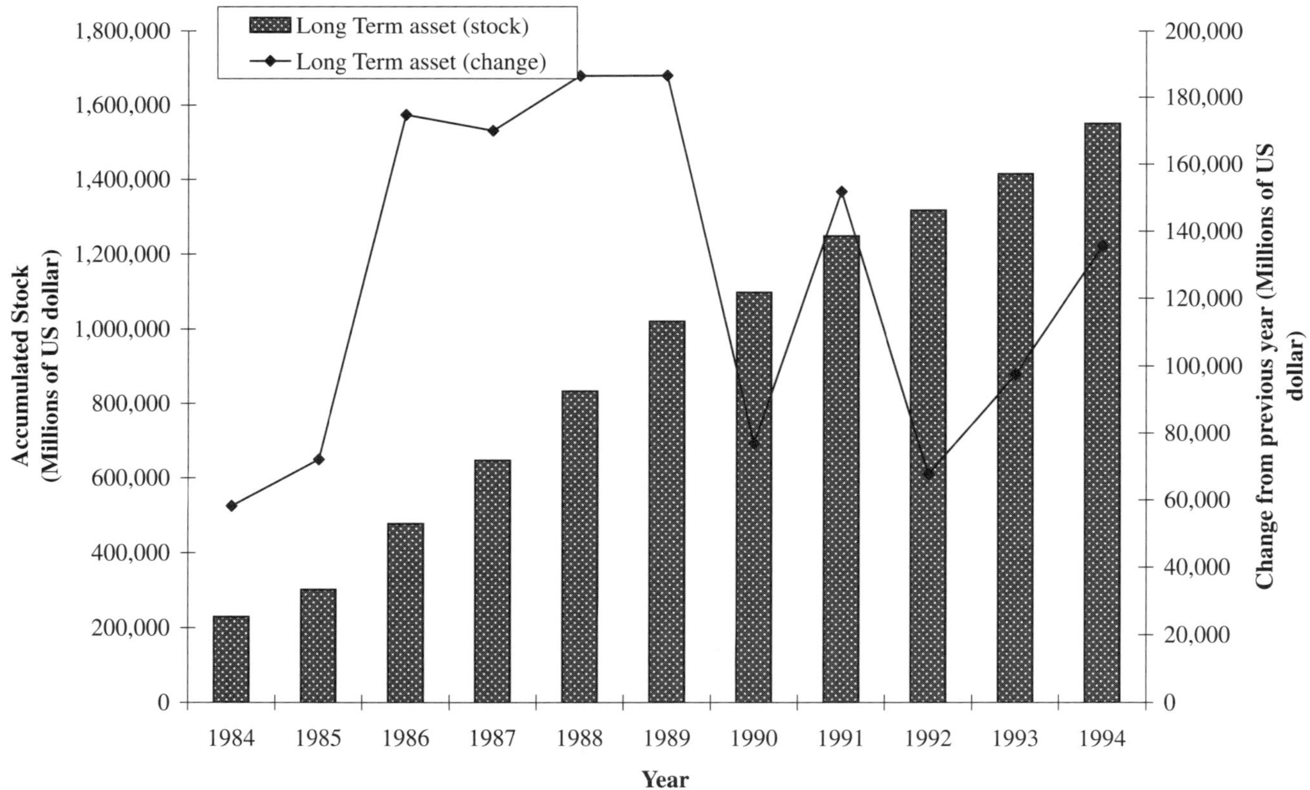

Fig. 2.11. Japan's long-term external asset: Stock and change, 1984–94. (From Bank of Japan, *Balance of Payments Monthly,* April 1995.)

TABLE 2.6. Composition and Geographical Distribution of Japan's Long-Term Net Capital Outflows, 1985–1991

	1985	1986	1987	1988	1989	1990	1991
World Total							
Direct investment	5,810	14,254	18,354	34,695	45,184	46,271	29,358
Security investment	43,032	101,432	93,838	66,651	28,034	5,028	–40,978
Trade credits	2,788	1,876	536	6,957	4,011	–671	–3,926
Loans	10,502	9,315	16,309	15,293	4,682	–16,930	–25,027
Other	2,410	4,584	7,495	7,334	7,335	9,888	3,516
Total	64,542	131,461	136,532	130,930	89,246	43,586	–37,057
United States							
Direct investment	2,043	7,774	9,018	19,568	22,768	24,986	15,302
Security investment	29,874	55,944	48,223	33,320	22,074	–19,849	–1,045
Trade credits	587	334	489	1,024	1,255	633	–314
Loans	716	690	1,663	2,830	4,761	2,783	2,569
Other	–57	908	1,637	2,518	3,003	3,166	1,846
Total	33,163	65,650	61,030	59,260	53,861	11,719	18,358
Twelve European Community countries							
Direct investment	1,480	2,594	3,476	5,693	9,419	9,921	7,344
Security investment	6,639	29,013	26,434	21,229	–24,562	9,409	–45,273
Trade credits	482	1,087	1,066	4,507	1,625	494	–843
Loans	835	1,038	2,091	1,768	–1,431	582	–1,876
Other	192	554	1,260	917	1,713	1,812	1,441
Total	9,628	34,386	34,327	34,114	–13,236	22,218	–39,207
Non-OECD/noncommunist countries							
Direct investment	1,913	3,055	3,972	5,842	7,802	6,864	4,627
Security investment	3,576	6,489	8,855	4,909	10,992	247	–10,436
Trade credits	1,447	1,111	–668	–741	–1,363	–2,246	–2,475
Loans	4,825	5,151	7,304	8,125	–3,406	–24,738	–26,389
Other	624	425	544	752	1,573	2,894	1,392
Total	12,385	16,231	20,007	18,887	15,598	–16,979	–33,281

Source: Kawai 1994, 96–98, table 5.8. Originally from Bank of Japan, *Balance of Payments Monthly,* April issues.

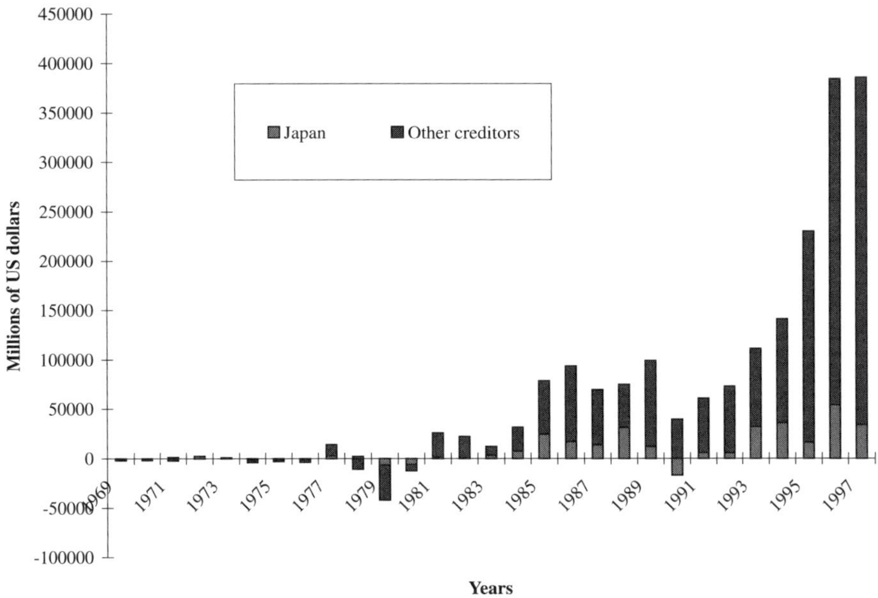

Fig. 2.12. US long-term net liabilities to Japan and other foreign countries, 1969–97. (From U.S. Treasury, *Treasury Bulletin.*)

up Japanese manufacturing firms and financial institutions in the United States, Japanese money, through purchases of U.S. long-term bonds and securities, financed not only American private firms but also U.S. government activities. From 1985 to 1987, large Japanese securities firms were among the principal investors in U.S. Treasury bonds, and they are said to have financed as much as 30 percent of the American government's budget deficit. The increasing trend in this area suffered a drastic decline in 1990 (see fig. 2.12).

The U.S. and Japanese economies became much more closely linked during this period, establishing the basis for the solid economic linkages discussed in chapter 1. Politically speaking, the two countries were living under a conflictive trade relationship, on one hand, and a symbiotic financial relationship, on the other. The United States became a net debtor in 1985 and the world's largest debtor in 1987. Japan became the major financier of U.S. debt throughout the 1980s. The Japanese private financial sector and other Japanese firms became heavily invested in the United States, as the strong yen and Japan's low interest rates made the purchase of U.S. stocks and bonds relatively profitable, and as exporting to the United States seemed more difficult due to exchange rates and strong protectionism in the United States. Economic interdependence, as well as economic linkages associated with these activities, led the

Japanese government to behave in support of the U.S. economy during this period. When Black Monday hit the U.S. stock market in 1987, for example, the Japanese government (the MOF) loosened (instead of tightened) regulations on Japanese investment in the United States in the aftermath of the market crash, so that the Japanese financial institutions could still invest in the country.[78]

As I noted earlier in this chapter, the bilateral dynamics of the foreign exchange rate between the United States and Japan have critically influenced both trade and capital flow issues. The Japanese government and its private sector have always preferred stability in Japan's exchange rate against the U.S. dollar, a preference tied to Japan's high dependence on the U.S. market and to the increasing importance of Japan's investment in the United States. In addition, many countries in Asia to which Japan exports have their currencies pegged to the U.S. dollar (or to the U.S. dollar-dominated currency basket). Such stability became harder to attain as the Bretton Woods fixed exchange rate system ended in the early 1970s. The exchange volatility further worsened in the 1980s (see fig. 2.13). A strong U.S. dollar and an accumulation of trade deficits in the United States in the early 1980s led to the 1984 Yen-Dollar Agreement, which liberalized Japanese capital markets for foreign capital inflow and internationalized the yen to correct the "artificially weak" yen. Although the exchange rate correction had to wait until the 1985 Plaza Accord, the agreement produced a fundamental transformation in Japan's external macroeconomic relations by increasing international capital mobility for Japan.[79] Despite various multilateral coordinating efforts through G-7 meetings and through bilateral negotiations and unilateral interventions, the yen strengthened (1978–81, 1985–89, and 1991–96) and weakened (1982–85, 1990, and 1997–98), influencing Japan's external economic activities.[80]

Finally, in the field of international development, in addition to its status as top ODA donor in the 1990s, Japan's influence has gradually augmented thanks to its own experience of economic success and its outstanding role in financing the economic development of many countries (as discussed earlier in this chapter). The Japanese government began to voice its reservations about prevailing development prescriptions through the forum of the IFIs, where the U.S. perspective traditionally dominated (i.e., the United States is considered a structural power here). The most prominent example of Japan's increasing initiative in that area is the World Bank's publication of *The East Asian Miracle* in 1993. This document gives more credence than usual to the idea that public policy and government intervention in the economy could play positive roles in economic development. In the publication, the World Bank and the United States, which wielded the greatest voting power in the institution, uncharacteristically compromise their "market-friendly approach."[81]

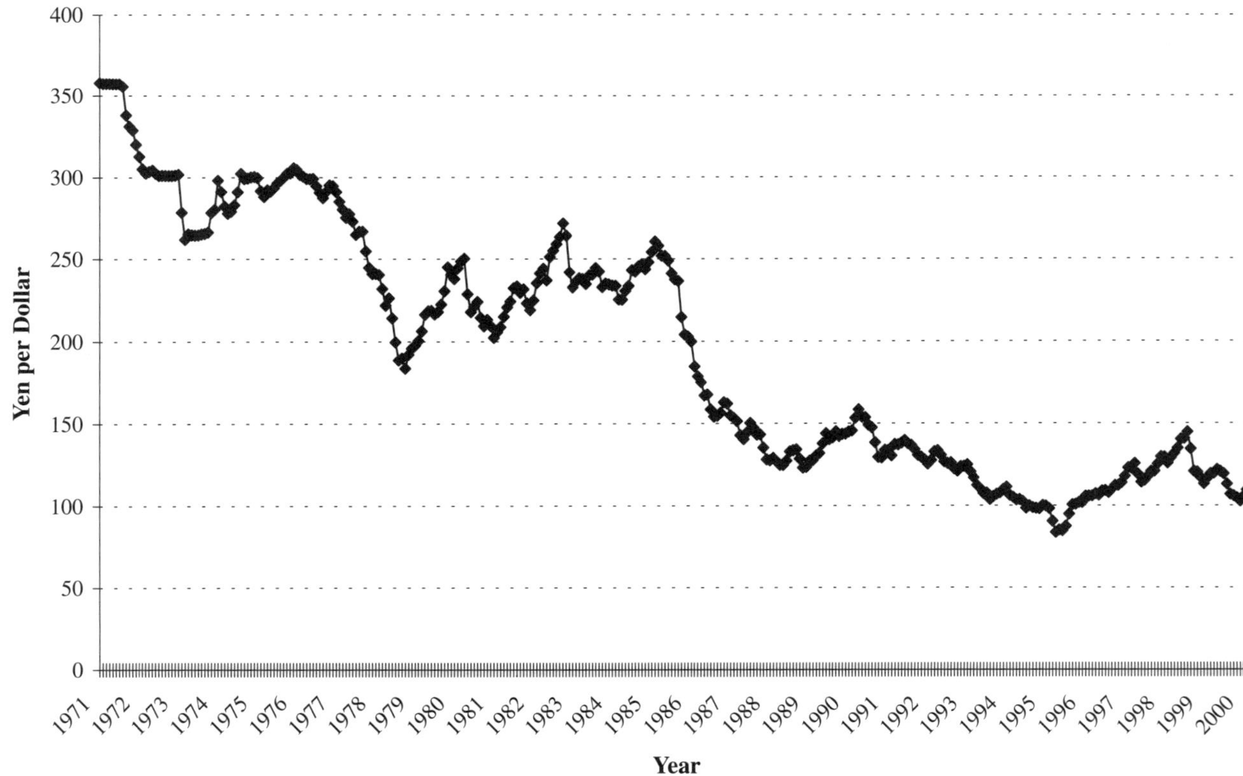

Fig. 2.13. Yen-dollar exchange rate fluctuation, 1971–2000. (From IMF, *International Financial Statistics.*)

Under the dramatic surge of Japan's economic power in the 1980s, some scholars saw something more than just an intensifying bilateral rivalry between the United States and Japan: they perceived a structural and hegemonic shift. Japan began to take on the function of a provider of international public goods as its relative economic size increased, with even the United States becoming dependent on Japanese financial resources. Rosecrance and Taw wrote in 1990:

> There are good reasons for Japan's present behavior: the leading economic power cannot escape the dangers of a possible collapse in the world trading and financial system. Today Japan sits atop the world financial pyramid; it must fall the farthest if the pyramid topples.[82]

Furthermore, Helleiner argued that given the way the Japanese government and business sector operate together to weather the adverse international economic environment and to guide, to some extent, the country's overseas business activities, Japan appears to be developing into an international (and structural) power.[83] This has led to a temporary surge in arguments that these developments are part of a power transition. The theory asserts that "international conflict is most likely to occur when the rate of development of the previous leading country is slowing down and when the rate of development of the previous lagging country is accelerating."[84] As the overriding power of cold war tension waned in the late 1980s, the Japanese "threat" was highlighted.[85]

As the 1990s clearly demonstrates, however, Japan never displaced the United States, while during the 1980s, economic interdependence between the United States and Japan strengthened. The Japanese government and its private sector became increasingly vulnerable to U.S. criticism and political pressure. Furthermore, under the structural power of the United States, discussion on Japan as a "reactive state" and on the country's responsiveness to *gaiatsu* (foreign pressure) gained wide recognition in the United States.[86] As Japan's recession in the 1990s lingered, it stemmed Japan's further rise in power. As the U.S. economy rebounded in the mid-1990s, the threat of Japan's overwhelming economic power waned. But concomitantly, given the widespread impact of Japan's economic problems in Asia and in the world, U.S. critics of Japan began to shift their focus from Japan's aggressive economic expansion to its apparent incapacity to put its own economic house in order.

Japan's Recession and U.S. Prosperity: The 1990s

International concern over the "rise of Japan" has waned slowly but definitely in the 1990s. From 1990 to 1991, Japan's "bubble economy" burst, revealing many negative effects; the economic performance of the United States, meanwhile, began to surpass that of Japan (see figs. 2.6, 2.7, and 2.8). Asher notes, "By 1992, it had become apparent to most observers that Japan faced a potentially comprehensive financial crisis, where problems in one area could migrate across the whole system."[87] Assessors of Japan's economic downturn in the 1990s may be divided into two groups, optimists and pessimists. The former group argues that slowdown of the Japanese economy is only a temporary phenomenon and that Japanese real economic power has not yet waned.[88] The latter group claims that the Japanese economic miracle is over and that the country requires a fundamental economic overhaul to get back on its feet.[89] The pessimistic view of the Japanese economic recovery gained more support both with the rise of criticism of the Japanese government's "too little, too late" approach in stimulating economic recovery during the past several years and with the ill-timed sales tax hike in 1997.[90]

Japan's economic problems are not limited to domestic problems. After the bursting of its economic bubble in 1990, Japan's external financial position also shifted. Although Japan has retained its large creditor status in the world (similar to the case of the late 1980s), the Japanese financial sector has become slowly incapacitated. The collapse of land and stock prices in Japan negatively affected the business performance of Japanese financial institutions and also caused them to accumulate bad loans. In addition, changes in the rules of international finance also impacted Japanese financial activities overseas. The most important change was the 1987 decision adopted by central bankers from the Group of Ten (G-10) countries who met at the Bank for International Settlements (BIS) to establish for all banks operating internationally a minimum ratio (8 percent) of self-capital to bank assets. The central bankers proposed to enforce this standard worldwide by the end of 1992. The fundamental purpose of introducing such a standard was to protect financial sectors from overexposing themselves to foreign lending. Often called the BIS capital adequacy (or bank capital adequacy) standard, the international rule has limited Japanese banks' overseas activities. The rule was particularly constraining to Japanese banks in regard to their future overseas lending activities, because the level of their capital to their assets was relatively low. Prior to the adaptation of the rule, such a low level of capital had given Japanese banks added risk and more competitiveness. In the 1990s, the introduction of the standard and the collapse of Japanese stock prices, which further lowered the Japanese banks' self-capital, hampered their overseas lending activities.[91]

Japanese investment in the U.S. securities market declined suddenly in 1990, and the net flow in this investment category became negative ($19.8 billion outflow from the United States, as illustrated in table 2.6). The reversal was partly the result of a temporary shift in Japan's monetary policy from a relatively

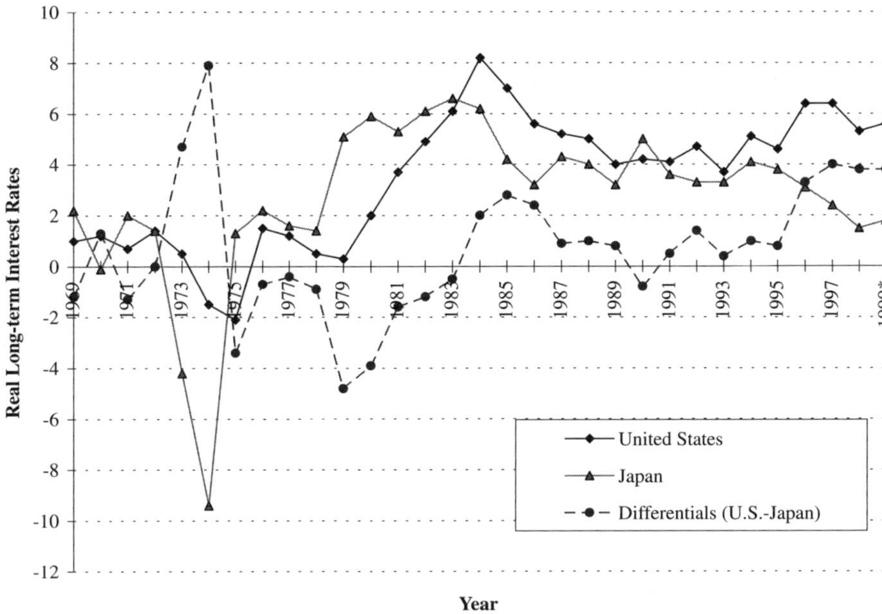

Fig. 2.14. Real long-term interest rates of the United States and Japan, 1969–99. (From OECD, *Historical Statistics.* *Long-term interest rates for 1999 are measured by the rate of central government bonds.)

loose policy to a tight one, a change that pushed Japanese long-term real interest rates to higher levels than those of the United States in 1990 (see fig. 2.14). The temporary weakening of the yen also threatened the profitability of Japanese investments in the United States (see fig. 2.13). In addition, an abrupt decline in the Japanese stock market decreased the capitalization of the Japanese banks and led some other financial institutions to withdraw investments from the United States to compensate for the domestic losses. Furthermore, there was a trend of regional concentration of Japan's lending and investment in Asia in the early 1990s, while the profitability of investment in the United States declined due to the U.S. recession and concomitant low interest rates until 1994.[92] Nevertheless, the financial ties between the United States and Japan remained solid (see fig. 2.12).[93]

During this time and despite Japan's financial problems, Asia kept attracting Japanese investment in the 1990s. After a moderate decline in capital outflow from Japan in the early 1990s, Japanese portfolio flows regained their strength, pushed by unprecedentedly low domestic interest rates at home and good investment and lending opportunities abroad. This outflow accounted for $84 billion by 1994, slightly down from its highest level of $113 billion in

1989. Not until the onset of the Asian financial crisis in 1997 did Japanese financial institutions curtail their financial exposure to the Asian economies.

Despite suffering a decade of recession, Japan is still the second largest economy and maintains its status as a major creditor in the world. However, it is clear, from its prolonged recession and from criticisms of the government's incapacity to move quickly to solve its economic problems, that the miraculous Japanese power that threatened to overtake the U.S. hegemonic position in the economic realm in the 1980s has waned. Japan thus remains the non-hegemonic major economic power. Going through a humbling experience of sifting through the country's major economic problems, Japanese policymakers and Japan's financial actors have struggled for answers to Japan's economic recovery problems. Japan's resentment against the United States increased in the 1990s in reaction to the intensification of U.S. criticism of Japan's economic mismanagement, which centers on Japan's economic turmoil and on the lack of effective solutions to such turmoil. This criticism, however, is derived from the fact that in the context of the firmly established economic interdependence between the two countries, Japan's lack of action would negatively affect not only the U.S. and Asian economies but also the stability of the world economy.

Summary

Japan's evolving relationships with the developing countries of the Pacific Rim and with the United States constitute important dimensions of Japan's external economic relations since World War II. We witnessed a dramatic increase of Japan's presence in both these regions in the 1980s. Although they are presented separately in this chapter, it is important to connect the two pictures to see how Japan's relationship with the United States has influenced Japan's involvement in developing countries, particularly at the time of their economic crises. It is also important, to a lesser extent, to note how Japan's relationship with developing countries altered U.S.-Japanese dynamics.

In the 1980s, the shift in U.S. position from the world's creditor to the world's debtor increased the pressure on Japanese creditors; subsequently, the Japanese government became more involved in the Third World debt crises occurring at that time. This led to an interconnection between the North-North debt crisis (although it was never the same type of payment crisis) and the North-South debt crisis.[94]

Considering Japan's involvement in the solution to the Latin American debt crisis, it is clear that the North-North relationship dictated a large part of Japan's participation. Although the decline of Japan's financial position in the world in the mid-1990s slowed, and occasionally reversed, Japan's overseas economic expansion, it has not quite altered the level of U.S.-Japanese economic interdependence or the economic stake of the Japanese financial sector in the stability of the international financial market. In this sense, examining a bilateral framework between Japan and the middle-income countries of the Pacific Rim under financial crises is not enough to understand the determining factors of Japanese foreign economic policy toward these countries and its motivation as a provider of international public goods. The strong interdependence between the United States and Japan in the late 1980s had special implications for the Latin American debt solution, and it continues to wield an influence in the 1990s. Collaboration or collusion among creditors—in this case between Japan and the United States—becomes a key factor in explaining financial crisis management dynamics. This collective action among creditors has given them greater leverage over debtors.[95]

Finally, the analysis in the following chapters emphasizes the active involvement of private economic actors in this triangular dynamic. The economic interdependence that has increased in recent years is not only of concern to governments but obviously of critical importance to private sectors. As the Japanese economy has become internationalized, the economic and political interests of Japan's private sector have become increasingly tied to its activities abroad. In particular, and as I discuss in the following chapters, the intensifying exposure of Japan's private financial sector to economic and political risks abroad has even changed the country's domestic political dynamics.

This evolution of Japan's economic relations with developing countries and with the United States sets the stage for the variation in the Japanese government's response to different financial crises in the past two decades. On one hand, shifting economic power dynamics and interdependence between the United States and Japan under continuing structural power asymmetry favoring the United States has led the Japanese government to respond differently to collective action with the United States. On the other hand, the varied regional context and the respective economic involvement of the Japanese private sector have become critical components affecting the decision-making process of the Japanese government.

CHAPTER 3

Quantitative Analysis

The Latin American Debt Crisis and Japan's Official Financial Flows

Japan became one of the most prosperous economies in the world in the 1980s. Concomitantly, and as the debt crisis deepened, the indebted economies of Latin America began to suffer from their limited access to the foreign capital on which they had previously relied. The Japanese government, in the mid-1980s, began to extend its official flows (OOF and ODA) to stabilize and help resolve the Latin American debt crisis. Particularly under the debt crisis situation, foreign aid (ODA) as well as OOF provided an important source of stable foreign capital inflows for the debtors, a trend that helped keep the debtors from defaulting. These funds thus contributed significantly to providing stability in international finance. In this special context, therefore, we can consider official flows as a cost in maintaining international public goods.[1] Japan shouldered a large portion of this cost of public goods provision. As Japan's total official flows to developing countries increased dramatically under the Capital Recycling Program initiated in 1986, Latin America received the second largest portion of such flows among the developing regions. A close examination of Japan's official financial flows, however, reveals the uneven allocation of such flows among the Latin American debtors.

This chapter examines Japan's involvement in the Latin American debt crisis through its official financial contributions. The quantitative method used in the chapter identifies and isolates important factors that influenced the Japanese government's decision to allocate official funds to Latin America. As I discussed in chapter 2, Japan's financial flows have constituted important channels for the past few decades, during which Japan has related to developing countries. Particularly as a financial crisis hit these countries, any positive financial flows (more likely from public sources than private) contributed to the stability of specific debtors and to the world of international finance in general. What were the major factors influencing the Japanese government's decisions regarding the disbursement and allocation of Japan's official financial flows during the debt crisis? With what criteria did the Japanese government (and its private sector, to lesser extent) decide which Latin American countries would receive a greater share of needed financial resources and which would receive less?

The analysis of these questions, in effect, tests the two hypotheses posed in chapter 1, hypotheses that aim to explain variance in Japan's behavior during different episodes of financial crisis management. This exercise probes how the hypotheses fare on the microlevel as they try to explain country variation of Japanese financial allocation in Latin America at the time of the debt crisis. In addition, by taking advantage of multivariate regressions, the quantitative method enables us to isolate and control for the influence of the variables included. The results provide unambiguous findings of the relevance of each variable.[2] The purpose of this quantitative chapter is therefore to clarify the sets of relationship among actors and forces involved in Japan's decision making in management of the Latin American debt crisis and to verify them statistically.

The Latin American debt crisis provides good experimental ground for quantitative analysis for various reasons. First, the actors involved in the genesis and resolution of the crisis are definable and quite limited in scope; the governments of the creditors, IFIs such as the IMF and the World Bank, the debtors (mostly governments and some private sector debtors), and transnational banks from the creditor countries. Furthermore, we can observe the fairly discernible resolution of this debt crisis, especially among the middle-income countries of Latin America (and some in Asia) in the early 1990s, after many of them experienced rescheduling and reconstruction of their debt through Brady deals or otherwise. This resolution enabled many of these economies to begin a successful return to the international financial market for at least several years, into the 1990s.[3] The second reason is more technical. Due to the relatively slow pace of its resolution and the large number of Latin American countries involved, the Latin American debt crisis presents a significant number of data points from which to run regression analysis.

In the first section of this chapter, I analyze Japanese–Latin American economic relations and the role of official financial flows (ODA and OOF) allocated to Latin America.[4] In the second section, I construct regression models to examine factors determining the decisions of the Japanese government and, to a lesser extent, Japan's private financial sector concerning fund allocation to the Latin American countries under the debt crisis. I include discussion on how I operationalize the variables used in the regression models. Five mutlivariate regressions are run, and results are reported. In the third section of the chapter, the results and findings are discussed. The quantitative analysis in this chapter indicates that the Japanese government's commitment to the management of the Latin American debt crisis was increased by three principal factors: (1) Japanese self-interest and the high private returns anticipated from the government's active involvement, including a desire to support U.S. economic interests in Latin America; (2) the strong institutional linkages constituted among transnational banks; and (3) the strong political leverage that banks had on the Japanese government's decision making at the time of the debt crisis.

Japan and Latin America

Due to extensive geographical distance and a lack of historical interaction, most of Latin America was unfamiliar to Japan until recently. In addition, the Japanese government considered the region to be within the U.S. sphere of influence, so it refrained from competing directly with U.S. economic interests there. Migration and bilateral trade dominated the early stage of interaction between Japan and Latin America.

The history of Japanese immigration to Latin America began with the migration of mostly poor Japanese farmers to Brazil in the 1920s and 1930s. Paraguay, Peru, Mexico, and other Latin American countries have also accommodated Japanese immigrants. Latin America currently has the largest Japanese population (estimated at 1.5 million) outside of Japan.[5] Approximately 250,000 Japanese chose to go and live in Latin America throughout the first half of the twentieth century, a flow that constituted 56 percent of total Japanese emigration.

Trade relations between Japan and Latin America became relatively important in the 1950s, when almost 10 percent of Japan's export and import exchange occurred with Latin America. However, Latin America's importance in Japanese trade has declined slowly and surely over time. As I noted earlier, total Japanese trade with Latin America looks much less impressive than Japanese trade with industrial democracies or countries in Asia (see chap. 2 and fig. 2.1).

Japanese FDI activities in the region followed a path similar to those of the United States during a large influx in the 1950s. Latin America was an attractive direct investment site because of its abundant minerals and natural resources and its relatively large but traditionally closed markets for manufactured goods. Japan followed the American example, but its firms arrived late in Latin America; balance-of-payments restrictions imposed by Japan's still capital-poor position limited Japanese FDI considerably until the 1970s. However, the "national project" format helped increase Japan's FDI in Latin America, partly by reducing private sector risk in investing in the region's natural resource projects (see chap. 2). For the Japanese government, these projects became important policy instruments in influencing private sector capital allocation in the developing world. For Japanese commercial banks, the government provided additional money for potentially lucrative but highly risky

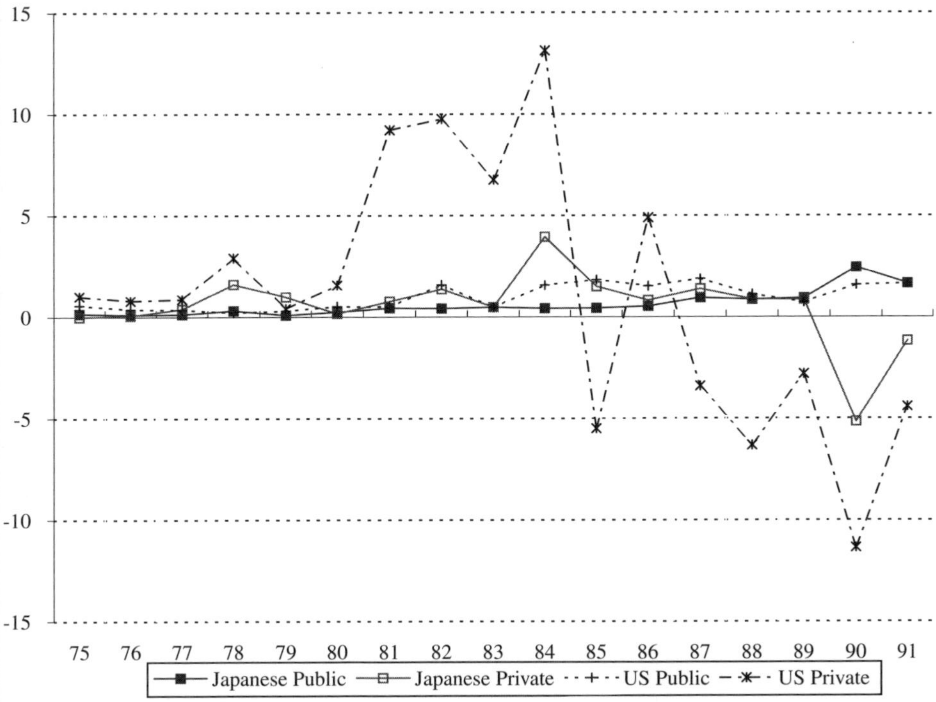

Fig. 3.1. Net financial flows to Latin America from the United States and Japan, 1975–91. (From OECD, *Geographical Distribution of Financial Flows to Developing Countries.*)

investments in natural resource extraction industries. Despite the policy efforts, Japan's FDI in Latin America did not become significant until the mid-1970s (see table 2.3).

The internationalization of Japan's financial activities since the mid-1970s led Japan to become increasingly actively engaged in Latin America (see fig. 3.1). Japanese banks began lending to the region and other developing countries as their foreign lending increased rapidly in conjunction with deregulation granted by the MOF. Heavy lending began in the latter half of the 1970s and continued until the early 1980s, as Japanese banks extended syndicated loans to Latin American and other governments in collaboration with American and European banks.[6]

There are several reasons for the significant increase in Japanese lending to Latin America. First, Japanese banks' eagerness to extend loans abroad had the same root as the global lending boom itself. Petrodollars accumulating in the foreign exchange accounts of some newly enriched oil-exporting countries were recycled and found their way into Japanese bank deposits. Hit additionally by the slump in domestic demand after the oil shock and the increased internationalization of the Japanese manufacturing sector, many banks saw no other option but to seek customers overseas. At the time, the Japanese government believed it was necessary to diversify its sources of raw materials, particularly oil, from countries beyond Asia and other than OPEC (Organization of Petroleum Exporting Countries) members. In the 1970s, after a brief period of a balance-of-payments deficit caused by the oil crisis, the Japanese economy managed to overcome its chronic balance-of-payments problems and was in a position to allow some outflow of capital.

Together, profit-maximization calculations, international competition, and medium- and long-term economic considerations made by the Japanese banks constitute a second reason that led the banks to proceed with lending to sovereign entities.[7] In many cases, Japanese banks followed the lead of American banks in forming syndicates, and they eventually became managers (leading banks) in syndicated loans. The MOF also guided such banks' behavior, encouraging them to act as leading banks in syndication.[8]

The Japanese government's overall development policy and pressure from the Japanese manufacturing sector comprise a third reason for increased lending to Latin America. The Japanese government played a major role in facilitating private lending to developing countries, particularly to a booming but traditionally foreign Latin America. Various official instruments (including the formation of "national projects," discussed in chap. 2) were used to encourage banks to lend to countries where they otherwise would not. The Japanese manufacturing sector also relied heavily on Japanese bank loans for investments abroad. Spindler notes,

> In essence, this general pattern has called for private Japanese industry to execute a given overseas project, relying on the Japanese government and a syndicate of Japanese commercial banks to provide a major share of the necessary financing.[9]

Furthermore, it is important to consider the essential relationship between trade and financial flows. The role of trading companies is crucial in this respect. On one hand, because of Japan's lack of natural resources, especially oil, a good part of Japanese investments or loans were provided to secure these raw material imports. Joint ventures between the Japanese government, banks, and trade and manufacturing companies were developed in the 1960s and 1970s to expand access to natural resources. On the other hand, such financial instruments as export credit or tied aid were also frequently used to expand Japan's export markets for its manufacturing goods.

Finally, the presence of the United States is an important factor in explaining Japanese banks' international behavior, particularly in the Latin American debt crisis. The U.S.-Japanese relationship was a major factor that led the Japanese private banks and the government to become heavily involved in the debt crisis. Interbank politics between the two countries were important in determining the volume and allocation of private capital flows. Devlin stresses that before 1979, those seeking loans (i.e., developing countries) faced a nearly flat commercial loan supply curve in Latin America. Devlin explains that this flat supply curve results from the competitive nature of banking and the "follow-the-leader psychology" among banks.

> Concentration of the debt crisis in Latin America may not be unrelated to market structure. The leaders in the oligopolistic market, especially in the initial phase of the 1970s expansion, were U.S. banks. These institutions have traditionally been most comfortable in Latin America. To the extent that the credit market was subject to interdependent decision-making and follow-the-leader psychology, Latin America may have been the developing region subject to the most intensive marketing pressures of the banks.[10]

In the evolution of syndicated bank loans, notes Devlin, "upstart banks relied heavily on the participation of other relatively *inexperienced* banks."[11] Japanese banks' involvement in Latin America increased, and they began taking a leading role in syndicated loan operations more often in the late 1970s and early 1980s, despite signs of impending disaster.

As the Japanese government was faced with the debt crisis in Latin America, a situation that threatened the stability of the international banking and financial sector, one primary means through which the government participated in the resolution of this financial crisis was to increase official financial flows to the region. Traditionally, official financial support from the Japanese government was limited to resource-related activities in Latin America, but the goals of Japan's official financial flows expanded as the region experienced a major financial crisis.

The Latin American countries were not, however, treated as like units. A close analysis of Japan's relations with individual Latin American countries reveals variance in Japan's interests. In addition, each country has had different and sometimes fluctuating politico-economic relations with the United States. All these factors influenced the Japanese government's decisions. Before I discuss these factors, it is worthwhile to analyze the dependent variable—Japan's official flow allocation in Latin America over time.

On the aggregated level, as figure 3.2 indicates, there was a gradual but

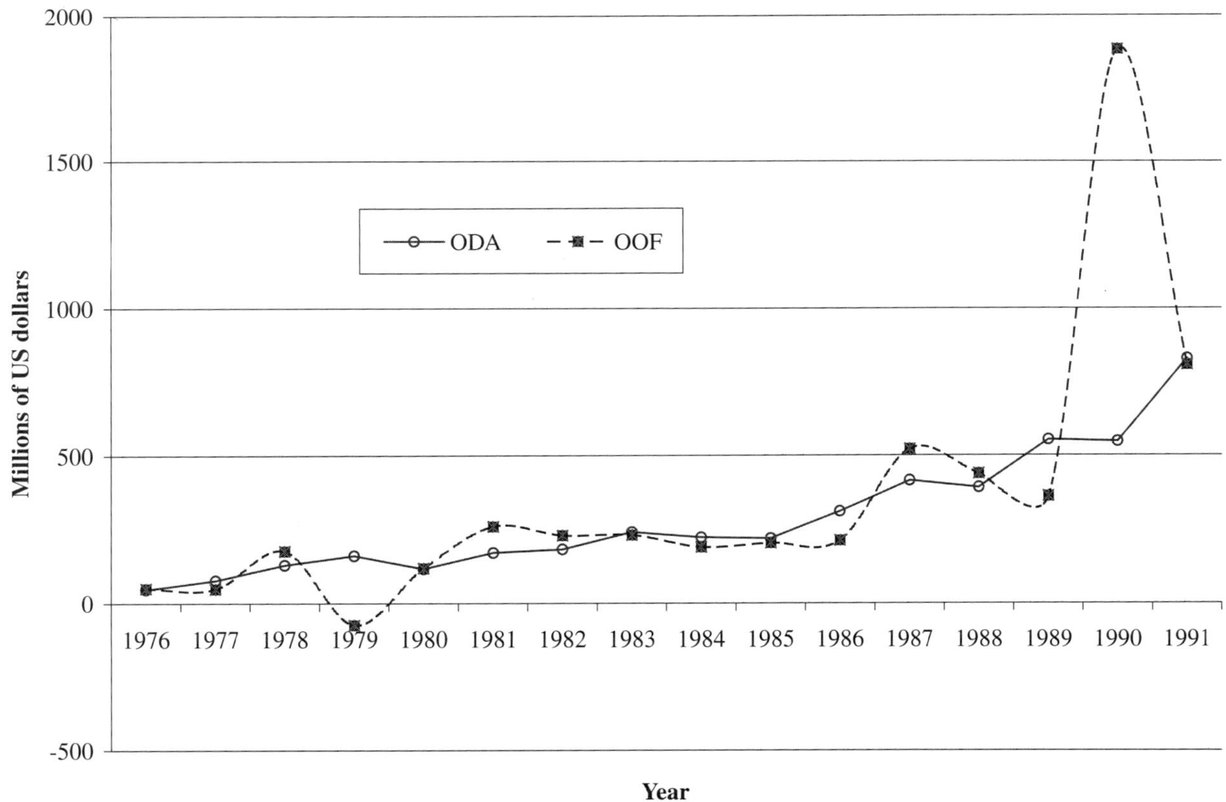

Fig. 3.2. Japan's ODA and OOF to Latin America, 1976–91. (From OECD, *Geographical Distribution of Financial Flows to Developing Countries.*)

steady increase in both ODA and OOF to Latin America, particularly after the onset of the debt crisis and since the initiation of Japan's Capital Recycling Program in 1986. The year 1990 shows a prominent peak in OOF disbursement to Latin America, which stemmed from the successful conclusion of the Brady deals with Mexico. The Japanese government contributed $1.9 billion in official loans to Mexico for this purpose. Table 3.1 demonstrates that certain Latin American countries, especially Brazil and Mexico, were consistently large recipients of Japan's official flows during this period. These two countries plus Venezuela and Argentina received the majority of Japan's OOF. ODA was distributed to smaller and poorer countries (with a large number of Japanese immigrants), such as Peru and Paraguay, as well as some Central American countries, including Honduras, El Salvador, and Costa Rica.

Three variables are plotted against Japan's official flow allocation (the average from 1983 through 1990) in Latin America: the outstanding debt of each Latin American country, the total trade of each country with Japan, and the country's respective per capita GNP. These variables are the usual suspects when it comes to Japan's aid allocation decisions. However, none of them give any clear indication of single-handedly attracting or repelling Japanese official flows. Three scatter plots (figs. 3.3, 3.4, and 3.5) provide an inconclusive picture of any of these factors as the single and dominant influence on Japan's official financial flow allocation. Therefore, we have every reason to proceed to run multivariate regressions.

TABLE 3.1. Top Five Latin American Recipients of Japan's ODA and OOF, 1976–1991 (averages in millions of US dollars)

	1976–80[a]		1981–85[a]		1986–91	
ODA						
1	Brazil	25.48	Brazil	37.04	Peru	86.48
2	Bolivia	13.16	Bolivia	29.58	Brazil	68.18
3	Peru	11.70	Peru	24.64	Bolivia	59.35
4	Paraguay	11.48	Mexico	23.72	Honduras	45.43
5	Ecuador	9.12	Paraguay	23.46	Paraguay	44.30
OOF						
1	Brazil	60.92	Mexico	151.22	Mexico	511.35
2	Trinidad	1.32	Colombia	46.80	Venezuela	110.30
3	Mexico	1.24	Argentina	12.14	Chile	67.62
4	Ecuador	0.96	Paraguay	6.08	Argentina	53.10
5	Jamaica	0.60	Brazil	3.54	Ecuador	19.27

Source: OECD, *Development Report,* various issues.
[a]Venezuela is not included during these years due to missing OOF data.

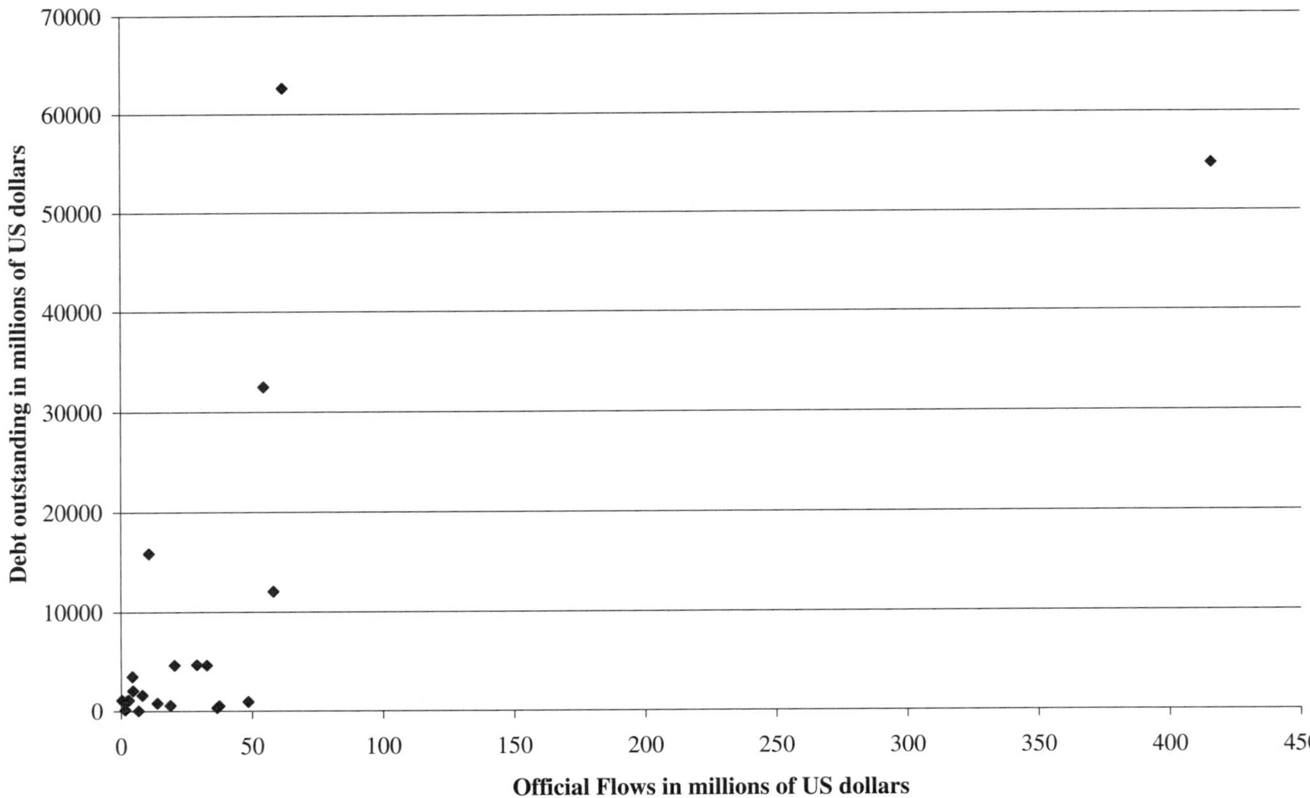

Fig. 3.3. Official flows (X) and debt outstanding (Y), average 1983–90. (From OECD, *Geographical Distribution of Financial Flows to Developing Countries,* and Japan Bond Research Institute, *Country Risk Information.*)

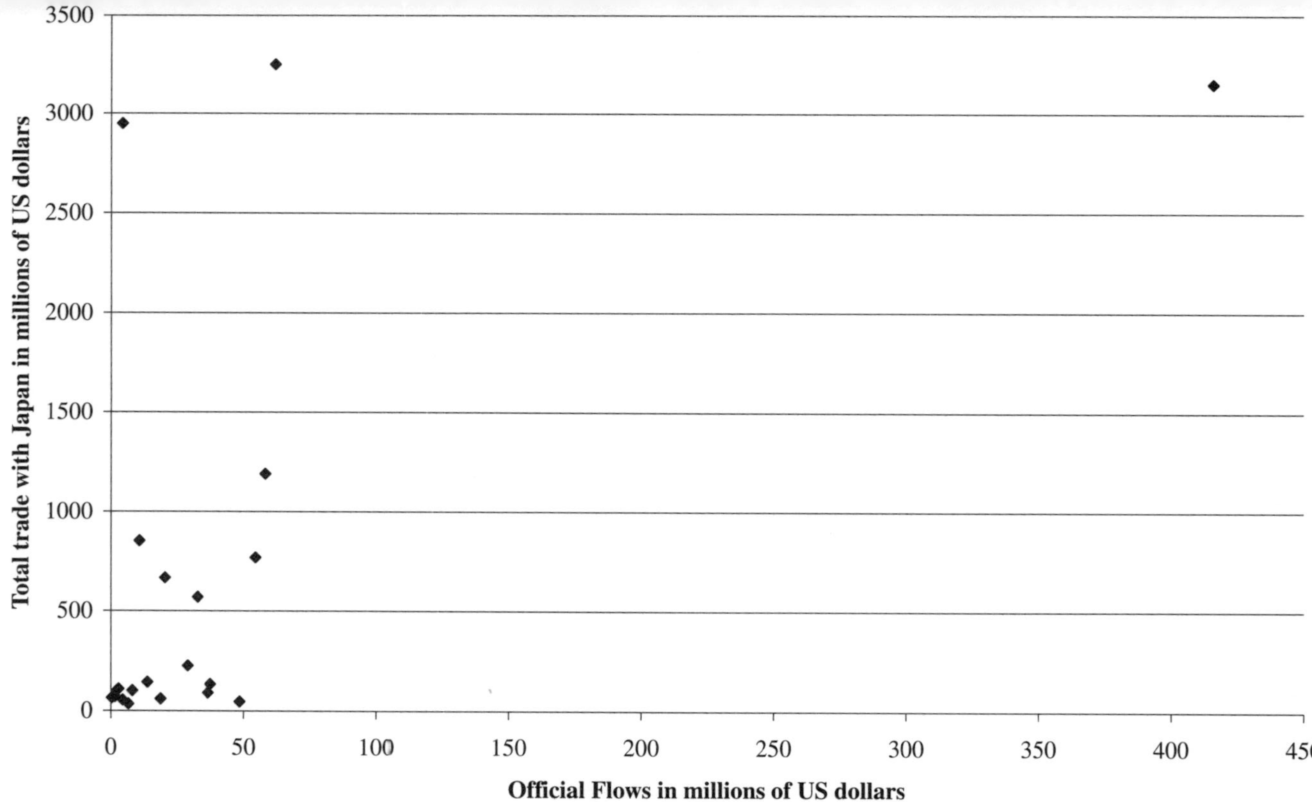

Fig. 3.4. Official flows (X) and total trade with Japan (Y), average 1983–90. (From OECD, *Geographical Distribution of Financial Flows to Developing Countries*, and IMF, *Direction of Trade Statistics Yearbook*.)

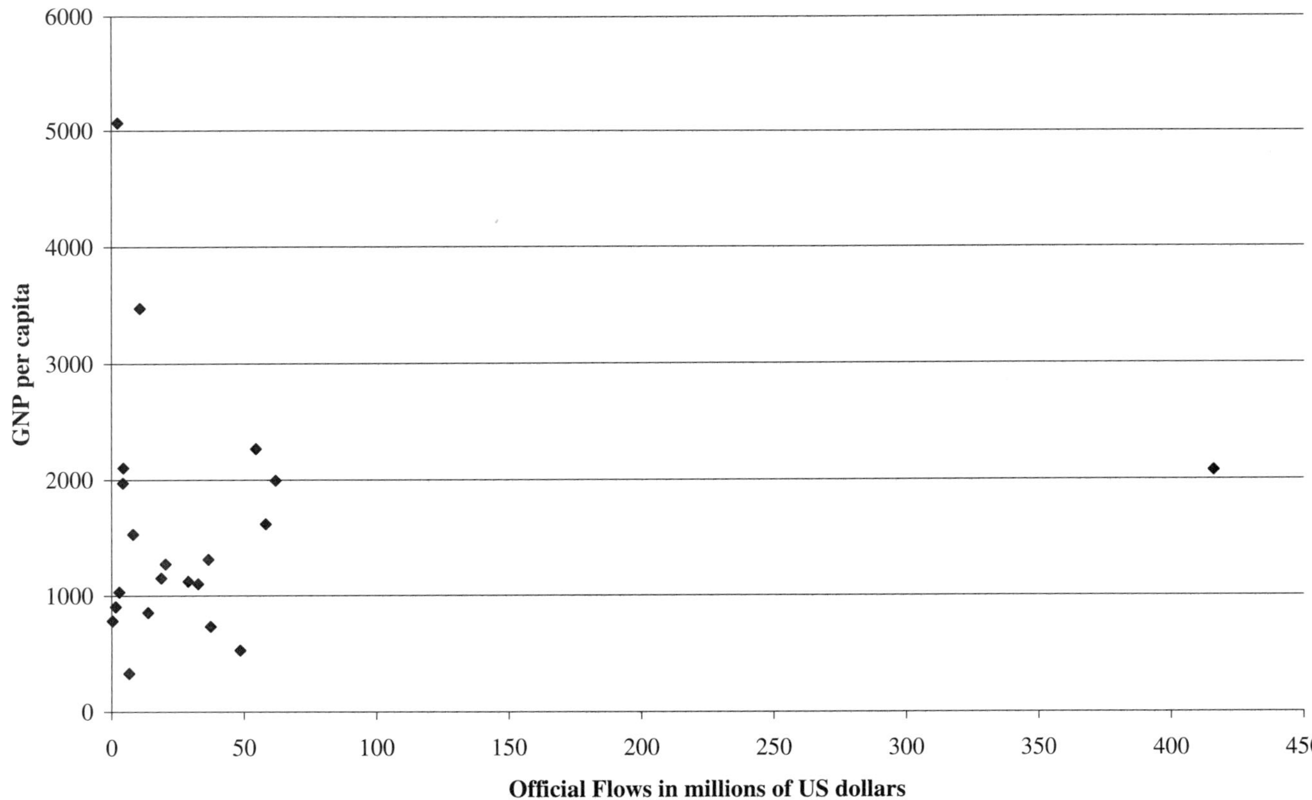

Fig. 3.5. Official flows (X) and GNP per capita (Y), average 1983–90. (From OECD, *Geographical Distribution of Financial Flows to Developing Countries,* various issues, and World Bank, *World Tables,* various issues.)

Regression Analyses

Variables of Interests

This study argues that two factors, the joint product nature of international financial stability and transnational linkages, are critical components of the Japanese government's decisions regarding involvement in financial crisis management. These two factors motivated the Japanese government when it allocated public funds to and among Latin American and Caribbean countries during the debt crisis. The first dimension arises from Japan's private interests. Japan's bilateral economic (trade and investment) and political (immigration) interests in certain Latin American countries have shaped Japan's private interests. In addition, Japan's relatively high financial exposure in these countries led the Japanese government to become involved in crisis management to protect Japanese financial institutions. The second dimension involves the economic and institutional linkages that connected Japan to Latin America, directly and bilaterally in some cases and indirectly, through the United States, in other cases. The involvement of Japan's financial institutions in Latin American lending also led to the establishment of institutional linkages between Japan and the United States that compelled the Japanese government to act. Finally, Japan's actions in Latin America clearly reflected U.S. interests in the region. The Japanese government and the business sector were concerned about the negative impact of the Latin American debt crisis on the U.S. economy. The detrimental impact of the Latin American debt crisis on the United States affected Japan in two different negative ways. The first involved the negative impact of the crisis on Japanese businesses exposed to the U.S. economy, and the second involved the bilateral pressure the U.S. government exerted on the Japanese government in relation to their bilateral trade imbalance.

Organizing Variables

This regression analysis involves two exclusive types of data, because important elements in the Japanese government's allocation decision making create two sets of variables of different characters. The substantive distinction among the variables is whether they capture Japan's relationship with Latin America as an aggregate unit (one-year one-data-point variable) or as individual countries (one-year *N*-data-point variable). For example, Japanese domestic conditions and U.S.-Japanese relations not concerned with Latin America only have one data point per year, so they belong to the former set. The variables that capture the importance of Japan's bilateral relations with each Latin American country, such as trade relations or immigration, belong to the latter set, containing as many data points as the number of individual Latin American countries included in the regressions.[12]

An obvious consequence of including these distinct variables is that it is hard to estimate their relationship in a single regression. These variables have to be grouped into two sets of regression models, and the organizational principle is that the data for certain variables are available for only one data point per year ($t \times 1$), while others have as many data points as the number of Latin American countries per year ($t \times N$). Regression models consisting of the former resort to time series ($t \times 1$) as the basis of estimation, and the latter provides an opportunity to run regressions based on time-series cross-section (TSCS) pooled data ($t \times N$). The first set of variables is estimated using twenty-one years of time-series data (1971–91), and the second set is estimated on a panel of twenty Latin American countries for seventeen years (1975–91). In addition, some TSCS regressions incorporate 0–1 dummy variables for certain time periods, as interaction terms to analyze the shifts in the relationship between dependent and independent variables during the different periods. The most obvious interaction terms indicate the precrisis period (1975–82) and the crisis period (1983–91).

Models with Financial Flows Disaggregated by ODA, OOF, and Private Flows

The dependent variable, capital flows from Japan to Latin America, is also disaggregated by type of flows, to avoid aggregation bias. Official financial flows, as I noted before, consist mainly of ODA and OOF. These two flows, in principle, have different objectives, different sources of funding, different implementing agencies, and different sets of constraints. During the Latin American debt crisis, however, there were cases where nonconcessional OOF was used to supplement Japan's ODA, because ODA has various noneconomic constraints, due to its heavier reliance on Japan's central budget.[13] ODA is more exposed to international and domestic pressure that it be appropriately used and to the mandates of the implementing agencies of ODA—the Ministry of Foreign Affairs (MOFA), the OECF, and the Japan International Cooperation Agency (JICA). Furthermore, the distinction between ODA and OOF comes from public scrutiny. Despite the fact that taxpayers' inquiry into the use of the central budget is weak in Japan compared to the Western nations, the Japanese government still has difficulty allocating a significant portion of its ODA for the purpose of "bailing out the banks with taxpayers' money." In comparison, OOF derives its funding largely from the Fiscal Investment and Loan Program (*zaisei-toyushi* or FILP), which is composed of the Japanese people's postal savings and pension funds managed by the government. Although this fund has to be repaid, the government and OOF-implementing institutions, such as the JEXIM

Bank, are under relatively weak public scrutiny in their use of this fund. This scrutiny was even weaker prior to the 1990s.[14]

Hence, disaggregation of these flows when running both time-series and TSCS regressions should improve the accuracy of the quantitative analysis by exacting the concrete dynamics that determine the flows and allocation of the two types of official funds to Latin America. One more time-series model is added, using as a dependent variable private capital flows dominated by bank lending from Japan to Latin America.[15] This allows me to empirically demonstrate influential factors that induced Japan's private flows to Latin America, factors that have increased total capital flows to the region.

Regression Models, Operationalization of Variables, and Results from Time Series (ODA, OOF, and Private Capital Flows as Dependent Variables)

The following three time-series regressions are run with three different dependent variables, all representing the needed foreign capital flows to debt-ridden Latin America as a region. The model specified under each category (Model A, B, or C) indicates the best and most interesting model from other slightly different specifications. The results from alternative specifications are also included in the regression result tables (tables 3.4, 3.5, and 3.6). Due to the small degrees of freedom in these regressions, I use Student's *t*-statistics to calculate the significance of each coefficient.[16]

For all three time-series regressions, unit roots are tested, and when found, as is the case for all of the variables, first differences are taken to detrend the series. No significant autocorrelation is found. Later, cointegration tests are conducted for all the variable pairs. Only one significant cointegrating pair is found (private capital flow model), and the lagged residual from this cointegrating regression is plugged back into the private capital regression model (Model 3C) as an error correction term.[17] Independent variables are lagged by one year to avoid a simultaneity problem. A lagged dependent variable has been added to each regression to control for the incremental nature of the capital flows.

Table 3.2 summarizes the variables and models from the time-series regression models discussed in detail in this section. Expected signs are also noted in the table. Appendix 1 details the data sources.

Models with Japan's ODA as the Dependent Variable (Model 1)

$$\text{JODA}_t = b1 + b2\ \text{DIFEX}_{t-1} + b3\ \text{BUDGET}_{t-1} + b4\ \text{LDPSP}_{t-1} + b5\ \text{CASURUS}_{t-1} + b6\ \text{USAID}_{t-1} + b7\ \text{TJODA}_{t-1} + e. \qquad \text{(Model 1B)}$$

TABLE 3.2. Models, Variables, and Their Expected Signs from Time-Series Models (one-year, one-data-point variables)

Dependent Variables	Independent Variables: Concepts	Independent Variables: Operationalization	Acronyms	Signs
Japan's ODA to Latin America as a region (JODA)	Japan's relative power gain	Difference in the world market share between the US and Japan	DIFEX	–
	US influence (1)	Japan's trade surplus vis-à-vis the US	CASURUS	+
	US influence (2)	Japan's vested financial interest in the US in government bonds	GVBOND	+
	US influence (3)	Japan's vested financial interest in the US in loans	LTFLW	+
	US influence (4)	Japan-US policy coordination in foreign aid; US foreign aid in Latin America	USAID	+
	Domestic constraint (1)	Total Japanese central budget	BUDGET	+
	Domestic constraint (2)	LDP popularity and support in Japan	LDPSP	+
	Importance of other regions	Japanese foreign aid (ODA) to Asia	ASIAID	–
Japan's OOF to Latin America as a region (JOOF)	US influence (1)	Japan's trade surplus vis-à-vis the US	CASURUS	+
	US influence (2)	Japan's vested financial interest in the US in government bonds	GVBOND	+
	US influence (3)	Japan's vested financial interest in the US in loans	LTFLW	+
	Government-bank linkage	Outstanding Japanese bank loans to Latin America	JOUT	+
Japan's private capital flows to Latin America as a region (JPRV)	Transnational bank linkage	Outstanding US loans to Latin America	USOUT	+
	Private sector interest in US	Japan's vested financial interest in the US in loans	LTFLW	+
	US commitment in region	US foreign aid to Latin America	USAID	+
	Government influence on banks	Japanese official flows as signs of commitment to Latin America	JOFF	+
	Profit motives of banks	Interest rate differentials between Japan and the international market	DIFINRT	+
	Link with Japan's MNCs	Japan's FDI in Latin America	FDIGR	+
	Yen power	Japanese yen's weakness vis-à-vis US dollar	YVSUSD	–

Note: For data sources and estimation procedures, see appendix 1.

For Model 1A, an additional variable, LTFLW, is added, and ASIAID is added for Model 1C.

DIFEX is a measurement of difference between the respective American and Japanese market shares of the world exports. This variable also captures Japan's increasing stake in a stable world economic system. DIFEX examines the hypothesis associated with the international systemic argument that Japan's official financial commitment to Latin America should have increased as Japan became a relatively large country. Scholars have been concerned, particularly in the second half of the 1980s, with the declining hegemony of the United States, and they have questioned the role of the supporting or challenging powers of Europe and Japan. From the Japanese government's perspective, as the Japanese role in the world economy increased, there should have been a greater demand for Japan to increase its commitment to the economic well-being of developing regions. Japan also had to become involved in regions where Japan had no direct economic or strategic concerns—for example, Latin America. Furthermore, as Japan became an increasingly "large country" capable of influencing the world economy, and as it increased self-interest in global economic stability, the Japanese government would have had far more incentive to make financial commitments.[18] Therefore, the hypothesis is that as the difference in the U.S. and the Japanese market share decreases (DIFEX), Japanese official financial flows to Latin America should increase, making the sign on this variable's coefficient negative.

The two following variables in the equation are controlling variables. BUDGET represents the government's budgetary conditions that finance Japan's ODA (General Account).[19] If there are enough budgetary resources available in the general account budget, one can expect greater ODA flows to Latin America. The elasticity of the Latin American allocation to the availability of budgetary resources was high: the more abundant available resources were, the more likely it was that ODA to Latin America would increase. ASIAID (Japan's ODA allocation to Asia as a region) is also included, because Asia takes the lion's share of Japanese financial resource flows. This share tends to be inelastic due to the region's political and economic importance to Japan. In contrast, the marginal increase in funding to Latin America during the 1980s depended on an increase in available financial resources.

LDPSP indicates the level of support for the Liberal Democratic Party (LDP), which was the ruling party throughout the period of analysis of this study. The support for this party influenced the legislative process and proved an important determinant of the control of resources used for official financial flows, such as ODA. The provision of public money to Latin America was a remote issue for most of the LDP's domestic constituents. When the party had more support from the public and thus a better chance of winning the next election, it had greater autonomy in responding to external demands, such as U.S. pressures to disburse money to Latin America. Strong popular support of the LDP also made it easier for the leading party to use official funds for purposes that did not appeal to its constituency, such as providing more funds to rescue Japanese banks in Latin America. However, if the Japanese financial sector, with its political contribution and support, was critical for the LDP's electoral success, the LDP might even have supported the banks' demands at the time of lower public support.

Finally, the increasing economic linkages between Japan and the United States in the 1980s undoubtedly influenced the behavior of the Japanese government. The government understood the impact the Latin American debt crisis would have on Japan's economic activities abroad, particularly in the United States. The transmission of U.S. influence could occur through explicit or implicit threats of protectionist retaliation by the United States against Japan and through linking financial issues to other economic and political tensions that existed in U.S.-Japanese relations. CASURUS, measured in terms of the size of Japan's trade surplus with the United States, is one way to operationalize the degree of economic tension between these two countries during this period. USAID represents the regional allocation of U.S. economic aid to Latin America, capturing the changes in the level of U.S. official commitment to Latin America, and LTFLW measures the amount of Japan's long-term investment in the United States, capturing Japan's direct financial interests in the country.

The Latin American debt crisis and U.S.-Japanese trade relations (CASURUS) were linked by the fact that the debt crisis caused a significant deterioration in the U.S. trade balance: Latin American debtors reduced their imports and adopted aggressive export-oriented strategies to improve their balance of payments and thus service their debt.[20] This decreased U.S. exports to the region and increased U.S. imports from the region. The deterioration of the external economic position of the United States became pronounced after 1982. Meanwhile, Japan kept accumulating its trade surplus against the United States, a factor that further intensified protectionist pressures against the Japanese.[21] Therefore, this trade imbalance (CASURUS) between Japan and the United States should have led to greater U.S. pressure on Japan, and it should have increased Japan's ODA flows to Latin America, making the sign on the coefficient positive.

Determining the amount of U.S. aid to Latin America (USAID) is an appropriate way to measure the region's importance to the United States. Assuming that the United States assists with foreign aid a region that the U.S. government perceives vital to U.S. interests, and assuming that the Japanese government responds to U.S. political considerations, an increased amount of U.S. foreign aid to Latin America should have increased Japanese ODA to the region. However, the Japanese government might have been more concerned about the decline of the U.S. economy, a condition that would hurt Japanese private investment in and lending to the country. The Japanese government might have tried to support the U.S. economy by shouldering more of the burden of the Latin American rescue, because of Japan's high financial exposure to the United States. In this case, the larger Japan's long-term capital flow (LTFLW) to the United States was, the more likely it was for Latin America to receive Japan's official economic assistance.

Table 3.3 summarizes the results from the regressions. Model 1B included the specification that performed the best, with all the variables of interests showing significance and with an adjusted R^2 of 0.5003.

TABLE 3.3. Times-Series Regression with ODA (JODA) as the Dependent Variable (Model 1: various specifications)

Independent Variables	Model 1A	Model 1B	Model 1C
Intercept	125.303	112.87	112.35
	(4.184)***	(3.802)***	(3.475)***
Difference in world	−57.227	−56.42	−56.79
market share (DIFEX)	(−2.317)**	(−2.200)**	(−2.059)*
Overall Japanese central	−0.032	−0.026	−0.026
budget (BUDGET)	(−2.898)**	(−2.467)**	(−2.319)**
Japanese foreign aid			0.002
to Asia (ASIAID)			(0.056)
Public support to LDP (LDPSP)	8.856	6.037	6.052
	(2.351)**	(1.830)*	(1.751)
Trade surplus vis-à-vis the US	−0.009	−0.007	−0.007
(CASURUS)	(−3.019)**	(−2.580)**	(−2.461)**
US foreign aid allocation	−0.226	−0.202	−0.201
to Latin America (USAID)	(−2.953)**	(−2.609)**	(−2.372)**
Japanese claims to US long-term	0.002		
securities (LTFLW)	(1.393)		
Lagged dependent variable	−0.195	−0.368	−0.375
(TJODA)	(−0.776)	(−1.625)	(−1.424)
Observations	18	18	18
Adjusted R^2	0.5367	0.5003	0.4551

Notes: Figures in parenthesis are *t*-statistics. With 11 degrees of freedom (Model 1B), the *t*-statistic at .975 level of confidence (two-tailed test) is 2.201.

Unit roots are found in all series; thus, the first differences are taken to detrend.

No significant cointegration is found among every pair of variables.

$^{*}p < .10$, $^{**}p < .05$, $^{***}p < .01$.

Models with Japan's OOF as the Dependent Variable (Model 2)

$$JOOF_t = b1 + b2\ JOUT_{t-1} + b3\ TJOOF_{t-1} + e. \qquad \text{(Model 2C)}$$

Models 2A and 2B include CASURUS. In addition, LTFLW is added to Model 2A, while that variable is replaced by GVBOND in Model 2B.

The model hypothesizes that OOF has been geared specifically to satisfy Japan's economic interests and that it is less constrained by Japan's domestic budgetary and political concerns. Among the economic interest variables, JOUT is the amount of outstanding claims by Japanese banks in Latin America each year, and it also measures the level of economic vulnerability and interests that the Japanese government had in protecting Japanese banks financially exposed to the region. If one of the Japanese government's objectives in providing public resources to Latin America came from its need to protect Japanese banks, the increased JOUT in Latin American would have invited more OOF from Japan, making the sign positive.

However, the strength of economic linkages arising from economic interdependence between the United States and Japan might have led the Japanese government to intervene actively in support of U.S. initiatives to resolve the Latin American debt crisis. Rather than focusing on the trade conflict (CASURUS), some (mostly Japanese) scholars have argued that there was an increase in financial support by the Japanese government for U.S. economic policies in the mid-1980s, a factor that prompted leading Japanese financial institutions to purchase a significant number of U.S. Treasury bonds.[22] This was allegedly the major contributing factor that enabled the U.S. government to sustain its large federal budget deficit for such a long time.[23] At the same time, the exposure of the Japanese financial sector to loan commitments in the United States created vulnerability on the part of Japan, particularly given oversensitive bilateral trade relations. This economic interdependence element is captured through variables constructed from the amount of either U.S. government bonds (GVBOND) or long-term securities in general (LTFLW) purchased by the Japanese financial sector. The former includes the political decision on the part of investors to support U.S. budget outlays, and the latter indicates more general economic considerations. As the Japanese financial sector became more involved in financing the U.S. debt, I would expect to see that there would be more funding made available to Latin America to help support a region essential to the U.S. economy. The coefficient of this variable should show a positive influence of the Japanese financial sector's economic involvement in the United States on increased capital flows to the indebted Latin American region.

The regression results indicate that the simplest model, Model 2C, is the best specification, capturing the most influential variable, JOUT. The adjusted R^2 from Model 2C is 0.8540.

Models with Japan's Private Capital Flow as the Dependent Variable (Model 3)

$$JPRV_t = b1 + b2\ YVSUSD_{t-1} + b3\ LTFLW_{t-1} + b4\ USOUT_{t-1}$$
$$+ b5\ USAID_{t-1} + b6\ TJPRV_{t-1} + e. \qquad \text{(Models 3B and 3C)}$$

Model 3A is a Japan-centered specification in which DIFINRT, JOUT, and JOFF are included to capture Japan's domestic dynamics that influenced Japanese bank lending to Latin America. Models 3B and 3C are U.S.-centered specifications. The only difference between Models 3B and 3C is that the error correction terms of USPRV is added to Model 3C to address the co-integration between USOUT and JPRV.

This regression model on Japan's private financial flow is a supplementary one used to ascertain how private and official financial flows interacted

TABLE 3.4. Time-Series Regression with OOF (JOOF) as the Dependent Variable (Model 2: various specifications)

Independent Variables	Model 2A	Model 2B	Model 2C
Intercept	138.52	135.19	155.22
	(2.870)**	(2.994)**	(3.378)***
Trade surplus vis-à-vis the US	0.007	0.006	
(CASURUS)	(1.127)	(1.023)	
Japanese claims to US long-term	−0.004		
securities (LTFLW)	(−0.953)		
Japanese claims to US		−0.0072	
government bonds (GVBOND)		(−1.555)	
Japanese bank exposure to Latin	−0.037	−0.035	−0.038
American debt (JOUT)	(−6.382)***	(−6.155)***	(−7.361)***
Lagged dependent variable	−0.933	−0.934	−0.934
(TJOOF)	(−7.403)***	(−8.064)***	(−7.917)***
Observations	18	18	18
Adjusted R^2	0.8508	0.8654	0.8540

Notes: Figures in parentheses are t-statistics. With 13 degrees of freedom (Models 2A and 2B), the t-statistic at .975 level of confidence (two-tailed test) is 2.161.

Unit roots are found in all series; thus, the first differences are taken to detrend.

No significant cointegration is found among every pair of variables.

$^{*}p < .10$, $^{**}p < .05$, $^{***}p < .01$.

and if institutional linkages among private financial sectors from the United States and Japan were important. YVSUSD is the strength of the Japanese yen against the major world currency, the U.S. dollar, an indication of the increased capability of Japan's economic power in the world. This factor should have positively influenced the behavior of the Japanese government and the private sector, resulting in a commitment to increased funding to the debt-ridden region.

For private capital flows, various economic and business-related variables need to be considered. The most obvious and important variable is the difference in profits (DIFINRT) between Latin American lending and Japanese domestic lending, which is measured using interest rate differentials. The standard economics literature suggests that an increase in an asset's expected return relative to that of an alternative asset, all other things being equal, increases the quantity demanded of that asset.[24] The expectation here is straightforward: when there is greater potential profit, there is more incentive for banks to lend to Latin America, leading to a strong positive relationship. However, Japanese private loans to Latin America might have been extended either in the form of defensive lending as Japanese banks' outstanding loans increased (JOUT) or in response to governmental signals or guidance as the Japanese government increased its official financial flows (JOFF) to the region. When there is a stronger commitment to the region by the private financial sector's home government, there should be increased private financial flows. The expected signs of the coefficients according to the hypotheses on these two variables (JOUT and JOFF) are both positive.[25]

Economic interdependence and institutional linkage between the United States and Japan might have influenced the behavior of Japan's private financial sector in several ways during this period. First, the Japanese financial sector's exposure to the U.S. economy in terms of long-term investment interests (LTFLW) might have prompted an increase in financial flows to Latin America in support of U.S. initiatives. Japanese banks' increased investment in the United States further enhanced the linkages among transnational banks from Japan and the United States, as Japanese banks relied on many American banks during the time of the Japanese buying spree in the United States in the mid-1980s.[26] Second, it is conceivable that there was a positive relationship between the amount of Japanese bank lending and the American banks' loan exposure (USOUT) in Latin America. Strong institutional linkages between American and Japanese banks were constructed during the height of the Latin American lending boom of the late 1970s into the early 1980s. As I discussed earlier, transnational banks bound their interests and tried, at least, to create a unified front to deal with the debtors.[27] These ties were strengthened through the very nature of the syndicated loans prevalent in sovereign lending to developing country governments before the crisis and through the BACs set up after the onset of the crisis, and this structure provided a legal and institutional framework for banks' conduct in financial crisis. Finally, Japanese private lending to Latin America might have responded to U.S. political commitments to the region. In the same way as in Model 1, this concept is here captured by the amount of U.S. foreign aid to Latin America (USAID). The expectation is that Japanese banks saw U.S. political commitment to the solution of the Latin American debt crisis as a positive element as they decided to increase lending to the region, making the sign on the coefficient positive.

Table 3.5 shows that none of the specifications produced a good fit. The poor results might be due to the relatively volatile nature of private financial flows, which cannot be captured by annual data. Nevertheless, Model 3C,

TABLE 3.5. Time-Series Regression with Private Capital Flows (JPRV) as the Dependent Variable (Model 3: various specifications)

Independent Variables	Model 3A	Model 3B	Model 3C
Intercept	−541.47	−820.60	−3020.1
	(−0.961)	(−1.723)†	(−5.106)***
Japanese yen exchange rate vis-à-vis US dollars (YVSUSD)	−22.34	−46.48	−43.45
	(−0.858)	(−2.218)**	(−3.198)***
Interest rate differentials between Japan and LIBOR (DIFINRT)	−101.25		
	(−0.377)		
Japanese bank exposure to Latin American debt (JOUT)	0.043		
	(0.665)		
Japanese official flows to Latin America (JOFF)	0.164		
	(0.114)		
Japanese claims to US long-term securities (LTFLW)		0.054	0.044
		(1.557)	(1.921)†
US bank exposure to Latin American debt (USOUT)		0.066	0.044
		(1.691)†	(1.693)†
US foreign aid to Latin America (USAID)		3.741	1.659
		(1.514)	(0.993)
Lagged dependent variable (TJPRV)	−0.488	−0.734	−0.266
	(−1.672)	(−3.420)***	(−1.515)
Lagged residuals from cointegrating regression (USPRV)			0.036
			(4.359)***
Observations	18	18	18
Adjusted R^2	0.0130	0.3488	0.7269

Notes: Figures in parentheses are *t*-statistics. With 11 degrees of freedom (Model 3B), the *t*-statistic at .975 level of confidence (two-tailed test) is 2.201.

Unit roots are found in all series; thus, the first differences are taken to detrend. One significant cointegrating pair is accepted (USOUT and JPRV; the *t*-statistic was −3.010, well beyond its critical value, 10 percent, of −2.65); its lagged residuals from the cointegrating regression is added as an error correction term in Model 3C.

† $p < .15$, * $p < .10$, ** $p < .05$, *** $p < .01$.

which has a cointegrated variable between USOUT and JPRIV, produced the best fit, with the adjusted R^2 of 0.7269.

Regression Models, Operationalization of Variables, and Results from Time-Series Cross-Section Data (ODA and OOF as Dependent Variables)

TSCS pooled data allow me to conduct a more in-depth analysis of the interactions among the Japanese government, individual Latin American countries, and the United States. Only two dependent variables (ODA and OOF) are used, because data on Japan's private flows to each Latin American country are not available for these years. In addition, given the nature of private flows, annual regression may not be an appropriate tool to assess the behavior of the Japanese private financial sector.

The two models are run on two different specifications. Model A includes independent variables run on the base period (1975–82) and some of the same variables with interaction terms that capture the "shift" after the onset of the debt crisis in 1982 (1983–91). The assumptions here are that both periods share a common structure and that the influence of some independent variables on the dependent variables should have shifted after the start of the crisis. Model B divides the entire time period (1975–91) into two pieces. First the regression is run for the whole period (Models 4Ba and 5Ba), and then two more regressions are run for 1975–82 (Models 4Bb and 5Bb) and 1983–91 (Models 4Bc and 5Bc). Here, the assumption is that there is a structural change in the regressions. A Chow test indicates that both ODA and OOF regressions experienced a structural shift (i.e., the coefficient vectors are not the same for the two time periods) between 1982 and 1983.[28] These regressions on TSCS data are run using panel-corrected standard errors (PCSE) after taking care of first-order serial correlation.[29]

Table 3.6 summarizes the variables and models from the TSCS regressions discussed in this section. Expected signs are also noted in the table. Appendix 1 details the data sources.

TSCS Models with Japan's ODA as the Dependent Variable (Model 4)

$$\begin{aligned} \text{JODA}_{xt} = {} & b1 + b2\ \text{IMMIG}_{xt-1} + b3\ \text{TRADE}_{xt-1} + b4\ \text{JLOANO}_{xt-1} \\ & + b5\ \text{USAID}_{xt-1} + b6\ \text{USTRD}_{xt-1} + b7\ \text{GNPPC}_{xt-1} \\ & + b8\ \text{OPEN}_{xt-1} + b9\ \text{POP}_{xt-1} + e. \qquad \text{(Model 4B)} \end{aligned}$$

TABLE 3.6. Models, Variables, and Their Expected Signs from Time-Series Cross-Section Models (one-year, *N*-data-point variables)

Dependent Variables	Independent Variables: Concept	Independent Variables: Operationalization	Acronyms	Signs[a]
Japan's ODA to a Latin American country ($JODA_x$)	*X*'s political importance to J	The number of Japanese immigrants in *X*	IMMIG	+
	X's economic importance to J (1)	Total trade between Japan and *X*	TRADE	+/±
	X's economic importance to J (2)	Japan's FDI to *X*	FDI	+/±
	X's political importance to US	US foreign aid to *X*	USAID	+/++
	X's economic importance to US	US total trade with *X*	USTRD	+/++
	X's economic policy	*X*'s economic openness to trade	OPEN	+
	J's government-bank relations	Japanese banks' exposure to loans to *X*	JLOANO	±/++
	Developmental needs of *X*	*X*'s per capita GNP as a measure of poverty	GNPPC	−
	The size of *X*	*X*'s population for buying influence	POP	−
Japan's OOF to a Latin American country ($JOOF_x$)	*X*'s economic importance to J (1)	Total trade between Japan and *X*	TRADE	+/±
	X's economic importance to J (2)	Japan's FDI to *X*	FDI	+/±
	X's economic importance to US	US total trade with *X*	USTRD	+/±+
	J's government-bank relations	Japanese banks' exposure to loans to *X*	JLOANO	±/++
	The size of *X*	*X*'s population for the size of the market	POP	+

Note: For data source and estimation procedures, see appendix 1.
[a]Multiple signs indicate that there are shifts in sign expected after the onset of the debt crisis in 1982.

For Model 4A, time interaction terms (0–1 dummy) are multiplied for all the variables except IMMIG, GNPPC, and POP, whose coefficients, I hypothesize, did not shift after the onset of the debt crisis.

Due to the great distance between Japan and Latin America and the shadow of the United States in the region, the Japanese government has not had a noticeable strategic presence or commitment in each Latin American country. However, the presence of Japanese immigrants (IMMIG) has constituted an important political consideration. Latin America has the largest ethnic Japanese population outside of Japan, and as the case of Peruvian president Alberto Fujimori indicates, Japanese ancestry has attracted special attention from the Japanese government.[30] The Japanese government has also made various special arrangements for the descendants of these immigrants.[31] Particularly since the late 1980s, Japanese Brazilians, Japanese Peruvians, and Japanese Paraguayans returning to Japan, either temporarily for working purposes or permanently, have established strong ties between the Japanese central and local governments and their native communities in Latin America. Therefore, it seems reasonable to assume that the more Japanese immigrants a Latin American country had, the greater was the ODA flow the country could expect, and this relationship should have been consistent over time.

Japan's economic interests in a given Latin American country are important determinants of the Japanese government's decisions, and these interests can be disaggregated into Japan's major economic activities in the region: trade, direct investment, and bank lending. Total trade (TRADE) with a Latin American country consists of the aggregation of both imports (in most cases, raw materials or agricultural products) and exports (mostly Japanese manufactured products for the Latin American market). Foreign direct investment (FDI) is understood here as the gross flow of FDI from Japan to each country.[32] The Japanese multinational corporations' vested interest in each country might have influenced governmental decisions in Japan, thus increasing official capital flows.

Japan's bank lending and its loan exposure to certain Latin American countries (JLOANO) embody an important dynamic between the government and the private sector in Japan, a dynamic that increases Japan's economic interests in certain Latin American countries. The higher the Japanese banks' stake in the economic conditions of a certain debtor country was, the more likely the country was to receive a larger contribution from the Japanese government. As the national lender of last resort, the Japanese government had reasons to be concerned about the exposure of Japanese commercial banks and their vulnerability to their outstanding loans in Latin America. Due to the symbiotic relationship between the Japanese financial sector and the government, the Japanese government felt the need to protect the Japanese financial sector as it became heavily exposed to the Latin American debt. Hence, as the outstanding loans increased, the Japanese government had more incentives to use its ODA resources to mitigate the financial crisis, thus reducing possibilities of a collapse of or severe damage to the Japanese financial sector. Moreover, Japanese banks themselves could have influenced the Japanese government's policies in terms of attracting increased ODA flows to a certain indebted country, financial resources the banks needed to prevent default.

The influence of both trade and outstanding loans on Japan's ODA allocation may have changed over time. The characteristics of Japanese ODA seem to have shifted in the late 1970s, in the form of the declining mercantilistic nature.[33] If this is an accurate observation, and if, consequently, the impact of the debt crisis on Japanese policymakers was that they gave more consideration to the "public good" function of Japan's official financial flows, the positive relationship between the trade variable (TRADE) and ODA flows (which represents Japan's mercantilistic behavior) should have weakened after the onset of the crisis. Furthermore, as the debt crisis deepened, Japan's outstanding loans in Latin America (JLOANO) might have positively influenced the allocation of Japan's ODA, as the Japanese government became increasingly motivated to financially support the countries to which Japanese banks had high exposure.

U.S. presence in Latin America seems to have influenced Japan's behavior in the region. This is partly because the Japanese government has had a high stake in maintaining a good relationship with the United States and partly because the Japanese government has explicitly coordinated its foreign aid policies with the United States. The amount of U.S. aid (USAID) to a country measures the country's importance to the United States. The logic is as follows: the United States assists with foreign aid countries vital to U.S. interests; the Japanese government adjusts its behavior according to U.S. political considerations; thus, the amount of U.S. economic and military aid to the important recipient countries during the debt crisis should have increased Japanese ODA flows to the same countries. In addition, an established consultation mechanism and informal channels set up to coordinate U.S. and Japanese economic assistance facilitated communication between the U.S. and Japanese governments. These provided opportunities not only for cooperation that was mutually agreed on but also for the transmission of demands from one partner to the other. Such a tendency might have grown after the onset of the debt crisis, making U.S. political concerns a vital factor influencing Japanese ODA flows. As the United States became more concerned, for security or political reasons, about the economic and political stability of particular Latin American countries, Japanese ODA should have likewise been more influenced, making the relationship significantly positive.

Due to the importance of U.S. economic health for Japanese overseas business activities (economic linkage), the Japanese government had strong motives to boost the U.S. economy, which was relatively depressed from the latter part of the 1980s through the early 1990s. USTRD (total American trade—the amount of U.S. exports and imports added—with a country) represents the U.S. economic interests. The stronger the U.S. economic interests in a Latin American country were, the larger Japanese ODA flows were, making the relationship positive.

Given the sizable trade imbalance between the United States and Japan at the time, it is conceivable that efforts were made to recycle Japan's trade surplus accrued against the United States via Latin America. Japan's official financial flows became a perfect channel for this mechanism. The Japanese government at least could have expected the U.S. government to be less demanding on bilateral trade issues when the Japanese government financially assisted Latin America by providing more foreign exchange resources. Congressional debate also supported the triangle that linked the issues of U.S.-Japanese trade to Japan's Latin American financing (see chap. 5). This consideration should make the relationship between U.S. economic interests and Japanese financial flows even more positive during later periods.

Three characteristics of each ODA recipient country should be influential in attracting or repelling Japan's ODA. First, GNPPC (each country's per capita GNP) represents the recipient country's development financial needs—an important factor for the allocation of Japan's ODA. This variable captures whether or not the Japanese government was concerned about the welfare of a country's population when it allocated and disbursed ODA in Latin America during this period. If, as stated in Japan's ODA Charter, humanitarian reasons were important factors in determining the allocation of ODA,[34] the poorer a country was, the more official financial support it should have received. This relationship should be stable over time.

Second, OPEN is a variable on the debtor country's openness to world trade, which operationalizes the impact of a Latin American debtors' economic policy on the Japanese government's aid allocation decisions. Creditor governments support those "exemplar" debtors who comply with the "rules of the game" set by the creditors to increase the debtors' ability to repay their debts through greater openness to trade. Most of the structural adjustment policies implemented in Latin America demanded a dramatic opening of these countries' economies to world trade through adjustment of exchange rates and elimination of trade barriers.[35] These changes were usually made to encourage exports and improve the countries' balance of payments. At the same time, openness to trade indicated a Latin American government's commitment to economic adjustment. Therefore, countries that have been consistent and trustworthy followers of such open-economy policies have tended to receive better external economic support, as the case of Chile illustrates.[36] The Japanese government rewarded the countries' adherence to these policies that aim to increase debt repayment capacity, a practice that in turn contributed to international financial stability. The likely outcome was that the more open a country's economy was, or the more closely it followed an orthodox adjustment policy, the greater ODA flows from Japan would be. For both measurements, the relationship between the independent and dependent variables should be positive and stable over time.

Finally, the population of a recipient country (POP) is a relevant variable concerning the Japanese government's decisions on ODA allocation. Existing literature on foreign aid suggests that foreign aid tends to be biased in favor of small countries.[37] In the case of Japan, this bias might exist for reasons of political effectiveness: the same amount of money can more powerfully influence a smaller country than a large one, thus making it easier for Japan to gain support for its goals in world forums, such as gaining permanent membership on the Security Council of the United Nations.[38]

The regression results are reported in table 3.7 and discussed later in this chapter.

TSCS Models with Japan's OOF as the Dependent Variable (Model 5)

$$\text{JOOF}_{xt} = b1 + b2\ \text{TRADE}_{xt-1} + b3\ \text{JLOANO}_{xt-1} + b4\ \text{USTRD}_{xt-1} + b5\ \text{POP}_{xt-1} + e. \qquad \text{(Model 5B)}$$

For Model 5A, time interaction terms (0–1 dummy) are multiplied to all the variables except POP.

Most of the independent variables included here should have a similar impact on the Japanese government's OOF allocation decisions as on Japan's ODA allocation decisions. A few differences in the influence of these factors in ODA and OOF warrant attention. Even though Japan's ODA is known (or alleged) to promote its economic interests, a substantial part of ODA allocation is still driven by stated humanitarian objectives. In comparison, OOF is actually designed to promote and support Japanese companies' economic activities abroad. The Japanese government thus does not have to be concerned about international criticism that Japan extends its OOF based purely on its economic self-interests and disregarding noneconomic criteria, such as GNP per capita and environmental or humanitarian considerations.

From the economic variables, then, the amount of Japanese trade (TRADE) and Japanese loan exposure (JLOANO) to Latin American countries should positively and significantly influence an increase in Japan's OOF. On the JLOANO variable, there should be evidence of a major shift in the impact of

TABLE 3.7. ODA (JODA) Allocation within Latin America, 1975–1991 (Model 4)

	Model 4A (with Time Shift)		Model 4Ba (No Time Shift)	Model 4Bb	Model 4Bc
Independent Variables	Base Period	1983–91 Shift	1975–91	1975–82	1983–91
Intercepts	12.641	10.610	17.802	10.048	24.466
	(3.703)***	(2.545)***	(6.872)***	(8.169)***	(6.131)***
Number of Japanese immigrants (IMMIG)	0.0007		0.0006	0.0007	0.0006
	(4.033)***		(3.495)***	(7.913)***	(2.577)***
Japanese trade with the country (TRADE)	0.0009	−0.0014	−0.0012	−0.0004	−0.0007
	(0.293)	(−0.359)	(−0.566)	(−0.347)	(−0.311)
Outstanding Japanese bank loans (JLOANO)	0.00006	−0.0013	0.00012	−0.0012	−0.0008
	(0.037)	(−0.707)	(0.117)	(−1.848)**	(−0.731)
Amount of US aid to the country (USAID)	−0.0241	0.014	0.0016	−0.016	−0.0218
	(−0.596)	(0.339)	(0.085)	(−1.118)	(−1.248)*
US trade with the country (USTRD)	0.00008	0.0008	0.0005	0.0005	0.0008
	(0.195)	(2.138)***	(1.597)*	(2.981)***	(2.246)**
GNP per capita of the country (GNPPC)	−0.0024		−0.0024	−0.0018	−0.0052
	(−2.709)***		(−2.621)***	(−3.030)***	(−2.304)**
Economic openness of the country (OPEN)	−0.0191	−0.065	−0.0693	−0.013	0.089
	(−0.300)	(−1.078)	(−1.108)	(−0.459)	(0.555)
Country's population (POP)	−0.00007		−0.00003	−0.00006	−0.00006
	(−0.779)		(−0.376)	(−1.118)	(−0.411)
Degrees of freedom	324		331	151	170
Total R^2	0.3804		0.2353	0.6797	0.2858

Notes: Figures in parentheses are *t*-statistics.
Corrections are made on heteroskadasticity, fixed effects, and autocorrelation. Panel-based standard errors are also corrected.
* $p < .10$, ** $p < .05$, *** $p < .01$.

Japanese banks' outstanding claims before and after the onset of the debt crisis. Before the crisis, or under normal financial conditions, Japanese official financial flows should not have followed private lending. The division of labor in providing finance to developing countries was usually such that private finance went to the higher-income developing countries with more business opportunities and lower risks, while public money, including foreign aid, went to countries with lower income. The relationship between the two variables should have been negative. However, once the financial crisis occurred, Japan's official financial flows should have gone to countries where there was greater bank exposure to assist these banks. In this event, the relationship between the two should have turned positive.

In relation to the United States, the argument applied to Japan's ODA allocation still holds: the Japanese government would allocate its official resources to help Latin American countries with strong trade ties with the United States (USTRD), because the Japanese government was concerned about the detrimental impact that the Latin American economic crisis had on the U.S. economy (which would then increase the pressure on the Japanese government regarding the bilateral trade imbalance). In contrast, there is no established coordinating mechanism between the two creditor governments on OOF; therefore, U.S. foreign aid allocation should not have influenced Japanese OOF allocation.

Table 3.8 summarizes the regression results.

Discussion of the Findings

Private and Public Benefits Constructing a Joint Product

The Japanese government's bilateral interests in each Latin American country appear to have increased its motivation to provide more funding to certain Latin American countries. As observed in the allocation model for ODA (Model 4), the presence of Japanese immigrants in a particular Latin American country increases Japan's ODA significantly and consistently (IMMIG). Thus, although it is said that the Japanese government has very limited political interests in this region, Japanese immigration captures a solid bilateral interest of the Japanese government in certain countries, leading to more ODA.

The variable representing the economic importance of Latin American countries in the form of their total bilateral trade with Japan (TRADE) reveals more complex and noteworthy effects on the allocation of Japan's OOF (Model 5).[39] During the period before the debt crisis (1975–82), the Japanese government allocated more of its OOF to countries trading substantially with Japan; the coefficient of this variable during this period was positive and

TABLE 3.8. OOF (JOOF) Allocation within Latin America, 1975–1991 (Model 5)

	Model 5A (with Time Shift)		Model 5Ba (No Time Shift)	Model 5Bb	Model 5Bc
Independent Variables	Base Period	1983–91 Shift	1975–91	1975–82	1983–91
Intercepts	−7.284	1.813	−9.510	−11.171	−5.208
	(−4.164)***	(0.783)	(−8.140)***	(−6.764)***	(−3.176)***
Japanese trade with the	0.0083	−0.015	−0.0052	0.0048	−0.0057
country (TRADE)	(2.520)***	(−3.678)***	(−2.521)**	(1.846)**	(−2.968)***
Outstanding Japanese	−0.0015	−0.009	−0.0074	−0.0179	−0.0097
bank loans (JLOANO)	(−0.831)	(−4.679)***	(−7.889)***	(−6.009)***	(−12.575)***
US trade with the	0.0025	0.0097	0.0093	0.0045	0.0123
country (USTRD)	(7.378)***	(27.854)***	(49.807)***	(12.087)***	(75.113)***
Country's population	−0.000012		0.00008	0.0007	−0.0001
(POP)	(−0.250)		(1.723)**	(10.978)***	(−2.633)***
Degrees of freedom	350		354	174	194
Total R^2	0.4498		0.3822	0.3437	0.4680

Notes: Figures in parentheses are *t*-statistics.
Corrections are made on heteroskedasticity, fixed effects, and autocorrelation. Panel-based standard errors are also corrected.
$^{*}\ p < .10$, $^{**}\ p < .05$, $^{***}\ p < .01$.

significant. This is as expected under the bilateral economic interest motivation. However, the coefficient turns negative and significant after the onset of the debt crisis (1983–91), both in the case of the shift (Model 5A) and in time-divided regressions (Model 5Bc). This means that as the debt crisis hit Latin American countries, the Japanese government began diverting its OOF away from countries with which Japan traded substantially. This quite intriguing result indicates that the Japanese government became less concerned about its direct economic returns after the onset of the debt crisis and started allocating its OOF distinctly, moving away from private gains from trade and toward more indirect benefits. This result is even more interesting, as I discuss later, because the allocation of Japan's OOF is heavily and positively influenced by the Latin American countries' high overall trade with the United States.

Private returns do not come only from satisfying Japan's bilateral political and economic interests in regard to certain Latin American countries. The increase of Japan's financial contribution to Latin America could stem from Japan's own increasing stake in the world economy, as some hegemonic stability theorists argue. In addition, the benefits of Japan's contribution could also have accrued from the direct payoffs that the Japanese government might have received from assisting the United States, the regional power in distress. In both cases, U.S. influence on the Japanese government's policy decisions should be measured to support this argument. The results from all the models must be integrated here to discuss this issue comprehensively.

Two variables that indicate Japan's increasing economic power are Japan's trade share in the world relative to that of the United States (DIFEX)[40] and the value of the Japanese yen vis-à-vis the U.S. dollar (YVSUSD).[41] Japan's trade share in the world influenced the Japanese government in terms of the disbursement of ODA to Latin America (Model 1), a region outside Japan's traditional sphere of interest. As Japan's trade share increased relative to that of the United States (DIFEX), Japan allocated greater ODA to the Latin American region (the sign is negative due to how DIFEX is measured). The strength of the Japanese yen, whether it represents an increase in Japan's economic power or merely indicates an increase in Japan's purchasing power, influenced the regional allocation of private financial flows to Latin America (Models 3B and 3C) positively (again the sign is negative due to the measurement of *YVSUSD*) and significantly. As the yen strengthened during this period, there were greater private capital flows from Japan to Latin America. Hence, the increase of Japan's economic power in the world positively influenced the Japanese government's ODA and private capital allocation to this indebted region. This is because the Japanese government and private sector became more concerned about the stability of the world economy and about the potential economic returns that Japan could accumulate from the region's economic health.

Additionally, the Japanese government was concerned that the strong yen against the U.S. dollar would have a negative impact on the country's exports, a concern that might have motivated the Japanese government to boost the dollar by assisting the Latin American economies.

As I described in chapter 2, the changing relative power between the United States and Japan is not the only possible influence on the Japanese government's behavior: Japan's economic linkage with the United States constituted a critical factor in the Japanese government's decision-making process. This was particularly the case when it came to the Latin American debt crisis, which had a major impact on the U.S. economy. The U.S. government and its private actors found various ways to influence Japan's behavior, because of the important political and economic ties between the two countries. Five regression models capture some interesting aspects in which this U.S.-Japan bilateral interaction influenced Japan's behavior in regard to debt crisis management in Latin America.

A few variables represent U.S.-Japanese bilateral relations, particularly in terms of the extent of the direct interest Japan has in supporting the U.S. economy for either economic or political reasons. The size of Japan's trade surplus with the United States (CASURUS) is conceivably the most prominent factor that would have caused the Japanese government to be concerned about the economic decline of the United States due to the deepening crisis in Latin America. In this rather passive way of responding to the debt crisis, the Japanese government attempted to avoid aggravating Japan-U.S. trade tensions.

But the coefficient on this variable does not show a significant influence on Japan's OOF disbursement to Latin America (Model 2). Even more puzzling, the ODA regression produces a significant but negative coefficient (Model 1). The time-series ODA model (Model 1) indicates that as Japan's trade surplus increased vis-à-vis the United States, ODA flows from Japan to Latin America decreased. This counterintuitive anomaly may be the result of the complex lag structure between Japan's trade surplus and its ODA disbursement to Latin America, a lag based on the way political pressures were transmitted from the U.S. government to the Japanese government. However, one can consider Japan's economic growth as a latent variable that influences both Japan's trade surplus with the United States and the amount of Japan's ODA. When Japan's economic growth slowed down, Japan would have decreased its imports because of less demand and would have possibly increased its exports to survive the economic downturn, thus increasing Japan's trade surplus against the United States. Concomitantly, a slowing of Japan's economy and a decrease in its tax revenues would have caused the Japanese government to cut ODA to Latin America (and possibly increase some to Asia, where there was more Japanese business); consequently, the relationship between Japan's trade surplus and Japan's ODA to Latin America became negative.

In addition, Japan's vested financial interest in the well-being of the U.S. economy, constituting their economic linkages, is represented by two variables regarding Japan's financial investment in the United States—in total long-term security investment (LTFLW) and in U.S. government bonds (GVBOND). These variables capture Japan's rather active interest in maintaining the health of the U.S. economy, in which the Japanese private sector as well as the government had substantial financial interests. However, neither of the variables performed well in influencing Japan's official flows (ODA in Model 1 and OOF in Model 2). None of the variables significantly influenced the flow of Japan's private capital to Latin America (Models 3B and 3C).

There is an indication that the U.S. political relationship with Japan and its financial commitment to Latin America clearly influenced the Japanese government's behavior in the region. The U.S. foreign aid commitment to Latin America—both to the region as a whole (Model 1) and to individual countries (Model 4)—influenced Japan's ODA allocation negatively, particularly in the aftermath of crisis (Model 4Bc). The coefficients on the U.S. aid variable (USAID) have negative signs, and many of them are significant (Models 1 and 4). This suggests that as a result of either explicit or implicit coordination between the Japanese government and the U.S. government, a division of labor arrangement was forming between the two large ODA donors in Latin America in two ways. On one hand (Model 4Bc), after the onset of the debt crisis, the U.S. government began taking care of certain Latin American countries considered of primary political (and to some extent economic) importance, by providing more U.S. foreign aid to them. The Japanese government, meanwhile, avoided those countries and provided more aid to countries that could not obtain sufficient foreign aid from the United States. On the other hand, Model 1 indicates that the Japanese government increased its ODA disbursement to Latin America as U.S. aid declined, to assure that a certain level of foreign aid flow was maintained.

Finally, the most significant and interesting statistical result is how the level of U.S. trade with certain Latin American countries (USTRD) influenced Japan's decisions to increase official flows in the forms of both ODA (Model 4) and OOF (Model 5). The coefficient of this variable, representing the Latin American countries' economic importance to the United States, shows a very significant positive influence on both ODA (particularly after the debt crisis) and OOF (for all time periods). The result strongly suggests that the Japanese official flows, both ODA and OOF, responded positively to the economic needs of the United States in Latin America. As I discussed earlier, there was no indication of the Japanese government responding directly to U.S. pressure in the form of increasing its official flows as Japan accumulated a trade surplus vis-à-vis the United States. However, this U.S.-Latin America trade variable demonstrates that the Japanese official flows were allocated to support certain Latin American countries that had strong trade relationships with the United States. Through this mechanism, the Japanese government indirectly contributed to the recovery of certain Latin American countries, a factor that would in turn favorably influence U.S. economic recovery.

The last variable representing a factor closest to a pure public good is the way in which Japan's financial contributions rewarded certain Latin American debtors for good behavior, increasing incentives for debtors to follow the "rules of the game" and accelerate their debt repayments. This variable is operationalized in terms of the debtor country's economic openness to world trade (OPEN). Unfortunately, this variable did not significantly influence Japan's allocation of ODA (Model 4) or OOF (the variable dropped from Model 5).

Thus far, regression results from the models indicate that both Japan's increased economic stake in the world economy under its strong yen and the Japanese government's bilateral relationship with the United States—in terms of both economic linkage and political interaction—influenced the Japanese government's official flow disbursement to and allocation in Latin America. These factors were considered private benefits that increased Japan's incentive to become more actively involved in the resolution of the debt crisis. Additionally, the Japanese government seems to have become actively, rather than passively, involved in the resolution of the crisis.

Transnational Linkage and Domestic Politics in Japan

Some variables clearly represent the influence of institutional linkages and of the direct political power of Japan's private financial sector on the Japanese government. First, the overall amount of U.S. outstanding loans to Latin America (USOUT) affected Japan's private flows to the region (Models 3B and 3C) only marginally, a trend predicted by the mechanisms of loan syndications and by the formation of BACs. An additional result worth noting comes from a pair of cointegrating variables: Japanese private capital flows to Latin America (JPRV) and the U.S. outstanding loans to the region (USOUT). As Model 3C demonstrates, the lagged residuals from the cointegrating regression between these two variables (USPRV) produced a strikingly significant positive coefficient (and boosted the adjusted R^2 of the regression from 0.3488 without it to 0.7269 with it). Thus, it can be interpreted that a visible long-term equilibrium trend between these two variables is captured in terms of level and that this trend significantly and positively influenced the behavior of Japan's private financial sector regarding Latin America. This indicates a close institutional linkage between the two private financial sectors across the Pacific.

A second aspect that connects institutional linkage among private sectors to the Japanese government's behavior toward Latin America is the domestic interaction between Japanese commercial banks (with links to American banks) and the Japanese government. In the regionally aggregated models, Japanese banks' exposure to Latin American debt (JOUT) shows a significant influence on the regional allocation of Japan's OOF (Model 2). The coefficient of JOUT is, however, not positive as predicted by the hypothesis (i.e., the higher the Japanese banks' exposure to Latin America is, the more OOF would flow from Japan to the region to protect the banks). Instead, it is negative (i.e., the lower the Japanese banks' exposure to Latin American debt is, the greater the OOF flows are). This is another counterintuitive regression result. One may interpret that the more the Japanese banks retreated from the Latin American debt, the more the Japanese government stepped up its official financial commitment to the region, for two reasons: (1) the official funding could compensate and justify the retreat of debt-injured Japanese banks, and (2) there would be a certain level of foreign capital inflows maintained to the indebted region. Qualitative analysis of the Latin American debt crisis supports this interpretation (see chap. 5), with qualitative information focusing on the process of bargaining between the Japanese government and its banks.

We can observe the same dynamic between Japan's official flows and the level of Japanese banks' outstanding loans to each Latin American country (JLOANO), particularly for the allocation of Japan's OOF (Model 5). This dynamic was much more prominent during the debt crisis, and it clearly illustrates the link between how the Japanese government became involved in the resolution of the debt crisis through its OOF allocation and the Japanese banks' demands for a secure retreat.[42]

Furthermore, Japan's private financial flow model (Model 3) shows that the sign of commitment given by the Japanese government in terms of its total official flows to Latin America (JOFF) did not influence the behavior of the Japanese private financial sector. This result suggests that Japan's private sector exerted a stronger influence on the Japanese government's behavior than vice versa—an interesting finding that runs counter to conventional explanations of Japanese government-business relations.

Controlling Variables

Japan's regional ODA allocation to Latin America (Model 1) is influenced by Japanese budgetary conditions (BUDGET). However, contrary to the hypothesis regarding this variable, its coefficient shows a significant, negative sign. This indicates that as Japan's overall central budget increased, there were decreased ODA flows to Latin America. It is conceivable in this case that economic growth was once again an underlying variable that drove both Japan's budget and its ODA. If the Japanese government increased its central budget to stimulate Japan's economy at the time of slow growth, and if such slow economic growth led to some decrease in Japan's ODA, the negative relationship between the two variables could be explained.[43]

The other controlling factor in Model 1 is Japan's political stability in terms of how much public support the country's majority party, the LDP, gained during this period (LDPSP). As the hypothesis predicted, the regression results indicate that when the LDP enjoyed higher popular support, more ODA flowed to the Latin American region. As I noted before, the relative domestic political freedom the LDP enjoyed because of the party's popularity made it easier for the Japanese government to allocate its ODA resources to particular needs (i.e., responding to pressures from both the United States and its own private financial sector).

The profit calculation by Japan's private sector, captured by the interest rate differentials (DIFINRT), did not influence Japan's private financial flows to Latin America as a region (Model 3A). In addition, it is interesting that the economic self-interest model for private capital flows (Model 3A) revealed a very weak fit to the data (with an adjusted R^2 of 0.013), while factors of U.S. influence captured a higher level of significance (Models 3B and, particularly, 3C).

Finally, the ODA allocation models (Model 4) including the level of economic development of the debtor countries (GNPPC)—a mandate for Japan's ODA allocation—showed a significantly strong relationship with ODA allocation. When the country's GNP per capita was low, it could expect more ODA from Japan. This is consistent with expectations. The country's population variable (POP) included in the ODA model (Model 4) failed to show any significant result. But the same variable included in the OOF model (Model 5) produced a positive, significant coefficient during the precrisis years (Model 5Bb) and a negative, significant coefficient during the crisis period (Model 5Bc). It is possible that during the time of normalcy before 1982, Japan's economic interest in allocating its OOF to more populous countries (and thus to a bigger market) influenced its allocation. But after 1982, the Japanese government and OOF-implementing agencies became much more concerned about the impact of OOF allocation on the debt alleviation of certain countries, so considerations of market size became secondary. This led these agencies to pursue an efficient resolution of the financial crises by targeting relatively small (or less populous) debtors.

Summary

The analysis of this chapter began by emphasizing that the Japanese government shouldered costs in providing international public goods in the form of international financial stability by increasing Japan's capital flows to Latin America at the time of the debt crisis. But the way in which the Japanese government allocated its financial resources to and within Latin America was not consistent over time. The question is, then, What factors influenced the Japanese government's fund allocation decisions? Many of the factors here identified have provided a quantitative support to the two hypotheses posed in chapter 1 of this study.

First, the Japanese government's commitment to increased funding to Latin America was supported by the fact that various private returns accrued to the Japanese government and its private financial sector through the process of debt crisis management. Such returns are notably found in the effects that some U.S.-related variables had on Japan's official flow allocation. The possibility that the Japanese government's actions might either please or directly assist U.S. economic recovery increased Japan's motivation to help the Latin American debtors. The regression analyses themselves do not provide any indication of the mechanism through which the Japanese government adopted these factors as an important aspect of its decision-making regarding official flow commitments to Latin America. But it is quite clear that significant attention was paid to the impact of Japanese policies on the U.S. economy (and possibly on U.S. political and diplomatic attitudes toward Japan).

Second, there is an indication that institutional linkage, which existed between American and Japanese private financial sectors, marginally affected the behavior of the Japanese financial sector and the Japanese government. Various linking mechanisms explained earlier helped form a relatively coherent and united front among Japanese banks and American banks, a connection that made prominent the influence of American banks on Japanese banks.

Finally, and as a complement to the second point, the regression results depict an interesting domestic dynamic between the government and the banks in Japan. This is not merely a straightforward dynamic in which the Japanese government protected its banks by increasing official flows to the debtors to which the banks were most exposed. Rather, the Japanese government's official funds were allocated in a way that made it easier for Japanese banks to retreat from the indebted region and countries, while allowing, at the same time, for additional official funding that maintained certain levels of foreign capital inflows to Latin America. This relationship between the Japanese banks and the government not only helped the banks but also provided public goods to Latin America to sustain a degree of stability at a time when private financial commitment was gradually declining.

PART 2

Latin America

CHAPTER 4

Introduction to the Comparative Case Study of Latin America

The following two chapters focus on Japan's actions in financial crisis management in Latin America. Two qualitative case studies examine factors that led Japan to respond differently to two crises that hit Latin America in the 1980s and the 1990s. The first crisis was the Latin American debt crisis of the 1980s (discussed in chap. 5, with a main focus on Mexico), and the second was the Mexican peso crisis of 1994–95 (discussed in chap. 6), which had repercussion in the Latin American region, particularly in Argentina.[1] There is a noticeable contrast in the way the Japanese government became involved in and committed to the solution of the two crises, particularly regarding the Japanese government's engagement in collective action with the United States. The Japanese government was quite active and collaborative with the United States during the debt crisis, but its response was quite reluctant and weak vis-à-vis the Mexican peso crisis. An empirical puzzle arises: What made the Japanese government become actively involved in the resolution of the first crisis but not the second?

The two hypotheses discussed in chapter 1 are tested through these case studies. The first hypothesis argues that the presence of high private returns increases the Japanese government's commitment and action in financial crisis management. The second hypothesis analyzes the role of transnational linkages between Japan and its most important economic partner, the United States. When such linkages are strong and ample, the Japanese government tends to be more responsive to crisis.

The following two chapters indicate that the absence of several critical conditions in the 1994–95 currency crisis made the Japanese government reluctant to play a role as a collective manager of that financial crisis, unlike the case of the debt crisis of the 1980s. High expected private returns from the management of the crisis—for example, economic benefits to Japan's private financial sector and a satisfying transnational coalition between the American and Japanese private financial sectors involved in the crisis—urged the Japanese government to become actively involved in the debt crisis in the 1980s, while the lack of those very factors limited the Japanese government's action in the 1990s.

Methodology

The purpose of this comparative case study, along with the quantitative analysis in chapter 3, is to investigate the validity of my theoretical claims by taking advantage of the synergy created by the two empirical approaches. Admittedly, both the quantitative analysis and the comparative case study of this book lean toward the variable-oriented approach described by Charles Ragin, through which I aim to test my hypotheses.[2] Nevertheless, the following two case study chapters include a fair amount of contextual and historical material. Moreover, they provide a better understanding of where the theoretically important factors in the analysis of international financial crisis management fit within the overall international political and economic dynamics of the time and within Japan's changing domestic environment.

The comparison of cases in different historical periods (time series) adds to each case temporal elements that cannot easily be controlled. But many of these temporal changes influenced the nature of the joint product and the strength of transnational linkages and thus are subsumed under my two major hypotheses. The cases are taken from the same region and are relatively close in time periods; thus they allow the study to explore the validity and impact of several important factors that led to contrasting outcomes. Many variables and their contexts are taken into account. Methodologically speaking, these variables can be placed into three categories: those controlled by the case selection, those that are historically contextual and have some impact on the variables of theoretical interest (and that often cannot be controlled), and those of theoretical interest.

The first group of variables that conceivably made a difference in Japan's response are controlled (i.e., unchanged or changed very little) by the research design. They include the weak political importance of the Latin American region to Japan (with exception of the Japanese immigrants there, a situation still unchanged) and Japan's relatively limited trade relations with the region.

Second are variables that represent the environment or context in which the Japanese actors make decisions and that indirectly influence the calculation of the theoretical variables. Although the factors of this second category are not central to my theoretical discussion, they still need to be analyzed on some level to illustrate how their evolution influences the theoretically important variables and the outcome. The chapter on the Mexican peso crisis (chap. 6) includes a section explaining these contextual variables, enhancing the strength of the analysis by adding a holistic dimension. The variables include (a) the end of the cold war and changes in U.S. attitudes toward economic regionalization; (b) economic, political, and budgetary changes in Japan since the early 1990s; (c) the creditor governments' and international financial community's learning and institutionalization regarding financial crises of large magnitude; and, probably most importantly, (d) changes in the nature of financial crises emerging from middle-income countries, particularly in terms of the speed of crisis evolution and the type of private actors involved. These variables are connected to the variables of theoretical interest. Domestic economic and political difficulties in Japan in the 1990s, for example, decreased Japan's relative private return from engaging in the solution of the Mexican peso crisis. This is because the Japanese government's stake in Mexico has diminished, not in absolute terms, but in relation to stability of the domestic economy.

Finally, there are two variables of theoretical interest, derived from the theoretical discussion (chap. 1). The first is the measurement of private returns the Japanese government expected and managed to obtain from its active involvement in the collective management of these financial crises. These private returns include improvement of U.S.-Japan relations and economic benefits to Japan's private sector. The other variable of theoretical interest addresses the level of involvement of transnational coalitions among private financial actors and the importance of economic linkages, as well as the domestic pressure that moved the Japanese government to respond to the respective crises. These two hypotheses are reiterated in the following discussion.

Crisis Management as a Joint Product

As I discussed in chapter 1, creditor governments are much more likely to engage in the collective management of financial crises to secure international financial stability when these actions also produce private returns to their respective home countries. These private returns range widely, including, to name a few, protection of the home country's private financial sectors exposed to the crisis, evasion of disruption in bilateral trade or payments, and an increase in the home country's political presence in or leverage over the crisis countries or in the international financial world. The combination of public purposes (which provide international financial stability) and private purposes increases the incentives for a creditor government to engage in the collective management of a financial crisis, making a government's participation in international cooperation much more likely.

In this sense, the realist prediction of relative gains inhibiting the possibility is at best partially applicable. Particularly when the private returns for a creditor government can be obtained without taking away any gains from another creditor government (e.g., financial stability in its home country), the likelihood of cooperation increases significantly. At the same time, it is clear that some crises produce much greater private returns to certain creditor governments than do other crises. In an extreme case, a resolution of a major financial crisis can fail to increase private returns to some creditor governments, although the lack of a solution to the crisis would threaten international financial stability, undermining a public return of management. For Japan, the contrast of the implications of the two crises in Latin America fit these respective cases and suggests the motivations behind the Japanese government's contrasting behavior.

Transnational Linkages and Domestic Dynamics

Transnational linkages lead creditor governments to increase their incentives to engage in collective management of financial crisis. On one hand, strong economic linkages increase private returns to the Japanese government as it supports the U.S. economy, in which Japan's private sector has a substantial vested interest (discussed earlier). On the other hand, institutional linkages among subnational actors have played a major role in increasing the Japanese government's involvement. When the Japanese government became an active crisis manager for the Latin American debtors in the 1980s, a strong domestic force represented by Japanese banks compelled the Japanese government to act. Furthermore, the power of the banks came not only from their own economic and political power in the country but also from the fact that institutional linkages with transnational banks in other parts of the world urged them to do so. The domestic dynamics of the crisis management of the mid-1990s was somewhat different. As is noted in chapter 6, the financial actors involved in the two financial crises changed, leading to differences in the way private actors influenced the Japanese government.

The private financial actors deeply involved in the 1982 debt crisis were commercial banks that had high exposure to developing country debts on syndicated loans in the 1970s and 1980s. Both lenders and borrowers were locked into those long-term loans. In the early 1990s, a large portion of capital flows took the form of bond and equity investments in emerging markets in Latin America. In the case of Mexico, J. P. Morgan estimated that the country enjoyed $26 billion (1992), $30 billion (1993), and $10 billion (1994) in capital inflows, most of them through such mechanisms. This type of financial flow, carried out by institutional investors, is mostly short-term flow and is significantly more liquid and more volatile than syndicated loans. The nature of these new investments (which do not lock in investors in the crisis countries), coupled with minimal pressure from domestic actors in Japan, weakened the Japanese government's motivation for collective action with the United States in the 1990s.

Summary

What factors motivated the Japanese government to get involved in solving the Latin American debt crisis in the 1980s but were lacking in the 1994 Mexican peso crisis? The following two chapters begin with this empirical question, which has led me to an analysis of the complex dynamics of collective financial crisis management among major creditors. Because international financial stability rests on the appropriate management of major crises like these, the possibility of international public goods provision in the world of finance can be understood by examining the motivation of the major creditor governments for becoming actively involved in this type of crisis management.

The analysis indicates the importance of understanding the nature of public goods in terms of joint products. The private returns accrued (or expected to accrue) from the collective provision of public goods become a critical component in the creditor government's decisions. The Japanese government was concerned with (a) the involvement of the private financial sector in the crisis, (b) the repercussion of the crisis on the U.S. economy and hence on Japan's economic and political relationship with the United States, and (c) Japan's status in the international financial world. As the active involvement in the resolution of the Latin American debt crisis provided satisfactory private returns, the Japanese government was quite willing to commit to crisis management. Although these private goods could have been separately produced, the Japanese government's active involvement in the management of the Latin American debt crisis produced these goods much more efficiently.[3]

Transnational linkages, both economic and institutional linkages, were also important in increasing the government's motivation for its involvement. Since the 1970s, there has been a trend toward increased internationalization of the Japanese private sector, deriving from structural and inherent causes in the Japanese economy that have fostered the private sector's interest in international affairs. The private sector demanded that the Japanese government intervene in situations that were stated to have potentially damaging effects on economic activities and profits. Particularly in the case of the debt crisis of the 1980s, Japanese commercial banks influenced Japanese foreign policy: they used their power to influence the Japanese government. Furthermore, collective action between Japan and the United States was facilitated by the common interests and common constituencies among transnational banks from each country, which transmitted pressures from the United States to the Japanese government.

As both of these influential factors were not strong in the case of the 1994–95 Mexican peso crisis, the Japanese government was not sufficiently motivated to become involved in crisis management, particularly given the different domestic political and economic circumstances it faced in the mid-1990s. Furthermore, the U.S. government was in a relatively good position economically, and the Clinton administration had a significantly elevated political motivation to act quickly, even by itself, to manage the Mexican peso crisis.

CHAPTER 5

Japan and the Latin American Debt Crisis

Japan was quite an important actor in the solution of the Latin American debt crisis. The Japanese government extended a significant amount of official funds to the indebted countries in need of foreign exchange income, and it also consistently supported the U.S. debt initiatives, thus facilitating collective action among creditor governments. In the late stage of the debt crisis, the Japanese government came up with its own debt initiative, the Miyazawa Plan. This plan finally gave rise to a tangible solution to the debt crisis for many countries, with the U.S. government adopting it in the form of the Brady Plan. Despite such involvement, very little of the abundant economic and political science literature analyzing the debt crisis in Latin America[1] examines Japan's role; nor does the majority of the literature explain how and why the Japanese government was willing and motivated to help Latin America and to support the United States in this crisis.[2]

This chapter argues that the Japanese government was motivated by the private returns it expected to gain from its active involvement in the debt crisis solution, frequently in support of the United States. After briefly describing Japan's actions during the debt crisis, the analysis of motivation is structured according to the hypotheses outlined in chapter 1. Both of these hypotheses, the joint product nature of international financial stability and the importance of transnational linkages, significantly influenced the behavior of the Japanese government during the debt crisis.

Japan's Involvement in the Latin American Debt Crisis (Dependent Variable)

The debt crisis of the 1980s, which began in Mexico in August 1982, was a major economic crisis that had the potential to destabilize the international financial system.[3] The crisis lasted for almost a decade, preoccupying the financial world and policymakers. On August 12, 1982, Mexican finance minister Jesús Silva Herzog informed the U.S. government and the IMF that Mexico would not be able to service interest payments on its debt. This sudden announcement shook the world of finance because of the magnitude of the creditors' loan exposure in Mexico, which stood at $80 billion, and because of the fear of repercussions on other major debtors, such as Brazil and Argentina. Smaller debtors, such as Bolivia and Ecuador, also requested debt rescheduling, in the fall of 1982.

As the crisis hit, policymakers in the creditor governments scrambled to get emergency and fresh loans and new lending to Mexico and other developing country debtors to alleviate their liquidity crises. Mexico's rescue package was immediately assembled by the United States and the IFIs; the first $2 billion from the United States was transferred on August 15, half in the form of a food credit (PL-480) and the rest as advance payments on future U.S. oil purchases from Mexico using the Treasury's Exchange Stabilization Fund (ESF). A few days after the initial package was released, negotiations between creditor countries' central bankers took place at the BIS headquarters in Basel, Switzerland, to assemble an international rescue package. Due to the potentially destabilizing effects of the Mexican crisis, central bankers from most creditor countries were sympathetic to the idea of a multilateral rescue package. They agreed to provide $1.85 billion (including the portion from the United States) in bridge loans until the IMF agreement shaped up.[4] The agreement between the Mexican government and the IMF was finally reached in November 1982. The Mexican government agreed to cut its budget deficit drastically by lowering subsidies and raising taxes, in exchange for $3.7 billion in IMF standby credit. By the end of the year, the formal rescue package for Mexico amounted to $8.25 billion.[5] In addition, the managing director of the IMF, Jacques de Larosière, practically twisted the arms of major transnational banks, such as the Bank of America, CitiCorp, and Chase Manhattan, to commit $5 billion of the new money, the amount needed to help cover the Mexican balance-of-payments shortfalls in 1983.[6]

During this phase, the Japanese government followed the consensus of the creditor community, led by the United States and the IMF. When the $1.85 billion rescue package was assembled through the BIS, then-governor of the Bank of Japan Haruo Maekawa "promptly obtained the approval of the Japanese government to participate on a scale second only to the United States."[7] Furthermore, the Japanese government also prevented Japanese commercial banks from exiting Mexican and Latin American outstanding debt in these early months. *Nihon Keizai Shimbun* reported on December 15, 1982, that when Japanese commercial banks refused to roll over part of their short-term lending to Mexico, the U.S. Federal Reserve Board, the Bank of England, and the Mexican government pressured the Bank of Japan to make the banks respond. The Japanese MOF agreed with the strategy of the United States and Great Britain, to avoid financial panic.

Despite this Mexican rescue package and other repeated debt relief agreements between the major debtors and private and public financial institutions between 1983 and 1984, there was no definite solution in sight.[8] By mid-1984,

Bolivia and Ecuador announced debt payment suspensions, and Peru stopped meeting its debt obligations. In June of that year, eleven Latin American debtors met in Cartagena, Colombia, to discuss the issue. The meeting caused some creditors to fear that the debtors might engage in collective action to strengthen their bargaining powers. Although the conference adopted a declaration that supported the creditors' debt relief strategies, debtors' frustration about prolonged economic difficulties resulting from their debt overhang was visible.[9]

At the World Bank/IMF annual meeting in Seoul, Korea, in October 1985, the Baker Plan, named after then-U.S. treasury secretary James Baker, was announced. This plan targeted fifteen of the most heavily indebted countries, ten of which were in Latin America, and announced three policy themes: (1) a continuing adjustment effort by these heavily indebted countries to produce economic growth, (2) greater collaboration between the IMF, the World Bank, and other regional banks to provide $27 billion to these countries over the following three years, and (3) increased lending from private banks, rising to $20 billion over the following three years.[10] The Baker Plan called for a greater flow of new money to heavily indebted countries, which represented the U.S. recognition of the need for more aggressive measures to provide adequate financing to Latin American countries so that they could recover from debt overhang.

Japanese and European banks responded to the Baker Plan somewhat reluctantly and suspiciously.[11] As I already noted, ten of the countries comprising the so-called Baker Fifteen were in Latin America (and twelve out of the expanded group of seventeen were in the region), where American banks had the most exposure. Moreover, the banks had already provided significant amounts of "new money" through involuntary lending to these high-risk countries. Despite these considerations, fourteen Japanese banks issued a statement to the World Bank on December 12, 1985, supporting the Baker Plan.[12]

But the plan failed to restore economic growth to the indebted countries, partly because the new money package did not restore large enough capital flows and partly because the plan did not lead to an expansion of productive capacity.[13] Some analysts then began to doubt the effectiveness of debt relief plans that presupposed illiquidity as the problem of the major debtors. They began to advocate some kind of debt forgiveness. U.S. senator Bill Bradley, for example, was skeptical about the effectiveness of the Baker Plan and of full payment of outstanding loans by the major debtors. He advocated a 3 percent interest cut on private and official loans for selected debtors that implemented successful structural adjustment led by the IFIs. At this stage, many Japanese bankers were not in favor of the debt-reducing nature of Bradley's proposal, and they emphasized market-oriented solutions to the debt problem.[14]

The payment crisis deepened once again for major Latin American debtors, such as Mexico and Brazil, between 1986 and 1987. The first major blow to the Latin American debt crisis solution occurred when, due to the decline of oil prices and increasing capital flight, the Mexican balance of payments, which had shown some signs of recovery, worsened in mid-1986. Mexico's international reserves decreased by $3 billion during 1987. It was reported that Mexico would require $9–10 billion in new loans to get the country's economy back on its feet. The IMF agreed to provide to Mexico an emergency stabilization loan package of $1.6 billion, which was part of a $12 billion multilateral rescue package. Rescheduling agreements between the Mexican government and commercial banks in September 1986 averted the worst outcome. The second major blow to the debt crisis solution was the Brazilian announcement on February 20, 1987, of a moratorium on its $67 billion commercial debt. The Brazilian balance of payments had also worsened during the latter part of 1986.

By this time, the attitude of policymakers in creditor countries had shifted. Previously, they had insisted that the developing country debt crisis should be characterized as a liquidity crisis, where more inflow of foreign capital was needed to resolve debtors' balance-of-payments problems. They had understood it as a temporary and short-term crisis. After the series of setbacks that occurred during 1986–87 despite efforts by creditor banks, creditor governments, and the IFIs, policymakers gradually became convinced that the problem was not merely a liquidity crisis: they were forced to acknowledge the insolvency of these governments as the fundamental problem.

The payment difficulties of these major debtors also triggered increased loan-loss reserves of American commercial banks that had high exposure to Latin America. The most influential response came from CitiCorp in May 1987, when it announced that it had set aside $3 billion in loan-loss reserves to stabilize its position in response to the Brazilian crisis. In December, Morgan Guarantee announced a plan to retire up to $20 billion of its Mexican debt through the exchange of outstanding loans for government bonds at a 50 percent discount. This scheme converted part of the Mexican bank debt into twenty-year bonds whose principal would be backed by U.S. government securities. In this way, Morgan Guarantee exited from large outstanding claims, and Mexico reduced its debt by persuading the banks to exchange their loans for U.S. government-guaranteed bonds at the discounted rate of two to one. The Morgan Guarantee approach was endorsed by the secretary of state, James Baker, and it constituted a model for future debt reduction schemes. The changes in perception and in the commercial banks' exposure positions were also reflected in a modification of the Baker Plan in 1987. At the World

Bank/IMF annual meeting in Washington, D.C., Secretary Baker called for a "menu approach" that enabled commercial banks to select from various options of the menu when supporting debt relief. The options ranged from trade and project loans to some debt reduction measures, such as debt swaps (with equity or for environment) and exit bonds.[15]

The Japanese government responded to the reemergence of the payment crises among major Latin American debtors by increasing its official financial commitment to the solution of the debt crisis, particularly with the objective of recycling Japan's current account surplus. Following the announcement of Mexico's economic difficulties, the Japanese finance minister announced, in October 1986, a $10 billion Capital Recycling Program over the next three years. Through this program, the Japanese government contributed $2 billion to establish the Japan Special Fund in the World Bank, $3.6 billion to the IMF, $3.9 billion to the International Development Association (IDA—a soft credit window of the World Bank) and the Asian Development Fund (a soft credit window of the Asian Development Bank [ADB]). This program was expanded from $10 billion to $30 billion in May 1987, after the Brazilian moratorium shock. Prime Minister Yasuhiro Nakasone announced that an additional $20 billion would be allocated among various IFIs committed to cofinancing, by the OECF ($8 billion), the JEXIM Bank together with the private sector and IFIs ($9 billion), and the JEXIM Bank's untied loans ($3 billion).[16] This $20 billion was announced as an *omiyage* (gift) on the occasion of a U.S.-Japanese bilateral meeting. In the United States, it was reported to be primarily targeted at Latin American countries.[17] This $30 billion Capital Recycling Program was well received at the Venice Summit in June of that year.[18]

Despite various debt reduction instruments made available to commercial banks, the banks were reluctant to participate because they doubted that even the reduced part of their claims would be fully honored by the debtor governments, due to the lack of foreign exchange income. The idea of increased creditor governments' financial involvement received a cold reception. Arguments against such action included political considerations regarding the response of creditor countries' taxpayers to bank bailout by public money; the moral hazard problem that public involvement creates for poorly behaved debtors and free-riding banks as they get bailed out with such support; and the budget implications of a large bailout plan, particularly for the U.S. government in the latter half of the 1980s.

In this context, the Japanese government took an initiative aiming to resolve the lingering debt problem. The so-called Miyazawa Plan, which included debt reduction schemes with public financial support, was informally introduced at a meeting of the IMF Interim Committee in April 1988 and then privately discussed among the G-7 finance ministers at the Toronto Summit that June.[19] Finally, the plan was formally announced during the World Bank/IMF annual meeting in Berlin in September 1988. This plan contained three major components. First, debtors would reach an agreement with the IMF on a structural adjustment program promoting economic growth. Second, the flow of bilateral and multilateral public funds for structural adjustment would be increased. Finally, banks and debtors would voluntarily convert a portion of debt to bonds and reschedule the remaining debt under suitable conditions once the structural adjustment program had been carried out. The debtor nations could securitize their debt by establishing a reserve account related to the proportion of debt converted to bonds and the proportion rescheduled. The management of this reserve would be entrusted to the IMF.[20] Analysts and policymakers then believed that the Japanese government would supply parallel lending to debtor countries, which would provide the reserves required for the collateral for exit bonds, thus creating official financial support for the bonds.[21] Japanese prime minister Noboru Takeshita lent support to this interpretation when he announced at the 1988 Toronto Summit that the Japanese government would begin a five-year (1988–92) ODA program involving over $50 billion, along with the $5.5 billion debt relief package for severely indebted countries.[22]

Although a few countries, including France and Canada, welcomed the Miyazawa Plan, and although it earned some support from scholars of the debt issue,[23] the plan received a cold reception from the other creditor governments. Some argued that the plan looked too much like "the public bailing out the banks," particularly using the IMF as a "debt purchasing facility."[24] For Washington, this debt underwriting function through the IMF was considered too ambitious and expensive. Due to the strained condition of its federal budget, the U.S. government was neither in a position to make a new infusion of money to the IFIs nor ready to relinquish its voice in these international organizations.[25] In addition, the concept of a public bailout would be resented much more in the United States than in Japan, given the U.S. political system's much stronger scrutiny over the government's use of taxpayers' money.[26] Some commercial banks joined in the criticism of the plan, arguing that it would distort the market and lead to moral hazard problems on the part of the badly behaved debtors that might benefit from the debt reduction.[27] The proposals of the Miyazawa Plan had to wait for the change in the U.S. administration in 1989 to be considered seriously.

During his visit to Washington in February 1989 right after President Bush took office, Japanese prime minister Noboru Takeshita confirmed that the United States and Japan would collaborate in their economic assistance efforts, particularly in Latin America and the Middle East. Referring to the allocation of Japan's ODA and support for debt relief, the prime minister noted that "Japan would like to expand the coverage of its ODA from the concentrated allocation to countries like China and the Philippines to a more widespread allocation toward Latin America and Africa."[28] President Bush was willing to revise the Baker Plan, and he promised that his administration would respond to the debt problem with flexibility. Washington became seriously concerned about the prolonged debt problem and the slow (or negative) growth of the heavily indebted countries.[29] This concern arose because of the negative impact on the national security of those countries arising from economic and social instability and because of the possible impact of these factors on the prospect for the democratization of some Latin American countries slated to hold elections during 1989–90.

The resulting debt strategy promoted by the Bush administration came in the form of the Brady Plan on March 10, 1989. The plan was formally called "the strengthened debt strategy" or "the new debt strategy"; it took on the name Brady Plan in reference to Treasury secretary Nicholas Brady. This debt reduction plan targeted heavily indebted middle-income countries by forgiving debt service to commercial banks and/or compressing the debt's principles. The plan conserved the principals of the Baker Plan, including the goals of (a) economic growth of the indebted countries, (b) structural adjustment of the debtors, (c) new money inflows from abroad, and (d) a case-by-case approach. However, the Brady Plan also emphasized debt reduction through various menu items and stipulated that the remaining portion of debt and new bond instruments were to be de facto guaranteed by the IMF and the World Bank. The plan also included penalties for commercial banks that did not abide by the Brady Plan; banks would have their interest and principal payments suspended for three years. The plan required the debtors to take measures to decrease their debt overhang by restructuring their economies, promoting capital inflows, and repatriating flight capital.

The Brady Plan very closely resembled the Miyazawa Plan. The Japanese government and the U.S. Treasury held consultations before its official announcement. At the end of February, a Treasury official, Charles Dallara, came to Japan and informed the Japanese government that the United States wanted to accept the Japanese proposal. The two governments then discussed the details of the plan.[30] When the Brady Plan was announced in March, Japan's finance minister Tatsuo Murayama told reporters:

> I would like to welcome the amply strengthened debt strategy just announced by Treasury Secretary Brady, and would like to support this new

> plan proposed by the United States that includes voluntary market-based debt and debt-service reduction and repatriation of flight capital. We have been in close consultation with the U.S. monetary authority on this issue, and this new American proposal incorporates fundamental ideas put forth by the Japanese government previously. Japan will collaborate closely with the United States and other governments concerned to implement this new debt strategy.[31]

The G-7 governments accepted the plan in April.[32] The heads of state at the Paris Summit in July also supported the plan. Japan was the strongest supporter of all. During the IMF meeting in April 1989, the Japanese government promised to support the Brady Plan by providing $4.5 billion through the JEXIM Bank in parallel financing with the IMF.[33] As debtor countries like Mexico, the Philippines, Costa Rica, and Venezuela entered negotiations with the IMF by the early summer of 1989, the Japanese government announced a contribution of $35 billion in addition to the $30 billion already committed to the Capital Recycling Program of 1986–87. This contribution increased the total of the Capital Recycling Program to $65 billion over fiscal years 1987–91, $10 billion of which was committed to debt relief.[34]

The first debt reduction negotiations commenced in April 1989 between various groups of creditors and the Mexican government. They reached agreement in July and concluded the details in September of that year. In the agreement, donor governments rescheduled their $2.6 billion in official loans. The IMF provided $1.6 billion through the Extended Fund Facility (EFF) and extended the World Bank $2.6 billion through the Sector Adjustment Loans (SECALs). The JEXIM Bank provided new untied loans totaling $1.9 billion—$1 billion in parallel financing with the IMF and $0.9 billion in cofinancing with the World Bank. Of medium- and long-term commercial bank debt, $48.5 billion was to go under the debt reduction scheme. Overall, 41 percent ($19.9 billion) of the total debt negotiated was reduced through discount bonds (reducing the principal by 35 percent), 49 percent ($23.8 billion) through par bonds (interest reduction to 6.25 percent per year), and only 10 percent ($4.8 billion) as a new money equivalent to a quarter of the old debts loanable in four years.[35]

During the ten years between 1987 and 1996, the JEXIM Bank alone provided $11 billion (or 23.6 percent of the JEXIM Bank's total) in untied loans to Latin America through the Capital Recycling Program (and its successor, the Development Initiative Program). Mexico (1989), the Philippines (1989 and 1994), Venezuela (1991), and Argentina (1993) benefited from the JEXIM Bank's untied loans parallel to the IMF agreement and successfully concluded their Brady deals (see table 5.1).

Crisis Management as a Joint Product

In the case of Latin America, the sense that the debt crisis threatened international financial stability was clear among the creditor governments. The list of indebted countries with the potential for debt moratorium or even default was extensive, and the exposure of many major creditor banks was alarmingly high. Because the major debtors involved in the crisis were concentrated in Latin America (beginning with Mexico), where the major banks of the United States were highly exposed, the United States was the first creditor government that sensed the crisis and acted to resolve it. The Japanese government was also drawn in, despite the fact that the center of this crisis involved geographically distant countries. In the end, the Japanese government positively contributed to collective crisis management to contain and resolve the Latin American debt crisis, committing substantial amounts of public funds in support of the U.S. government's initiatives.

The abundance of the private returns promised by this crisis management drove the Japanese government's strong interests and commitment. Although the region in crisis was far away, Japan's political and economic position in the middle and late 1980s provided ample grounds for the involvement of the Japanese government in the management of these economic problems in an unfamiliar region. The private returns to the Japanese government can be categorized into three groups: domestic economic stability in Japan; a smooth and fast recovery of the U.S. economy, in which Japan had vested economic and political interests arising from economic linkages between the two countries; and an increase in Japan's status and power in IFIs, particularly in the IMF.

Domestic Economic Stability in Japan

The first private return served the Japanese government's concern for its own domestic economic stability, particularly for the health of the Japanese financial sector, mainly the banks.[36] The private return for the Japanese government

TABLE 5.1. JEXIM Bank's Support to the Brady Plan with Signing Dates and Amounts (in millions of dollars, equivalent)

Recipient Country	Signing Date	Amount
Mexico	November 1989	1,000
Philippines	November 1989	300
Venezuela	March 1991	300
Argentina	February 1993	300

Source: Export-Import Bank of Japan, *EXIM Japan Bulletin* (November 1997).

emerged from the fact that successful management of the crisis could have led to financial security for the Japanese banks exposed to foreign debts, particularly in Latin America. Thus, such management enabled the Japanese government to maintain the stability of the country's domestic financial system. Obviously, the MOF has long been the protector of the well-being of Japanese banks.[37]

During the period of large commercial bank lending (1975–82), the MOF had regulatory concerns about commercial banks' rapid accumulation of outstanding loan claims to developing countries. MOF officials were also concerned about banks' excessive competition, which lowered the spread over these loans. By July 1979, the MOF and the Bank of Japan had prepared comprehensive rules to increase their control over Japanese banks' foreign lending.[38] Furthermore, the MOF advised banks to be more selective in their lending activities to developing countries. One way for banks to reduce their risk was to develop cofinancing arrangements with multilateral financial organizations, such as the World Bank and the Inter-American Development Bank (IDB), with the IMF working as an information provider.[39]

The concern of the MOF about the health and management of the Japanese banks was well founded. As Japanese bank profits increased 16.6 percent in the third quarter of 1979, their reliance on foreign exchange and foreign lending as sources of profit also increased significantly. The Bank of Tokyo had an exceptionally high rate of foreign lending, since it was once the only foreign exchange bank and was traditionally very internationally oriented. Its rate of profit from overseas activities in 1979 was 77.5 percent. Other major banks also expanded their proportion of overseas activities. The average rate of profit on these activities for the twelve city banks, excluding the Bank of Tokyo, increased from 9.24 percent to 10.33 percent during 1979. Several of the largest banks derived 10 to 17 percent of their profits from foreign exchange and foreign lending activities.[40]

However, the MOF's guidance occasionally increased the risk Japanese banks were taking. Although Japanese banks were at first followers of the American banks' lead in forming syndicate loans, they eventually became managers (leading banks) in such loans. The Bank of Tokyo handled $753 million as the leading bank by 1981, and other, less internationally experienced Japanese banks began to play the role of leading bank in the latter half of 1981. Sumitomo Bank increased the number of syndicated loans it led from one worth $50 million to seven worth $617 million, and the Long-Term Credit Bank of Japan led its first three such loans, worth $217 million, during this period.[41] The MOF encouraged the Japanese banks to act as leading banks in syndication, because of the greater commission fees they could earn.[42]

In 1982, when the debt crisis struck, all transnational banks feared the repercussions of a Mexican default throughout the rest of Latin America. Exposure to Mexican debt ranged anywhere between 40 percent to 67 percent of bank capital for major American banks.[43] A less-known but nevertheless striking fact about the Japanese banks' involvement in this Mexican debt was their high exposure. The U.S. banks' familiarity and expertise in Latin America (and possibly their knowledge of the U.S. government's political commitment) contributed to the concentration of debt in the region and in Mexico in particular, and that affected Japanese banks' lending practices.[44] The Bank of Tokyo's exposure level in Mexico was 83 percent of its capital, and the exposure of other major banks ranged from 28.3 percent (Mitsui Bank) to 53.6 percent (Long-Term Credit Bank of Japan).[45]

With these alarmingly high rates of exposure, the Japanese government's role as a protector became even more important. Various rescheduling agreements during 1983 and the fear of a Brazilian moratorium continued to shake the financial world. In July 1983, the MOF reported that Japanese banks' outstanding loan claims had significantly increased since the previous July, mainly due to an increase in short-term lending to maintain debtors' interest payments. The increase totaled $16 billion among the heavily indebted countries, bringing Japan's total lending to Mexico to $10 billion, to Brazil to $7.5 billion, and to Argentina to $4 billion.[46] Assisted by an appreciation of the yen, the increase in Japanese banks' exposure to Latin American loans continued until 1987 (see fig. 5.1).

Despite the high exposure, Japanese banks seldom defected from agreements set up under BACs after the Mexican debt crisis, nor did they exit from bad loans (see fig. 5.1). The reasons may be that the banks' asset base in Japan was expanding rapidly during the period (so they possessed significant hidden assets) and that the yen was getting much stronger against the dollar.[47] These factors made it somewhat easier for Japanese banks to maintain a high level of exposure in Latin America. However, from the MOF standpoint, Japanese banks were still less competitive than other major banks in the world and needed to be protected through the MOF's tight rein so that they would not incur huge losses and possibly create a domestic financial panic.[48] In return, the MOF made various gradual concessions domestically in the form of increases in the tax-deductible rate on debt losses and increased official financial commitment to the indebted region.[49]

Late in 1987, Japanese banks' outstanding loans to major Latin American countries became a bigger problem for the Japanese government, and the solution to the problem thus became a larger private return. The Cooke Committee of the BIS came to an agreement in December 1987 that member country banks operating overseas, including Japanese banks, would adopt a bank capital-asset ratio of 8 percent by 1992. Because other OECD countries had

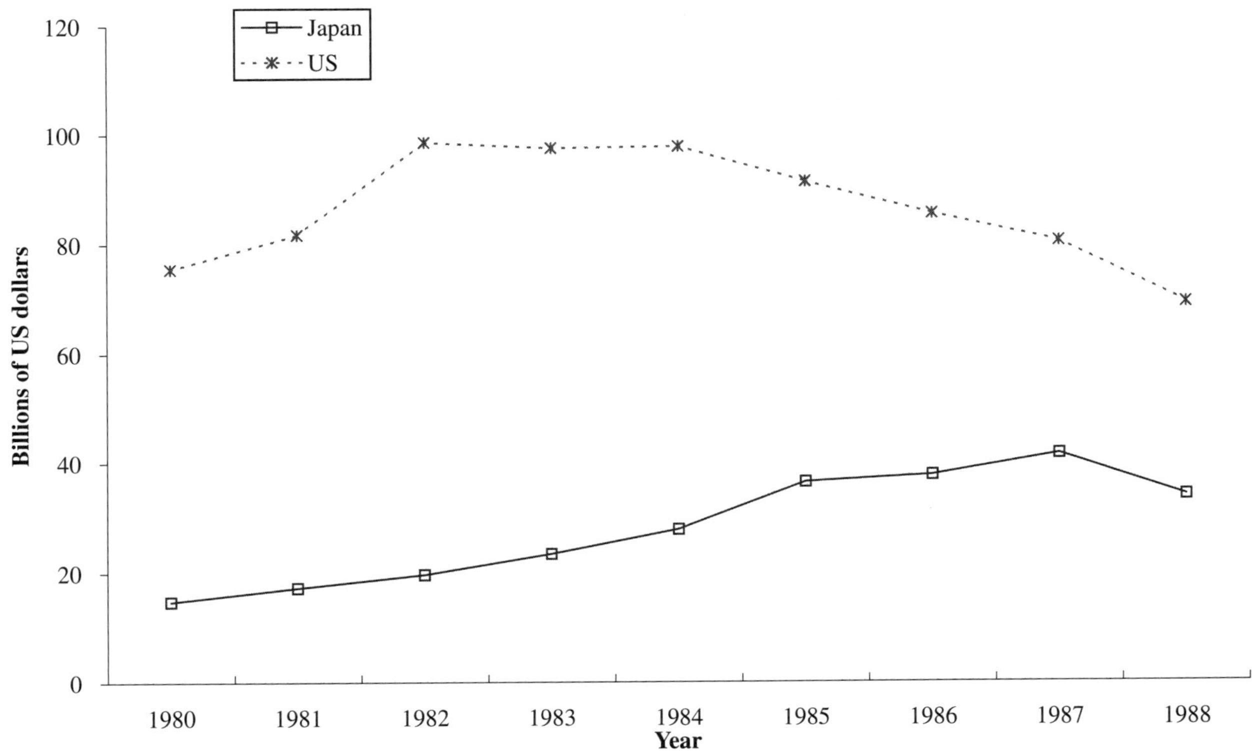

Fig. 5.1. Bank loans outstanding in Latin America, Japan, and the United States, 1980–88. (From Federal Financial Institutions Examination Council, *Country Exposure Lending Survey,* and Japan Bond Research Institute, *Country Risk Information.*)

criticized the Japanese banks for unfair competitiveness deriving from a low capital-asset ratio, the Japanese banks and the MOF feared that failure to comply with the standard would invoke retaliatory exclusion of Japanese banks from international operations.[50] At least a portion of the Japanese banks' large loans to Latin American debtors, for whom they had no prospect of swift repayments, had to be repatriated to improve the Japanese banks' compliance with the BIS standard.

The timing of the appearance of the Miyazawa Plan, a debt reduction proposal first publicly advocated at the IMF Interim Committee meeting in April 1988, reveals the MOF's concern over the course of Japanese banks' bad loans in the region. In addition to proposing the Miyazawa Plan, the Japanese government poured $30 billion into the Capital Recycling Program, a sum expanded in 1989 to $65 billion (with half of the additional money earmarked for Latin America).[51] Rosenbluth notes that through these schemes, "the Japanese government had purchased for Japanese banks a clear path for retreat" from Latin America.[52] At the same time, this policy intervention supported the resolution of the debt crisis by increasing available financial resources for the parties involved.

Japan's Concern over the U.S. Economy

The second type of private return that the Japanese government perceived as accruing through collective management of the Latin American crisis was the smooth and fast recovery of the U.S. economy in the latter half of the 1980s. The Japanese government could consequently expect a stable relationship with the United States, which was (and is) by far Japan's most important economic partner in the world. The Japanese government could also expect milder political pressure on Japan's one-sided trade surplus with the United States, as Japan supported the U.S. debt initiatives and contributed to the recovery of the U.S. economy.

The Latin American debt crisis not only gave rise to a fear of domestic financial collapse in the United States due to the heavy exposure of many major American banks in the region but also led to a deterioration in the U.S. trade balance.[53] Japan had a large trade surplus against the United States, ranging from $30 billion to $60 billion between 1984 and 1990. Therefore, those who dealt with developing country debts and the problem of liquidity expected Japan to recycle its current account surplus either to the United States or to debt-ridden Latin America. For example, Harvard economist Jeffrey Sachs calculated that if Japan recycled its surplus capital to Latin America by $2.5 billion each year for three years, there would be an improvement of the U.S. overall trade balance by $1.15 billion per year. This recycling method recommended itself as a much more effective way of improving the trade balance with the United States than would be the expansion of Japan's domestic fiscal expenditure by the same amount or the recycling of the same amount of capital to non–oil-developing countries in general.[54] In addition to the direct effect of a capital recycling program on the U.S. trade balance, such recycling, if it stimulated significant capital outflow from Japan, could be expected to have some effect on reversing or slowing the yen appreciation, which the Japanese government faced after the Plaza Accord in the fall of 1985. This perspective permeated the thinking of Japanese policymakers, and it inspired Japan's Capital Recycling Program. Although the program's target was not solely Latin America, this indebted region, with its major impact on the U.S. economy, constituted an important part of the scheme.[55]

There are some indications that the Japanese government's commitment to the Capital Recycling Program aimed mainly to please the United States (and Japan's own financial sector, as I noted earlier) rather than the debtors themselves. This perspective emerged in response to discussions during U.S. congressional hearings that outlined what American policymakers wanted and what they feared about Japan's capital recycling. In 1987, when the U.S. Senate Committee on Finance (Subcommittee on International Debt) discussed the impact of the Latin American debt crisis on the United States, some lawmakers strongly urged the U.S. government to link the issue of U.S.-Japanese trade to Japan's supportive involvement in the solution of the crisis. One report noted:

> In particular, economically powerful nations with large trade surpluses vis-à-vis the United States should be encouraged to make major commitments to a resolution of the debt crisis. Though they are certain to resist, it is ultimately in their interest to cooperate with the United States in providing debt relief, because the alternative may be a protectionist U.S. trade policy. Japan, specifically, could ease some of the current trade tensions with this country by cooperating in Third World debt restructuring.[56]

A few years later, however, in the spring of 1989, when the announcement of Japan's large financial commitment to Latin America was perceived as a threat to the United States, a U.S. congressman expressed his concerns that "[in Latin America, w]e may find that the major increased role of the Japanese in lending will cause them, by mixed credit arrangements or by the conditions they place on their foreign assistance, to capture significant commercial markets that we once had."[57] U.S. lawmakers wanted the Japanese government to become actively involved in the crisis management, but they did not want this involvement to threaten privileged U.S. economic ties to Latin America. This is not to say that the Japanese government and its private sector did not have any direct trade interests in mind when the Japanese government stepped up capital recycling to Latin America. But the modality of the capital recycling program, which totally relied on untied loans, demonstrates the Japanese government's desire to please the United States so that it could reduce political pressure.[58]

To meet such political objectives, the Japanese government resorted to an active initiative to recycle its current account surplus. The Japanese government used untied loans from the JEXIM Bank and cofinancing arrangements with IFIs to enhance private capital flows to Latin American countries that were heavily indebted. The Capital Recycling Program included activities of the OECF, the agency that deals with Japan's foreign aid loans. The OECF, however, faced some constraints in providing official capital resources to some Latin American countries, because the basic laws of the OECF did not allow it to provide concessional yen loans to countries with relatively high GNP per capita.[59] Therefore, the Japanese government needed a new funding instrument to recycle capital to such countries in Latin America. The MOF envisioned that at this stage, approximately $4 billion in capital should flow between Japan, on one hand, and Latin America and the Caribbean countries, on the other.[60] An examination of bids for these aid projects in Latin America reveals that American firms have been very successful. In 1990, two large aid projects in Mexico were contracted by American companies: railroad repair totaling approximately $44 million by General Electric Co. and General Motors Interamerica Corp., and Mexico City air pollution reduction totaling approximately $495 million by HRI Inc. and Japan Plant Kyokai. Seminars were held in Tokyo about business opportunities involving Japanese aid, and the International Trade Administration in the U.S. Department of Commerce published a booklet titled *Japanese Foreign Aid Program: Opportunity for U.S. Business* in 1991. Together with the increased implementation of PBL during this period (see chap. 2), the fungibility of governmental financial flows from Japan has helped some American firms conduct business in Latin America with Japanese funds. In this way, the Japanese government could appease and please the United States through engaging actively in the management of the debt crisis, which was considered an important gain for the Japanese government.

Furthermore, the economic returns that would have resulted when the United States regained its economic health were also in the minds of Japanese policymakers. Strengthened economic linkages between Japan and the United States increased Japan's vested interests in the U.S. economy dramatically from the early 1980s onward. A direct investment boom and an increase in mergers and acquisitions by Japanese companies in the United States increased the economic stake of both manufacturing and financial sectors invested in the country.[61] In addition, a strong yen, the progress of Japan's financial liberalization, and low interest rates in Japan (see fig. 2.14) led a large Japanese capital outflow to the United States in the latter half of the 1980s (see fig. 2.12), with Japan purchasing U.S. Treasury bonds as well as corporate bonds.

In short, the Japanese government had a high stake in the U.S. economy, with the intent of avoiding more protectionist pressure on the trade front and maintaining the economic stability of the country in which Japan had substantial investment. The U.S. economy was in a relatively weak position throughout these years. Thus, helping to reinforce the U.S. economic recovery (and being perceived as doing so) by resorting to measures that did not cause major domestic backlash in Japan (e.g., opening Japan's rice market could have caused a major protest by Japan's politically strong agricultural sector) was a private return that the Japanese government welcomed from this crisis management.

Japan and IFIs

The third type of private return to the Japanese government from collective management of the Latin American crisis was the possible enhancement of Japan's status in IFIs, especially in the IMF, where voting power is based on capital subscriptions (or quotas). Since Japan joined the IMF immediately after it regained its political independence in 1952, the rapid increase in Japan's economic power (to which the amount of IMF capital subscriptions should be closely linked) has led to some reshuffling of the major countries' voting shares in the IMF.[62] Starting out below 4 percent, Japan's IMF quota increased to 4.75 percent in 1983 and remained there for the rest of the 1980s. Japan held 4.47 percent of the voting rights in the IMF during this period, placing it in the fifth most powerful voting position, after the United States (18.9 percent), the United Kingdom (6.55 percent), Germany (5.72 percent), and France (4.75 percent).

With Japan having already acquired the position of the second largest economy and ODA donor in the world, the Japanese government saw as problematic the gap between Japan's position within the IMF and the burden of international development cooperation that Japan was bearing, especially in relation to the power Japan wielded in the IFIs.[63] The Japanese government fought for an increase in its subscription quota in the IMF between 1987–89, but it faced reluctance from the other major powers, who feared that an increase in Japanese power would relatively decrease theirs.[64] Meanwhile, the Japanese government stepped up its capital infusion to the IFIs through various parallel financing and cofinancing channels; it also channeled its official flows directly to heavily indebted countries in the name of financial crisis management. But neither of these moves counted toward an increase in Japan's capital subscription to the IMF. This intensified the Japanese government's frustration and dissatisfaction regarding its status in the organization.

The breakthrough for the Japanese government came in April 1989, when the United States finally relaxed its opposition to proposals that would increase overall IMF quotas with revisions of national quotas and voting shares. This change placed Japan (tied with Germany) in the second position of voting strength. As Rapkin and Elston observe, the timing of this reversal occurred "during the same week that Japan announced it would provide $4.5 billion to support the U.S.'s Brady Plan for developing country debt relief."[65] This redistribution, agreed on in 1990 and implemented in 1992, shifted the order of the voting shares: first was the United States (19.6 percent), followed by Japan and Germany (tied at 6.1 percent) and then Britain and France (tied at 5.48 percent). The story in the World Bank is similar. The increase of Japan's contribution (but not its subscription) to the World Bank's soft window IDA and Japan's cofinancing resources, used in part to deal with the debt problem, were explicitly and implicitly linked to Japan's increased voting share in the institution.[66]

Although the process and negotiations of such private returns to Japan were long and complicated, the Japanese government's active role in the debt crisis management, especially its support for U.S. initiatives, such as the Brady Plan, helped Japan achieve its goal in the IFIs. Because the Japanese government neither expects nor wants the number one voting position in these institutions, the country's major goal was already achieved by the early 1990s.[67]

Transnational Linkages and Domestic Dynamics

Two noteworthy aspects of bank lending in the 1970s and early 1980s influenced the way the Japanese government responded to the 1982 Mexican crisis and the Latin American debt crisis. The first aspect was the strong ties existing among those transnational banks that had high exposure to developing country debts. The second was the effective lobbying power of Japanese banks on the Japanese government. The banks demanded that the government take up the lender-of-last-resort function and protect financial stability. The pressure from the international financial community on the Japanese government was transmitted in two steps: first from overseas to Japan through private sector channels, then from the powerful domestic actors to the government.

Institutional Linkages

During the Latin American lending boom prior to 1982, and in the aftermath of its debt crisis, cross-border linkages between American and Japanese transnational banks were formally and informally institutionalized. The linkages established before the crisis included the very structure of syndicated loans, with their cross-default clauses. After 1982, BACs were set up among the creditor banks in each debtor country to deal with their debt negotiations. BACs transmitted transnational pressures in dealing with various major debtors in Latin America, and Japanese banks were obligated to follow the agreements for rescheduling or forced to provide new money despite their desire to exit. In this process, the Bank of Tokyo, the traditionally outward-looking foreign exchange bank with a large exposure to Latin American debt, with the help of the MOF, served as a major channel of pressure among the transnational bank community carrying loan exposure.[68] It also served as a key coordinator of international cooperation for debt relief.[69] In addition, the Japanese banks' tendency to follow the American banks' lead, particularly in Latin America, created higher reliance and responsiveness of the Japanese banks to the needs and strategies of the American banks.[70]

Gaiatsu (foreign pressure) successfully influences foreign governments when the one who pressures has a strong domestic supporter in the country it is pressuring.[71] Such institutional links and the dynamics between private Japanese financial institutions and the Japanese government greatly influenced Japanese decisions whether or not to become involved in financial crisis management. This linkage and the natural convergence of interests among transnational banks in dealing with the debtors transmitted demand from abroad to the Japanese government. Furthermore, the financial sector became more dominant and less dependent on the government's support, a trend that increased its bargaining power as the sector became internationalized, expanding "its ability to seek out overseas sectoral allies"; in short, "[f]inance is mobile, it can easily search out overseas complements," and this cross-border alliance "has strengthened their respective hands domestically."[72] Such transnational linkage and leverage translated into positive and more involved actions of the Japanese government in the debt crisis management, because of domestic dynamics.

Domestic Dynamics

The relationship between the banks and the government in Japan was crucial during the debt crisis. As I discussed earlier in this chapter, when the Mexican debt crisis struck in 1982, not only were the major American banks highly exposed to Latin American debt, but Japanese banks also had a similar or even higher debt exposure. Thus, during the debt crisis years, Japanese banks put pressure on the government. They needed governmental support to secure an exit from their heavy exposure to the Latin American debt and to create a better environment for absorbing such debt without excessively impairing their business performance. Japanese banks felt locked in and forced to contribute to debt relief for two reasons: (1) Japan's stringent regulations on loan-loss reserves and the tax deductibility of such reserves[73] and (2) the pressure of the agreements produced by the BACs with various major debtors in Latin America.

In the first five years of the Latin American debt crisis, commercial banks, creditor governments, and IFIs strove to contain this international financial problem and to later support the recovery and economic growth of the Latin American debtors. Although the debt crisis affected developing countries in other regions, it was obvious that the United States was most concerned about the problems of its neighbors to the south, where U.S. bank exposures were the highest and where its security concerns were also substantial. The Baker Plan and its modification to a menu approach mostly targeted Latin America, and all plans attempted to restore private capital inflow to the debtors with some help from the creditor governments and the IFIs. In 1986 and 1987, the deterioration of the balance-of-payments conditions of the two largest debtors, Mexico and Brazil, shifted the perspectives and strategies of commercial banks and led them to prepare for their exit. The Japanese government, which had quietly supported U.S. initiatives during these first five years, began to show increased commitment to the solution of the Latin American debt crisis, particularly by supporting Japanese banks and increasing official lending to the region.

Larger Japanese city banks and long-term credit banks have exerted a powerful influence over the Japanese government.[74] They are a tight-knit group with homogenous views and preferences about Japan's foreign economic policy. They have also been the critical actors shaping the Japanese economy, in collaboration with the government. This relationship has created strong ties with the government. Regarding international financial matters, the Bank of Tokyo functioned as a coordinator, which made the collaboration among the banks easier. Politicians also channeled the banks' demands to bureaucrats, with whom they have customarily close relationships. The bureaucrats are accustomed to reading the LDP Diet members' interests and positions and responding to their needs and wishes.[75]

A big agenda on which Japanese banks confronted the MOF during the 1980s debt crisis involved loan-loss reserves. Japan's low loan-loss reserve under the domestic regulatory environment was one major factor that led the

Japanese banks to hesitate from exiting the Latin American debt, and ever since 1982, Japanese banks had pressed the MOF for provisions to cover possible loan losses to developing countries. Unlike some European countries where banks could set aside almost 50 percent of their developing country loans as loan-loss reserves to hedge possible default, Japanese banks had no such provisions. This made it very difficult for them to tolerate any losses in developing countries, since these losses would not be covered by a reserve and would directly affect the value of the banks' assets.[76] Finally, beginning in March 1983, Japanese banks were allowed to accumulate a 5 percent loan-loss reserve for loans to countries the MOF considered high risk. Initially, these reserves were completely taxable. The banks pressed both for an increased loan-loss reserve and for its tax deductibility.[77] In 1984, thanks to heavy lobbying by the banks, the arrangements were modified: 20 percent of the loan loss reserve—1 percent of total loans—became tax deductible.

The Japanese government's role as lender of last resort and as the banks' protector was stretched further when the Latin American debt problems resurfaced in 1986 and 1987. The banks reacted strongly and wanted to get out of this never-ending spiral of financial problems, which included the moratorium by Brazil and various rescheduling arrangements. The banks became increasingly impatient with the MOF for not letting them quickly exit from this long debt ordeal. After four months of negotiation, the banks and the MOF struck a deal setting up a holding company, JBA Investment, Inc., in the Caribbean tax haven of the Cayman Islands. The company bought the Japanese banks' Latin American debt at a discounted rate. Under the new arrangement with the MOF, banks' losses were now tax deductible. The precise amount involved was tailored to make it the equivalent of a loan-loss reserve tax deductible by 5 percent—exactly the amount that the banks wanted.[78] These negotiations created the first opportunity for the Japanese banks to reduce their outstanding loans to heavily indebted countries in Latin America without paying tax on the loss.[79] The rate of reserve was increased in 1988 to 10 percent of the book value of high-risk loans, in 1989 to 15 percent, and later to 35 percent.[80]

Japanese banks' impatience with the burden of the prolonged debt problem made the Japanese government increase its private returns by minimizing banks' dissatisfaction and shortening the time that it took to resolve the problem. This led the government to propose alternative solutions. The first stage came in the form of a 1987 study by the World Institute for Development Economics Research (WIDER) in Finland and the United Nations University (UNU) in Japan, calling for a large Japanese capital recycling program. *Mobilizing International Surpluses for World Development: A WIDER Plan for a Japanese Initiative*, produced by a group chaired by the prominent Japanese internationalist Saburo Okita, proposed the recycling of the Japanese current account surplus—$125 billion over five years—to developing countries.[81]

Following the same line of thought, the Japanese government produced a practical alternative to the U.S. solution of the debt problem, an alternative that allowed Japanese banks to exit from the Latin American debt burden. The Miyazawa Plan, as I noted earlier, was formally announced during the World Bank/IMF annual meeting in Berlin in September 1988. Although the plan was not adopted, it marked a clear commitment by the Japanese government to alleviate the debt overhang in the severely indebted countries.

For Japanese banks that wanted to exit from Mexico, the 1989 Brady Plan came as a blessing. Twenty-nine Japanese commercial banks with outstanding loans to Mexico opted not to put up new money but to write off some of their Mexican debt. The outstanding stock of Japanese loans to Mexico was stable at the $11 billion level in 1988.[82] From the three options of the 1989 Brady Plan,[83] most Japanese banks chose the principal reduction option, and they converted $8 billion worth of principle into discount bonds and almost immediately sold them on the secondary market, even at a loss. About 83 percent of the Japanese banks' outstanding debt to Mexico was converted into discount bonds and then written off through this option, while only 41 percent of the total of Mexican debt reduction by other creditors was carried out through this channel. The Japanese government supported the principal reduction option, which "made it easy for [the banks], counting effectively 100 percent of their losses as tax write-offs and giving the banks flexibility in when to record their losses."[84] No new money came from Japan through the new money option, while about 10 percent of other creditors' debt to Mexico followed this option.[85] Transnational banks thus exited from Mexico by swapping their debts for bonds at a discounted rate or writing them off. Private creditors' outstanding amount of long-term debt to the Latin American countries declined slowly after this period. In the process, the Mexican debt swaps, along with a Mexican privatization scheme, invited new investments. Japanese banks and institutional investors, however, did not get on this bandwagon.

In short, transnational linkages were established among major banks highly exposed to the Latin American debt crisis, and their political power in Japan has proven to be very influential in the process of the Japanese government's policy-making. Despite the much discussed characterization of the Japanese polity as a developmental state or autonomous bureaucracy, the Japanese government was still very responsive to the pressures coming from its powerful financial sector. Institutional linkages among the transnational banks made such pressures particularly effective on Japan's decision making.

Conclusion

During the time of the debt crisis, Japan demonstrated an increasing presence in financial crisis management in the developing world, particularly as a source of development finance. Even Latin America, which was traditionally outside Japan's sphere of interest and did not have strong economic links with Japan, developed more ties with Japan, particularly on the financial side of economic exchange. Especially between 1988 and 1991, the Japanese government made an unprecedentedly strong initiative to help resolve the debt crisis, initiating and supporting debt reduction schemes both politically and financially. Japan's active involvement in providing official financial support to resolve the debt crisis made the Japanese government an important supporter in financial crisis management. Many heavily indebted countries in Latin America succeeded in reducing their debt through the Brady deals and other debt reduction measures. In turn, they began to attract private (mostly portfolio) investment based on their bond issuance and privatization. The so-called emerging markets of Latin America started booming in the early part of the 1990s, and the Latin American financial crisis appeared to have finally been solved.

The Japanese government became actively involved in the solution of the Latin American debt crisis because its actions in Latin America directly or indirectly would accomplish private returns. Its actions could protect the Japanese financial system and allow Japanese banks to exit gradually, without a major disturbance or criticism, from Latin American debtors. Its active participation also supported the United States, possibly improving Japan's most important bilateral economic and political relationship, and making it easier for Japan to enhance its power and influence in IFIs. Finally, the tight institutional linkages among transnational banks secured the meeting of private sector needs through the Japanese government's active provision of official financial resources to the region. The quantitative and microlevel analysis in chapter 3 provides support for this picture arising from the analysis of the Japanese actions in the Latin American debt crisis. The variables associated with Japan's private financial sector involvement and U.S. economic interests in Latin America increased Japan's official financial commitment in the region as well as in particular countries in the region.

The remaining task on hand is to compare the Japanese government's behavior and the factors that led to the government's active involvement in the Latin American debt crisis to those in the case of the more recent Mexican peso crisis (1994–95). This comparison should illuminate with increased robustness the importance of the level of private returns and transnational linkages.

CHAPTER 6

Japan in the Mexican Peso Crisis and Its Repercussions

By 1992, thanks to the Brady Plan, to which the Japanese government contributed billions of dollars, the prospect of Mexican and Latin American recovery looked bright. David Mulford, who pushed the Brady Plan through in 1989 as undersecretary for international affairs at the U.S. Treasury, wrote triumphantly in the *Wall Street Journal* that the U.S. economy had benefited from restored economic growth in the Latin American region and that the United States had begun to expand its new trade partnerships in the Western Hemisphere.[1] The *Economist* was also cautiously optimistic about the positive outcome of the Brady Deals, noting, "The Brady gamblers win, for now."[2]

Good times arrived to many Latin American countries in the early 1990s, as international investors became increasingly attracted to bond and equity issues by these ex-debtors. The Mexican economy started to become even more integrated continentally than before, thanks to the successful negotiations of the North American Free Trade Agreement (NAFTA), which came into effect in January 1994. Mexico became one of the success stories of the emerging market countries, and in 1994 the country even became a member of the OECD.

When the currency and financial crisis hit Mexico in December 1994, the U.S. Clinton administration, along with the IMF, was ready to help, while the Japanese government and the Europeans were quite reluctant.[3] Why was the Japanese government so active in resolving the Mexican debt crisis, with a large official fund committed to the country's debt solution in 1989–90, but so inactive in the Mexican peso crisis?

From the 1980s into the 1990s, a few major changes in the international financial environment and in Japan's political and economic conditions influenced the Japanese actions. First, regarding the international financial environment, the type of financial flows to middle-income developing countries shifted from predominantly bank lending to portfolio investment in stocks and bonds. This shift changed not only the speed of capital movement in and out of the country but also the financial actors involved in the transaction. These changes in the financial actors and the implication of these changes on the strength of institutional linkages among creditors come under my second hypothesis in chapter 1. Beyond that, the apparent changes in the international financial environment has not transformed the fundamental nature of the creditor-debtor dynamics or the necessity for financial crisis management.

Second, the changes in Japan's economic and political conditions have contributed to decreasing the private returns that the Japanese government could expect from international financial crisis management in the 1990s. The relative decline of Japan's economic strength vis-à-vis the United States, with Japan suffering an extended period of recession in the 1990s and with the United States experiencing a long economic boom, might have made the Japanese government reluctant to assist the United States. This shift in relative economic positions has influenced the Japanese government's calculation of its private gains, and thus its behavior in the Mexican peso crisis, in three ways. First, weakening bilateral trade tensions (despite an increasing trade imbalance) decreased the Japanese government's sensitivity to U.S. demands in other fields. Second, Japan's domestic financial weakness abated economic linkages between Japan and the United States, as the Japanese financial sector withdrew from the United States; concomitantly, the U.S. economic strength eliminated one major reason for the Japanese government to intervene in financial crises in Latin America—to boost the U.S. economic recovery (see chaps. 3 and 5). Third, the Japanese government began focusing on Japan's domestic economic and financial problems, which have represented more urgent concerns for the government than have the economic problems of Mexico. In a way, recovery of Japan's economy would, in the mid-1990s, contribute more to the stability of international finance than would the recovery of Mexican finance.

Finally, Japan's domestic political changes, including the LDP's loss of parliamentary majority in 1993, have further influenced the Japanese government's behavior. As political instability continued into the second half of the 1990s, the highly symbiotic relationship between the LDP, the financial bureaucracy (especially the MOF), and Japan's financial sector has transformed, making it less likely for the Japanese government to respond consistently and favorably to Japanese banks' pressures. This domestic political change in Japan contributed to weakening the transnational pressures via institutional linkages as these pressures tried to permeate the Japanese government's policy regarding the peso crisis rescue.

This chapter examines the factors that resulted in the Japanese government's inaction or its lack of involvement in the management of the Mexican peso crisis. The analysis of the chapter uses the same framework as the chapter on the Latin American debt crisis, to illuminate the determining influence of the two major factors affecting the Japanese actions—the presence of private returns and the presence of transnational linkages. After describing the actions taken by Japan and other creditors, particularly the U.S. administration and the IMF, the study examines which factors made the Japanese government a reluctant player in this financial crisis management case. As I have already discussed, a few changes in the domestic and international political economy surrounding Japan from the end of the 1980s into the 1990s changed the Japanese government's attitudes toward the Mexican financial crisis management by reducing Japan's private returns and weakening the power of transnational linkages. In addition, a few other particular factors associated with the Mexican peso crisis, such as U.S. political interests and the corresponding Mexican government's policy, also changed Japan's attitudes toward the crisis.

Japan's Limited Involvement in the Mexican Peso Crisis and the Repercussions of the Crisis (Dependent Variable)

On December 20, 1994, the Mexican government was forced by market pressure to leave the band in which the peso had fluctuated against the U.S. dollar. The Mexican peso was devalued by 15 percent, compelling the Mexican government to change the ceiling of the exchange rate band. Two days later, on December 22, Mexico was forced to allow the peso to float. As Mexico abandoned its pegged exchange rate and moved to a floating currency, the peso continued to come under attack, with corresponding effects on its stock and bond prices. Investors withdrew capital from Mexico during the first few days of the peso devaluation, leaving Mexico's foreign exchange reserve as low as $6 billion.[4] At the same time, Mexico's dollar-denominated short-term bonds, Tesobonos (Bonos de la Tésoreria de la Federación), were maturing—from January through March 1995—and fear existed that Mexico could exhaust its dollar foreign exchange reserve in only a few weeks.[5] Over the next few months, the Mexican stock market dropped by 68 percent in dollar terms (between December 19, 1994, and its low on March 9, 1995).[6] The speed and magnitude by which portfolio capital flows exited from Mexico especially in 1994 sent shock waves through the international financial community.

An international rescue package for Mexico, led by the United States and the BIS, was negotiated during the last few days of 1994. On January 2, 1995, the package was expanded to $18 billion, including $6–9 billion of the U.S. swap facility,[7] $5 billion through the BIS, about $1 billion from Canada, and $3 billion from commercial banks. The U.S. Treasury was quoted as stating that Japan was to contribute "$0.6 to $1 billion" through the BIS arrangement.[8] Unlike Japan's support to the Brady Plan only five years earlier, the amount of Japan's commitment was relatively small within the package and did not come in the form of a bilateral pledge.

To the distress of the Mexican authorities and the creditor governments that agreed to contribute to the rescue package, the peso continued to drop during the first few weeks of January 1995, pulling down the Mexican stock market. Contagion effects were felt in various emerging markets of other middle-income countries, such as Argentina, Brazil, and the Philippines. To stabilize the situation, President Clinton of the United States requested congressional authorization on January 12 to provide Mexico with $40 billion in the form of loan guarantees. At the same time, the administration called for expanding the multilateral rescue package from $18 billion to $25 billion.

As the U.S. Congress stalled its authorization due to domestic opposition during the last weeks of January, the market responded negatively to efforts by Mexico and others to restore credibility. The IMF announced the provision of $7.8 billion (the maximum of the Mexican cumulative limit, equivalent to 300 percent of its quota) in an eighteen-month standby credit for Mexico on January 26, but this did not contain the crisis. In the last weekend of January, the Mexican external balance dropped to a dangerous level, and the Mexican authorities informed the United States and the IMF that Mexico might be forced to default on some of its payment obligations.

In response, the Clinton administration immediately announced a multilateral assistance package of $48.8 billion to manage the Mexican financial crisis, including up to $20 billion in currency swaps and securities guarantees from the U.S. Treasury's ESF. The package also included an increase in the IMF's eighteen-month standby arrangement, to $17.8 billion. This amount was equivalent to 688.4 percent of Mexico's IMF quota, the highest proportion ever allowed to any member country up to that date. The Clinton administration and the IMF also counted on $10 billion through the BIS (i.e., double what was originally discussed) and $1 billion from Canada. In addition, the administration was hoping for $1 billion in currency swaps from Argentina, Brazil, Chile, and Colombia, but this did not materialize. Three billion dollars in new loans from commercial banks were also promised but were never called on by the Mexican government. The World Bank and the Inter-American Development Bank (IDB) also extended a total of $3 billion in loans.[9]

Japan was reluctant to act. Although the Japanese government generally supported the United States, it expressed reservations in this case, as did several European governments.[10] These governments viewed the 1994–95 Mexican financial crisis as a problem for the Americans, who had by far the largest stake in economic interests, political legitimacy, and security concerns (discussed later in this chapter).[11] Nevertheless, Japan at least appeared ready to collaborate with the U.S. initiatives.[12] During a meeting of finance officials from the G-7 countries on February 1, 1995, a Bank of Japan official was quoted as saying that Japan had decided to provide $1.3 billion for the BIS aid package to Mexico.[13] In addition, four Japanese commercial banks—the Bank of Tokyo, the Industrial Bank of Japan, Sumitomo Bank, and Fuji Bank—were petitioned by the U.S. banks to contribute a total of $1.2 billion to the package arranged by commercial banks, led by CitiCorp and Morgan Guarantee. The final commitment these four Japanese banks accepted on January 25, however, was only $0.4 billion.

Thanks to the impressive U.S-IMF rescue package, the Mexican crisis wound down in mid-1995, with some components of the package left unused. In June 1995, the Mexican government declined the BIS loan package, which was, in effect, available only on paper, with its need for high repayment guarantees and stringent restrictions on its use. Mexico also declined the package assembled by the commercial banks in March 1995. Japan showed a few gestures of support for the Mexican rescue during the summer of 1995. For example, the Japanese trading companies extended $0.5 billion in loans to the Commercial Bank of Mexico (Bancomext), with the support of trade insurance by the MITI.[14] The JEXIM Bank resumed loans to Japanese companies intending to invest in Mexico.[15] When the Mexican government floated bonds between July and September 1995, one in U.S. dollars ($1.0 billion) and the other in Japanese yen ($1.1 billion worth), four major Japanese banks (the Bank of Tokyo, Fuji Bank, the Industrial Bank of Japan, and Sumitomo Bank) each bought $20 million.[16] In addition, a new development project through the OECF, including a project for Mexican sewage treatment, began in the fall of 1995. However, it is still striking that Japanese involvement in the Mexican peso crisis was very limited, especially after Japan's significant financial support of the Brady Plan implemented for Mexico just a few years before. Not until June 1996, during Japanese prime minister Ryutaro Hashimoto's visit to Mexico, did the JEXIM Bank extend its untied loans to Mexico, promising $0.5 billion for Mexico's export promotion.[17]

The Mexican peso crisis severely curtailed Mexico's economic growth, but thanks to the devalued peso and booming U.S. economy and to U.S. efforts in terms of both the rescue operation and increased imports, the Mexican external balance stabilized by early 1996 without significant economic support from Japan. On January 16, 1997, Mexican president Ernesto Zedillo announced that Mexico had repaid its entire debt from the rescue package to the U.S. Treasury and thus had concluded the major part of its financial obligations arising from the crisis. Although there remained various economic problems, the most crucial of which was high unemployment, Mexico recorded a strong economic growth of 7 percent by 1997.

The repercussions of the Mexican peso crisis were not, however, limited to Mexico. Argentina had signed the Brady Plan agreement in April 1993, after more than a year of tough negotiations with the IMF and commercial banks. The JEXIM Bank at that time supplied $0.8 billion of the $3.2 billion provided by IFIs to support the purchase of zero coupon bonds. The Mexican Peso crisis of December 20, 1994, severely affected the external financial balance of Argentina. The regional contagion effect, often referred to as the "Tequila Effect," was strongly felt in the country.[18] There was a strong similarity between Mexico and Argentina in the way that the balance of payments was maintained during their booming years of the early 1990s. The Convertibility Plan of a fixed nominal exchange rate inevitably made the Argentine peso expensive, thus making it harder to export and easier to import.[19] This, along with the booming economy, led to a significant current account deficit, but that deficit was compensated by inflowing capital from international investors attracted to Argentina's bonds and equities (thus turning Argentina's capital account positive). As U.S. interest rates rose after February 1994, such external capital flows began to dry up, gradually making Argentina's current account deficit hard to sustain.

As the crisis struck Mexico, foreign capital flows were reversed in Argentina, and international reserves dwindled from an already low $16 billion in December 1994 to $11.2 billion in May 1995. Facing election for a second presidential term in May 1995, Argentine president Carlos Menem and his administration engaged in crisis management immediately after the Mexican crisis.[20] Despite these efforts, the attack on the Argentine currency and stock market continued during the first few months of 1995. Argentina finally turned to the IMF and other public institutions for help. On March 13, 1995, Argentina's economy minister, Domingo Cavallo, announced that Argentina had agreed to receive a loan package of $4.7 billion from the IMF ($2.4 billion), the World Bank ($1.3 billion), and the IDB ($1 billion). The IMF portion came in the form of a twelve-month extension of Argentina's already established EFF credit of $6.3 billion.[21]

To solicit additional bilateral support, Economy Minister Cavallo flew to Tokyo on March 31 to request a rescue package of $1.2 billion from the JEXIM Bank and six Japanese commercial banks (the Bank of Tokyo, Daiichi Bank, Sumitomo Bank, Fuji Bank, the Industrial Bank of Japan, and Long-Term Credit Bank).[22] The JEXIM Bank responded favorably to the Argentine request. The two parties signed a letter of agreement in June, through which the JEXIM Bank pitched in $0.8 billion in untied loans parallel to the IMF's EFF on June 22. In addition to this multilateral and bilateral financial support, the Argentine government privatized hydroelectric dams, nuclear power installations, and petrochemical plants, raising $1 billion. It also subscribed to a "Argentine bond" of $2 billion arranged by thirty transnational commercial banks. Among the Japanese banks, only the Bank of Tokyo participated in the scheme, arranging for $50 million.[23]

In sum, the Japanese government showed hesitation and resistance during the Mexican Peso crisis, although some positive action was taken at the time of the contagion crisis in Argentina. The next sections of this chapter analyze the forces that influenced the Japanese government's behavior.

Crisis Management as a Joint Product

The U.S. Engagement in the Mexican Peso Crisis

Following the December 1994 devaluation of the Mexican peso and its accompanying financial crunch, Mexican foreign minister José Angel Gurría visited Japan. He came to Japan not to request any direct financial rescue package from the Japanese government but to assure Japanese investors that the crisis would not affect foreign investment in Mexico.[24] However, some signs of the spreading crisis kindled serious concerns about the possibility of international financial disaster during the first quarter of 1995.[25] If the crisis continued to threaten both Asia and the value of the U.S. dollar (thus leading to yen appreciation), a major systemic crisis might ensue.[26] Because the Mexican government alone could not contain the problems of rapid devaluation and the decline of its stock prices, trends that could precipitate the departure of billions of dollars from the country, it needed outside forces to conduct crisis management of some sort.

The U.S. government pressured Japan and the other OECD countries, particularly during the early stage of the crisis. Within ten days after the Mexican peso devaluation, a preliminary rescue plan was set up through the BIS. The suggested total amount of this package expanded from $18 billion (January 4) to $40 billion (January 25). The Clinton administration faced two stumbling blocs in attaining the use of the funds. First, the U.S. Congress itself was not easily persuaded by the president's call to rescue Mexico and further burden the U.S. budget, which Congress wanted to balance. In addition, Congress insisted that Japanese and European creditor governments participate in the expanded Mexican rescue plan as a prerequisite to authorization of the rescue package.[27] Second, the other creditor governments, especially in Europe, had become increasingly resentful of the Clinton administration's attempt to ram the Mexican package down their throats.[28] The prolonged debate in Congress and resistance from the other industrial countries negatively influenced the Mexican peso and its stock market.

As the crisis deepened at the end of January 1995, the Clinton administration assembled the final rescue package of $48.8 billion without resorting to authorization from Congress. Germany and five other European countries reacted bitterly against overt U.S. pressure and the hastily arranged rescue deal through the IMF: they debated their withdrawal from the deal at the beginning of February. Japan was not a part of this European group, nor was it very active in these efforts toward collective crisis management. Although one might consider the 1995 response to Mexico by the IMF and the U.S. administration an important instrument that contained the spread of the crisis and produced public goods of international financial stability, the crisis itself was perceived, even by the Japanese, as "the problem of the Americans."[29] This was mainly because many saw that despite possible "public good" implications, successful crisis management would not produce any measurable returns to creditor governments other than the United States.

The Clinton administration considered Mexico its priority and showed an utmost willingness to support the rescue plan. U.S.-Mexican economic relations strengthened from the late 1980s into 1994, as NAFTA was signed in December 1992 and ratified by the U.S. Congress in November 1993. This agreement became effective in January 1994, creating a relative advantage for American producers to expand their market shares in Mexico. NAFTA exempts American and Canadian manufacturers from Mexican tariffs in stages, and it makes it difficult for Japanese products to penetrate Mexico.[30] Mexican trade with the United States has always been substantial, accounting for more than 60 percent of the Mexican total trade value (imports plus exports) during the 1980s. With NAFTA, Mexican trade dependence on the United States increased further, accounting for 74.9 percent of its total trade value in 1994.[31]

The Clinton administration, which had strongly supported this trade arrangement with Mexico, faced elections in 1996. Thus, the administration had to orchestrate a quick Mexican recovery to maintain its credibility. Political considerations drove the U.S. government's—particularly the executive branch's—support of Mexico throughout the rough months.[32] The flow of illegal immigration and drugs from Mexico has also made the country an important security concern for the United States. When divisions in Congress delayed the commitment of a Mexican rescue package of $40 billion, hurting Mexico's currency, the support by the executive branch became unambiguous. The Clinton administration dropped the debate and turned to the Treasury's ESF (normally used for U.S. intervention in the foreign exchange market) to contribute $20 billion without congressional authorization.[33] Furthermore, the Mexican government was aware of the elevated level of U.S. commitment to Mexico. This explains why Mexican government leaders did not even extend an official request to the Japanese government regarding concrete actions in the rescue plan.[34]

Private Returns for Japan

In contrast to the case of the Latin American debt crisis, the Mexican peso crisis presented limited private returns for Japan and thus limited incentive for the Japanese government to share the burden of public goods provision. None of the three kinds of private returns that had previously encouraged the Japanese government to engage actively in the Latin American debt crisis (see chap. 5) were strong factors in the 1994–95 Mexican peso crisis. Meanwhile, the changes in the international and domestic political and economic environment led the Japanese government to focus less on support of the United States or Latin America and more on its own economic weakness.

Three important factors that raised the stakes for the Japanese government at the time of the Latin American debt crisis were (1) the exposure of Japan's private financial sector to the Latin American debtors, (2) the imbalance in the bilateral U.S.-Japanese economic relations and its associated U.S. political pressure, and (3) Japan's own ambitions in the IFIs. None of these factors were strong in the case of the Mexican peso crisis.

The investment and involvement of the Japanese financial sector was quite limited, particularly relative to that of the United States, when the crisis struck Mexico. By the end of 1994 (December), commercial bank loans to Mexico from Japan reached $4 billion, compared to $22.2 billion from the United States.[35] In the Samurai market, there were only a few bond issues from Mexico, totaling ¥55 billion ($550 million at U.S.$1 = ¥100).

The U.S. economy was experiencing a strong boom in the middle of the 1990s, particularly in comparison with the Japanese economy. By 1992, U.S. GDP growth overtook that of Japan (see fig. 2.6) and continued to increase steadily, while Japanese economic growth stagnated notably in the 1990s. Hence, despite Japan's persistent economic interests in the United States, the Japanese government did not have to worry about propping up Latin American countries, including Mexico, to support U.S. economic recovery.

Finally, having acquired the second largest voting position in the IFIs, the Japanese government did not have a pressing agenda to promote in the IMF or the World Bank. The Japanese government did not see substantial gain in acting more positively (beyond quietly supporting the U.S. initiatives by not opposing them), especially considering the major split between the United States and other major powers from Europe in the institution.

International and Domestic Change and Japan's Motivation

Changes in the international and domestic environment from the 1980s into the 1990s further reduced the Japanese government's motivation to become actively involved in support of the United States in the peso crisis management. The end of the cold war in 1989–91 impacted the developments of the international financial market. On one hand, the "triumph of liberalism" or the loss of an alternative economic model gave rise to a market-centered developmental "consensus" in the world and limited the options of developing countries.[36] Developing countries in economic distress in the 1990s had no other choice but to rely on IFIs and request financial assistance from the capital-rich countries of the OECD members. This might have reduced the importance of constructing a solid united front among the creditor governments to keep the debtors in check.[37] On the other hand, the post–World War II anti-communist or anti-Soviet front among the countries of the "West" unraveled. Observations have surfaced that this change was particularly important for U.S.-Japanese relations, because many of the security arrangements between the two countries were made under the cold war structure.[38] As the cold war ended, the real or imaginary threat of the Soviet Union ceased, for the most part, to affect the foreign policy agenda. Japan's growing influence on the IFIs and an increase of regional arrangements in Asia are also attributed somewhat to the post–cold war environment.[39] This type of arrangement among major powers in the world economy has led the Japanese government to promote an alternative model in development.[40]

The change in Japan's economic position in the world between the 1980s and the 1990s led the Japanese government to reevaluate its policy priority. Since the early 1990s, Japan has experienced a severe recession, which came on the heels of a 1990 decline in stock prices when overheated land speculation ended. The dramatic slowing of Japan's annual GDP growth (see fig. 2.6) and the decline in real gross fixed capital formation (see fig. 2.7) are clear signs of Japan's economic slowdown starting in 1992. The recession also caused the government's revenue to decline, and it simultaneously increased the need for public investments to boost the economy.[41] Due to the squeeze from both the supply and demand sides of its budget, the government's reliance on public bonds expanded, from a relatively low level of about 10 percent of its budget in fiscal year 1988 (April 1988–March 1989) to 18.7 percent in fiscal year 1994. In this tight budgetary environment, the growth of Japan's General Account expenditure turned negative in fiscal year 1994 (−5.2 percent) and again in fiscal year 1995 (−2.9 percent). Overall, the national budget moved from a 1 percent GDP surplus in 1993 to an 8 percent GDP deficit in 1995–96.

Missing in the case of the Mexican peso crisis was not, however, the

Japanese government's capacity but its motivation. Despite the tight budgetary condition and the country's economic downturn, Japan's strong economic role in the world of the late 1980s still carried momentum in the first half of the 1990s. Japan has remained a major figure in aid flows to developing countries and a major financial contributor to multilateral organizations, such as the United Nations and the IFIs.[42] Since 1993, Japan has been the largest ODA donor, contributing more than $13 billion a year to Third World development, and Japan's presence in the IFIs has also become prominent, particularly because Japan contributes substantial funds under cofinancing arrangements with the World Bank, the IDB, and the IMF. Japan's voting share in the IMF and the World Bank has increased, and Japan maintains the second most powerful vote in both institutions.[43]

In the private financial sphere, Japanese portfolio investment to the rest of the world increased significantly from the early 1980s through the end of the decade: it rose from $3.7 billion in 1980 to its highest level of $113 billion in 1989.[44] Although this capital outflow declined somewhat in the early 1990s, Japanese portfolio flows regained outflow levels, reaching $82 billion in 1994. Appreciation of the yen in 1994–95 contributed to the increase in the nominal amount of Japan's capital outflows, and the relocation of Japanese firms to cope with the strong yen meant Japanese money followed. In addition, persistently low interest rates in Japan, coupled with Asia's dynamic economic expansion, reversed the previous trend of Japanese capital retreat.[45]

Even at the time of economic downturn in the mid-1990s, Japan's economic capacity to extend financial assistance was not seriously undermined. The Japanese government was not inhibited from allocating resources when it was regarded as absolutely necessary. In August 1997, as the Thai currency crisis affected the Asian economies, the Japanese government took initiatives to assemble a relief package of $17.2 billion, with Japan contributing $4 billion in parallel financing with the IMF.[46] This effort emphasizes the importance of the Japanese government's motivation—particularly in terms of pursuing its private returns under different economic priorities—as the determinant of Japan's behavior toward Mexican peso crisis management.

The speed with which the emergency package for Mexico was assembled made it difficult for the Japanese government to respond. Scholars examining Japanese policy response at the time of the Persian Gulf crisis have noted that the structure of Japanese decision making, which lacked a top-down mechanism, prevented the Japanese government from moving quickly at the time of emergency.[47] The United States could not wait long to solve the Mexican crisis, and the pace it established prevented any solid pressure, external or internal, from permeating the Japanese government's decision-making process. Yet it is puzzling that the Japanese government was able to respond to the 1997

Thai crisis with little more than a one-month span between its currency devaluation and the establishment of the package. Thus, again, the Japanese government's willingness to become involved in such actions becomes the center of the analysis.

The Case of Argentina

The rescue package to Argentina requires explanation, since the overall environment of the crisis was the same for Argentina as for Mexico but Argentina obtained more financial support from Japan. As in the Mexican situation, crisis management in the Argentine case would not have produced a high level of joint products for Japan. But the Japanese government did step in, albeit with small steps, to assist the Argentine government.

Two unique factors in the case of Argentina led the Japanese government to become more engaged. The first factor, which produced private returns in the form of gaining favors from the United States, was the complete immobility of the U.S. Congress in March and April 1995, the time when Argentina needed relief most. After the Clinton administration bypassed Congress and tapped the Treasury's ESF for the U.S. rescue package of $20 billion to Mexico, some U.S. lawmakers furiously attacked the administration's use of "the obscure Treasury fund," claiming it violated the law. The most vehement opponent, Republican Senate Banking Committee chairman Alfonse D'Amato of NewYork, remarked, "[The ESF] is not the president's personal piggy bank," and called for a hearing on the matter.[48] Having been so closely scrutinized in the case of the ESF and facing strong resentments among lawmakers regarding the "Latin American bailouts," the U.S. government became virtually incapable of responding to the Argentine crisis on a bilateral basis. This provided an opportunity for the Japanese government to extend its bilateral political favors to the U.S. administration under siege.

The second factor reveals the shadow of the United States on Japan's decision making: a commitment to the United States is reflected in the minds and attitudes of the policymakers of the countries in crisis. Although the Japanese government received visits from top ministers from both countries, Mexico and Argentina, soon after the crisis hit, the purposes of their visits and the attitudes involved were quite different. Economic Minister Cavallo of Argentina, knowledgeable of the problematic prospect of the U.S. contribution to the Argentine rescue, went to Japan to formally request assistance; Foreign Minister Gurría of Mexico, meanwhile, counting on high U.S. involvement, visited Japan largely to underplay the extent of the crisis.[49] The Japanese government, with its foreign policy gains vis-à-vis both the United States and Argentina in mind, responded to the Argentine request favorably.

Transnational Linkages and Domestic Dynamics

Transnational Institutional Linkages among Financial Sectors

According to a famous phrase by former IMF managing director Michel Camdessus, the debt crisis of the 1980s was the last global financial crisis of the twentieth century, and the Mexican peso crisis represented the first crisis of the twenty-first century.[50] Despite his statement, there is an abundance of commonalties between the two crises. Elements common to both crises are (a) the sequence of a strong surge of capital inflows into the middle-income countries and dramatic outflows following a "crisis of confidence" (in both cases initiated by Mexico) and (b) a heightened financial integration of these middle-income economies into the global capital market via capital flow from major industrial countries (particularly the United States) and repercussions of the crises due to such a link. However, there is an important difference: the presence and absence of transnational institutional linkages among the financial sectors. This contrast has a major implication on the necessity and modality of international crisis management by major creditor governments.

Prior to both crises, there was a dramatic increase of financial flows from capital-rich industrial countries to capital-hungry industrializing Latin American countries within a relatively short period of time.[51] The competition among the lenders and/or investors became quite fierce in the final stage of both booms, when spreads narrowed on the bank lending and newly issued bonds. After awhile, the repayments on such huge loans became unsustainable. This occurred particularly because of the debtors' increasing trade deficits, which resulted from such factors as changes in the external economic environment (e.g., declining terms of trade for goods); real appreciation of the debtors' currencies, which makes their goods less competitive; and increases in debtors' consumption through imports. Significant jitters among all investors followed as a major capital recipient country (Mexico in both cases) demonstrated signs of economic distress in the form of a suspension of interest payments in 1982 and a de-pegging of the currency against the dollar in 1994. An alleged "herd mentality" of investors led to a massive financial retreat from the country as quickly as possible to minimize losses, a process that in turn caused a major financial panic.

Although this dynamic of manias, panics, and crashes[52] seems quite similar in the two crises, there are a few critical differences in terms of what constituted these foreign capital surges to the region. Table 6.1 demonstrates that foreign capital inflow to Latin America just prior to the 1982 crisis was made up mostly of long-term commercial bank lending that functioned as a channel to recycle petrodollars from the bank accounts of industrial countries to the governments of the newly industrializing developing countries in the latter half of 1970s. This was sovereign lending whereby the borrowing governments acted as guarantors of the debt, which took the form of syndicated loans with cross-default clauses for avoiding selective defaults by the debtors.[53] By contrast, after the debt crisis dried up the debtors' access to banks' voluntary lending in the late 1980s, a much higher proportion of foreign capital flows to the region in the early 1990s came through FDI, bond issues, and portfolio equity flows (see table 6.1).[54]

In accordance with the different types of capital flows in the two cases, the financial actors obviously changed. The case of the Latin American debt crisis involved transnational commercial banks engaged in Latin American lending, while the major financial actors involved in the capital surge of the early 1990s included investment banks and such institutional investors as mutual funds, pension funds, and insurance companies.[55] Cline explains:

> In short, the moribund commercial bank financial market for lending to Latin America was being replaced by portfolio security financing. . . . nationals repatriating flight capital provided an important part of the demand for the new, securitized flows to Latin America. There was even a change in vocabulary that signaled the transformation: "emerging markets" becomes the Wall Street phrase to describe Latin America and Asia, with psychological connotations far more buoyant than "LDC debt."[56]

The hedging device for the risks associated with investment in Latin America also changed in the 1990s, which had a major impact on the strength of institutional linkages. From the 1970s into the 1980s, sovereign guarantees, variable interest rates, and cross-default clauses established a (false) sense of lowered risk, and banks were linked to each other through syndication. In the 1990s, the highly liquid nature of portfolio equity flows (sometimes described as "hot money") gave investors quick and easy ways of entrance into and exit from their investments. The former finance minister of Mexico Jesús Silva Herzog characterized this phenomenon as a "twenty-one year old pushing a button," leading to the exit of billions of dollars from Mexico in a matter of seconds in the aftermath of its peso devaluation.[57] Although the behavior of investors fleeing from Mexico appeared uniform, their behavior was united not by institutional linkages but by the herd mentality. Each investor was free to move independently.

The second general similarity between the two periods of capital surge and reversal is the fact that the capital importing countries had become closely integrated into the international capital market and that the economic envi-

TABLE 6.1. Comparison of Net Capital Flows to Seven Latin American Countries, 1982–1997 (in billions of US dollars)

	1982	1983	1984	1985	1986	1987	1988	1989	1990	1991	1992	1993	1994	1995	1996	1997
Total	**26.57**	**4.39**	**6.48**	**1.90**	**7.99**	**12.25**	**−1.10**	**3.94**	**16.19**	**29.44**	**54.37**	**37.97**	**36.81**	**68.22**	**64.58**	**69.81**
Foreign Direct Investment	4.81	3.08	2.85	3.91	2.88	3.60	5.21	5.98	6.53	11.08	13.28	11.98	25.30	27.45	38.88	57.29
IMF	0.99	4.95	2.72	2.59	1.67	1.94	−1.36	−0.30	2.74	−0.98	−2.04	2.51	0.88	15.65	1.30	0.66
Official	3.33	2.54	3.44	3.34	3.93	2.47	2.66	1.56	5.22	1.40	−0.23	2.05	−1.80	8.53	−8.52	−7.12
Banks, long term	18.03	9.61	7.95	2.34	−1.00	2.04	0.23	−6.38	1.80	2.80	10.10	1.13	2.08	3.13	1.42	2.99
Interest arrears	0.00	0.84	1.61	0.85	0.69	3.80	2.48	6.98	7.89	3.01	0.60	−3.80	−5.42	−0.39	−3.76	1.07
Bonds, public & publicly guaranteed	3.96	−0.81	−1.09	−0.91	−1.40	−2.05	−1.53	−1.27	0.10	2.66	−2.46	6.30	6.00	8.17	22.39	8.02
Bonds, private	0.00	0.00	0.00	0.00	0.00	0.00	0.00	0.15	0.61	2.01	7.68	14.33	7.82	3.41	7.20	5.42
Subtotal	**31.12**	**20.21**	**17.48**	**12.12**	**6.77**	**11.80**	**7.69**	**6.72**	**24.89**	**21.98**	**26.93**	**34.50**	**34.86**	**65.95**	**58.91**	**68.33**
Residual	−4.55	−15.82	−11.00	−10.22	1.22	0.45	−8.79	−2.78	−8.70	7.46	27.44	3.47	1.95	2.27	5.67	1.48

Source: For years between 1982 and 1992: Cline 1995, 435, table 8.3. For years after 1993: *Global Development Finance,* 1999.
Note: The seven Latin American countries include Argentina, Brazil, Chile, Columbia, Mexico, Peru, and Venezuela.

ronments were driven predominantly by the capital-exporting industrial economies. A heated debate has taken place in international circles of development and finance regarding how capital movements are affected by "push" (low interest rates and unfavorable domestic investment conditions pushing money out from capital-rich countries into the emerging markets) and "pull" (policy reforms, favorable investment conditions, and robust economic fundamentals attracting money from abroad). The debate seems, however, to tilt toward the substantial influence of the economic conditions of industrial countries on the outflow of capital into middle-income regions (the "push" factor).[58]

As I noted in chapter 5, the excess of petrodollars in bank accounts of rich nations and major recessions in the developed world turned capital flows toward the capital-hungry industrializing nations of Latin America in the second half of the 1970s. In the early 1990s, a prolonged recession and low interest rates, along with pressure on the institutional investors to earn good returns, guided the capital to flow to the "emerging markets," with expected high returns.[59] Many argue that, along with the political instability following the assassination of Mexico's presidential candidate Donald Colossio, improvements in U.S. economic conditions, which led to a rise in interest rates in the spring of 1994, triggered significant capital flight from Mexico back to the United States, paving the way to the peso crisis.[60] Although the economic fundamentals and economic policies of emerging market countries do matter, the international financial environments are critical factors that trigger crises.

As a rapid reversal of foreign capital flow occurs after an initial shock, it produces economic and financial repercussions beyond a country's borders, leading to a fear of systemic crisis. These shocks were transmitted through various channels, such as explicit or implicit trade and financial linkages, and through demonstration or contagion effects in the early 1980s. Many developing countries sank along with Mexico. Because of the widespread practice, started in the 1970s, of sovereign and syndicate lending to many developing countries, most of the countries in Latin America, as well as such countries as Cote d'Ivoire and Nigeria, became problem debtors in the 1980s. The list further expanded to the poorest nations of Africa. Most of the countries entered into debt negotiations with creditors, intensifying the threat of systemic crisis.

In the early 1990s, only about twenty countries were referred to as "emerging market" countries, where more than 80 percent of private capital concentrated. Most of these countries were located in Latin America and in Asia, along with some in Eastern Europe.[61] In hindsight, the crisis turned out to be not as serious as the debt crisis of the 1980s, but many unknown factors existed at that point, including the magnitude of the contagion, which made the option of inaction highly dangerous. Contagion effects of the Mexican peso crisis hit other Latin American countries, particularly Argentina. In Latin America, a concentration of Brady deals, a privatization boom, and the intense reinsertion of the Latin American economies into the international capital market in the early 1990s contributed to creating a regional wave of crisis.[62]

The lack of institutional linkages among new actors who have invested in Mexico influenced the way the Japanese government behaved in the peso crisis. Even when the portfolio investment of bonds and securities in Latin America became a hot market, Japanese financial institutions did not have in the region strong institutional ties that would lead them to become underwriters of these instruments. Involvement of Japanese investors had been minimal, and there had not been much structural innovation to engage these investors in the Latin American market. The emerging market in Latin America became, rather, a captured market for those with strong information and institutional channels to the region, capabilities that are concentrated in the United States. As I discussed earlier, in response to the 1994 Mexican crisis, J. P. Morgan and CitiCorp tried to arrange a rescue package of $3 billion among commercial banks. Four major Japanese banks were asked to contribute.[63] The four grudgingly agreed to contribute $0.4 billion, but such requests were a "nuisance" for the Japanese banks, which had already eliminated most of their outstanding debt to Mexico.[64]

Domestic Dynamics

Japan's financial sector has remained cautious about Mexico and Latin America in the 1990s. With a more rigid personnel and institutional structure than that characteristic of the United States, Japanese banks are slow to forget the experience they had lending to the region. In addition, the BIS capital adequacy requirements present a major obstacle.[65] At the same time, as the Asian markets became more stable and attractive and as the Japanese manufacturing sector started operating more in the region, the banks geared their activities toward Asia. Several interviewees commented that the banks' international operations should be seen in a global context; that is, if there is a more profitable, stable, and promising region closer and more familiar to Japan, there is no reason for Japanese banks to go to Latin America.[66] Institutional investors were also cautious toward Latin American investment. Despite government relaxation of the quality guidelines and of quantity of investment abroad, these Japanese investors are still keeping their traditionally risk-averse postures.[67]

By the end of 1994, there were small signs of Japanese mutual fund investment in Mexico, but it was a very limited amount.[68] When the Mexican currency devaluation shocked the world, no Japanese financial institutions were heavily exposed or committed to the country. Thus, there was no pressure from Japanese domestic actors on the Japanese government to rescue them from the crisis.

Because there was no measurable pressure from Japan's financial sector urging the government to act, one cannot analyze the channel through which the domestic pressure worked its way into the decisions regarding the government's commitment to this financial crisis. It is conceivable, however, due to some institutional and political changes in the relationship between the politicians, the bureaucracy, and major business groups, that the link has weakened. Japan's political instability was an important underlying factor contributing to shifts in the early 1990s. In August 1993, the LDP lost its majority position in the lower house of the Diet for the first time in thirty-eight years, and Morihiro Hosokawa, a former LDP member and the leader of the New Japan Party (Nihon Shinto), became Japan's prime minister. Since then, the Japanese Diet has undergone various shufflings and shakings of coalitions.[69] This political instability directly affected the daily business of the Japanese government, causing such difficulties as delays in budget decisions. More important, in the arena of international finance, the close relationship that the longtime governing party, the LDP, had with the Japanese government bureaucracy was disrupted by this change. Some argue that resistance to "reforming" the MOF waned as the LDP—the party that benefited most from its close ties with the MOF—lost its footing in the Diet.[70]

Actually, the underlying forces of change in domestic political constellations in Japan did not come about all at once in 1993; this evolution dated back to the 1980s. Some careful watchers of Japanese politics noted a certain "disincorporation" in Japan, or a "regime shift," much earlier than 1993.[71] Japan's "embedded mercantilism," a characteristic of a typically late industrializer that was supported by the fairly inclusive conservative alliance, began to give way to international liberal economic forces in the mid-1970s. Pressured externally by the appreciation of the yen and by political tensions with its trading partners, and pressured internally by Japan's internationally competitive big businesses, this once powerful conservative alliance began to fall apart piece by piece.[72] Pempel explains that this trend gained salience "as the economy slowed (in the 1990s), as the continuation of once relatively easy intraregime adjustments became increasingly problematic."[73] This issue is further discussed in chapter 8, when I examine the dynamics of the Japanese government's involvement in the management of the 1997 Asian financial crisis.

In sum, strong institutional linkages among transnational banks during the first debt crisis helped translate external pressures from the United States into internal ones in Japan. These linkages were strong in terms of both maintaining well-established rules and arrangements to deal with the debtors and keeping the junior partners, Japanese banks, in line with the interests of American banks. In the 1994 crisis, although a similar follow-the-leader mentality persisted in the Japanese financial sector in dealing with Latin America, neither transnational institutional linkages nor interest in the Mexican rescue were strong. Therefore, the crisis did not generate domestic support from the financial sector to shift the Japanese government's decisions toward active involvement in the rescue plan. Furthermore, and as discussed more in chapter 8 on the Asian financial crisis, the domestic political changes weakened the close and symbiotic relationship between Japan's financial sector and the government, making it harder than before to coordinate actions between Japan's private sector and the government.

Conclusion

The Japanese government's involvement in the Mexican peso crisis was very limited despite the U.S. government's keen interests in managing the financial crisis. The Japanese government, although supportive of the U.S. initiatives, was very reluctant in providing funding to Mexico on a bilateral basis, and Japanese banks also resisted participating in the commercial rescue package. With the European resistance to involvement, the U.S. government and the IMF ended up shouldering the bulk of crisis management costs this time.

The analysis of the Mexican peso crisis indicates conditions required for the Japanese government to act. The Japanese government needed a high level of private returns from the rescue package, in relation both to the United States and to Japan's private financial sector. Such returns did not exist in the case of the Mexican peso crisis. In addition, due to the changes in the international financial environment and the lack of Japan's private sector exposure to Mexico, no transnational linkages were urging the Japanese government to become actively involved in this financial crisis management.

The contrast of the Japanese government's behavior in the Latin American debt crisis and the Mexican peso crisis emphasizes the importance of private gains and pressure channels. A high level of both made the Japanese government active in the debt crisis, while a lack of both made the Japanese government quite reluctant to become involved in the peso crisis.

PART 3

Asia

CHAPTER 7

Introduction to the Case Study of Asia

This study of international financial crisis management will now shift its geographical focus from Latin America to Asia, analyzing the motivation and behavior of the Japanese government as it engaged, fully or partially, in collective action with other creditor governments and IFIs in the management of the 1997–98 Asian financial crisis.[1] The Asian crisis provides an excellent additional case to reexamine the hypotheses, which have so far been applied to Latin American cases (chaps. 4–6), regarding the sources of Japan's collective action in financial crisis management. This case also supplements quantitative analysis and the case study on financial crises in Latin America (chap. 3) by strengthening the generalizability of important dynamics in different regional settings.

This chapter outlines the contrast between the interests that Japan has in Latin America and in Asia, then it briefly summarizes how this contrast has influenced the Japanese government's motivation to become involved in financial crisis management in Asia. On one hand, regional and temporal changes transformed several factors leading to the changes in the Japanese government's incentives in the Asian case. These factors include Japan's interests in the regions, the level of structural power between the United States and Japan, the shifting dynamics of U.S.-Japanese interactions from the 1980s into the 1990s, and changes in the domestic political dynamics in Japan, especially in the relationship between the MOF and the Japanese financial sector. On the other hand, the Asian case, though embracing a stark regional contrast to the Latin American cases, seems to lend support to the two hypotheses, with a few caveats. The large private returns motivated the Japanese government to step in actively, supplying public goods in the form of international financial stability (i.e., joint product). But the divergent interests among the Japanese government and its private sectors occasionally led to the Japanese government's immobility. The transnational linkages, which were strong in some stages and weak in others during the Asian crisis between the spring of 1997 and the end of 1999, help explain the characteristics and shifts in Japan's involvement during different stages.

Contrasts: Latin America and Asia

The change in the geographical region of the crisis' epicenter from Latin America to Asia is obviously an important element in the Japanese government's decision making. The Asian financial crisis came as a surprise in the context of the previous few decades of impressive economic development in Southeast and East Asia (hereafter Asia), economic growth that turned many of these economies from low-income to middle-income countries, creating the so-called East Asian economic miracle. The near double-digit economic growth rates in the region in the 1980s were impressive, and the economic success story of these countries was often contrasted with the "lost decade" in Latin America, a parallel period of economic stagnation, riveting international debt, and economic problems.[2] Yet the financial crisis in Asia and the crisis in Latin America demonstrate unmistakable similarity, especially when it comes to the incentive structures of the lenders and the borrowers of large sums of foreign capital and the power dynamics between the creditors and the debtors.[3] Through a comparison between the two regional crises themselves, we can distinguish three major facets contrasting between the Asian case and the Latin American cases, which are relevant in analyzing the Japanese government's behavior in respective crises.

First, both the Japanese government and the private sector view their relationship to the Asian countries and to the economic prosperity and stability of the region to be much more important than their relationship to Latin America. As I outlined in chapter 2, Asia ranks as the region of top priority for Japan in terms of trade (see figs. 2.1 and 2.2), investments (see tables 2.3 and 2.4), and other interactions, such as foreign aid (see figs. 2.3 and 2.4; table 2.2). In addition, a strong trend toward economic regionalization has occurred in Asia since the latter half of the 1980s. Beginning in the late 1980s, the Japanese private sector increased its investments in many countries of the region, further fueling this trend (see table 8.2). Additionally, to support the operations of Japanese manufacturing companies in the region, the Asian countries received a significant number of loans from Japan during the 1990s (see table 8.1).[4] All of these factors reveal the strong economic interests that Japan's private sector, both financial and manufacturing, had in the region at the time the crisis hit. This involvement was much more widespread, deep, and serious than during either of the Latin American crisis cases.

Likewise, the political interests of the Japanese government are much stronger in Asia than in Latin America. The Japanese government has striven to cultivate amicable and close relationships with the Asian countries, particularly with the original five ASEAN members (Indonesia, Malaysia, the Philippines, Singapore, and Thailand) and Korea during the past several decades and with China and Vietnam in recent years. Once Japan regained its sovereignty in 1952, it began reparation payments. Japan's efforts to repair these relationships strengthened in the late 1970s, after Japan failed to establish friendly relations with these countries. Damages inflicted by Japan before and during

World War II still manifest themselves through major scars in these relationships.[5] In addition, the Japanese government considers any opportunity to show its "leadership" role in Asia as a diplomatic achievement. This is particularly the case as an earlier regional hegemon, China, has gained ground as a rival to Japan in recent years.[6]

Second, the regional contrast raises the associated question regarding the roles that respective regional powers play in crisis management and the possibility that the "number two" power would lead to collective action with the leading power in support of successful crisis management with a unified front. Here, the dynamics between Japan and the United States become critical. After all, despite its strong foreign reserve position, Japan remains the number two power (along with Europe), following the United States, in the field of international finance. Asymmetry of power exists, therefore, between the United States and Japan, especially when it comes to structural power in international finance influencing the international financial system.

In the Latin American triangle (consisting of the United States, Japan, and Latin America) during the debt crisis and the peso crisis, the power dynamics between the United States and Japan were "natural," so to speak; that is, the United States, the regional power in Latin America, was in a position to induce the support, financially or otherwise, of the number two power, Japan, both regionally and globally. In contrast, in the Asian triangle (consisting of the United States, Japan, and Asia), the regional power, Japan, had to either work independently without the explicit support of the United States (as in the AMF case) or support the initiatives and conditions originating from the extra-regional structural power, the United States. The tension that has risen from an asymmetry of power between the two leading countries seems to have influenced the form of collective crisis management in the Asian case.

The United States, the longtime global hegemon and the world's strongest "structural power" (see chap. 1), continues its quest to sustain or extend its direct influence and is reluctant to relinquish its existing power and presence in regions beyond the Western Hemisphere. This U.S. behavior inevitably influences the behavior of the regional power in Asia—Japan. There are indications, however, that the United States has been willing to engage in collective action with Japan and other creditors, in both official and private realms, to create a united front and effectively manage the Asian financial crisis with adequate financial resources. In some respects, the United States has also sought to support Japan's economic recovery, by taking a softer stance in its trade relations. Nevertheless, the global-level asymmetry of power in favor of the United States has led to an ultimate difference in the motives and behavior of the United States in the management of the Asian crisis compared to those of Japan in the management of the Latin American crisis.

This dynamic is particularly prominent in the third phase of the Asian crisis, beginning in the latter half of 1998. The inescapable U.S. supremacy in economic crisis management in the 1990s in any part of the world has led to a frustration among the Japanese because they have been forced to submit to U.S. dominance in Asian crisis management. As the U.S. predominant presence withdrew from Asia due to crises elsewhere by mid-1998, the Japanese government and the governments of the Asian countries began reasserting independence from U.S.-led crisis solutions.

Finally, the timing of each crisis and the economic strength of respective regional powers—the United States in the case of the Latin American crises and Japan in the Asian case—are important factors. The Latin American debt crisis of the 1980s in particular provides an instructive comparison to the 1997–98 Asian financial crisis. The respective regional powers were each constrained economically when they faced the momentous task of financial crisis management in neighboring regions, in which they had high economic, political, and security stakes.[7] At the height of the Latin American debt crisis in the latter half of the 1980s, the United States was suffering from extensive budget and trade deficits. Various debt solutions were introduced and implemented under the U.S. initiative, and the Japanese government, which held high stakes in the economic well-being of the United States, actively supported these debt initiatives and pumped funds into the Latin American region (see chaps. 3 and 5). The Japanese government also generally supported U.S. crisis management initiatives during this period. There were instances of Japanese initiatives, such as the 1988 Miyazawa Plan, aimed at managing this debt crisis. But these initiatives were constructed in such a way that they would not have challenged or intentionally threatened the dominant role of the United States, nor would they have provided alternative avenues for debt negotiations (see chap. 5). In this sense, collective action between the two creditor governments was very much intact.

But when the Asian crisis threatened the already weakened Japanese economy in 1997, U.S. actions were quite different from those taken by Japan during the Latin American debt crisis. The United States was never a big supporter of independent crisis solutions proposed by Japan or the Asian countries. Despite "talk" by U.S. policymakers that the Asian region had to take care of its own economic problems,[8] the United States was, in reality, one of the most forceful opponents of the AMF idea when it was first proposed by the Japanese (see chap. 8). The shadow of U.S. influence, along with the dominance of IMF-led crisis management, loomed large in the resolution of the Asian financial crisis, particularly during the AMF controversy, which coincided with the period when Indonesia began to experience serious financial problems.[9]

Japan's Motivation in Financial Crisis Management

Although the regional difference introduces new factors in the analysis of the motivation of the Japanese government's involvement in financial crisis management, the fundamental forces behind the Japanese government's decisions seem to remain quite similar in both regions. On one hand, the Japanese government weighed its diverse private returns as it determined its appropriate actions and level of leadership in the different phases of the Asian crisis. On the other hand, the transnational financial sector, when it could produce a united stance among creditors, promoted greater collaboration between the two governments.

Chapter 8 analyzes the factors behind the shift of the Japanese government's actions throughout the Asian financial crisis from mid-1997 through 2000, by focusing specifically on the dynamics within Asia. The book's conclusion revisits further questions about the intercreditor government dynamics that emerge from the regional contrast between Asia and Latin America and contemplates possible future research directions.

CHAPTER 8

Japan and the United States in the Asian Financial Crisis Management

Not even the Asian countries, with their "miracle economies," could escape the financial turmoil of the twenty-first century.[1] In 1997, Thailand, the Philippines, Malaysia, Indonesia, and Korea all experienced attacks on their currencies and stock markets, and their governments could not, on their own, manage these attacks or stabilize their economies. In response, the IMF, with the participation of Japan, the United States, and other governments, assembled international financial rescue packages in an effort to stabilize the international financial market. The combined total of aid committed through multilateral and bilateral channels reached more than $110 billion by the end of 1997.

Japan's involvement in the management of the Asian financial crisis[2] presents a much more complex picture than its involvement in the series of Latin American crises analyzed in chapters 5 and 6. First, the Japanese government's actions and the style of leadership in managing the Asian crisis shifted over time from active and independent (early summer through fall 1997), to passive but cooperative (fall 1997 to mid-1998), to active with cautious independence (mid-1998 through 1999). Second, the Japanese government demonstrated ambivalence in cooperating with the United States and the IMF, by sometimes fully supporting their initiatives (e.g., in the second phase) and sometimes providing (or attempting to provide) alternative solutions to the crisis. This chapter analyzes the reasons for the variance in the Japanese government's actions in Asian crisis management by applying the same theoretical framework as chapters 5 and 6: the importance of joint product and transnational linkages.

This chapter first introduces a historical narrative of Japan's behavior in the three phases of the Asian financial crisis, to explain what constitutes the dependent variable. The chapter continues by examining the actions and motivations of the Japanese government and its financial sector, based on the hypotheses posed in chapter 1, which were tested on the Latin American cases in chapters 5 (debt crisis) and 6 (peso crisis), as well as chapter 3 (quantitative analysis of the debt crisis). The joint product nature of crisis management seems to provide a domestic and international environment for the Japanese government to act distinctively in different phases of the crisis. This hypothesis also provides a good basis for understanding Japan's ambivalence. Different levels of institutional linkages among transnational financial sectors operating in different countries—weak in Thailand and particularly strong in the case of South Korea—help explain the variance in Japan's behavior. Finally, this chapter concludes with a discussion of the lessons learned from the new Asian case study. The following conclusion to the book expands the discussion, explicitly contrasting Japan's actions in Latin America and Asia.

In relation to the Asian crisis, a great deal of academic and policy literature is being produced concerning (a) the causes of the Asian crisis; (b) appropriate solutions to the crisis, including questions about the role of the IMF; (c) implications of the crisis for the "Asian miracle" and the global economy; and (d) how to prevent future crises.[3] It is not in the scope of this study to discuss these issues; the focus here is the role of the Japanese government as a crisis manager in the Asian financial crisis.[4]

The Japanese Government in the Asian Financial Crisis (Dependent Variable)

Japan at Center Stage: The Thai Crisis and the Debate over the Asian Monetary Fund (Phase 1)

The first phase of the crisis represented a period of Japanese leadership. During this phase, the Japanese government undertook strong crisis management initiatives along with the IMF. The Japanese government promoted both multilateral and bilateral support to resolve the Thai crisis as promptly as possible, and Japan also helped assemble a financial rescue package of $17.2 billion for the country in August 1997. Furthermore, based on the Thai rescue format, a collective rescue package for which the United States did not provide any financial commitment, the Japanese government proposed, at the time of World Bank/IMF annual meeting in September 1997, a fund for balance-of-payments support to the countries in the region, the Asian Monetary Fund (AMF). This represented a new financial mechanism, understood as an Asian version of the IMF.

As the economic fundamentals and the country's ability to defend its peg were in doubt in May 1997, the Thai currency came under attack. The Bank of Thailand (central bank) spent billions of dollars to defend its pegged currency, but by May 15, the authorities had no alternative but to impose informal exchange controls to defend the baht. According to the promise made among the Asian countries eighteen months before,[5] the central banks of

Singapore, Malaysia, and Hong Kong also supported the baht in the currency market on May 14, but the attack continued. With its weakened economy, the Bank of Thailand could not help but let the baht float on July 2, 1997. The currency came under a severe attack on that day and lost about 17 percent of its value against the U.S. dollar. Contagion effects were a prominent feature of the crisis, as in the 1994–95 Mexican peso crisis. Within a few weeks, the Philippine peso and the Malaysian ringgit were forced to devalue, and ripple effects were also felt in the currency and stock markets of other Asian countries.[6]

Among these Asian countries, the Philippines was the only country that immediately turned to the IMF, because it had already agreed on an IMF program several years earlier. The Filipino government obtained an agreement with the IMF for $1 billion in the form of EFF credit and other financial programs on July 18, only a week after its peso came under severe attack. This support measure used the newly established New Arrangements to Borrow (NAB) under the Emergency Financing Mechanism of the IMF.[7]

The government of Thailand was initially reluctant to resort to IMF financial support, which comes with stringent conditionality. Thailand's new finance minister, Thanong Bidaya, and central bank governor, Rerngchai Marakanond, visited Tokyo on July 17 and 18, 1997, to meet with twenty-one Japanese commercial banks to explain the economic situation in Thailand. They also met with Japan's finance minister, Hiroshi Mitsuzuka. During that meeting, the Japanese government agreed that it would intervene in the foreign exchange markets to defend the baht. Even at this point, Thanong was reportedly explicit that he did not intend to request financial support from the IMF.[8] But as the attack on the Thai currency and outflow of foreign capital continued in the last week of July, the Thai government had no other alternative but to shift its policy and turn to the IMF. By August 4, 1997, the government of Thailand and the IMF reached a basic agreement. An international conference was held in Tokyo, led by the IMF, to hammer out concrete terms for the Thai rescue package. Japan's MOF was supportive of Thailand as it reached an agreement with the IMF. The package finally assembled totaled $17.2 billion, in which Japan (providing $4 billion through the JEXIM Bank untied loans) and the IMF (providing $4 billion) contributed the largest components. Many Asian countries also contributed to the package, as did the World Bank (with $1.5 billion) and the Asian Development Bank (ADB) (with $1.2 billion).[9] The United States was the one significant party that did not take part in this rescue package. Although an American delegate was present at the IMF-led conference in Tokyo, the U.S. government did not commit any financial support at the time.

There are two well-recognized reasons for the U.S. reluctance in the Thai case. The first was that many U.S. financial policymakers had an inaccurate understanding regarding the nature of the crisis at the time. The policymakers thought that the Thai crisis was an isolated incident and that the IMF package, with some help from Asian neighbors, would be enough to contain regional financial turmoil, without major contagion to emerging market countries in Asia or in other parts of the world. This U.S. behavior was described as follows:

> When the IMF put together a $17.2 billion bailout package for Thailand in August, the United States helped craft the conditions—including sharp austerity requirements that have sparked protests in Thailand—but did not contribute funds. Treasury Department officials argued that a direct financial contribution from Washington was not called for in Thailand's case because it appeared at the time that there was little risk that the country's financial troubles—fueled by speculative attacks on its currency—would spread to other markets.[10]

The second reason has to do with U.S. domestic politics. After the Mexican bailout of $20 billion in early 1995, for which the Clinton administration used the ESF, there were mounting criticisms from Congress on how the administration disregarded the congressional debate and unilaterally conducted the Mexican rescue (see chap. 6). Congressionally imposed restrictions on future use of the ESF made it difficult for the U.S. administration to provide bilateral financial contributions to the Thai rescue package.[11]

From the Thai currency crisis and the rescue in the summer (July/August) of 1997 through the Indonesian currency crisis and the rescue in the fall (October/November), an interesting tug-of-war emerged between AMF advocates and the IMF-centered Western coalition that opposed the AMF. In stark contrast to the 1995, American-led Mexican rescue package, Thailand's rescue package demonstrated collaborative action among Asian financial authorities, with a solid Japanese initiative and in the absence of U.S. leadership. This rescue package was seen by many as a "precursor of future standard arrangements"[12] for this type of crisis in the region; concomitantly, the lack of U.S. presence concerned the Asian countries. By August 18, the Thai foreign minister was reported as saying that he would like to propose the establishment of an ASEAN Monetary Fund (the name was tentative) to support Asian currencies against foreign speculators.[13] The finance secretary of the Philippines picked up the idea in September at an ASEAN finance ministers' meeting. The Asian Fund scheme was considered a counterpart to the IMF, with Japan as the major contributor.

Japan's finance minister at that time, Mitsuzuka, mentioned Japan's interest in collaborating if Asian governments put forth such requests.[14] Finally,

Mitsuzuka put the idea of an Asian Fund on the table at the World Bank/IMF annual meeting in Hong Kong on September 21. In his meeting with ASEAN financial ministers, he proposed the establishment of a fund of $100 billion (tentatively called the Asian Fund) that would be financed and run by Asian countries to help the region's governments cope with currency crises. The arrangement would be based on the Thai rescue package put together by the Asian countries and Australia. He also suggested that the IMF be the model for the operation of such a fund.[15]

The IMF and the governments of the United States and Europe did not react favorably to Japan's proposal. As is discussed later in this chapter, these entities considered that an alternative institutional mechanism aimed at solving the Asian financial crisis would jeopardize the effectiveness of the IMF programs and invite a moral hazard problem. The IMF and major creditor countries, other than Japan, were further agitated about the timing of the proposal. The G-7 finance ministers had recently reached a compromise agreement to increase the IMF's capital base by a more-than-expected 45 percent, precisely to prepare the IMF to address possible currency crises in emerging market countries—the type of crises that had just occurred in Asia. As a result of this capital increase, the IMF voting powers of Japan and many Asian countries, including Korea, Malaysia, and Thailand, were to be expanded.[16]

The AMF issue was continuously debated during October and November, as many Asian currencies, including those of Indonesia and Korea, became targets of attacks by the market. The Japanese government maintained its support for the Asian governments' idea, to counter "foreign speculators," the emergence of whom many believed was a result of liberal economic prescriptions designed by the IMF and the United States.[17] One of the most influential officials in Japan's MOF, Eisuke Sakakibara, became quite vocal in deploring the damage that the "Washington consensus" on development had caused. Although there was no explicit mention that the Asian Fund would be more lenient to the countries under crisis, Sakakibara emphasized the "flexibility" that such a fund could bring to the operation of emergency funding.[18]

As discussed more extensively later in this chapter, the lack of support from the financial community, both international and domestic, along with opposition from Washington, led to the retreat of the Japanese (and Asian) idea. The AMF proposal was finally put to rest, at least for the time being, at a meeting of APEC finance ministers in Manila on November 18–19,[19] before the APEC annual meeting in Vancouver. Although the participating finance ministers agreed on the need and desirability of a framework for regional cooperation to enhance prospects for financial stability, they basically concluded that the emergency funding scheme should be based solely on the IMF. Additional financial assistance would be possible for the countries in financial distress only after they fully negotiated conditionality with the IMF. This became known as the Manila Framework.[20] After the APEC meeting, ASEAN senior financial officials who met in Kuala Lumpur on November 30 affirmed, "at this level, [the proposal] is on the backburner."[21] The idea did not die but was "revived" a year later.

Despite its withdrawal from the AMF idea, the Japanese leadership and its active commitment to support Asian countries in financial crisis during the first four months after the outbreak in Thailand was significant. Successful or not, the Japanese government clearly demonstrated its willingness to become a lead crisis manager in the region, either regardless of the U.S. participation or because of its absence. This leadership position might, however, have reflected a default in a situation where there was a lack of involvement by other parties, particularly the United States. This circumstance made Japan's active engagement in crisis management far more essential. Note that although collective action among major creditor governments was present via IMF commitments, the U.S. reluctance to act bilaterally on the Thai rescue package came as a shock to many Asian countries.[22]

Japan Supports U.S. Leadership: The Indonesian and Korean Crises (Phase 2)

The Asian financial crisis spread to much larger economies in the region, such as Indonesia and Korea, during the fall of 1997. As Hong Kong's currency came under attack by speculators, the financial world, including the United States, began to recognize the risk of further contagion and the chilling fact that the Asian crisis was real and here to stay, at least for a while. This was when the second phase of Japan's involvement in the financial crisis management began to take shape. The role of the U.S. Treasury Department and the IMF became much more central during the process of assembling financial rescue packages for Indonesia and Korea to calm the market, deter attacks on their currencies, and stop or slow capital flight. Japan's role then became more subordinate, supporting solutions led by the IMF and the United States with major financial contributions but without strong alternative initiatives. A change in the U.S. government's attitude toward the Asian currency crises came, on one hand, as a response to the emerging regional schemes to address the Asian economic problem. On the other hand, it came from the realization by U.S. policymakers that Thailand was not going to be an isolated case and that there was a high risk of a contagion effect from the crisis. The United States also became particularly concerned when the Indonesian crisis pulled down prices in the stock markets of such Latin American countries as Brazil and Argentina.[23]

As Indonesia's currency came under attack and the Indonesian government, after repeated attempts to avoid IMF involvement, finally turned to the IMF, leading to an agreement on October 31, 1997, the U.S. government promised to contribute $3 billion of the $14 billion in bilateral contribution pledges. This bilateral contribution was considered part of the "second line of defense,"[24] in case the first line of defense, consisting of $10 billion from the IMF, $4.5 billion from the World Bank, and $3.5 billion from the ADB, failed to stop the run on the Indonesian currency.[25] The Japanese government's financial contribution made Japan one of the two biggest bilateral contributors to the Indonesian rescue. Along with the government of Singapore, the Japanese government committed $5 billion dollars. In addition to such financial contributions, the Japanese and Singaporean monetary authorities stepped into the Singapore currency market in early November to prevent the Indonesian rupiah from falling further. Despite the IMF package agreed on, Indonesia's unwillingness to adjust its macroeconomic policies according to the IMF agreement caused its currency to continue its problematic course into the first half of 1998.

The last major IMF-led rescue package in the series of the Asian financial crises was assembled for Korea, the eleventh largest economy in the world. By November 1997, with a vicious attack on its currency and plummeting stock market prices, it was obvious that Korea needed some kind of financial help.[26] The Korean government and its policymakers, however, vehemently denied rumors that Korea would go to the IMF in the first weeks of November.[27] The Korean government, meanwhile, attempted to arrange financial rescue packages bilaterally with Tokyo and other creditor governments without turning to the IMF, but this effort failed.[28] As the Korean won dropped below 1,000 to the dollar from 910 just a month before, and as its financial stabilization package, announced on November 19, failed to restore overseas confidence, the Korean government turned to the IMF, asking for $20 billion in emergency loans on November 21, 1997. On the same day, Korea's deputy prime minister, Yim Chang-yol, called on Japanese finance minister Mitsuzuka, requesting additional financial support from Japan.[29]

Facing the biggest economic threat among the series of the Asian crises that occurred in 1997, and acknowledging that the Korean government finally decided to involve the IMF, the Japanese government responded quickly and positively. On November 24, during the APEC forum in Vancouver, Japanese prime minister Hashimoto met with outgoing Korean president Kim Yong-sam and promised to assist South Korea financially in cooperation with the IMF. Furthermore, various high-ranking officials from Korea visited Japan during the last weeks of November to increase the chances and the amount of emergency funding from Japan. It is reported that the Korean government was hoping for a commitment of $20–30 billion from Japan.[30] The Korean rescue package of $57 billion, the largest ever assembled, was agreed on with the IMF on December 3.[31] It included $21 billion from the IMF (which constituted 1,939 percent of Korea's quota, the highest ratio ever for IMF lending), and $10 billion and $4 billion from the World Bank and the ADB, respectively, as the first line of defense. In addition, more than $20 billion for a second line of defense came from Japan ($10 billion), the United States ($5 billion), and other OECD countries.[32] Korea also got some breathing space from external financial pressure as it secured agreements with foreign commercial bankers and investors to suspend temporarily the repayments of $15 billion in loans by the end of December and as it started to convert some of its short-term loans to bonds with long-term maturities.[33]

In both the Indonesian and Korean cases, the U.S. government's policies were clearly behind the IMF agreements. Unlike the Thai rescue package, the United States also committed a large bilateral financial contribution to a second line of defense, in case the crises deepened. Moreover, the Clinton administration began to put significant pressure on the Japanese government to support the ailing Asian economies both directly, by contributing financially to these countries and allowing some delay of repayments, and indirectly, by stimulating its own economy in recession with an expansionary fiscal package, preventing the Japanese yen from falling, and buying more from those countries in crisis. In the face of the U.S. assertion of its leadership role in the Asian currency crises, the retreat of the Japanese government's independent position, particularly after the failure of the AMF scheme, was quite striking. Only a limited version of the AMF idea was adopted as part of the Manila Framework. The framework outlined a form of response to this new type of financial crisis, including the Supplemental Reserve Facility (SRF), which would enable the IMF to respond to short-term financial crises with more flexibility. The Japanese government had to relinquish its own initiative—which, in exchange for a large financial commitment to the new regional funding mechanism, would have given Japan greater power in the region—because of strong opposition to the idea by the IMF and other creditor governments, including both the United States and China. Additionally, since the beginning of crisis management in the summer of 1997, the Japanese government consistently insisted that the reluctant Asian countries go through the IMF before Japan committed itself to help them financially. Japan even took a lead in assembling the IMF rescue package for Thailand, and Japan supported the crisis management operations for Indonesia and Korea led by the United States and the IMF.

This pattern of financial crisis management between the United States and Japan continued into early 1998 as the Indonesian government rebelled against the IMF-led solution to the country's economic crisis. Into 1998, the Japanese government remained supportive of initiatives by the United States and U.S. efforts to revive the Asian economies. However, there were indications of subtle conflicts, disagreements, and resentments on the part of the Japanese, which materialized in the form of Japan's renewed assertiveness in late 1998.

The economic problems in the region continued into the early months of 1998 despite the efforts by creditor governments, their financial sectors, and the IFIs to stabilize the financial crises suffered by various Asian countries. Korea suffered from a significant illiquidity problem due to the country's massive short-term debt, until its government finally reached an agreement with a group of thirteen banks to extend the maturities of the short-term loans totaling $24 billion owed by the country's local banks.[34] The problems with Indonesia, however, were not so quickly or easily resolved. The tension between that country and the IMF emerged on January 6, 1998, as Indonesia's president, Suharto, announced the national budget for fiscal year 1998, which included a large public spending program against the budget austerity "medicine" given as a condition of the IMF loans. This led the currency to take a nosedive until a new agreement between the Indonesian government and the IMF was announced ten days later. This was but one of Indonesia's rebellious attempts against the IMF-led prescription to its economic crisis.

In February, economically damaged by the ever declining rupiah, Suharto revealed his interest in pursuing the idea of a "currency board," a foreign exchange pegging mechanism used by Argentina, Hong Kong, and others.[35] The plan was strongly criticized by the IMF and the United States as an infeasible scheme that would be detrimental to Indonesia's already depressed economy. There was also skepticism about Suharto's commitment to carry out the IMF-led reform, because the economic reforms Indonesia had agreed on under IMF loan conditions were not making progress. The IMF came to a decision on March 6 to suspend its second loan installments of $3 billion. Along with the IMF loan suspension, loans from the World Bank and other bilateral donors, such as Japan, were also frozen. Soon after, Suharto was forced to give up his pursuit of a currency board.

With the aim of persuading Suharto (who was reelected as Indonesia's president for the seventh time on March 10, 1998) to cooperate with the IMF, special envoys and top officials from both the United States and Japan flew to Jakarta during the first weeks of March. During these missions, both the United States and Japan urged Indonesia to stick to the IMF reforms so that the country could restore market confidence for its currency. Nevertheless, the manner in which this message was conveyed varied between the two creditor governments. When U.S. special envoy Walter Mondale, a former vice president, visited Jakarta, his message was strong and clear that the United States would not support Indonesia if it continued resisting the IMF reforms. In comparison, at the time of his meeting with Suharto on March 14, Japanese prime minister Hashimoto promised Indonesia additional food and financial aid amounting to several billion dollars if Suharto cooperated with the IMF and smoothly enacted necessary economic reforms.[36] It took another three months—until June 4—to settle Indonesia's private debt problem. Various meetings between the Indonesian government and major foreign creditor banks, which formed a bank steering committee, occurred between March and June, and they finally reached an agreement in Frankfurt, Germany to restructure $80 billion of Indonesia's foreign debt.[37] Meanwhile, Indonesia's economic problems led to the demise of its long-term president: Suharto was forced to step down on May 21, naming as his successor his former vice president, B. J. Habibie.[38]

During the first half of 1998, criticism against Japan's lack of leadership in the resolution of the Asian crisis mounted both in Japan and abroad, coming especially from the United States.[39] At the meeting of G-7 finance ministers in London on February 21, 1998, the notion of the "threat of a weak Japan" *(Nihon-no fu-no kyoi)* was vigorously discussed. Foreign criticism focused on Japan's weak yen (which increased Japan's export competitiveness at the expense of the Asian exports) and its depressed economy (which further hindered Japan's imports from the Asian countries), both of which were allegedly derived from Tokyo's unwillingness to adequately stimulate its economy.[40]

The Japanese government struggled to defend its actions in helping the Asian countries, and it insisted that it was doing the best it could to assist these countries' economic recovery. It also sought to construct a solid consensus among creditor governments and IFIs toward an increased commitment to resolve the Asian crises. The Japanese government emphasized several aspects of past and future Japanese contributions to the resolution of the Asian crisis, and it increased its public relations campaign in its defense. Obviously, the first and foremost of the Japanese government's arguments was the sizable amount of money that Japan contributed to the financial rescue packages of the three Asian countries (Thailand, Indonesia, and Korea). Japan, until then, contributed a total of $19 billion in financial commitments for these emergency loans, while the United States, the second largest contributor, committed less than half of that—$8 billion in total.

At the G-7 meeting, the Japanese government demonstrated its active support of the Asian countries by responding to calls for extensive trade insurance and export credit to stabilize these economies. Two days before the G-7 London meeting, the Japanese government decided on its plan to help stabilize Asian economies by implementing economic policies. These measures included (a) more flexible use of Japan's Fiscal Investment and Loan Program to augment the pool of JEXIM untied loans by ¥30 billion ($2.5 billion) during Japan's fiscal year 1997 (i.e., before March 1998); (b) easier access to JEXIM Bank's trade finance for the Japanese companies operating in Asian countries, particularly in Indonesia; and (c) provisions of at least \$3 billion in trade insurance in fiscal year 1997. Increased technical cooperation and support to Southeast Asian students studying in Japan were also included in the support plan.[41]

Furthermore, the Japanese government included in the country's own fiscal stimulus package of \$128 billion announced on April 24, 1998, about ¥700 billion (\$5.8 billion) as part of a financial support plan for Asia. A special fund was again set up at the JEXIM Bank for fiscal year 1998, amounting to ¥650 billion (\$5.4 billion), mostly to support Japanese companies operating in these Asian countries. In addition, increased policy-based yen loans are expected to be used to financially assist Asian countries that suffered a dramatic depreciation of their currencies of over 30 percent.[42]

Finally, and along with these financial measures to boost Japan's support to crisis countries, the MOFA published in April 1998 a report in English entitled "Misperception and Truth about the Economies of Asia and Japan," which emphasized Japan's contribution to Asia and defended Japan's position in Asian financial crisis management.[43] Despite efforts by the Japanese government, international criticism continued. Then, in June, concerns for the very weak yen (and for the possibility that, as a result, the Chinese government might devalue its currency) invited the United States to intervene in the foreign exchange market, jointly with Japan, in support of the Japanese yen.

Although the Japanese government was constantly put in the place where it had to defend its inaction, the Japanese government did not seem to have completely relinquished its desire to take a leading and independent role in the Asian crisis, even during this second phase. Many Japanese policymakers and analysts became forceful critics of the IMF conditionality imposed on the Asian countries in crisis.[44] They also denounced the failure of the Japanese government (particularly of the MOF) to establish what they considered a more appropriate framework for crisis management and economic recovery in the region.[45]

The U.S. administration, however, was concerned about the slow progress in containing the Asian crisis and its possible contagion of major Latin American economies, such as Brazil. Constrained by congressional checks on the use of taxpayers' money in bailout packages, the United States pressed Japan and other Asian countries to step up their efforts to contain the crisis, particularly through increased financial commitment. But it seemed quite obvious, especially after the AMF debate, that the United States was not willing to concede its ultimate power over the modality of Asian crisis management in exchange for financial contributions from Japan or other Asian countries.

Reemergence of Japan's Initiatives: The New Miyazawa Initiative and Beyond (Phase 3)

The third phase of Japan's involvement in the Asian crisis management, from the latter half of 1998 into 1999, reflects the undercurrents of the post-AMF controversy and Japan's frustration over repeated criticisms, mostly from the U.S. government, that Japan was not doing enough to help its Asian neighbors. In addition, as the hands of the IMF and the United States became tied by major financial crises taking place in Russia and Brazil in the fall of 1998, the Japanese government devised active policies in economic crisis management in Asia. These policies, during the third phase, constituted Japan's independent initiative in the region, albeit with coordination and consultation with the United States. The most prominent sign of Japan's move in this direction was the $30 billion in funds that the New Miyazawa Initiative targeted to six East and Southeast Asian countries, as announced at the World Bank/IMF annual meeting in Washington, D.C. in October 1998. Furthermore, various additional financial commitments aiming to support the Asian economic recovery were announced from 1998 through 1999.

In the months after July 1998, a sense of worldwide financial crisis became dramatically heightened. The Russian crisis came partly as the Asian crisis contagion threatened to make investors flee emerging markets all together, making it difficult for the Russians to attract foreign capital.[46] The crisis also stemmed from the many difficulties Russia has had in transforming its economy to capitalism, including the country's huge budget deficit and political problems. By May 1998, signs of Asian contagion were visible in Russia as it became impossible to attract external capital or even stop the capital outflow with exceptionally high interest rates, which soared as high as 150 percent. In efforts to contain this economic fallout, Russian president Boris Yeltsin signed an austerity package to stabilize the budget and cut spending at the end of the month. Foreign investors demanded a much stronger "shot in the arm" for the Russian economy through the IMF stabilization package. The IMF and Russia had already agreed to a loan package of $9.6 billion in March 1996, and $670 million of this package was to be disbursed, but it was not enough to calm the market. After repeated negotiations with the IMF in June, and with political support from the Clinton administration, Russia managed to secure an additional $17.1 billion from the IMF, the World Bank, and the Japanese government, $12.6 billion of which would be delivered during 1998.[47] Even international efforts like this did not manage to restore foreign investors' confidence in the country, and Russia was forced to devalue its currency, the ruble, and partially default on its external debt in August. The country's economic crisis continued into 1999.[48]

In addition to the Russian economic disaster, Brazil, another relatively large economy, experienced financial turmoil before and after its presidential election in October. In response to this crisis, U.S. Treasury secretary Robert Rubin noted: "Brazil is very important to the economic well-being of the region, the United States and the international community, and all of us are very much focused on seeing how we can be helpful."[49] Offering financial assistance to Brazil before its economic problem got out of hand—a so-called precautionary aid approach proposed by the United States—was touted as a new strategy to cope with instability in the world economy. The Brazilian government, the IMF, and other supporting governments came to an agreement on November 13, and announced a package of $41.5 billion to stabilize the country's economy. The IMF would contribute $18 billion (600 percent of Brazil's IMF quota), the United States promised $5 billion from its ESF, and Japan pledged $1.45 billion.[50] On January 13, 1999, "the gamble over Brazil" seemed to have failed as the country abandoned its currency peg and devalued its real, triggering further capital outflow and a decline in its stock market.[51] The Brazilian economic problem emerged, and it became obvious that the Brazilian government could not execute the fiscal discipline it promised as a condition for the IMF loan package.[52]

As the economic troubles of these relatively large economies and continuing concern about the more-than-yearlong Asian economic crisis pulled the U.S. stock market down in the summer months of 1998, concerns over a possible global depression emerged among policymakers. When Japan's new prime minister, Keizo Obuchi, met with U.S. president Clinton in New York on September 22, they reportedly agreed on an arrangement by which "Japan would draw up a blueprint of Asia's economic reconstruction."[53] The Japanese media interpreted this agreement as an indication of an emerging regional division of labor between Japan and the United States for rescue and reconstruction efforts to support the emerging market countries in economic distress. It was partly because the U.S. government and the IMF needed the Japanese government to take up more of the cost of Asian crisis management as they faced challenges from other parts of the world.

The Japanese government's willingness to support the Asian economies following the Obuchi-Clinton meeting was manifested in the New Miyazawa Initiative (formally called "A New Initiative to Overcome the Asian Currency Crisis"). On September 30, 1998, Japan's finance minister Kiichi Miyazawa (who was also the advocate of the 1988 Miyazawa Plan for the resolution of the Latin American debt crisis) unveiled a package of $30 billion consisting of medium- and long-term financial support ($15 billion) and short-term trade finance and currency swap arrangements ($15 billion). The fund aimed to aid six troubled Asian nations (Thailand, Indonesia, Malaysia, the Philippines,

Singapore, and Korea).[54] Like the AMF idea rejected a year earlier, the initiative aimed to protect Asian countries against speculative attacks and to provide financing for their long-term structural reform. The New Miyazawa Initiative was formally announced at World Bank/IMF annual meeting in Washington, D.C. three days later, and the G-7 finance ministers continued to discuss mechanisms to cope with existing and future international financial instability.[55] The entities that opposed the earlier Japanese AMF proposal—the U.S. government, the IMF, and the World Bank in particular—welcomed the initiative, partly because the announcement came at an opportune time when these entities were overwhelmed by Russia and Brazil, and partly because the Japanese government maneuvered carefully this time to earn solid support on the proposal before its announcement.[56]

While uncertainty lingered, the Japanese government's active financial engagement in the resolution of the Asian crisis continued, under some coordination with the United States, during the annual APEC summit held in Malaysia on November 14–18, 1998. During the summit, Washington and Tokyo announced a joint debt restructuring and refinancing initiative (the so-called Asia Growth and Recovery Initiative [AGRI]) that would provide an additional $10 billion to the Asian economies.[57] Furthermore, Japan's strong gestures continued as Prime Minister Obuchi announced at the ASEAN summit in Hanoi on December 16, 1998, the establishment of a special framework for yen loans, involving ¥600 billion ($5 billion), for Asia during the next three years. This fund was set up to incorporate part of the loans planned under the New Miyazawa Initiative, to support efforts both to internationalize the use of yen and to promote human capital development in the Asian countries.[58] Prime Minister Obuchi also pledged $20 million for establishing a Japan-ASEAN "solidarity fund." In the end of January 1999, the Japanese government announced the expansion of the amount committed to the New Miyazawa Initiative to accommodate the yen credit worth $2.4 billion and untied JEXIM loans requested by Indonesia. As the funds for the plan dried up in May of that year, the Japanese government announced its bond guarantee program of ¥2 trillion ($16 billion)—in addition to the New Miyazawa Initiative funds—through the Japan Bank for International Cooperation (JBIC), to support Asian governments issuing yen-denominated bonds.[59]

The Japanese government's financial support initiatives to the Asian countries during this phase and through the response of the Asian governments reveal that the core ideas of the AMF died hard. Occasional comments from the Asian leaders advocating a revival of the AMF by Japan circulated, and many inside and outside of Japan considered the New Miyazawa Initiative a watered-down version of the AMF, without a multilateral/regional institutional framework.[60] As of the end of 2000, two indications of alternative (or supplementary) mechanisms to the IMF-led solution to financial crisis were emerging in Asia, slowly and cautiously. The first was the establishment of the Asian Currency Crisis Support Facility set up within the ADB in March 1999, with $3 billion in funds from Japan, to provide credit guarantees in the case of financial emergencies.[61] The second and more recent move was the establishment by the members of the ASEAN+3 (the ten ASEAN member countries plus China, Korea, and Japan) of regional swap facilities that member countries could tap during financial crises. This scheme was discussed at the APEC symposium in July 1999, supported by Asian deputy ministers at the ASEAN meeting in Manila in November, and finally and officially announced at the annual ASEAN+3 meeting in Brunei on March 24, 2000. The announcement stirred up further controversy between the regionalists in Asia and the "Washington consensus advocates," despite the Asian leaders' emphasis that this facility would not compete with the IMF but supplement it.[62] At the ASEAN+3 meeting in Thailand in May, the scheme was agreed upon in the form of expanded swap arrangement and repurchase agreement facilities among the participating countries. The agreement is currently called the Chiang Mai Initiative.[63]

In sum, even though the Japanese government's financial commitment in alleviating the Asian crisis has consistently been high, with more than $80 billion in contributions pledged in the two years after the onset of the crisis, the Japanese government's initiatives in managing the Asian crisis were not consistent over time. In Phase 1 (summer 1997 through fall 1997), the Japanese government was an active and independent leader from the time of the Thai crisis through the announcement of the AMF. During Phase 2 (fall 1997 through summer 1998), it was passive but cooperative as the world faced financial crises in Indonesia and Korea, leaving the leadership role to the IMF and the United States. Then, in Phase 3 (fall 1998 through 1999–2000), the Japanese government regained its active position with cautious independence as it announced the New Miyazawa Initiative and stepped up its financial assistance to Asian countries in distress. The following sections of this chapter examine the causes of this variance in Japan's behavior via two hypotheses: the joint product nature of public goods and the role of transnational linkages.

Asian Crisis Management as a Joint Product

Japanese Interests in Asia

A quick restoration of financial stability and vigorous economic recovery in Asia in the aftermath of the crisis would undoubtedly have provided critical private benefits to Japan. As I have already discussed, the Japanese government considers Asia a region of critical importance in terms of Japan's economic and political interests. Successful Asian crisis management represents private returns to Japan in addition to producing international public goods in the form of international financial stability (i.e., joint products). According to the first hypothesis outlined in chapter 1, this should create a perfect condition for the Japanese government to become actively involved in crisis management, either with the United States or on its own. Thus, the Japanese government should have had strong incentives to be actively engaged in Asian crisis management and to do so consistently. The first phase of Japan's involvement in the Asian crisis management, for Thailand, supports this explanation. The Japanese government exhibited its initiative by putting together, along with the IMF, a financial rescue package for Thailand, and later Japan proposed regional mechanisms for responding to financial emergencies, even without the discernible involvement of the United States. Phase 3 also fits the picture. However, Japan's weaker initiative in the second phase as compared with the first and third phases is puzzling, particularly when we recall the growing perceptions of the Asian crisis as a major threat to the stability of global finance and to the world economy. What else shaped Japan's interests in Asian crisis management during this phase?

In contrast to the management cases of the series of Latin American financial crises, Japan's multidimensional interests in Asia make it difficult to clearly define what constituted private return for the Japanese government in the case of Asian crisis management. Disaggregating "Japan's interests" into at least two major components helps partially explain the changes in the Japanese government's attitudes during the different phases of Asian financial crisis management and its occasional ambivalence. The first factor is the desire and priority on the part of the Japanese government as it faced the opportunity to take a leadership role in the region when its own country was confronting the worst domestic economic crisis. The second factor involves the diverse interests of various private sectors in Japan in maintaining the profitability and stability of their business operations in the region.

The Japanese government has long striven to score high on the Asian "leadership" scale through its diplomatic support and foreign aid to the region, and its desire to pursue this private return was apparent in its support to Thailand and in its AMF proposal during the first phase. However, from late October to early November 1997, the Japanese government (particularly the bureaus of the MOF) was forced to give up ambitious regional leadership actions, because the country's domestic economy faced an eminent possibility of major financial turmoil. In early November 1997, two major financial institutions, Yamaichi Securities and Hokkaido Takushoku Bank, failed, causing a large disruption in Japan's financial and real economy. As the domestic financial priority became urgent, the MOF had to suspend its financially burdensome fund idea, at least for awhile. Finally, Japan's active and independent initiatives were revived, including the announcement of the New Miyazawa Initiative in the latter half of 1998, as the Japanese government slowly emerged from the initial shock of the country's domestic financial crisis of 1997.[64]

The Japanese private sector, both finance and manufacturing, has maintained a high stake in procuring stability and prosperity in Asia. Confronting the Asian financial crisis, however, Japan's banking sector and manufacturing sector pursued different goals as management of Asia's financial crisis evolved. Japanese banks, already vulnerable because of their domestic bad loan problems, were highly exposed to these Asian countries in crisis in 1997 (see table 8.1), and they wished to exit from Asia as quickly and with as little harm done as possible. To achieve this goal, the Japanese banks needed the Japanese government to channel increased official funds to Asia, and they welcomed other measures to stop the financial run on these countries. The banks first applauded the Japanese government's active role in managing the Thai crisis and then quietly supported the government's initiative during the AMF debate (discussed later in this chapter). But the involvement of the United States and the IMF during the second phase, along with the transnational pressure from their counterpart banks in the United States and Europe (in dealing with Korea, in particular), made Japanese banks reluctant supporters of a multilateral solution. Even if the Japanese banks wished to act on their own to exit from Korea, strong institutional linkages among transnational banks would have made such a move impossible (as is discussed later in this chapter). Finally, with the crisis behind them, Japanese banks sought as much support as possible from the Japanese government as they rapidly exited from the Asian countries in 1998 and 1999. Their loan exposure to Asia decreased dramatically from 1997 to 1999 (see table 8.1). During this third phase, the dynamic between the Japanese banks and the government was similar to that of the later stage of the Latin American debt crisis. It paved the way for the Japanese financial sector to retreat from the region by contributing large official funding to Asia (see chap. 5).

Japan's manufacturing sector and trading companies maintained a long-term perspective on Asia as they faced the crisis. Although we observe a large decline in new FDI from Japan to the region in fiscal year 1998 (see table 8.2) due to the hardship the Asian economies were experiencing, the MITI's white paper on international trade indicates that the Japanese companies operating in Asia are there to stay.[65] Japan's manufacturing sector, in turn, hoped for restructuring of the Asian economies to suit their agenda when the Japanese

TABLE 8.1. Japan's Bank Claims in Asia, Year-End 1996 through Year-End 1999 (in millions of current dollars)

	1996		1997		1998		1999	
	(December)	Share (%)[a]	(December)	Share (%)[a]	(December)	Share (%)[a]	(December)	Share (%)[a]
All countries (excluding offshore)	169,999	17.1	163,435	14.6	127,533	11.8	102,813	9.2
Offshore banking centers	219,690	33.1	216,367	29.6	151,895	24.0	161,528	28.3
Asia[b]	264,847	34.7	249,666	31.7	154,065	27.8	122,407	25.4
Hong Kong	87,462	42.2	76,272	36.0	38,669	29.4	36,328	32.3
Singapore	58,809	31.1	58,649	30.1	29,474	23.6	21,029	21.4
Thailand	37,525	53.5	33,180	56.4	22,437	55.1	13,075	46.0
South Korea	24,324	24.3	20,278	21.5	16,925	25.9	12,592	20.8
Indonesia	22,035	39.7	22,018	37.7	16,402	36.6	12,491	30.7
People's Republic of China	17,792	32.3	19,589	31.0	15,115	26.0	11,789	25.3
Malaysia	8,210	36.9	8,551	31.1	6,623	31.8	6,029	33.3
Taiwan	2,683	12.0	3,516	13.4	2,143	10.2	2,652	13.2
Philippines	1,558	11.7	2,624	13.3	2,324	14.4	2,921	17.5

Source: Bank for International Settlements, *The Maturity, Sectoral, and Nationality Distribution of International Bank Lending.* The publication title changed in the November 1998 issue to *BIS Consolidated International Banking Statistics.*

[a] Share of Japan's bank claims to the country's total outstanding loans.

[b] Asia includes Hong Kong and Singapore, two countries categorized under offshore banking centers by the BIS.

government engaged in Asian crisis management. Rather than just bailing these economies out of the crisis through financial support, Japan's manufacturing sector wanted to use the situation to remove domestic obstacles to Japanese business operations in these countries, including corruption and traditional exclusion of foreigners (discussed later in this chapter). The Koreans, in particular, were quite disturbed as they sensed that the American and Japanese were taking advantage of the Korean crisis to pry open the country's economy and buy up its precious industrial base.[66] In addition, Japan's manufacturing sector, including the construction industry, urged the Japanese government to use its official fund exclusively for Japan, especially for the private sector, by "tying" the aid and by promoting infrastructure that would benefit these sectors.

The way in which the Japanese government has calculated its private return in managing the Asian financial crisis has been complex due to the strong, but not unified, interests that various Japanese actors have in Asia. The divergence of respective goals and of preferred methods regarding the crisis solution became most apparent during the second phase of the crisis, when (a) the Japanese government itself became immobilized due to the country's domestic financial crisis, (b) Japanese banks experienced high domestic and transnational pressure to cooperate with other international creditors, and (c) parts of the Japanese manufacturing sector sided with the Washington consensus to reform the economic environment of some of the Asian countries.

TABLE 8.2. Japan's Foreign Direct Investment in Asia, FY 1995–FY 1998 (in millions of current dollars)

	FY 1995	FY 1996	FY 1997	FY 1998	Accumulated by March 1999
Total	51,398	49,728	54,739	40,747	658,514
Asia	12,361	12,027	12,355	6,527	119,074
Indonesia	1,605	2,500	2,550	1,076	24,627
Hong Kong	1,147	1,540	705	601	17,821
People's Republic of China	4,478	2,600	2,015	1,065	18,798
Singapore	1,185	1,155	1,850	637	14,332
Thailand	1,240	1,453	1,894	1,371	13,093
Malaysia	575	592	803	514	8,821
South Korea	449	430	449	302	6,572
Taiwan	455	540	456	224	5,342
Philippines	718	579	531	379	5,004

Source: MOF, *Kokusai Kiyukyoku Nenpo.*

The U.S.-Japanese Relationship and the U.S. Presence in Crisis Management

The changes in U.S. presence during different phases of the Asian crisis are obviously a key to explaining shifts in Japanese behavior. The U.S. absence in the first phase and its presence and management initiatives, along with the IMF, during the second phase of the Asian crisis seem to have impacted the Japanese government's behavior. Analysis of the Latin American debt crisis in the 1980s (see chap. 5) suggests that the Japanese government might have been expected to step up its involvement in managing that crisis as the U.S. presence and the urgency of crisis management increased. In the Asian crisis, however, the increase in the U.S. presence from the first to the second phase deterred the Japanese government from taking a more active role in crisis management. As the IMF and the U.S. government became preoccupied with problems in Russia and Brazil during the third phase, Japan began to readdress the Asian crisis in an independent way that could have caused tension with the United States. The Japanese government was not solely reacting to U.S. demands but walked on a fine line between supporting the United States and emerging as the independent leader in Asia. Why did the Japanese government prefer a strategy that would make its attitude appear inconsistent and its leadership difficult?

To answer this question, it is important to examine the evolution of U.S.-Japanese relations in the 1990s, particularly in comparison to Japan's increasing involvement in Asia's regional economy. The intense economic interdependence and economic linkages between the United States and Japan, which created another important set of private returns, increased incentives for the Japanese government to cooperate closely with the United States during the Latin American debt crisis (see chap. 5). Some changes in the U.S.-Japanese economic relationship became noticeable, however, beginning in the early 1990s, due to the U.S. economic recovery and the reversal of the economic power balance between the United States and Japan. The U.S. economic recovery and the solution of its savings and loan problems in the early 1990s created a major economic boost for the country, and the U.S. economy entered the longest peacetime expansion in its history (see figs. 2.6 and 2.7). Despite some glitches, such as the summer of 1998 (the period of "correction in the market," according to investors), the U.S. stock market has continued to post record highs into the year 2000.[67]

The changes in the relative economic conditions between the two countries were first manifested in a gradual lowering of tensions in bilateral trade relations between the United States and Japan throughout the first half of the

1990s. Japan's large trade surplus vis-à-vis the United States increased the Japanese government's political sensitivity to U.S. demands in the 1980s (see chaps. 2 and 5), and this trade imbalance continued into and throughout the 1990s (see fig. 2.9). However, as the United States gradually recovered from its recession and its economy continued to boom, the Japanese share of the U.S. deficit decreased drastically from 69 percent in 1992 to approximately 30 percent in the mid-1990s. This was partly a result of greater U.S. trade diversification (see fig. 2.10 and table 8.3).

The weight and importance of U.S. trade with Japan decreased from the mid-1990s because of the booming U.S. economy (see table 8.3), and bilateral trade tensions between the United States and Japan became less of a political battlefield between the two countries. Some occasional and conspicuous bilateral disputes between the two countries occurred during this period, particularly in the areas of auto parts and dealerships (1995), photographic film (1996–97), steel, rice, forests, and fisheries (1998). Nevertheless, U.S.-Japanese trade issues began to take a backseat as Japanese economic problems worsened in 1997.[68]

The trading of economic places between the United States and Japan also affected the Japanese financial sector. As the Japanese banks faced severe domestic economic conditions and the worsening condition of their books, the capital flow trend from Japan into the United States in the 1990s reversed. Japanese bank money slowly retreated from the United States (see table 8.4), despite the fact that the Japanese private sector still had a higher accumulated direct investment in the United States than anywhere else in the world.[69]

Such factors as declining profits and the volatility of yen-dollar exchange rates have contributed to the Japanese financial sector's retreat from the United States. In addition, the BIS capital standard rules for asset positions of commercial banks operating abroad forced the Japanese financial sector to be more conservative and thus more reluctant to extend loans abroad.[70] Japanese banks, which agreed to comply with the BIS rules by March 1993, were under pressure to reduce their lending. Declining levels of capital, due to very low prices of shares and the bad loans banks had accumulated during the previous decade, made the BIS rules a high hurdle to clear.[71] The trend of decreasing Japanese financial presence in the United States was exacerbated by the Daiwa Bank incident. In 1995, Daiwa Bank became ineligible to operate in the United States after its bank manager was found to have hidden $1.1 billion of the banks' U.S. operational losses from unauthorized bond trading. It also turned out that Japan's MOF failed to inform U.S. financial regulators of the incident for forty days. Finally, during the Asian crisis and as the collapse of two major financial institutions in Japan was announced in November 1997, Japanese banks began suffering from higher "Japan Premium" on their loans

TABLE 8.3. Changes in US Total Trade with Different Regions, 1991–1997 (in billions of current US dollars)

Regions	1991		1992		1993		1994		1995		1996		1997	
Industrial countries	556.9	59.8%	580.5	58.1%	617.6	56.4%	686.6	57.1%	763.0	56.4%	794.9	55.2%	858.6	54.1%
Japan	143.1	15.4%	147.3	14.7%	158.4	14.5%	176.0	14.6%	191.5	14.2%	185.5	12.9%	189.9	12.0%
Africa	21.0	2.3%	21.5	2.2%	21.6	2.0%	20.9	1.7%	22.5	1.7%	26.1	1.8%	28.0	1.8%
Asia	176.2	18.9%	200.2	20.0%	246.3	22.5%	256.0	21.3%	305.8	22.6%	319.6	22.2%	348.1	21.9%
Developing Europe	11.7	1.3%	12.6	1.3%	15.8	1.4%	17.3	1.4%	19.6	1.4%	21.0	1.5%	24.1	1.5%
Middle East	35.5	3.8%	37.2	3.7%	36.8	3.4%	36.3	3.0%	38.4	2.8%	43.0	3.0%	47.3	3.0%
Western Hemisphere	129.3	13.9%	147.6	14.8%	156.3	14.3%	184.4	15.3%	203.4	15.0%	235.6	16.4%	278.7	17.6%
Total	930.6	100.0%	999.6	100.0%	1094.4	100.0%	1201.5	100.0%	1352.7	100.0%	1440.2	100.0%	1584.8	100.0%

Source: IMF, *Direction of Trade Statistics Yearbook.*
Note: Because of rounding, percentages do not always add up to 100.

(i.e., high interest rates were imposed on international borrowing by the Japanese financial sector), making it difficult for them to access dollar loans.

While the business activities of Japan's financial sector in the United States were declining, Japanese economic interests in the Asian region continued to increase (as I discussed earlier) up until the crisis. Thus, protecting Japan's vested interests in the U.S. economy directly and indirectly was no longer the only imperative for Japan's financial sector, nor was it the overriding concern of the Japanese government. The economic linkages that had tied the Japanese financial sector to the U.S. economy and to the fortune of the U.S. dollar so closely in the 1980s lost their dominant position of importance in the 1990s. The outbreak of the Asian crisis, particularly in light of its spread to Hong Kong, Indonesia, and Korea, raised major concerns among U.S. economic policymakers at the end of 1997, and it detrimentally affected the U.S. trade balance with the region. The U.S. trade deficit grew with an increase in imports from these countries coupled with a drastic decrease in U.S. exports to the region. Nevertheless, catastrophic economic repercussions did not reach the United States. The yen-dollar exchange rate, which Japanese policymakers frequently worry about, shifted temporarily in favor of a strong dollar and a weak yen under the crisis (see fig. 2.13). In short, Japan was affected much more severely by the Asian crisis than was the United States, and Japan's economy has become much weaker.[72] Since a large portion of Japan's manufacturing sector welcomed a weak yen, the shift in the exchange rate removed an-

TABLE 8.4. Changes in Japan's Financial Asset Position in the United States by Investment Category, 1980–1995 (in millions of current US dollars)

Year	Direct Investment	Security Investment	Trade Credits	Loans	Others	Total
1980	729	−3,001	−15	409	224	−1,654
1985	2,043	29,874	587	716	−57	33,163
1986	7,774	55,944	334	690	908	65,650
1987	9,018	48,223	489	1,663	1,637	61,030
1988	19,568	33,320	1,024	2,830	2,518	59,260
1989	22,768	22,074	1,255	4,761	3,003	53,861
1990	24,986	−19,849	633	2,783	3,166	11,719
1991	15,302	−1,045	−314	2,569	1,846	18,358
1992	8,914	8,490	−322	4,838	922	22,842
1993	6,755	21,957	−364	5,676	−143	33,881
1994	6,193	15,097	−308	2,006	348	23,336
1995	8,192	15,863	−771	−340	1,703	24,647

Source: Bank of Japan, International Department, *Balance of Payments Monthly,* various April issues; Kawai 1995, 96–98.

Note: Due to changes in the statistical compilation from the year, no comparable data are available from 1996.

other motive for the Japanese government to intervene in the crisis in support of the United States and its stronger dollar.

Such factors as decreased trade tensions, Japan's increased economic interests in Asia relative to the United States, and the reversed economic positions between the two countries were of course already present at the time of the 1994–95 Mexican currency crisis. These factors certainly contributed to discouraging Japan from actively collaborating with the United States in managing that situation. The decline of the Japanese financial sector's interests in the U.S. economy became even more prominent in 1997, when several Japanese banks failed and the real magnitude of their bad loan problems were revealed.

In sum, the economic tension between the United States and Japan that had enhanced Japan's willingness to collaborate closely with the United States in the 1980s evolved into something more complex in the 1990s, particularly in the face of the Asian financial crisis. The types of private returns accrued by Japan from engaging in crisis management, which used to converge toward an active engagement in and collaboration with the United States in the 1980s, become more diffuse in the 1990s. Both the regional shift of the crisis from Latin America to Asia and changes in U.S.-Japanese economic relations contributed to Japan's independent actions in the first and third phases of the Asian financial crisis management. In particular, the tension between Japan's regional interests in Asia and its economic interests in the United States seems to have caused the Japanese government to become ambivalent regarding the issue of collective management of the Asian crisis.

The Case of the AMF Scheme

The Japanese government's multiple private returns that produced a joint product from its management of the Asian financial crisis explain the curious way in which the AMF idea emerged in the summer of 1997 and then retreated by late fall. The Japanese government's expected private returns came from (a) its own economic and political interests in Asia, (b) its positive relationship with Japan's private sector, and (c) its positive relations with the United States. In addition, the relative weakness of transnational linkages among international financiers, particularly in the earliest phase of the Asian financial crisis, prevented the formation of a strong position among transnational banks.

First, the AMF idea appears to have been partially a construction of the MOF. It was specially formulated in the MOF's International Finance Bureau, with strong support from some Asian countries. China notably opposed it. One MOF official explained four major reasons for the emergence of the AMF around the time of the Thai crisis:

1. Concerns about the possibilities of contagion.
2. Awareness that there were limited money sources available outside of Asia.
3. Awareness that there was limited access to the IMF funds, particularly for Asian countries, due to their small IMF quotas.
4. Difficulty of some countries, like Australia, to justify case-by-case bilateral support of rescue packages in domestic political arenas, thus creating the need for an established regional fund for this purpose.[73]

In addition, the MOF took into consideration the interests and needs of Japan's private sector in its planning process, even though there was only limited consultation with Japan's financial sector (mostly "information exchange" *[joho kokan]*) and no vigorous input of ideas from it.[74] Of course, behind the official AMF initiative was a strong desire by the Japanese government to take a leadership role in Asia, particularly in the economic sphere.[75]

Second, Japan's private sector actors' ambivalent positions on the AMF during the first phase contributed to the uncoordinated way that the AMF idea emerged, as presented by Japan's finance minister in September 1997 in Hong Kong. Many Japanese bankers with high exposure to the Asian economies in trouble quietly welcomed the idea, hoping that the Japanese government would use such a fund to help them withdraw from Thailand and possibly from other financially troubled countries in Asia without accruing significant loan losses.[76] However, such support was rarely stated publicly. In contrast, many Japanese businessmen, particularly from the manufacturing and exporting sectors, demonstrated their doubts about the AMF. They were aware that it would be dangerous to provide easy money in the name of an Asian rescue that could undermine the reforms and adjustments usually demanded by the stringent conditionality of the IMF. They were also aware that support of the AMF might result in the loss of opportunities for further liberalization of the Asian markets.[77] Even in Japan's financial sector, those supporting the solutions through the IMF argued against the AMF because "such a fund as the financial last resort creates a psychology of dependence."[78]

Finally, the dynamics between the Japanese government and the major creditor governments of the United States and Europe seem to have impacted the fate of the AMF. As the AMF scheme was officially announced in late September, the reaction from IMF supporters in the United States and Europe and from the IMF itself was negative and skeptical. It was clear that the U.S. government and the IMF did not want to relinquish their powers to push the Washington consensus via the only international financial institution that could assist balance-of-payments problems. Western European countries, in addition, were concerned about the major moral hazard problem that such an arrangement could incur. They all were also worried about constructing a divided authority in international monetary matters, which would diminish the consistency and effectiveness of the IMF programs implemented in borrower countries, and which could also invite increased risk of moral hazard problems among the private lenders.[79] IMF deputy managing director Stanley Fischer criticized the proposal, stating that it could undermine the authority and effectiveness of the IMF itself. In addition, congressional constraints faced by the Clinton administration in allocating large funds to a new financial organization made the U.S. critical of the idea of a new fund, which, without active U.S. contributions, would threaten U.S. influence in Asia.[80]

This incoherence and opposition led to the "defeat" of the AMF in November 1997. Instead, the IMF-led solution to the Asian crisis emerged as the Manila Framework, preserving some components of the AMF idea.[81] Nevertheless, the idea of a regional fund did not die, and it has subsequently been revived both through the ADB and in the ASEAN+3 forum (discussed earlier in this chapter). There are indications that the Japanese government started to revive strong initiatives to resolve the Asian financial crisis—for example, through its announcement of the New Miyazawa Initiative. Unlike the case of the AMF debate, however, Japan's renewed initiative took a form that did not conflict directly with the creditor coalition or the United States—a mostly financial facility without establishing a new institution. Besides making financial contributions, Finance Minister Miyazawa has engaged himself in a debate on appropriate financial crisis solutions as part of a "new international financial architecture" discussion in international forums, such as the G-7 finance minister's meetings and APEC meetings.[82]

In sum, the independent initiative by the Japanese government in proposing the AMF emerged from the desire by the Japanese government (particularly the International Finance Bureau of the MOF, in this case) to show leadership in Asia at a time of apparent U.S. reluctance. But the Japanese government could not sustain this independent initiative, because of the fragmented position of the Japanese private sector on the issue and because of opposition from the Washington consensus. Meanwhile, tension between Japan's interests in Asia versus its interests in the United States remains and has led the Japanese government to resent the creditor coalition based on the Washington consensus, which was highly critical of Japan's contribution (or alleged lack thereof) and its failure to bolster the Asian countries' economic recovery. At the same time, the IMF-led reforms of the economies of the region seem to have taken the opportunity of the Asian crisis, forcing the countries to restructure their economies.[83]

Institutional Linkages and Domestic Dynamics

Financial Actors in the Asian Crisis

The composition of capital flows to middle-income (or emerging market) countries changed between the 1970s–1980s and the 1990s. A prominent feature of the first Latin American debt crisis was the important role of commercial bank lending, particularly syndicated loans. The amount of these loans shrank in the 1990s, when other portfolio flows (bond purchase, equity investments) became the major financing instruments, particularly for Latin America (see table 6.1). I have argued in chapter 6 that this shift in the 1990s led to the changes in the cast of financial players, reducing the strength of transnational linkages among financial institutions, and weakening their power to induce collective action among creditor governments in financial crisis management.

The change in the composition of capital inflows to emerging market countries was not as marked in Asia as in Latin America. A comparison of the foreign capital inflow composition between Asia and Latin America in the 1990s reflects Asian countries' propensity for direct debt (see figs. 8.1a and 8.1b). This contrast arises partly from the fact that, unlike most of the Latin American countries, many Asian countries did not experience severe debt crises in the 1980s and thus had not suffered a major withdrawal of commercial banks and their loans from the region. The contrast is also partly due to the fact that many Asian economies have always depended more on debt financing (bank loans) than on financing from the market (securitized debt), making Asian firms much more reliant on bank lending than on stock or bond markets.[84]

Dominant participation of commercial banks tends to increase linkage, as was seen in the Latin American debt crisis, and thus it should increase the positive motivation toward collective action among creditor governments, particularly between Japan and the United States (see chaps. 1 and 5).[85] Indeed, one can observe examples of such institutional linkage in the management of the 1997–98 Asian financial crisis: in particular, the establishment of bank steering committees among international banks with outstanding loans to Indonesia and Korea during the first half of 1998, which enabled banks to deal collectively with these countries (see discussion earlier and later in this chapter).

The level of transnational institutional linkage among commercial banks provides one important element necessary to understanding the changes in the nature of collective action between the Japanese government and the United States during the Asian crisis. Of the three phases outlined earlier in this chapter, the second phase, when creditor governments and the IFIs were faced with the financial crisis management of Indonesia and Korea, was the period when Japan showed the closest collaboration with U.S.-led financial crisis management. It does not appear to be a coincidence that during this phase, the creditor governments were dealing with the countries where a fairly tight institutional linkage existed among commercial bank creditors.[86]

This correlation is particularly interesting when the second phase is contrasted with the first instance of Asian financial crisis management—the Thai crisis—during which such close collaboration among transnational banks was not a prominent feature of the financial solution. As is shown in figure 8.2, Thailand accrued a disproportionately large debt to Japanese banks at the time of the crisis, while Indonesia and particularly Korea accrued foreign debts from banks in a wider range of major industrial countries.

Because of the wider range of lender country involvement, more creditor countries were interested in resolving the crises in Indonesia and Korea than in Thailand. Concomitantly, the institutional linkage and transmission of pressures on creditor governments to engage in collective action to stabilize the market was much stronger in these two countries. In some ways, the Thai crisis appeared to both private lenders in the United States and Europe and their creditor governments as a problem for the Japanese to solve, a situation that draws an ironic parallel to the case of Mexico and the United States in 1994–95 (see chap. 6). These circumstances enabled the Japanese government to take an independent stance because of the lack of intervention by other creditor governments except for the IMF, whose intervention, according to Japan's official perspectives, was absolutely necessary to stabilize the situation.[87]

Japan's Domestic Politics

An aspect of crisis management involvement that relates closely to the institutional linkages among financial institutions and loosely with my earlier discussion of the Japanese government's private returns is the level of political influence that various financial institutions can place on the Japanese government's foreign policy formulation at the time of crisis (and, occasionally, that the government can place on financial institutions). The level of such influence is derived from two factors: (1) how effectively the Japanese financial sector manages to transmit its demands, in accordance to its counterpart abroad, to its home government; and (2) how responsive the Japanese government is to these private institutions. These influences are always transmitted through Japan's domestic political process, and if both factors are high, they should af-

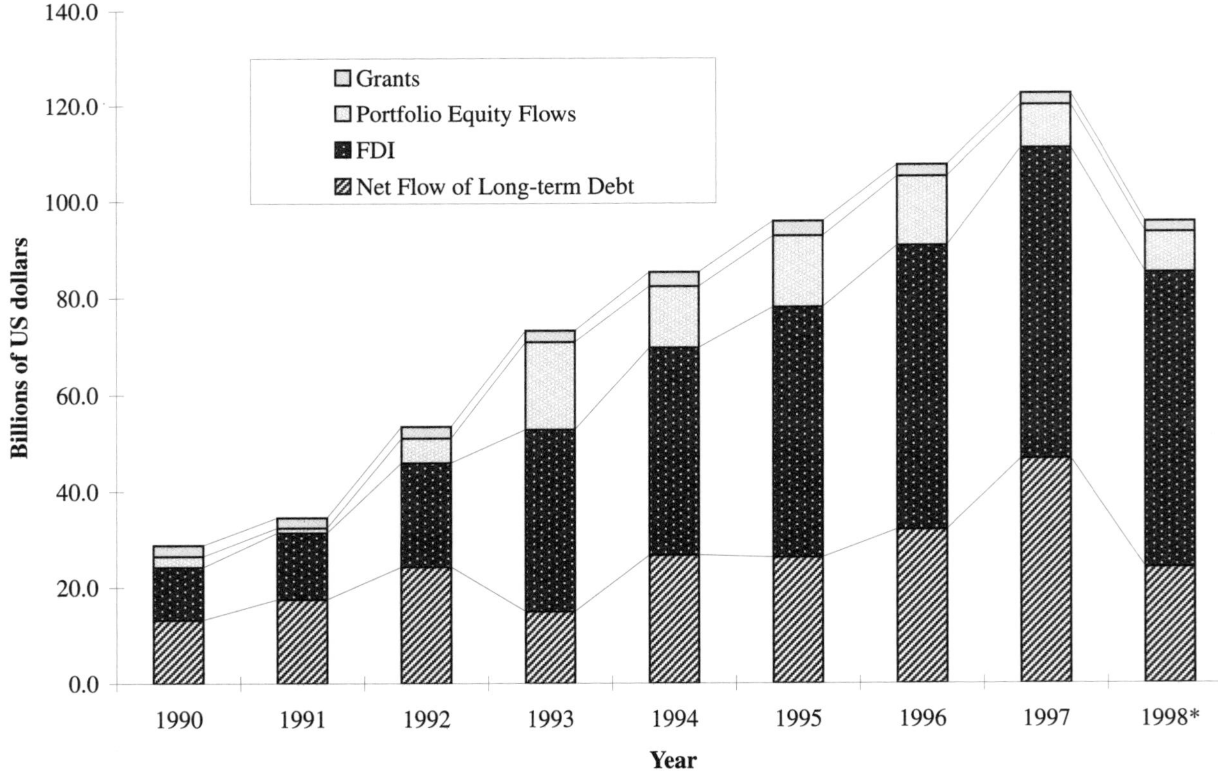

Fig. 8.1a. The composition of foreign capital inflows into Asia, 1990–98. (From World Bank, *World Debt Tables*, 1990–94, and *Global Development Finance*, 1995–98. *World Bank staff estimate for 1998.)

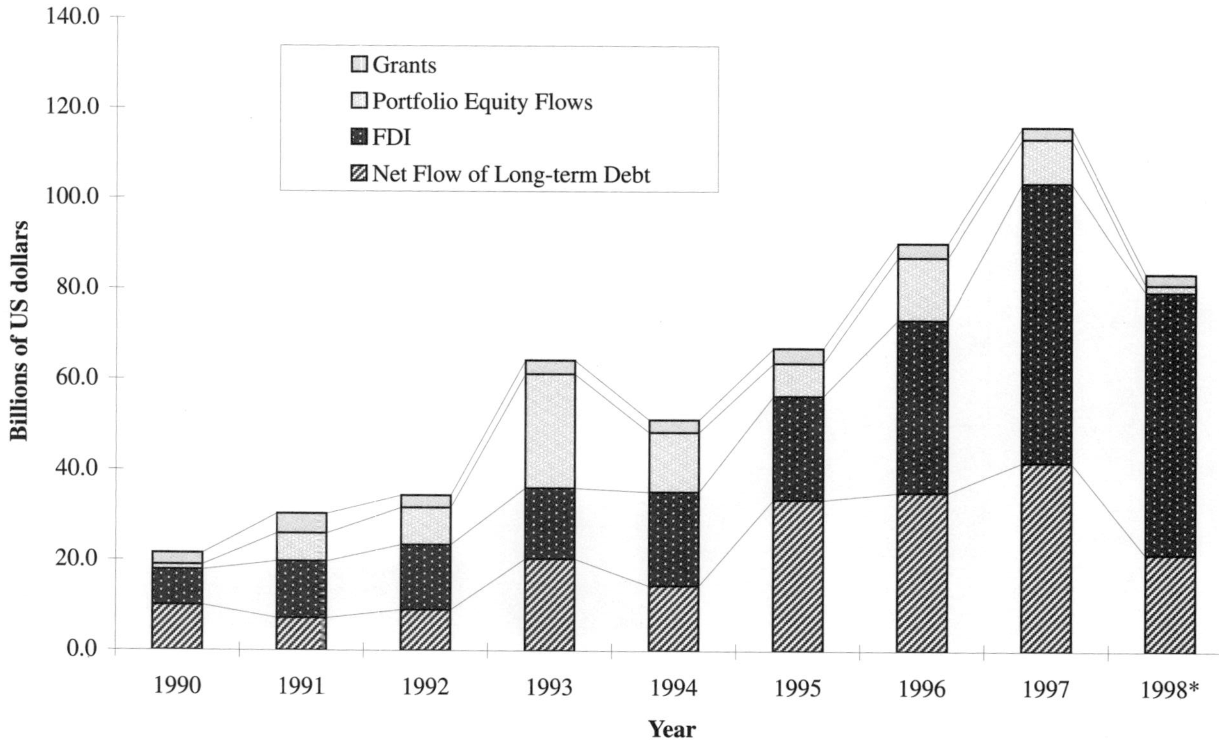

Fig. 8.1b. The composition of foreign capital inflows into Latin America, 1990–98. (From World Bank, *World Debt Tables*, 1990–94, and *Global Development Finance*, 1995–98. *World Bank staff estimate for 1998.)

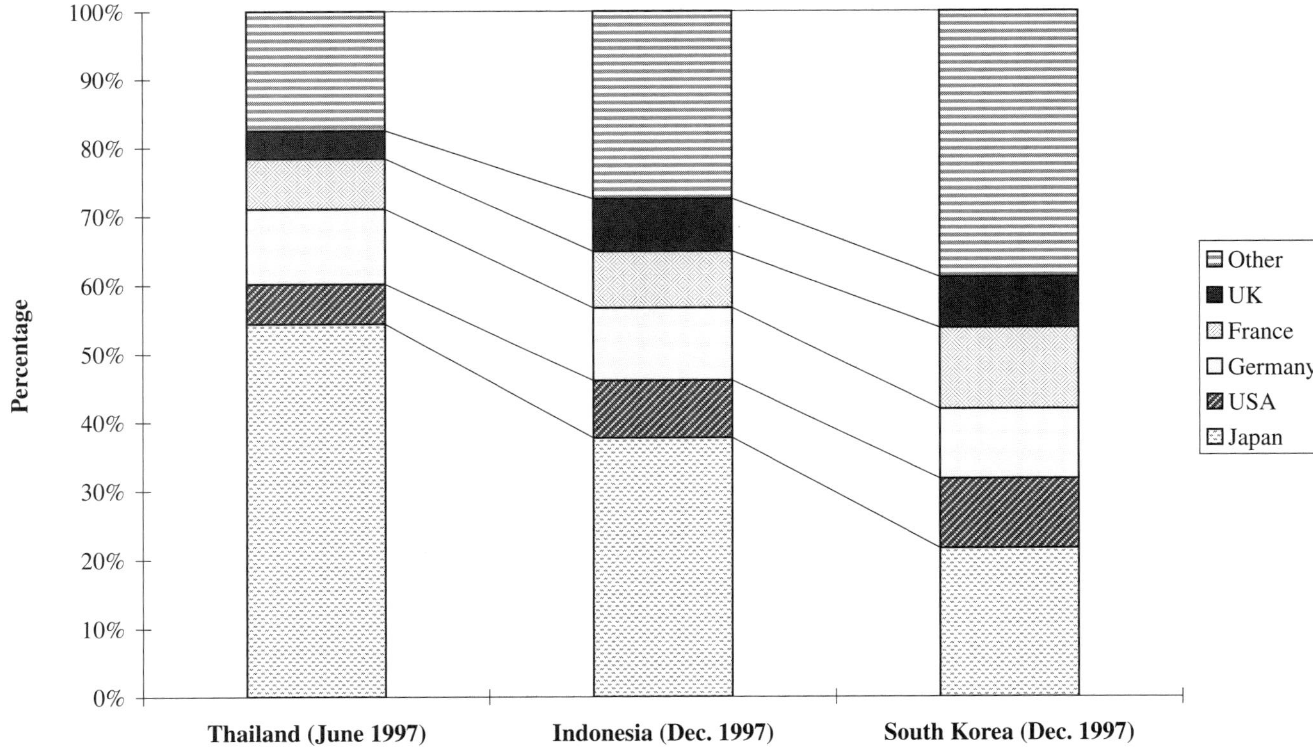

Fig. 8.2. Country origin of bank debt in Thailand, Indonesia, and South Korea in 1997. (From Bank for International Settlements, *The Maturity Distribution of International Bank Lending*, table 2.)

fect the Japanese government's behavior and involvement in Asian crisis management. The changing dynamics between Japan's financial sector and its ministry in charge, the MOF, in the 1990s, thus became a critical component.

Japan's financial sector and Japan's arguably most powerful ministry, the MOF, maintained a very close and symbiotic relationship throughout Japan's post–World War II economic recovery and into the 1980s. Many times, Japanese banks had been urged to make loans that served Japan's foreign policy purposes, and in return the MOF provided an implicit guarantee for Japanese banks against bankruptcy. This close relationship led the Japanese government to actively support Japanese banks during the Latin American debt crisis, as is supported quantitatively in chapter 3 and qualitatively in chapter 5. This so-called convoy approach *(goso sendan hoshiki)* under the MOF's careful protection of the Japanese financial sector, along with the close collaboration between the two sectors, faced a major challenge in the 1990s due to several changes taking place in Japanese economics and politics. These changes made it difficult for both the MOF and Japan's financial sector to transmit their usual influence or to exchange candid opinions and information during the Asian crisis, a factor that hindered the Japanese government from interpreting the banks' positions and desires accurately.

Some changes in the relationship between the MOF and Japan's financial sector have evolved gradually since the late 1970s. As I have already discussed, financial deregulation and the internationalization of the Japanese economy, particularly of its financial activities, tipped relative bargaining power in favor of Japan's financial sector (see chaps. 1 and 5). However, after the mid-1990s, the symbiotic relationship between the financial sector and the Japanese government (MOF) began to show signs of weakening. The early signs came slowly during the first few years of the 1990s. A collapse of the Tokyo Stock Exchange and of Japan's property market came soon after interventions by the MOF and the Bank of Japan in 1990 to deal with Japan's overheated economy. They raised discount rates and changed regulations to curb land speculation, interventions perceived to be failures.[88] To shed its tarnished reputation and revive the vigor of Japan's economy, the MOF intervened in Japan's stock market, financially assisted loans made in both corporate and household sectors, and changed regulatory and tax laws in favor of land purchased from 1993 through 1995.[89]

Thanks to this intervention, the MOF seemed to have regained its power by mid-1993. This recuperation was boosted particularly by the temporary demise of the LDP—the thirty-eight-year ally of the MOF that had also kept the MOF in check—as the party lost its majority status in the diet.[90] The powerful position of the MOF, however, did not last long. Various major scandals and mismanagement by the MOF shook Japan's financial circles between 1995 and 1998, and the trusted and close (and usually personal) linkages nurtured between the MOF and Japan's financial institutions began to disconnect.[91] The MOF also began distancing itself by implying an end to the government's implicit guarantee of all banks. The MOF stated in 1995 that it would withdraw its guarantee of the security of all deposits after a five-year interval.[92]

The failure of two major financial institutions in Japan in November 1997 clearly led to a loss of mutual trust between the leading decision makers of the Japanese financial sector and the MOF and also to the loss of a close channel of communication between the two sets of actors. Furthermore, just when resolution of the Asian financial crisis became critical in early 1998, the financial sector lost its personal channels to the MOF as the ministry's corrupt relationship with banks and other financial institutions were revealed. Harsh public criticism of the collusion between the government and banks followed.[93] Public and media scrutiny inhibited Japan's financial circles from transmitting demands or even information to the Japanese government, making the Japanese position on the Asian financial crisis management less coherent.[94]

In addition to the loss of informal communication channels between the MOF and the banks, a mega–bank merger between the Bank of Tokyo and Mitsubishi Bank in April 1996 removed one of the established communication channels between the group of banks dealing with international financial issues and the MOF. As is noted in chapter 5 and discussed in detail by Stallings,[95] the role of the Bank of Tokyo had been critical in creating both a strong international channel with other transnational banks and a coordinated domestic pipeline to influence the Japanese government at the time of the 1980s debt crisis. The Bank of Tokyo was considered the bank with the strongest international outlook in Japan. It had fifty years of experience as a specialized foreign exchange bank, seventy offices overseas, and an average of 60 percent of its profits from international business. This bank merged with the "domestic" and dominant Mitsubishi Bank (with 70 percent of its total profits earned at home). The confusion at the time of this transition and the power dynamics within the new Bank of Tokyo-Mitsubishi removed some of the important functions previously performed by Bank of Tokyo managers and international experts.[96]

The Korean Crisis

Following the initial and possibly prematurely executed Japanese response during the first phase of the Asian crisis management, particularly represented by the first attempt at floating the AMF idea, the second phase included management of the Korean crisis. This represented a period of relatively strong collaboration, both among major creditor countries and between the Japanese government and its financial sector. The high level of collaboration during this phase can be explained by the transnational pressure exerted by the United States and by the domestic dynamics between the Japanese government and its financial sector. Obviously, the magnitude and impact of the Korean crisis made a difference. As I noted earlier, Korea has a fairly large economy, and its decades of economic success had attracted investors. Hence, Korea's accrued debt from creditors was quite evenly distributed among many industrial countries (see fig. 8.2). In addition, the Korean crisis emerged after the U.S. government became seriously involved in Asian financial crisis management at the onset of the Indonesian crisis.

The response of Japan's financial sector to the Korean crisis revealed changes from the earlier crisis: Japan's financial sector was much more involved in the Korean crisis solution negotiated by the foreign banks in collaboration with the MOF. The pressure on Japanese banks apparently came both from the government and from transnational financial sector linkages. Japanese banks also had much to gain from successful collective management of the crisis, which enhanced their motivation to cooperate. The Japanese government, in turn, collaborated with the United States to support the actions of the private sector, thus strengthening collective action, though weakening its own independent initiatives.

Despite the large IMF rescue package, the Korean government had to approach international creditors again during the third week of December 1997 to inform them of the dire condition of Korean banks due to the massive exit of short-term capital, which had not halted. This led to actions by financial sectors from Japan, the United States, and Europe. Many of the Seoul-based foreign bankers, forty to fifty representatives from big international banks, began their own loan extension discussions for Korea in mid-December.[97] The deal was set, finally, on Christmas Day, and a formal agreement to roll over the country's $15 billion in outstanding loans, while the IMF released $2 billion in loans to the country, was finalized a few days later.[98]

The U.S. government was not unified. Actually U.S. Treasury secretary Robert Rubin was not in a hurry to rescue Korea in the middle of December, and he publicly noted that the economic problems of Korea would stabilize as soon as the Korean government faithfully implemented the IMF-reforms agreed on a few weeks earlier. Evidently, the security wing of the U.S. government (the State Department, the Department of Defense, and the national security advisor) was much more worried about the collapse of the Korean financial market and its negative implications for Korea's social and political conditions under the newly elected president, Kim Dae Jung. In particular, they were concerned that such instability would raise the risk of a major conflict between South and North Korea. Given this divided opinion on the Korean rescue, the strong lead taken by transnational banks with significant stakes in Korea had an impact on America's Korean policy, making it imperative that the Treasury Department cooperate in the Korean rescue. Such a gesture by the private banks bearing some of the burdens of the rescue gave the U.S. administration a good incentive to become actively involved. The gesture thus deflected criticisms from U.S. taxpayers and from Congress, which had often opposed using U.S. money, on the ground that such an operation would only bail out rich bankers.[99]

This international coalition among actors in the private financial sector also had an impact on the way Japanese banks behaved toward the Korean financial crisis and on the Japanese government's willingness to follow the U.S. lead. Because of the business connection between Japanese banks and U.S. and European banks operating in Korea, transnational peer pressures on the Japanese banks in the case of the Korean rescue attempt were strong. In addition, the long-term interests of the Japanese banks in the stability and recovery of the Korean economy made it important for the Japanese banks to commit to the resolution of the country's financial crisis. Despite a major coordination problem among the banks, due to the "loss" of the Bank of Tokyo, ten major Japanese banks managed to commit to a united front, promising to maintain their current outstanding loan balance until the end of March 1998.[100]

A substantial part of the management of the Korean financial crisis was conducted through private sector channels in a way that paralleled the official rescues conducted by the IMF and by creditor governments. The coordinated position taken by the Japanese banks also came about with the help of the MOF and the Bank of Japan, which enhanced the incentives for banks to get actively involved in the crisis management and to avoid free-riding. In return for the Japanese banks' concessions on Korean loans, the MOF promised three things: (1) responsibility for increased debt would be absorbed by Japan's official sector, (2) the credibility of their performance in front of their shareholders would be supported by the MOF, and (3) there would be actions by G-7 countries to guarantee the recovery of extended outstanding loans.[101]

Furthermore, some Japanese banks were at that time suffering from the "Japan Premium," a condition that made the banks' access to U.S. dollars very expensive. This coincided with a period of a very weak yen in early December (see fig. 2.13). Thus, the banks were given temporary access to U.S. dollar deposits in the MOF's Foreign Exchange Fund Special Account *(gaikoku kawase shikin tokubetsu kaikei)*. This measure aimed to relieve the pressure on major Japanese banks caused by insufficient U.S. dollars in their accounts. As the MOF granted such measures to Japanese banks, it hoped to prevent the banks from retrieving their dollar-based assets abroad, including assets from Asia, and to enable them to withstand issuing new loans or extending loan amortization periods to such countries as Korea.[102]

In short, strong institutional linkages enhanced Japan's involvement in Korean crisis management in collaboration with the U.S. actors during the second phase of the Asian crisis management. This dynamic closely resembles Japan's involvement in the Latin American debt crisis, where the coalition of transnational financial sectors bound the two creditor governments closer together toward collective action in crisis management. The difference between the two cases, however, comes from the change in the region, which altered Japan's independent and regional self-interests. The regional contrast is discussed further in this book's conclusion.

Summary

The 1997–98 Asian financial crisis has posed many challenges to the Japanese government. Despite the Japanese government's desire to show active, reliable, and consistent leadership in Asian crisis management, its behavior shifted over the course of two years, as the scope of the crisis and the IMF/U.S. policies to the region evolved. Japan's high stakes in the region arising from its close and historically important economic and political relationships have produced varied and sometimes conflicting private returns for the Japanese government. The Japanese government could not even induce a coherent position among Japan's private sector in relation to support on the AMF scheme, and thus any alternative to the IMF-led crisis solution led by Japan was slow in coming.

The changes in the level of U.S. presence in Asian financial crisis management were also influential on the Japanese government's behavior, although not in the determining way predicted by Japan's "reactive state" thesis (see chap. 1). Due to the structural power that the United States still disproportionately possesses in the world of finance, the alternative solution proposed by the Japanese government could not be sustained once the IMF and the United States (or Washington consensus actors) appeared on the scene during the second phase of crisis management. However, the central idea of the AMF—establishing a regional emergency fund—was never abandoned by the Japanese government or the governments of many Asian countries, and it reemerged in the third phase as the crises in Russia and Brazil took the focus of attention of the IMF and the U.S. government away from Asia.

Finally, institutional linkages seem to produce results in favor of transnational actors that can impose pressure across countries. The contrast between the Korean case and the Thai case has indicated that the interests of the transnational financial sector, especially commercial banks, swayed crisis management modality.

Conclusion

International Cooperation and Financial Crisis Management

Why do major powers engage in collective action to manage some financial crises but not others? How do nonhegemonic powers decide to support or not support such collective actions? With these questions in mind, this study has examined the factors that determined the behavior of the Japanese government and its private financial sector when confronted with major financial crises in the Pacific Rim over the past two decades. The cases include the Latin American debt crisis of the 1980s, the 1994–95 Mexican peso crisis, and the Asian economic crisis beginning in 1997.

This study has defined international financial stability as a prominent international public good that needs to be produced at the time of financial crises (see chap. 1). It also asserts that creditor government actions, particularly in the form of collective action, hold the key to some kinds of solutions to these crises. In crises arising from the middle-income countries incapable of stabilizing the situation by themselves, outside intervention and management is required. Otherwise, the crises could spread and destabilize the world of finance. In other words, the formation of collective action among the creditors is an important step toward providing international financial stability in the aftermath of a crisis.

Japan's involvement in crisis management has varied significantly across cases. Active involvement of the Japanese government, particularly in coordination with U.S. debt initiatives, helped solve the Latin American debt crisis by the early 1990s. But the Japanese government was reluctant to become involved in the Mexican peso crisis in the mid-1990s, despite substantial U.S. interest in resolving it. Finally, Japan's ambivalent and irresolute behavior during different phases of Asian crisis management has been puzzling, given Japan's much stronger interest in stabilizing Asian economic turmoil than in solving Latin America's economic problems. These observations of Japanese behavior led this study to analyze empirically the factors that determine these differences in Japan's behavior. Japan's collaboration is very important for the supply of international public goods. Japan has been a major provider of financial resources to middle-income developing countries over the past few decades (see chap. 2), and even during its prolonged recession beginning in the 1990s, Japan is still the largest creditor country in the world.

This study has organized around two interrelated hypotheses regarding various empirically specific factors that appeared to have influenced the behavior of creditor governments in financial crisis management. The first hypothesis states that financial crisis management often produces a joint product—a combination of private and public returns. The production of substantial private returns, such as domestic financial stability or improved bilateral relations with one's largest trading partner, would induce a creditor government to become actively involved in crisis management. The second hypothesis emphasizes the influence of transnational linkages among the private sectors of different creditor countries. In general, economic linkages arising from economic interdependence among major economic powers increase creditor governments' stakes in maintaining the economic stability of other countries, including major creditors affected by the financial crisis. The institutional linkages arising from international financial activities help establish subnational channels that transmit pressures from one part of the world to another; the strong domestic influence of these private financial sectors, in turn, affects the actions of the creditor governments in crisis management. This domestic dynamic also helps increase the private returns each creditor government receives from its active involvement.

As a result, the most favorable conditions for coherent collective action by creditor governments in financial crisis management arise when, on one hand, there are substantial private returns for a creditor government from its involvement and, on the other hand, there are strong and coherent transnational linkages among the private sectors, which augment pressure on the creditor governments to act collectively. The coalition of private sectors can transmit demands domestically to their respective home governments to obtain strong collective management of the crises.

The Latin American debt crisis provided these conditions for the Japanese government (see chap. 5), while the Mexican peso crisis lacked both of them (see chap. 6). The Asian financial crisis (see chap. 8), an additional case study of crisis management situated in a different region, has supported the thrust of two hypotheses but highlights the importance of the issue of power asymmetry between the two creditor governments, the United States and Japan. The regional contrast provides important insights into the dynamics among the major creditor powers interested, to a different degree, in their respective "backyards." This issue of regional arrangement is discussed further later in this conclusion.

In short, international cooperation or collective action among major powers for international solutions of financial crises emerges when the decision makers of the creditor countries find adequate private returns that drive their actions. The modality of crisis management needs to satisfy the creditor countries' private sector with its strong institutional linkage and domestic political power, adding significant private returns to the creditor governments' actions.

Other Explanations

Three common explanations regarding the possibility of collective action and public goods supply with particular focus on the number two power (like Japan in this study) are outlined in chapter 1. Having empirically examined the dynamics of the Japanese government's involvement in two financial crises in Latin America and one in Asia, it is time to revisit these theories to consider how they fare as explanations of creditor governments' behavior.

Systemic Explanation of International Cooperation

If international cooperation or supply of public goods in the world is maintained due to the emergence of an international regime, even after the relative decline of a hegemon, a pattern of financial crisis management should emerge under which any one of the major economic powers in the world would act consistently to resolve all crises. A particularly interesting puzzle that arises from this perspective is the Japanese government's active collaboration in the Latin American debt crisis case and its inactivity in the Mexican peso crisis. Furthermore, the shift of Japan's "leadership" position during different phases of the Asian crisis poses a challenge to the theory. These contrasts in Japan's behavior require a better explanation than the presence or absence of an international regime. Moreover, regime theory in the neoliberal institutionalist tradition states that an international regime should be strengthened through repeated interactions and accumulated experiences.[1] This did indeed take place through the IMF modality and other arrangements during the ten-year ordeal of the Latin American debt crisis and in the following crises. If such a regime existed and was strengthened through the Latin American debt crisis, becoming a major influence or intervening factor affecting the creditor governments' behavior, a stronger and more organized regime should have enhanced collaboration among the creditor governments at the time of the Mexican peso crisis and the Asian crisis. This did not happen.

Rational calculations by the members of a "k-group" might provide a basis for cooperation.[2] There are indications that the Japanese government deliberated the costs of international financial collapse, particularly in terms of the implications for Japan's vested economic interests. It seems apparent, however, that such an abstract, hypothetical notion of world financial collapse, with its unknown future costs, was not enough for the major powers in the "k-group" to act immediately or concertedly. Rather, the known and concrete private returns (which come from the calculation of the direct costs at the time of the crisis) and the tangible pressures thrust on creditor governments compelled their decisions.

As the contrast of the two Latin American crisis cases clarified, the Japanese government had much more to gain and faced stronger pressure—both domestically and externally—in the Latin American debt crisis. Staying aloof was relatively easy in the case of the Mexican peso crisis. This invites a modification of the "k-group" argument to include concrete and situation-specific diagnostics of costs and benefits for individual participants.

Japan's ambivalent position in the Asian crisis also casts doubt on the imminent formation of the "k-group." The Japanese government demonstrated, in the form of the AMF proposal, that a major power might sometimes initiate independent actions for the solution of crises without forming a "k-group." These plans could conceivably help manage the crisis (by providing public goods), but other powers could retreat from joining the scheme unless it satisfied their private interests. As discussed more extensively shortly, the very characteristics of power asymmetry among major participants in crisis management (the United States and Japan in this study) may occasionally deter the prospects of "k-group" formation.

Regionalism

If private returns gained through international financial crisis management drive the behavior of creditor governments, then when crises are regionally concentrated, a regional solution may be appropriate. But a few important factors could lead to cross-regional involvement of other creditor governments. These factors include strong institutional linkages among private financial sectors and the disproportionately strong impact many regionalized crises have with the region's major economic power. In addition, extraregional contagion, as it becomes apparent to extraregional powers, is an essential component of international finance.

As is evident from the case of the Latin American debt crisis, Japanese banks were heavily involved in Latin American lending due to supposedly risk-lowering financial instruments, such as syndicated loans and cross-default clauses. At the resolution stage of the crisis, such mechanisms as BACs prevented Japanese banks and many major banks from other parts of the world from exiting the Latin American debt. BACs successfully pressed the banks into minimum but meaningful involuntary lending. A mutually acceptable resolution of the Latin American debt crisis became the common goal for those private creditors involved, and such institutional linkage translated into pressures on their home governments, despite the regional unfamiliarity of these governments.

The second important factor leading to cross-regional involvement arises from the very fact that regional economies are much more integrated compared to cross-regional ones. The economic conditions and/or policies of major regional economic powers can trigger a regional crisis, and the regional crisis would be most detrimental to the economy of the regional superpower. In that sense, the Latin American debt crisis was typical in that the region was heavily influenced by U.S. economic policies but, at the same time, the crisis strained U.S. economic recovery in the late 1980s. The Asian crisis likewise illustrated the close economic linkages and interdependence between Japan and the Asian region.[3] In such circumstances, a regional solution that counts on unitary contributions from the regional power becomes more difficult, and support from other creditor governments, particularly those that have strong interests in the well-being of the regional power in question, becomes critical. In sum, in typical circumstances, the nature of regionalized crisis itself complicates a regional version of hegemonic stability theory as a valid solution. There are exceptions, however. The Mexican peso crisis was a case where, though it was partly brought on by the rise of interest rates in the United States in the spring of 1994, the regional power, the United States, was economically strong at the time it became involved in crisis management. In such a case, crisis management within the region is possible, and the need and ability of the regional power itself can deter others (with private returns in mind) from getting deeply involved.[4]

Additionally, two features of international finance make regionally based crisis management difficult. On one hand, the strong regional contagion of a financial crisis makes a regional fund like the AMF problematic at the time of crisis, as many countries in the region would be hit by market attacks at the same time.[5] On the other hand, the possibility of extraregional contagion makes it necessary for extraregional powers to intervene in the way a regional crisis is managed, though usually without providing major financial contributions to the solution. Furthermore, the strong ties among regional powers produce cross-regional ties, and the economic and political dynamics among these powers inhibit regional solutions (see the regional contrast later in this conclusion).

An Outside-In View of Foreign Policy Formation on the Unit Level

Overall, this study has supported the outside-in view, in which external environment and cross-border pressure has substantial impact on the behavior of major powers. It is evident that the financial crises forced the governments to react one way or the other. The policy outcome, however, results from a complex process through which effectiveness of transnational linkages and domestic political dynamics forms the direction of governmental interests.

Moreover, Japan is not always a reactive state. The case of the Mexican peso crisis has demonstrated that the Japanese government does opt not to follow or "react" to U.S. demands. Japan's move toward independent actions in the first phase of the Asian financial crisis and the emergence of management tensions between Japan and the United States in the third phase are additional examples of proactive or nonreactive moves by the Japanese. Common in these cases, when the Japanese government did not collaborate with the United States despite U.S. demand, are weak transnational linkages, in terms of both economic interdependence and institutional linkages among financial actors. Furthermore, Japan's occasionally ambivalent position in Asia also came from the country's diverse interests in Asian financial crisis management: Japan wanted both to support the U.S.-led solution and to demonstrate independent leadership by proposing alternative crisis solutions. The domestic political channels between Japan's financial sector and the government, which weakened in the latter half of the 1990s, made it even more difficult for Japan to adopt a coherent position as a creditor country, especially during the Asian financial crisis management (see chap. 8).

Regional Contrast

As the scope of the empirical cases expands from Latin American financial crises (see chaps. 3–6) to include the Asian crisis (see chaps. 7 and 8), a few important questions emerge. The questions have implications for the future refinement of the two major hypotheses of this study. One question regards the level of consistency in private returns produced through collective action in each case, and the other related question concerns the impact of the dynamics between the two regional powers, the United States and Japan, given the power asymmetry between them.

First, the Asian case has indicated that inconsistency in the set of private returns made it difficult for the Japanese government to form a solid crisis management position. The Latin American debt crisis case presented a straightforward set of consistent private returns that directed the Japanese government to act positively in crisis management in concert with the United States. Japanese banks (with strong transnational ties) demanded that the Japanese government support U.S. debt solutions, the U.S. pressured Japan to step up its commitment, and the Japanese government was interested in earning political points (both within the IMF and vis-à-vis the United States) through active involvement in support of the United States. The Japanese economic and central budgetary positions were quite strong, and the relationship between the majority party (LDP) and banks was close and stable. These Japanese actions faced no strong opposition among other, rather indifferent, private sectors.[6] Contributing to these factors was the time period of the crisis (the latter half of the 1980s): then, the Japanese economy was booming, creating strong trade tensions with the United States, and the Japanese government still had strong links to its private financial sector (see chaps. 5 and 6).

Another important element derives from regional variation. Japan's governmental and private sector interests in Latin America were historically limited (see chap. 2), and during the time of the crisis, Japan had very narrow and well-defined direct economic involvement in Latin America, consisting of scattered direct investment, but overwhelmingly large bank exposure throughout the region. In addition, Japan's concerns regarding the U.S. economy influenced the Japanese government's behavior during this crisis.

Asia presents a much more complex picture than Latin America, producing multiple and sometimes conflicting sets of private returns. In Asia, Japanese private sectors, both financial and real, have vital and vested interests (see chaps. 2, 7, and 8), and the Japanese government has economic and political ambitions to establish itself as an acknowledged leader in the region. Moreover, these various actors often enter into conflict in the context of deciding which type of returns should be pursued first and more vigorously. For example, at the time of the AMF proposal, the Japanese government wanted to demonstrate its resolute leadership role, in any way possible, before the Asian countries in crisis, particularly in the first phase, when U.S. presence was limited. The Japanese banks mostly hoped for added liquidity to Asia, allowing them to retreat from their exposure in the region without damaging these economies or their own long-term relationship with these countries. But some Japanese manufacturing firms, which have struggled to penetrate and compete in these Asian markets, expected increased liberalization via the IMF-led solution to the crisis. Such disagreement infused the Japanese government's action with surprising weakness and ambivalence, especially during the second phase of crisis management, when the AMF scheme was put to rest at least temporarily (see chap. 8).

In addition, the failure to establish the AMF exemplifies the existence of strong tensions between Japan's self-interests satisfied by its independent crisis management actions in the region and those satisfied by collective crisis management with the United States. This type of tension was never a prominent problem for crisis management cases in Latin America, in which Japan had a strong interest in improving U.S.-Japanese bilateral relations and in boosting U.S. economic health. In the Asian case, however, Japan as the regional power could not gain much support for its independent leadership to help solve the region's economic problems from the United States or, most of the time, from other creditor governments.

This leads to the second factor providing a clear regional contrast between Latin America and Asia: the dynamics between the two regional powers, the United States and Japan. As a financial crisis hits a region, a regional creditor government with higher stakes in the region first becomes engaged in crisis management. If this regional power can induce support from other creditor governments, collective action forms smoothly. If the power distribution among the major creditors is symmetrical, transnational linkages and economic interdependence should enhance creditor collaboration regardless of which major powers lead and which ones follow. But power distribution is rarely symmetrical, and in the five decades since the end of World War II, the United States has enjoyed unsurpassed structural power (see chap. 1). Collective action seems to emerge as long as the structural power leads and others follow. The leader-follower dynamic in the Latin America debt crisis was a clear case of this combination, in which Japan fairly consistently supported the U.S. leadership (see chap. 5).

The case of the Asian crisis introduces a reverse combination (see chap. 8). The United States, the structural power, is not the regional power in Asia, while Japan, a nonhegemon lacking structural power, is. As the crisis deepened, asymmetry of power frustrated the regional power, Japan, as it was forced to follow the lead of the United States in collective action. This frustration came about partly because Japan became torn between its interest in helping resolve the regional economic problem under its independent leadership and its interest in maintaining close relations with the United States. But the frustration also came from the fact that the Japanese government, despite its desire to present an alternative modality or solution to the Asian financial crisis, was highly constrained in doing so because there was no international institutional arrangement supporting Japan's initiatives.

Furthermore, taking advantage of the opportunity created by Asia's economic downturn, the IMF, with the support of the United States, actively attempted to "reform" the economic structures of many Asian countries to fit more closely "Western" models.[7] A bumper crop of discussions have emerged on how the "East Asian miracle" and the economic models that supported it failed and how "Western" models should become the dominant economic policy frameworks for these countries in the future.[8] Consequently, it has been argued, "[n]ot only will the new Asia that is struggling to be born look much more like America, but the United States will probably also find its international economic and political dominance enhanced."[9] As the Japanese government ventured to create a new modality to circumvent these challenges in the region, opposition from the established structural power was insurmountable.

The preceding discussion supports the validity of a triangular perspective as an analysis of the dynamics of international financial crisis management among creditor countries. Bilateral relationships (such as the one that exists between the United States and Mexico) can be a dominant factor in influencing creditor governments' decision making in crisis management, but the dynamics among creditor governments commonly shape the way an instance of crisis management, particularly a collective one, is conducted.

The regional contrast presents an interesting insight into the two hypotheses of this study. The case studies from the two Latin American financial crises (see chaps. 5 and 6) have demonstrated that two important factors—joint product and transnational linkages—are essential to understanding the determinants of Japanese collaboration with the United States. The first factor involves Japanese banks' exposure and Japan's direct stake in U.S. economic well-being, due to Japan's economic linkages and its desire to avoid excessive political pressure from the United States arising from Japan's significant trade surplus over the last few decades. The second factor involves the strength of institutional linkages that underscore the Japanese government's decision-making process, creating a unified front to pressure governments in the crisis. Both factors were strongly present in the Latin American debt crisis case, while there was only a weak presence of the first and near absence of the second in the Mexican peso crisis.

As the analysis of Japan's behavior extends to various phases of the Asian financial crisis management, direction as to how one can modify the hypothesis of joint product becomes clear. The Asian case adds support to the importance of the second factor, the presence of institutional linkages among creditors (see chap. 8). The impact of the first factor, however, becomes uncertain at best, because of the complexity of how one can define "private return." Japan's economic interdependence and linkages with the United States remain important for Japanese policymakers, but two elements made the Japanese actors less responsive to U.S. demands in the Asian crisis. On one hand, the United States did not require Japan's economic support at the time of the Asian crisis, because U.S. economic strength had consolidated by the mid-1990s. This is particularly so in comparison to Japan. Thus, economically supporting or boosting the U.S. economy became an unimportant factor for Japan's actions. The United States was not, however, very willing to support Japanese initiatives (such as the AMF) in the same way that Japan supported the U.S. solution in Latin America ten years earlier. On the other hand, Japan revealed an ambivalent attitude regarding crisis management modality, because the Japanese government became torn between its strong economic and political interests in Asia, divided interests among Japan's private actors, and its interests in maintaining its good relationship with the United States.

In short, the regional contrast in this study has helped illuminate how major nonhegemonic regional powers (i.e., major powers except for the United States) endure conflicting interests and structural pressures as they propose regional alternatives to preexisting international institutional, legal, and political arrangements. More research into this question would enhance our understanding of international public goods.

Looking into the Future

As financial globalization has closely integrated many economies in the world in the past two decades, concerns over international financial collapse have led policymakers to focus on the important question of how the world can manage the negative consequences of this process. Despite the continuing (or reemerging) dominance of the United States during this period, it is clear that the United States would not be able or willing to single-handedly manage major global (or even regional) economic crises, a reality that is reflected in the dynamics of both the Latin American debt crisis and the Asian financial crisis. The magnitude and multiplicity of financial transactions and the impact of resulting contemporary financial crises outstrip the management capacity of any single country. Although various international modalities and arrangements exist via IFIs to address international financial problems, the involvement and support of major financial powers is essential. International cooperation and collective action among major economic powers in international financial and monetary relations will thus remain crucial in the foreseeable future.

This study has found empirical evidence of a vital influence imposed by transnational linkages on the formation of collective action among creditor governments and of the strong incentives arising from the joint product nature of collective financial crisis management. These factors substantially influence the behavior of supporting powers, such as Japan. Furthermore, the power asymmetry among the major creditor countries and the associated possibility or impossibility of regional crisis management are intriguing issues when we think about the modality of future financial crisis management. The analysis of the Asian crisis has introduced us to these prominent new avenues for future research.

Although it is still premature to conclude where the tensions arising from this asymmetry will lead Japan, but one should not dismiss the role of nonhegemonic but major regional powers like Japan in formulating alternatives. The cold war is over, but at the same time, the "triumph of liberalism a la

Washington Consensus" seems still tentative.[10] Recent movement toward the establishment of a regional financial arrangement in Asia reveals that the Asian countries, particularly Japan, have learned from the experience of the Asian financial crisis of the detrimental consequences of lacking crisis management alternatives as they face the repercussions of increased financial globalization. In this context, the question of what constitutes an acceptable modality of financial crisis management or of international public goods provision among the major powers remains essential and in need of further investigation.

Appendixes

APPENDIX 1

Data Sources, Calculation, and Estimation of Five Multivariate Regressions

Models 1, 2, and 3: Time Series with Japan's ODA, OOF, and Private Capital Flows as the Dependent Variables

Dependent variables

JODA	OECD, *Geographical Distribution of Financial Flows to Developing Countries*
JOOF	OECD, *Geographical Distribution of Financial Flows to Developing Countries*
JPRV	Calculations from OECD, *Geographical Distribution of Financial Flows to Developing Countries*

Independent variables

ASIAID	OECD, *Geographical Distribution of Financial Flows to Developing Countries*
BUDGET	IMF, *Government Finance Statistics Yearbook*
CASURUS	Calculations from IMF, *Direction of Trade Statistics Yearbook*
DIFEX	IMF, *Direction of Trade Statistics Yearbook*
DIFINRT	IMF, *International Financial Statistics*
FILP	Bank of Japan, Research and Statistics Department, *Economic Statistics Annual*
FDIGR	MOF, *Kokusai Kinkyukyoku Nenpo*
GVBOND	U.S. Treasury, *Treasury Bulletin.*
JOFF	OECD, *Geographical Distribution of Financial Flows to Developing Countries*
JOUT	Japan Bond Research Institute, *Country Risk Information,* 1980–1982; MOF, *Kokusai Kinyukyoku nenpo (Annual report of the International Finance Bureau),* 1983–91; extrapolation for other years based on the region's total outstanding debt from OECD/BIS, *Statistics on External Indebtedness,* annual issues, and OECD, *External Debt of Developing Countries: 1982 Survey*
LDPSP	Asahi Shimbun, *Asahi Shimbun Seron Chosa,* various issues
LTFLW	U.S. Treasury, *Treasury Bulletin*
PORTF	IMF, *International Financial Statistics*
USAID	U.S. Agency for International Development, *U.S. Overseas Loans and Grants and Assistance from International Organizations*
USOUT	Federal Financial Institutions Examination Council, *Country Exposure Lending Survey*
YVSUSD	IMF, *International Financial Statistics*

Models 4 and 5: TSCS Models with Japan's ODA and OOF as the Dependent Variables

Dependent variables

$JODA_x$	OECD, *Geographical Distribution of Financial Flows to Developing Countries*
$JOOF_x$	OECD, *Geographical Distribution of Financial Flows to Developing Countries*

Independent variables

FDI	MOF, *Direct Investment Abroad by Country and Region*
GNPPC	World Bank, *World Tables,* annual issues
IMFWB	IMF, *IMF Survey;* World Bank, *Annual Report*
IMMIG	MOFA, *Japanese Emigrants and Their Destination*
JLOANO	Japan Bond Research Institute, *Country Risk Information,* 1980–88; intrapolation of outstanding debt to each country for other years based on the allocation of available years and total outstanding debt for these countries from OECD/BIS, *Statistics on External Indebtedness,* annual issues, and OECD, *External Debt of Developing Countries: 1982 Survey*
OPEN	National Bureau of Economic Research, *Penn-World Tables,* 1975–89 and linear extrapolation for other years
POP	National Bureau of Economic Research, *Penn-World Tables,* 1975–89 and linear extrapolation for other years
TRADE	IMF, *Direction of Trade Statistics Yearbook*
USAID	U.S. Agency for International Development, *U.S. Overseas Loans and Grants and Assistance from International Organization*
USTRD	IMF, *Direction of Trade Statistics Yearbook*

List of Latin American and Caribbean Countries in the Regression; Justification for Omission of Some Countries

Countries used in regressions

Argentina, Bolivia, Brazil, Chile, Colombia, Costa Rica, the Dominican Republic, Ecuador, El Salvador, Guatemala, Honduras, Jamaica, Mexico, Panama, Paraguay, Peru, Trinidad and Tobago, Uruguay, and Venezuela.

Countries omitted in regressions due to heavy missing data

The Bahamas, Belize, Bermuda, Cuba, Guyana, Haiti, Nicaragua, and Surinam.

Countries omitted due to small size, lack of information, or lack of relevancy

Anguilla, Antigua and Barbuda, Barbados, Dominica, Granada, Netherland Antilles, St. Christopher Nevis, St. Kitts, St. Lucia, and St. Vincent.

APPENDIX 2

Interviews and Contacts

Tokyo, Japan

Institutions	*Date(s)*
Asahi Shimbun	June 1998
Bank of Japan	April 1993
Bank of Tokyo	April 1993, May 1996
Bank of Tokyo-Mitsubishi	June 1997, June 1998
Bank of Tokyo Research International, Ltd.	May 1996, June 1997
Economic Planning Agency	April 1993
Embassy of Mexico in Tokyo	April 1993
Engineering Consulting Firms Association	May 1996
Export-Import Bank of Japan	April 1993, October 1995, May 1996, June 1997, June 1998
Hitotsubashi University	April 1993
Hose University	June 1997
Industrial Bank of Japan	April 1993, May 1996, June 1998
Institute for International Monetary Affairs	June 1998
Institute of Developing Economies	April 1993, May 1996, June 1998
Inter-American Development Bank Office in Tokyo	May 1996
International Monetary Fund, Regional Office for Asia and the Pacific in Tokyo	June 1998
Japan Bond Research Institute	April 1993
Japan Center for International Finance	April 1993, May 1996, June 1998
Japan International Development Organization, Ltd.	April 1993
Jochi University (Sophia)	April 1993, May 1996
Kobe University	May 1996
Long-Term Credit Bank of Japan	April 1993
LTCB Research Institute, Inc.	October 1995, May 1996, June 1998
Ministry of Finance	April 1993, June 1997, June 1998
Ministry of Foreign Affairs	April 1993, June 1998
Ministry of International Trade and Industry	April 1993
Mitsubishi Trust and Banking Corporation	April 1993
National Defense Academy	June 1998
Nihon Keizai Shimbun	April 1993
Nomura Research Institute	April 1993, June 1998
Overseas Economic Cooperation Fund	April 1993, May 1996
Temple University Japan	April 1993
Tsukuba University	April 1993
United Nations University	May 1996

University of Tokyo	April 1993
Waseda University	June 1998

United States (Universities Excluded)

Institutions	*Date(s)*
Federal Reserve Bank (Washington, D.C.; New York; Richmond)	April 1993
Institute of International Finance, Inc. (Washington, D.C.)	May 1997
InterAmerican Development Bank (Washington, D.C.)	April 1993
International Monetary Fund (Washington, D.C.)	April 1993, May 1997
Japan Center for International Finance, Washington representative office (Washington, D.C.)	May 1997
Japan Economic Institute (Washington, D.C.)	May 1997
Nikko Research Center, Inc. (Washington, D.C.)	May 1997
World Bank (Washington, D.C.)	April 1993, May 1997

Mexico

Institutions	*Date(s)*
Banco de México	December 1997
Bancomext	December 1997
Cámara Japonesa de Comercio e Industia de México	December 1997
Centro de Investigación y Docenca Económica (CIDE)	December 1997
Colegio de México	October 1992
Commisión Económica para América Latina y el Caribe, Mexico office	December 1997
Export-Import Bank of Japan	December 1997
Industrial Bank of Japan, Ltd., Mexico rep. office	December 1997
International Monetary Fund, Mexico office	December 1997
Japanese Embassy in Mexico	December 1997
Japan External Trade Organization	December 1997
Japan International Cooperation Agency, Mexico	December 1997
Long-Term Credit Bank of Japan, Ltd., Mexico rep. office	December 1997
Secretaría de Hacienda y Crédito Público	December 1997
Secretaría de Relaciones Exteriores	October 1992

APPENDIX 3

Sources of Statistics and News Data

Statistics

Asahi Shinbun, *Asahi Shinbun Seron Chosa,* various issues.

Bank for International Settlements, *The Maturity, Sectoral, and Nationality Distribution of International Bank Lending.* The publication title changed in the November 1998 issue to *BIS Consolidated International Banking Statistics.*

Bank of Japan, Research and Statistics Department, *Balance of Payments Monthly,* monthly issues.

Bank of Japan, Research and Statistics Department, *Economic Statistics Annual,* annual issues.

Export-Import Bank of Japan, *EXIM Japan Bulletin,* various issues.

Federal Financial Institutions Examination Council, *Country Exposure Lending Survey,* annual issues.

Financial Times Business Ltd., *The Banker,* July issue.

International Monetary Fund (IMF), Annual Report, annual issues.

IMF, *Balance of Payment Statistics Yearbook,* annual issues.

IMF, *Direction of Trade Statistics Yearbook,* annual issues.

IMF, *Government Finance Statistics Yearbook,* annual issues.

IMF, *IMF Survey,* various issues.

IMF, *International Financial Statistics,* annual issues.

Japan Bond Research Institute, *Country Risk Information,* various issues.

Japan Center for International Finance, *Shiryo: 82 Nen Iko no Ruiseki Saimukoku ni taisuru Kinnyu Shien Sochi Ichiran Hyo* (Tokyo: JCIF, 1991).

Ministry of Finance (MOF), *Kokusai Kinyukyoku Nenpo,* annual issues.

MOF, *Zaisei Kinyu Tokei Geppo,* various issues.

Ministry of Foreign Affairs, *Kaigai Zairyu Houjin su Chosa Toukei,* various issues.

Ministry of International Trade and Industry (MITI), *Kaigai Jigyo Katsudou Kihon Chosa: Kaigai Toushi Toke Soran,* various issues.

National Bureau of Economic Research, *Penn-World Tables,* annual issues.

Organization for Economic Cooperation and Development (OECD), *Development Co-operation: Efforts and Policies of the Members of the Development Assistance Committee,* annual issues.

OECD, *Economic Outlook,* annual issues.

OECD, *External Debt of Developing Countries,* annual issues.

OECD, *Geographical Distribution of Financial Flows to Developing Countries,* annual issues.

OECD, *Historical Statistics,* annual issues.

OECD and Bank for International Settlements, *Statistics on External Indebtedness: Bank and trade-related non-bank external claims on individual borrowing countries and territories,* semiannual issues.

United States Agency for International Development, *U.S. Overseas Loans and Grants and Assistance from International Organization,* annual issues.
United States Department of Commerce, *Survey of Current Business,* various issues.
United States Treasury Department, *Treasury Bulletin,* various issues.
World Bank, *Annual Report,* annual issues.
World Bank, *Commodity Trade Statistics,* annual issues.
World Bank, *Financial Flows to Developing Countries,* quarterly reviews.
World Bank, *Global Development Finance,* annual issues.
World Bank, *World Debt Tables,* annual issues.
World Bank, *World Tables,* annual issues.
World Event Interaction Survey [WEIS] Data, provided by Professor Rodney Tomlinson from the U.S. Naval Academy.

Publications from Government and Research Institutions

Ajia Keizai Kenkyujo (Institute of Developing Economics), "Mekishiko no Tsuka Kiki to Ajia he no Kyoukun," *Ajiken Kinkyu Report,* special issue, 1995.
Economic Planning Agency, "Ajia Tsuka Kiki Tokushu," *Economic Research,* special issue (June 1998).
Federal Reserve Board, "Bank Lending to Developing Countries: Recent Developments and Some Considerations for the Future," *Federal Reserve Bulletin* 70, no. 10 (October 1984): 755–83.
Helsinki World Institute, *The Potential of the Japanese Surplus for World Economic Development* (Helsinki: Helsinki World Institute, 1986).
Japan Center for International Finance (JCIF), *Kantori Risuku Mondai to Waga Kuni Kinyuu Kikan tou no Taiou* (Tokyo: Japan Center for International Finance, 1984).
JCIF, *Beikoku no Shin saimu senryaku to detto maketto* (Tokyo: Japan Center for International Finance, 1990).
JCIF, *Ruiseki Saimu Mondai no Genjou* (Toyko: Japan Center for International Finance, 1992).
JCIF, "Yomigaeru Raten Amerika," *Kikan Henkakusuru Sekai* 1 (1992).
JCIF, *Beikoku no Shin Chunanbei Senryaku to Seno Keizai heno Eikyou* (Toyko: Japan Center for International Finance, 1993).
JCIF, *Chunanbei Shuyokoku no Saimu Mondai to Shikinn Furo* (Toyko: Japan Center for International Finance, 1993).
JCIF, *Nishihannkyu ni okeru Chiuki Keizai Kyoryoky to Oubei shokokuno Taiou: Mekishiko Kinyuu Kiki no Eikyo wo fumaete* (Toyko: Japan Center for International Finance, 1996).
Japan External Trade Organization (JETRO), "Inversiones Directas Extranjeras de Japón y del Mundo," 1989.
Japan Productivity Centre, *Chunanbei: Keizai Toushi Kankyo Chosadan Hokokusho* (Tokyo, 1992).
Japan-United States Economic Relations Group. Memo from Tadayoshi Yamamoto to Jack Button on U.S.-Japan cooperation in economic assistance, August 8, 1980.
Ministry of Finance, *Kokusai Tokei Geppo,* monthly issues.
Ministry of Finance, *Wagakuni Shihon Yushutsu wo meguru Shomondai ni tsuite: Gaikoku Kawase tou Shingikai, Kokusai Kinyuu Torihiki ni okeru Shomondai ni kansuru Senmonbukai Chuuka Hokoku* (Tokyo: Kinyuu zaisei jijo kenkyukai, 1990).

Ministry of Foreign Affairs (MOFA), *Wagakuni no Seifu Kaihatsu Enjo,* annual issues.
MITI, *Wagakuni no Keizai Kyouryoku no Genjo to Mondai ten,* annual issues since 1971.
MITI, *Tsusho Hakusho* (White Paper on International Trade, [Soron, 1999]).
Overseas Economic Cooperation Fund (OECF), *OECF Research Quarterly,* seasonal issues.
OECF, *Annual Report,* annual issues.
United States General Accounting Office, "International Financial Crises: Efforts to Anticipate, Avoid, and Resolve Sovereign Crises," report to the chairman of the Committee on Banking and Financial Services, House of Representatives, GAO/GGD//NSIAD-97-168, June 1997.
United States General Accounting Office, *Mexico's Financial Crisis: Origins, Awareness, Assistance, and Initial Efforts to Recovery,* report to the chairman of the Committee on Banking and Financial Services, House of Representatives, GAO/GGD-96-56, February 1996.

Publications from International Organizations

Comisión Económica para América Latina y el Caribe, Naciones Unidas (ECLAC), *América Latina y el Caribe: Opciones para Reducir el Peso de la Deuda* (Santiago, Chile: CEPAL, 1990).
ECLAC, *Towards New Forms of Economic Co-operation between Latin America and Japan,* Cuadernos de la CEPAL, no. 51. (Santiago, Chile: ECLAC, 1987).
ECLAC, *La Evolución Económica del Japón y su Impacto en América Latina,* Estudios e Informes de la CEPAL, no. 70 (Santiago, Chile, 1988).
ECLAC, *Políticas Macroeconómicas y Brecha Externa: América Latina en los Años Ochenta,* (Santiago, Chile: CEPAL, 1989).
International Monetary Fund, *Determinants and Systemic Consequences of International Capital Flows: A Study by the Research Department of the International Monetary Fund,* IMF Occasional Paper 77, Washington, D.C., March 1991.
IMF, *International Capital Markets: Developments, Prospects, and Key Policy Issues,* 1997.
Sistema Economico Latinoamericano. (SELA), *Situación y Perspectivas de las Relaciones Económicas entre América Latina y el Japón* (Caracas: Ediciones de la Flor, 1987).
United Nations, "Foreign Direct Investment in Latin America: Recent Trends, Prospects, and Policy Issues," ST/CTC/SET.A/3, New York, August 1986.
World Bank, *East Asia: The Road to Recovery* (Oxford: Oxford University Press, 1998).
World Bank, *The East Asian Miracle: Economic Growth and Public Policy* (Oxford: Oxford University Press, 1993).
World Institute for Development Economics Research of the United Nations University, *Mobilizing International Surpluses for World Development: A WIDER Plan for a Japanese Initiative,* Study Group Series, no. 2 (Helsinki, 1987).

Magazines and Newspapers

Asahi Shimbun
Congressional Press Releases
Economist
Euromoney

Export-Import Bank of Japan Press Release
Far Eastern Economic Review
Financial Times
Foreign Broadcast Information System (FBIS) (*Bangkok Business Day, Bangkok Matichon, Bangkok The Nation, Hong Kong AFP, Korean Times, Kyodo News, Maeil Kyongje Sinmum, Nikkei Weekly*)
IMF Press Release
International Herald Tribune
JEI Report
Los Angeles Times
Minichi Shimbun
New York Times
Nikkei (Nihon Keizai) Shimbun
Wall Street Journal
Washington Post
Yomiuri Shimbun

Mimeographed Papers and Speeches

ASEAN+3 Finance Ministers, "Joint Statement of the ASEAN+3 Finance Ministers Meeting," Chiang Mai, Thailand, 6 May 2000.

Camdessus, Michel, "International Financial and Monetary Stability: A Global Public Good," speech made at the IMF/Research Conference on Key Issue in Reform of the International Monetary and Financial System, Washington, D.C., May 28, 1999.

Camdessus, Michel, "Prospect and Challenges in Our Globalized World Economy," speech made at the Wharton School of Business, University of Pennsylvania, Philadelphia on April 4, 1995.

Council on Foreign Exchange and Other Transactions (Gaikoku Kawase tou Shingikai), "Ajia Keizai, Kinyu Saisei Neno Michi: Nijuisseiki no Jizokutekiseicho to Tasouteki na Ikinai Kyoryoku Netto Waku no Kouchiku" (June 20, 2000, mimeographed).

Council on Foreign Exchange and Other Transactions (Gaikoku Kawase tou Shingikai), "Ajia Tsuka Kiki ni Manabu: Tanki Shihon Idou no Risuku to 21 Seigata Tsuka Kiki" (May 1998, mimeographed).

Ministry of Foreign Affairs (MOFA), "Misperception and Truth about Economies of Asia and Japan" (April 17, 1998, mimeographed).

Miyazawa, Kiichi, "Towards a New International Financial Architecture," speech made at the Foreign Correspondents Club of Japan, December 15, 1998.

Nagatani, Yashutaka, "Reisen-go no Keizai Kyoryoku" (Economic Planning Agency, 1993, mimeographed).

Sakakibara, Eisuke, "Reform of the International Financial System," speech made at the Minila Framework Meeting in Melbourne, March 26, 1999.

Terada, Kousuke, "1990 Nendai ni okeru Wagakuni no tai Chunanbei Seisaku" (Central–Latin American Department, Ministry of Foreign Affairs, 1993, mimeographed).

Yanagihara, Toru. "Ajia Tsuka Kiki to AMF he no Michi" (The Asian currency crisis and a road to the AMF). (Tokyo, ADB Institute, mimeographed).

Notes

Introduction

1. In this international economic environment, the ability of governments to manage their macroeconomic policies effectively is also constrained. For examples, see Keohane and Milner 1996; Cohen 1996; Andrews 1994.

2. For historical accounts of various financial crises, see Kindleberger 1989; Galbraith 1994. I acknowledge the general argument by economists that public intervention in the market has, in many cases, led to a moral hazard problem and thus may be more detrimental than a laissez-faire policy. However, the international financial market has also been known to be unstable. John Maynard Keynes, for example, advocated in the 1920s an international mechanism to provide a multilateral lender-of-last-resort function.

3. The recent financial crises include the Third World debt crisis of the 1980s (which continued for some countries into the 1990s), the 1987 Black Monday stock market crash, the 1992–93 EMS (European Monetary System) crises, and a major currency crisis in Mexico in 1994–95. Most recent has been the global crisis that began in several East and Southeast Asian (hereafter Asian) countries in 1997–98 and has since spread to Russia, Brazil, and elsewhere.

4. The basic definition of public goods has two parts: that they are jointly supplied and that exclusion is impossible. The first part means that one person's consumption of the good does not reduce the amount available for anyone else, and the second means that it is impossible to prevent relevant people from consuming it (see Hardin 1982, 17). On the international level, these goods are known to be the basis for the smooth operation of multilateralism and an open international economic order.

5. Charles Kindleberger (1989, 201) notes that in an international arena "with no government, no world central bank, and only weak international law, the question of where last-resort lending comes from is a crucial one."

6. Many scholars have tackled the question of peace and stability after the relative decline of the United States. Their explanations range from the formation of international regimes, to the role of privilege groups, to coerced cooperation.

7. This study focuses on the dynamics between Japan and the United States as an important component of international financial crisis management. However, the focus does not translate into the discussion on whose policy is right and whose policy is wrong. In addition, I have no intention of engaging myself in the polemic of keeping score as to which country is winning points and becoming the number one power in the world. From observing Japan's position in the world of international finance in recent decades, the study starts out defining Japan as a nonhegemonic supporting power in this issue area.

8. For discussion on Japan's role as a major economic power in the world, see Inoguchi 1988.

9. In a way, a major nonhegemonic power has strong relational power but not so strong structural power. See my discussion on this distinction in chapter 1.

10. Cooperation is generally defined as "when actors adjust their behavior to the actual or anticipated preferences of others, through a process of policy coordination" (Keohane 1984, 51–52). Cooperation also means something opposed to conflict.

11. For example, following requests from the Argentine government after it suffered from capital outflows and attack on its currency in the spring of 1995, the JEXIM Bank agreed to extend $0.8 billion in untied loans. In the summer of 1996, the JEXIM Bank signed an agreement for $0.5 billion in untied loans to Mexico at the time of the Japanese prime minister's visit to the country.

12. The New Miyazawa Initiative, announced in October 1998, would provide $30 billion in financial support to Asian countries in crisis. In December 1998, the revival of the AMF was once again suggested by Japan's finance minister (see *Financial Times,* December 16, 1998), and, finally, the regional fund scheme in the case of financial crises was officially agreed upon. The agreement on May 6, 2000 among the Association of Southeast Asian Nations (ASEAN) plus three members was called the Chiang Mai Initiative (see chap. 8).

13. In the 1994–95 Mexican peso crisis, the Europeans disagreed with the assertion by the Clinton administration that this crisis was systemic. This issue is discussed in chapter 6.

14. More theoretical discussion on this point is included in chapter 1.

15. Furthermore, although the nature of each crisis differs to some extent, the need for some kind of external intervention to contain and resolve the crisis remains the same.

16. Therefore, the distinction between public and private here does not correspond directly to the distinction between the state sector (public sector) and the private sector.

17. At the time of the Asian crisis, the United States enjoyed stability and growth in its own economy, but it had to respond to the fact that its major economic partner was hurt by the regional crisis, a factor that threatened the overall stability of the international economy.

18. For the first complete discussion of "complex interdependence," see Keohane and Nye 1977.

19. The first factor belongs to the hypothesis of joint product, and the remaining factors belong to the hypothesis of transnational linkages.

20. See King, Keohane, and Verba 1994, 3–7.

21. The typical example, particularly relevant to the issue of this study, is the sign of a coefficient. Suppose that Latin American country A received more foreign aid from Japan as its foreign aid receipts from the United States rose. The coefficient shows a positive sign. But does this mean that Japan is competing with the United States for influence in country A or that Japan is cooperating with the United States to help country A because it is considered important for the United States?

Chapter 1

1. Former managing director of the IMF Michel Camdessus also emphasized this notion of international public goods in his speech "International Financial and Monetary Stability: A Global Public Good" (IMF/Research Conference on Key Issue in Reform of the International Monetary and Financial System, Washington, D.C., May 28, 1999).

2. James Boughton (1997) discusses the historical role of the IMF as crisis manager. He argues that the IMF was only pulled in to deal with the crisis. The big turning point came at the time of the 1982 debt crisis, when the IMF was set in the center stage.

3. The problem associated with fungibility of economic resources is best described by David Baldwin in his discussion regarding foreign aid as a strategic good. When a good is fungible (freely exchangeable for or replaceable by another of like nature or kind in the satisfaction of an obligation), the good can contribute to something different from the intended use. For example, foreign aid disbursed by a donor to build a bridge in a developing country can be fungible. If there has already been some money set aside in that country for the construction of this bridge before the country receives aid, the economic resource provided from outside frees up the original budget, which would then be used for other purposes (see Baldwin 1985, 304). In the simplest case of bailout, funds provided by creditor government A can be used to pay back debts from private creditor B first. Thus, creditor B will benefit immediately while the benefit to creditor A is uncertain and probably less than that allocated to creditor B.

4. See Grieco 1988 on the theory of relative gains and international cooperation.

5. On the debtor side, the crisis management and bailout packages can often reward problem debtors. They mismanaged their economies, severely indebted themselves, and have not committed seriously to the country's economic reforms or its repayment obligations, both of which are often politically difficult. It is true that the rescue packages—above all, those implemented by the IMF—come with stringent conditionality and stabilization programs, but prolonged crises in relatively large countries, such as Brazil or Russia, give debtor countries much more leverage not to adjust. On the investors' side, such rescues may end up encouraging those investors and transnational banks to take repeatedly high risks in their investments and lending decisions. By creating the perception that they will be bailed out every time the financial crisis gets out of control, many critics argue, these bailout packages lower financial institutions' risk consciousness, thus increasing the likelihood and the magnitude of future financial crises. Incidentally, some argue that the action of creditors (particularly the U.S. government) in the 1995 Mexican peso rescue encouraged investors to be more aggressive in Asian investments and thus invited the 1997 Asian financial crisis. For further discussions of problems with rescue packages, see Goldstein and Calvo 1996.

6. See, for example, my discussion of the AMF scheme and of the criticism of the IMF in chapter 8.

7. For an excellent narrative of the negotiation on the form of new institutions, see Gardner 1980. See James 1996 on the evolution of the role of the Bretton Woods institutions from the time of their establishment through the present.

8. The Group of Ten (G-10: France, Germany, Japan, the United Kingdom, the United States, Canada, Italy, Belgium, the Netherlands, Sweden, and Switzerland) was actually the first group to form, in 1962, to organize an extraordinary lending system called General Arrangements to Borrow (GAB) via the IMF. The Group of Five (G-5: only the first five countries from G-10) came together in 1973 to provide a forum among the countries' finance ministers. G-7 (G-5 plus Canada and Italy) formed after the Tokyo Summit in 1986. From the Denver Summit (1997), Russia joined G-7 as a special member on political issues, leading some to address this group as the Group of Eight. The first summit among the heads of state was held in 1975. See Bergsten and Henning 1996, 18; James 1996.

9. For the classic texts on the hegemonic stability theory, see Kindleberger 1986b and Krasner 1976.

10. Robert Keohane's well-known discussion in *After Hegemony* (1984) emphasizes that international regimes play a key role in maintaining stability. Others attribute sta-

bility to collective action among major powers and to international cooperation; see, for example, Oye 1986.

11. Mancur Olson (1971, 35) notes that "there is accordingly a surprising tendency for the 'exploitation' of the great by the small." In addition, a hegemon can ensure that everyone plays by the rules.

12. See this point in Milner 1992, 480 and n. 26; Snidal 1985, 588–90. Also on the discussion of involuntary cooperation (coerced cooperation) involving economic sanctions, see Martin 1992.

13. Lisa Martin (1992, 15–45) provides a succinct contrast of the forms international cooperation take under different theoretical perspectives. The realist tends to see international cooperation as coercion by the strong, the liberal thinks cooperation occurs as a coincidence of interest, and the neoliberal institutionalist looks at cooperation as co-adjustment arising from mutual policy adjustment.

14. This perspective originates in Keohane and Nye 1977. In contrast to "realist" ideal types, complex interdependence emphasizes the interaction of subnational actors and argues against the assumption of security supremacy.

15. Peter Haas (1990, 55) coined the term *epistemic community,* defining it as "a professional group that believes in the same cause-and-effect relationships, truth tests to assess them, and shares common values. As well as sharing an acceptance of a common body of facts, its members share a common interpretative framework, or 'consensual knowledge,' from which they convert such facts, or observations, to policy-relevant conclusions."

16. Grieco 1988, 499–500; 1990, 47.

17. Krasner 1985, 3.

18. Here I follow the criticisms of regime theory by Susan Strange (1983).

19. Snidal 1985.

20. This is not to contradict the assumption of the anarchic nature of international relations. All students of international relations learn in IR101 that anarchy is not the opposite of order and that anarchy in the international arena means the lack of an overseeing world government. Some, such as Helen Milner (1992), argue this point to be problematic. In the context of my analysis, I am merely pointing out that units (states) in international relations are neither equally powerful nor equally motivated.

21. Robert Keohane and Joseph Nye (1977, 15) define this distinction earlier as process-level and structural-level power of interdependence, and they discuss sensitivity and vulnerability in a country's interdependent relationship with others.

22. Strange 1994, 24–25.

23. See Cohen 1977, 56–57. This point is discussed further in the section on regionalism that follows.

24. See Stallings and Streek 1995.

25. Discussion on international sources of regionalism includes functionalism and neofunctionalism, emphasizing the role of expansion of economic activities in regional economic integration. International institutions and ideational change can explain regionalization. But domestic interest groups and societal pressures can also promote regionalization. For a summary, see Mansfield and Milner 1997, 4–14. For summaries of various theories on regionalism, see Hurrell 1995.

26. See Yarbrough and Yarbrough 1994, 108; 1987.

27. For an application of club theory on regional arrangement, see Padoan 1997.

28. There are various nonregional arrangements among G-10 countries in the form

of the General Arrangements to Borrow (GAB) (see James 1996, 161–65). Recently, the New Arrangements to Borrow (NAB) was established to deal with balance-of-payments problems of emerging market countries.

29. In the case of Asia, discussion of this type of arrangement was widespread in the aftermath of the 1994 Mexican peso crisis, and some achievements were made in this area (see chap. 8). The currency swap lines established were, however, not sufficient.

30. Risse-Kappen 1995, 15–16.

31. Milner and Keohane 1996b. Benjamin Cohen (1996) discusses the contrast between outside-in and inside-out perspectives regarding the rise of financial globalization.

32. See Calder 1988.

33. The early work of T. J. Pempel (1978) and a new contribution by Frances McCall Rosenbluth (1996) provide alternative explanations focusing more on the domestic sources of foreign policy.

34. Schoppa 1993, 383.

35. This study distinguishes the two, when necessary, by calling the former "transnational institutional linkages" and the latter "economic linkages."

36. Stephany Griffith-Jones (1991, 111) notes that "stable external financial flows to fund development and stability of the banking system are 'public goods' that cannot be provided by private market agents acting individually." Although funds themselves are excludable and thus are not pure public goods, one can use such financial flows as necessary costs in providing public goods (i.e., international financial stability).

37. As I discussed earlier, classic collective action literature suggests that financial stability will always be undersupplied when there are many actors involved. The larger a group is, the more motivated its members will be to free ride on the public goods without contributing. See Olson 1971, 9–16. Note the argument of relative gains by Grieco (1990), who disagrees that a larger number of group members could enhance cooperation.

38. Sandler 1992, 11.

39. Lawrence Broz uses this analysis to explain the formation of the Bank of England (1998) and the Federal Reserve Bank (1999), and Leonard Dudley and Claude Montmarquette (1976) analyze foreign aid in this light.

40. Broz (1999, 40) notes that "the crucial requirement of the model . . . is that the private and public goods in question cannot be disaggregated due to some prevailing supply constraints." Although I agree with the importance of the "joint" nature of the product, I argue that if private goods can, by the very nature of their connectedness to the public goods supply, be most effectively or cheaply supplied when tied to public goods provision, there is a clear reason why the suppliers prefer the joint product to a separate one.

41. Logically, one can also argue the reverse sequencing of public goods–private goods provision and that creditor governments are much more concerned about providing public goods in terms of international stability so that, as the externality, their own private financial sectors can be saved from financial collapse (I thank Benjamin Cohen for pointing this out). I argue, however, that as a single creditor government decides its policy regarding crisis management, there is enough uncertainty as to whether or not sufficient stability would be produced through its own actions so that the government would not be driven initially or solely by the production of public goods.

42. Kenichi Ohmae (1991, x) notes that "[the Interlinked Economy] is becoming so powerful that it has swallowed most consumers and corporations, made traditional na-

tional borders disappear, and pushed bureaucrats, politicians, and the military toward the status of declining industry." David Andrews (1994, 197–203) notes that capital mobility is becoming a systemic constraint in international relations.

43. For further discussions on the way in which these new inventions facilitated capital flows to developing countries and invited the collapse of the world of development finance, see Wood 1986.

44. See Lipson 1985.

45. Devlin 1989, 217–18.

46. The issue associated with asymmetry of power is relevant here. Even though this type of economic linkage binds two major economic powers, the negative impact of the U.S. economic downturn influences the Japanese economy much more than vice versa. This asymmetry arising from the powers' bilateral relations in both economic and security realms, therefore, leads the Japanese government to act more on behalf of U.S. economic recovery than the other way around.

47. See Gourevitch 1978.

48. For details on the history of the Japanese government's role in forming Japan's economy, see Johnson 1982 and Hollerman 1988a.

49. Henrik Schmiegelow and Michele Schmiegelow (1986, 582) note that "the government can use instruments of domestic policy to stimulate, control, guide, and promote autonomous households and firms to save, consume, invest, or undertake research and thereby become, through such private actions, factors of structural change on the global scale."

50. See Spindler 1984, 121. Koichi Hamada and Akiyoshi Horiuchi (1987, 260) argue that coordination by the authorities *(nemawashi)* has created a situation in which most participants are prepared to conform smoothly to the new rules. The relationship between the Ministry of Finance (MOF) and the banks in Japan is also known as the "convoy system" *(goso sendan hoshiki).*

51. See, for example, Pempel 1987.

52. Evans 1992, 165.

53. See Stallings 1990b.

54. See Yamamura 1994 and Rosenbluth 1996 on how internationalized private sectors, such as large manufacturing firms and commercial banks, gradually won the support of the Liberal Democratic Party (LDP) over the domestic sectors, such as farmers and small and medium-sized businesses.

Chapter 2

1. There is some increase in the trend of Japan importing manufacturing goods from developing countries, particularly from Asia since the late 1980s. However, as Edward Lincoln argues (1993, 86), Japan's imports of manufacturing goods as a percentage of its gross domestic product (GDP) remains very low (3.8 percent in 1990) compared to other industrial countries, whose figures range from 7.8 percent (United States) to 50.8 percent (Belgium). In addition, the ratio of manufactured goods within the U.S. total imports (not GDP) have been higher (averaging 75 percent between 1990 and 1993) than that of Japan (averaging 46 percent between 1990 and 1991) (see OECD, *Handbook of International Trade and Development Statistics,* 1994).

2. See, for example, Rosecrance and Taw 1990; Helleiner 1989.

3. A comprehensive analysis of Japan's economic activities in developing countries is beyond the scope of this book. Recent books that focus on this issue include Koppel and Orr 1993; Nester 1992; Yasutomo 1995.

4. See Bergsten and Cline 1987; Bergsten and Noland 1993a.

5. Such a trade deficit is partly due to the increase of Japan's FDI in the region since the mid-1980s, through which the Japanese manufacturing firms overseas increased their imports of intermediate goods and inputs for production. Despite some increase in the amount of exports due to manufacturing production, the level of manufacturing exports from these Asian countries to Japan is still limited, particularly in comparison to that of the United States. See Bernard and Ravenhill 1995, 200–202; Naya 1990, 181.

6. See Lincoln 1993, 87–93.

7. See Pyle 1992 for detail. The gist of the so-called doctrine originated right after Japanese independence in 1952, when Japanese foreign policy rested on two pillars: (1) Japan will concentrate on its economic recovery and growth after World War II, and (2) Japan will minimize its military expenditure and resort to the U.S.-Japan security alliance for its defense needs.

8. See Teranishi 1986.

9. See Johnson 1995.

10. Historically, the Japanese government has preferred to refer to all of its financial flows to developing countries as "economic cooperation." This category includes funds from both the government and the private sector. In comparison to *foreign aid,* the term *economic cooperation* emphasizes Japan's comprehensive and multidimesional economic interaction with the recipient countries. Alan Rix (1980, 226) notes that the term *economic cooperation* constructs a program that would not be identified with the view of a single ministry and that it is more appropriate for the Japanese foreign aid administration, which is a consortium of several ministries. They include the four major ones (MOF, Ministry of Foreign Affairs, Ministry of International Trade and Industry, and Economic Planning Agency). In addition and as noted by Hanabusa (1991, 90), the government and private sector entities dealing with developing countries are considered "partners in development," as their interests have often converged.

11. Early writings include Rix 1980; Hasegawa 1975; Yasutomo 1986, 1995; Inada 1989; Orr 1990; Brook and Orr 1985. In the 1990s emerged a new generation, including Arase 1995; Ensign 1992; Katada 1997; Kato 1996, 1998; Miyashita 1999; Wan 1995.

12. Burma first reached an agreement on reparations with Japan in 1954; the agreement took effect in 1955. The Philippines (1956), Indonesia (1958), and South Vietnam (1959) followed. Additionally, Laos, Cambodia, Thailand, Burma (in addition to the previous agreement), and Korea received Japan's quasi-reparations grants during the 1960s. The last installment of reparations officially ended in 1977. See Hasegawa 1975 for accounts of Japanese foreign aid during these early years.

13. See Yanaga 1968.

14. Until 1961, Japanese foreign aid was implemented by the JEXIM Bank, which was set up in 1950 to encourage commercial banks to finance exports, imports, and overseas investment. In 1961, the OECF was established specifically to handle foreign aid loans. The two organizations merged in October 1999 and established the Japan Bank for International Cooperation (JBIC).

15. Throughout the 1970s, the OECD publication *Development Co-operation* kept mentioning that Japan's foreign aid failed to meet the terms recommended by the De-

velopment Assistance Committee (DAC), and the publication criticized that Japan's foreign aid had a very high concentration in Asia.

16. Brook and Orr (1985, 326) note that the concept of ODA was not firmly established until the early 1970s.

17. Aid-doubling plans were conducted in 1978–80, 1981–85, 1986–92, 1988–92, and 1993–97. See Arase 1995, 217.

18. However, due to Japan's high gross national product (GNP), the country has never met the UN target of ODA contribution relative to its GNP, 0.7 percent. Japan has always scored below average (0.3 percent) in this measurement.

19. Representative cases in the 1980s include Korea (1982), Egypt (1977–80, 1983), Jamaica (1980–83), Pakistan (1980, 1982, 1984), Sudan (1982, 1984), Ethiopia (1984), the Philippines (1984), China (1979, 1984), and some Central American countries (1985). See Orr 1988; Yasutomo 1986, 81–105.

20. See Brook and Orr 1985, 323.

21. MITI 1977, 123, my translation.

22. Yasutomo 1986, 5. The notion of comprehensive security has been best described by its advocate Prime Minister Ohira when he explained in July 1980 that the days were gone when Japan could count on an international system maintained single-handedly by the United States, either in the realm of military security, politics, and diplomacy or in that of the economy. He said that Japan must now contribute to the maintenance and management of the system as an influential member of the free world. There has been a shift from a world of "Pax Americana" to the world of "peace maintained by shared responsibilities" (cited in Pyle 1992, 206).

23. Japan-U.S. communiqué, May 8, 1981.

24. Inada 1989, 402.

25. See Kato 1996, 100–101.

26. OECF, *Nenji Hokoku Sho* (Annual Review) (1992), 13–14. In 1991, the only remaining tied loans are called "LDC tied," which means that only firms from the less developed countries (LDCs) or Japan can participate in the bidding. Some scholars argue, however, that there is still de facto tying of Japanese aid in many parts of Japan's development projects (see Ensign 1992). In addition, some Japanese industries pushed toward more "tied aid" in the late 1990s to increase their business opportunities (see chap. 8 in this book).

27. Japan became the top ODA donor for the first time in 1989. The United States apparently overtook Japan from 1990 through 1992, when Japan returned to the postition of number one aid donor. However, if you subtract the non-ODA debt forgiveness from U.S. ODA figures in these three years, Japan has kept its position as number one aid donor.

28. Another noteworthy issue in the first half of the 1990s is that in 1992, after facing long-standing criticism for not having a clear philosophy or guidelines for its foreign aid, the Japanese government announced its ODA Charter. The charter contains four pillars: (1) environmental protection and sustainable development; (2) no use of aid for military purposes; (3) diversion of ODA from countries that have excessive military expenditures, production of weapons of mass destruction, and arms trade; and (4) promotion of a market economy, democratization, and human rights.

29. For more on government-business relations in Japan's foreign direct investment in the Asia Pacific, see Hatch and Yamamura 1997.

30. The OECF has restrictions on its concessional loans to countries whose GNP per

capita is higher than an upper middle-income country as determined by the World Bank every year. In 1997, for example, the threshold for GNP per capita was $3,126.

31. Most of the JEXIM Bank's loan sources come from the Fiscal Investment and Loan Program (FILP). FILP consists of postal savings (which is 30 percent of Japan's savings deposits) and has traditionally been used to fund Japan's economic reconstruction. Due to Japan's economic recovery and the decreased need for infrastructure projects, the Japanese government was facing declining demands on this fund (sometimes called the Japanese government's shadow budget). During the mid-1980s, the MOF agreed to lend the excess liquidity of FILP to developing nations. Thus, the demand from indebted countries and the supply of JEXIM Bank untied loans happily met. See Calder 1997, 38.

32. For illustrations in various financial activities, see Schmiegelow and Schimiegelow 1986; Spindler 1984; Hatch and Yamamura 1997.

33. For discussion on the Japanese model of FDI in Asia, see Hatch and Yamamura 1997.

34. The compilation of FDI by notification to the MOF started in 1951. This statistic is the accumulation of 1951–80. See Jun et al. 1993, table A-4.

35. The aggregate amount of Japanese FDI in Latin America is quite deceiving: it is strongly dominated by Panama and other tax-haven countries where Japan has significant investment in finance and insurance as well as in flag-of-convenience ship registrations (see Jun et al. 1993, 17–19). In addition, a substantial amount of Japanese investment in Mexico has been made by Japanese subsidiaries in the United States and is not captured statistically as Japanese investment (interview with a Japanese businessman, Mexico City, December 1997).

36. One banker noted: "[the banks] felt that we were contributing to Japan's national interest by investing in these projects. We felt proud to work for the benefit of our country, since there was a sense of urgency to secure the source of minerals and oil through these projects" (interview with a Japanese banker, Tokyo, April 1993). Although bankers' feelings of patriotism spurred their involvement in these "national projects," the accompanying public financing also reduced their risk.

37. Akamatsu 1937.

38. Kojima 1978b; the definition of the "flying geese pattern" is from Bernard and Ravenhill 1995, 171. Bernard and Ravenhill argue that this pattern does not apply to Asian development.

39. Ozawa 1979.

40. See Encarnation 1992, 169.

41. See Encarnation 1992, 169–74; Yoon 1990, 13; Lincoln 1993.

42. See Yoon 1990, 12. In 1990, 41 percent of long-term debt to implement Japan's FDI in the manufacturing sector of Asia was financed by Japanese investors or Japanese banks, and the rate was 45 percent for Latin America (see MITI, *Kaigai jigyou katsudo kihon chosa* [1991], 33).

43. See Ozawa 1989.

44. See Frieden 1981.

45. The MOF officials thought that in comparison to FDI, capital flows in the form of bank lending were relatively free from potential friction and conflict in investment-receiving countries (or against other investors in these countries). See Fujioka 1979, 222, 248.

46. Fujioka 1979, 181, emphasis added.

47. See Spindler 1984, 182.

48. See Ozawa 1989, 41.

49. See Rosenbluth 1989, 52–95; Pauly 1988; Healey 1991, 131–34.

50. Nakao 1995, 63. This maturity transformation also enables banks to make financial profit from the difference between the short-term borrowing and long-term lending.

51. See MOF, "Wagakuni Shihon yushutsu wo meguru shomondai ni tsuite" (1990), 22. This was also pointed out by Healey (1991, 133–37).

52. See MOF, "Wagakuni Shihon yushutsu wo meguru shomondai ni tsuite" (1990), 51.

53. See Schadler et al. 1993. For discussions on push factors and pull factors of capital flows to developing countries, see Chuhan, Claessens, and Mamingi 1993; Fernandez-Arias 1996. Sylvia Maxfield (1998) contributes to the discussion of "push" and "pull" by adding the level of "patience" of different types of portfolio capital to developing countries.

54. For the conservative and illiquid characteristics of Japan's Samurai (yen-dominated) bond markets, see Shilling 1992, 98.

55. Chuhan and Jun (1995) list various explanations for why Japanese institutional investors were slow to tap into Latin American emerging markets, including Japan's administrative guidance that is conservative on political risk.

56. For example, Mike Mansfield, former ambassador to Japan, has repeatedly emphasized that the U.S.-Japanese relationship was the most important bilateral relationship in the world. See Mansfield 1989.

57. The two countries' combined economic weight in the world economy is significant, with the aggregate exports of the United States and Japan reaching over 20 percent of total world exports in the 1980s. These two countries have been the top two aid donors to developing countries since the mid-1980s. They also wield the top two voting positions in IFIs, such as the IMF, the World Bank, and the Asian Development Bank (ADB).

58. The well-cited literature on the U.S.-Japan relationship in the area of political economy includes Destler et al. 1976; Destler and Sato 1982; Bergsten and Cline 1987; Prestowitz 1988; Volcker and Gyohten 1992; Encarnation 1992; Bergsten and Noland 1993a; Iida 1993b; Schoppa 1997.

59. See H. Schmiegelow 1986, 222–38.

60. The emphasis of this book is more on the first and second dynamics and less on the third.

61. This study does not focus on the question of Japan's "leadership" role, and it assumes that there is a power asymmetry between the United States and Japan in the U.S. favor. Well-known scholars of Japan-U.S. relations have already produced a collective work on the analysis of U.S.-Japan leadership sharing (Sato and Destler 1996). In that volume, Sato defines leadership as "the initiative taking in leading or getting others to do what one wants them to do (or to move toward a certain goal)" (14). For further discussion on the different types of leadership, see Young 1991.

62. For a historical account of Japan's external economic policy from the 1950s through the mid-1970s, see Krause and Sekiguchi 1976, 411–40.

63. See Borden 1984; Schaller 1997.

64. Some have claimed that Japan is still a free rider, particularly in the field of international security, a trend well exemplified during the 1990–91 Persian Gulf crisis. For a discussion of the three scenarios of Japan's international role in relation to the United

States, in terms of Japan becoming a free rider, challenger, or supporter to the United States, see Inoguchi 1988.

65. Kindleberger 1986a, 9.

66. For example, see Nau 1990.

67. This was the time when Ezra F. Vogel's book *Japan as Number One* (1979) and his article "Pax Nipponica?" (1986) attracted the attention of the public from both the United States and Japan. Many anti-Japan campaigns emphasized the threat of Japan's economic dominance, see Fallows 1994.

68. The Japanese yen appreciated rapidly between 1985 and 1988, from ¥250 to ¥125 to a dollar; thus the relative strength of the yen against the U.S. dollar doubled within three years.

69. The information is compiled in Inada 1993.

70. See Ito 1993; Janow 1994. In this recent stage of U.S.-Japan trade negotiations, the revisionist perspective on the Japanese system is said to have influenced U.S. policymakers. The revisionists argue that Japan's unique domestic structure is maintained in such a way that it is difficult for any foreign goods to penetrate and reach its consumers; they thus argue that to change the trade imbalance, there has to be a clear target with which Japan must comply (see Ito 1993, 409; Uriu 2000). The revisionist perspective is best presented by Chalmers Johnson (1995).

71. Edward Lincoln (1993, 87–92) and others argue that Japan's lack of intra-industrial trade is making the "Japan problem" much worse than is indicated by the trade numbers themselves. Nevertheless, it is worth noting that thanks to a strong yen and to repeated trade negotiations, Japanese imports of U.S. manufacturing goods doubled between the mid-1980s and the mid-1990s.

72. For example, see Tyson 1992. David Richardson (1990) has a good overview of the main characteristics of strategic trade theory.

73. The U.S. trade dependence on Japan for certain goods like semiconductors has led to a serious discussion about the security threat this represents for the United States: Japan could potentially curtail this supply, affecting U.S. defense capabilities. See Morita and Ishihara 1989.

74. In terms of profitability per capital or asset, no Japanese banks rank high. Fukushima Bank is the only one that was ranked in the top ten (twice) around the mid-1990s.

75. Shigeo Nakao (1995) discusses two theories regarding the rise of Japanese banking in the 1980s: threat versus statistical exaggeration. The original argument on the "hegemonistic threat" comes from David Hale (1990). Others who discuss the threat of Japanese yen power in the late 1980s include Daniel Burstein (1988) and R. Taggart Murphy (1989).

76. Nakao 1995, 103.

77. Yamamura 1996, 29. Yamamura also continues to argue that the capital flow from Japan to the United States was further facilitated by Japan's developmentalist state policy to boost its economy with artificially low interest rates in the 1980s, a trend that led to its "bubble economy."

78. Interviews with Japanese bankers, Tokyo, June 1997.

79. For the details of the Yen-Dollar Agreement, see Frankel 1984.

80. For an excellent account of Japan's monetary policy, with strong emphasis on its exchange rate policy against the U.S. dollar from the 1970s through the early 1990s, see Henning 1994, 121–75.

81. For the details of the discussion, see Stallings and Streeck 1995, 85–87. See also World Bank 1993; Wade 1996b.

82. Rosecrance and Taw 1990, 208.

83. Helleiner 1989. Schmiegelow and Schmiegelow (1986) also note the importance of the dynamics between government and domestic actors in determining Japan's global power.

84. The original thesis is from Organski 1958, 300–316; the quote is from Chan 1993, 109.

85. For example, James Fallows (1989) calls for the need of "containing Japan."

86. See Calder 1988.

87. Asher 1996, 220.

88. The debate surrounds the "Japanese model of development" led by a strong bureaucracy. Many Japanese policymakers and scholars, such as Ryotaro Komiya (1996) and Eisuke Sakakibara (1997), as well as some American analysts, such as Peter Drucker (1993a, 1998), assert that Japanese fundamentals are still strong and that its bureaucracy can lead Japan, one way or the other, into future recovery. Also see a debate between Helweg (2000) and Mulgan (2000).

89. However, many American observers are attacking Japan's model as "what not to do" (Desmond 1997). The critiques include Posen 1998 and Lincoln 1998.

90. For an example of such criticism, see "Reviving Japan: Time to Wake Up," *Economist* 348, no. 8087 (September 26, 1998): 21–23.

91. See Kapstein 1989, particularly on the competitiveness of Japanese banks before the rule (327). Since this standard is not applied to those banks operating solely domestically (their capital-asset ratio guideline is 4 percent instead of 8), some banks, such as Nissaigin (Nippon Credit Bank), weakened by the recession and lack of profitability abroad, retreated from international operations.

92. The United States, however, started to pour its portfolio investments into the emerging Latin American markets, particularly in Mexico, where the United States was concluding NAFTA negotiations between 1992 and 1993 (they came into effect in January 1994).

93. The relationship is not merely one-sided. When the Daiwa Bank ran into problems due to its illegal dealing in 1995, the U.S. Federal Reserve offered to support the Bank of Japan in dealing with the financial sector problems.

94. See Padoan 1990.

95. For further bargaining analyses of debtor-creditor negotiations under the debt crisis, see Aggarwal 1996.

Chapter 3

1. See the discussion on public goods in chapter 1.

2. However, regression analysis involves costs, including difficulties in operationalizing concepts and data limitation.

3. The Third World debt crisis of the 1980s is not over for many severely indebted low-income countries, such as those in Africa. Hence, it makes more sense to limit the case to the Latin American region.

4. The definition and distinction between ODA and OOF did not become clear until the early 1970s. Currently the standard definition of ODA (or foreign aid) is the financial assistance provided by the public sector for development objectives and with higher

concessionality (25 percent of grant element or more). The official flows that lack the second and third components are considered OOF. In the case of the Latin American region, from 1975 to 1991, the proportion of ODA within the official financial flows has ranged between 40 and 60 percent. The source for these calculations is OECD, *Geographical Distribution of Financial Flows to Developing Countries* (various issues).

5. See Iyo Kunimoto, "Japanese Migration and Its Consequences in the Context of Modern Japanese-Latin American Relations" (paper presented at a conference "Agenda on the Pacific Rim" Northwestern University, October 16–18, 1997), 23, table 4.

6. A syndicated loan involves the combined activities of a number of banks (ranging from a few to 200) in the assembly of a relatively large loan to a single borrower under the direction of one or several banks serving as lead manager. See Smith and Walter 1997, 22.

7. Interviews with Japanese bankers, Tokyo, April 1993. Devlin (1989, 99–100) notes that the insertion of Japanese finance in Latin American lending since 1976 increased competition among lenders, lowering the loan spread.

8. The MOF seemed to be in favor of the Japanese banks becoming leading banks, since the banks could earn more commission fees this way, thus offsetting the low profit margin of overseas lending. In 1980, a qualitative guideline introduced by the MOF favored the banks' role as leading banks in syndicated loans.

9. Spindler 1984, 162.

10. Devlin 1989, 122.

11. Devlin 1989, 154, emphasis added. Devlin continues with an example: "Wells Fargo drew heavily on Japanese banks which contributed approximately one-third of the funds raised in syndication by this institution."

12. See appendix 1 for the list of Latin American countries included.

13. See the discussion in chapter 2. On the one hand, noticeable fungibility exists between ODA and OOF. They serve the same purpose when it comes to increasing Japan's financial flows to indebted countries. On the other hand, the stated purpose of and forces overseeing these respective flows are different, and thus they should be disaggregated.

14. Scrutiny on the use of FILP as well as its existence (which is argued to have crowded out private financing) has dramatically increased in the 1990s.

15. Due to the data constraints, I was not able to disaggregate flows of Japanese bank lending from OECD data or to find such data from Japanese sources. Therefore, the private capital flow variable includes any private capital flows except FDI.

16. The level of confidence at 2.5 percent for the two-tailed test changes from 1.96 (degrees of freedom higher than one hundred) to 2.228 (degrees of freedom of ten).

17. See Kennedy 1992, 247–67. See also Harvey 1990; Dickey and Fuller 1981; Engle and Granger 1987.

18. As noted in chapter 2, Richard Rosecrance and Jennifer Taw (1990) have argued the importance of Japan's increasing concerns for world affairs as the size of the Japanese economy has increased. Despite Japan's increasing economic power, however, the structure of the power hierarchy of international finance in the 1980s was not altered, with the United States remaining at the top.

19. However, OOF is financed largely by FILP. FILP was once added as a control variable in OOF regression, but due to its insignificance, it was dropped.

20. Jeffrey Sachs (1989b, 17) calculates that 25 percent of the deterioration in the U.S. trade balance in the 1980s was attributed to the collapse of international finance in Latin America.

21. The U.S. Congress urged Japan in 1987 to import more from Latin American countries to provide them with foreign exchange. The link between debt and trade increased the incentive for Capitol Hill to enact trade legislation against the Japanese. See *JEI Report* 29A (July 31, 1987).

22. For example, see Mototada Kikkawa, *Mane-i Haisen, Bhunshun Shinsho,* no. 2 (Tokyo: Bungei Shunju, 1998).

23. See, for example, Yamamura 1996.

24. See Mishkin 1992, 96–97. The expected return on portfolio investment (including bank lending) is determined by the interest rate differentials plus the spread to cover the risk factor and commissions that the financial institutions charge for these transactions. The ideal way to measure this interest rate differential is to compare the domestic discount rate, which is strongly related to the domestic interest rate for bank lending, to the international interest rate, usually represented by the LIBOR (London Interbank Offered Rate—the rate of interest offered on loans to first-class banks in the London Interbank Market for a specified period, usually three to six months) plus the specific margin. This is particularly relevant for the syndicated loans of the 1970s and early 1980s.

25. Additionally, Japanese banks' relations with Japanese multinational corporations might have influenced Japan's private capital flows to the region. Because of the "follow-the-customer" mentality of Japanese banks, Japanese corporations' overseas direct investment is thought to induce Japanese bank lending to a particular region or country (see Yoon 1990). The MITI reported in 1989 that in Latin America, $1 billion (45 percent) of $2.26 billion in long-term lending for Japanese direct investment to the region was financed directly by investors, while $0.7 billion (32.5 percent) was financed by the Japanese banks. Therefore, the hypothesis is that larger Japanese FDI in a particular region should lead Japanese banks to expand their financial activities in that region. This variable, however, had to be dropped from the regression due to a severe multicollinearity problem.

26. Interview with a Japanese banker, Tokyo, June 1997.

27. For a game theoretic analysis of bargaining dynamics among the debtors, the banks, and the governments, see Aggarwal 1996.

28. The F ratio for ODA regression (Model 4B) is 7.501 (critical value at 0.5 percent, 1.88), and that for OOF regression (Model 5b) is 9.413 (critical value at 0.5 percent, 2.10). See Kennedy 1992, 108–9; Chow 1960; Greene 1990, 211–14.

29. See Beck and Katz 1995. I also run these TSCS data using TSCS regressions (the Park method) and the Weighted Least Square method (suggested by Greene [1990]). The results, particularly the signs and significance of the important coefficients, are almost the same.

30. See *Wall Street Journal,* March 18, 1992. Fujimori's presidency attracted a significant amount of Japanese ODA. Peru ranked as the tenth largest Japanese ODA recipient in 1992.

31. Arrangements include the issuing of work permits in Japan, scholarships, and training (interview with a MOFA official, Tokyo, April 1993).

32. This FDI variable had to be dropped from the model due to a severe multicollinearity problem.

33. See Brook and Orr 1985, 325; Nakai 1989.

34. Various discussions on this issue can be found in government publications on economic cooperation and from the ODA Charter (*Seifu Kaihatsu Enjo Taiko*), announced on June 30, 1992.

35. There is a vast literature on the development model that Latin America pursued prior to the debt crisis (especially in comparison to the East Asian model) in terms of trade and industrial policies. For example, see Haggard 1990; Gereffi 1989. Also note Frieden 1981.

36. Interviews with Japanese bankers, Tokyo, April 1993. This notion of economic structural change can also be measured by looking at whether or not a country agreed to follow orthodox economic prescriptions under structural adjustment policies designed by IFIs, such as an SAL (Structural Adjustment Loan by the World Bank) or an SAF/ESAF (Structural Adjustment Facility and Enhanced Structural Adjustment Facility by the IMF). But when I ran regressions using these variables, they came out insignificant, so they were dropped.

37. For example, see Chenery and Strout 1966.

38. Obtaining permanent membership in the UN Security Council is noted to be one of the most important foreign policy goals of the MOFA in recent years (interview with a MOFA official, Tokyo, April 1993). Because the General Assembly of the United Nations adopts a one country–one vote system, the greater the number of countries that the Japanese government can influence is, the better its chances are.

39. No significant relationship was found between Japan's ODA allocation and its total trade with a Latin American country (Model 4, TRADE).

40. Note that since the variable measures difference between the U.S. and Japanese trade shares, DIFEX will be smaller as the Japanese trade share increases relative to that of the United States. Thus, the expected relationship between DIFEX and the dependent variable is negative.

41. Like DIFEX, YVSUSD is denominated in such a way that the Japanese yen is counted per dollar. Thus, as the yen strengthens, there will be fewer yen per dollar, making the expected relationship between YVSUSD and the dependent variable negative.

42. For ODA allocation (Model 4), the negative relationship between JLOANO and ODA is more prominent during the predebt crisis (Model 4Bb). This indicates that before the crisis, there was a clear division of labor between Japan's capital flows; that is, Japan's ODA refrained from going to some rich Latin American countries (prone to have accumulated more debt exposure to Japanese banks), while poor countries with more aid from Japan did not get much private financing.

43. Japan's ODA allocation to the Latin American region could be influenced by its ODA allocation to other regions (particularly influential is Asia, where usually more than 60 percent of Japanese ODA is allocated). Model 1C includes the variable of Japanese foreign aid to Asia (ASIAID), but it did not produce any significant results.

Chapter 4

1. Throughout this chapter, I distinguish between these two crises as the "1982 crisis," or "debt crisis," and the "1994–95 crisis," or "peso crisis."

2. On the strength of the synergy between the variable-oriented approach and the case-oriented approach, see Ragin 1987, 69–84.

3. All three concerns could have been addressed individually, but that would have been more problematic: helping the private financial sector would be problematic due to the negative reaction of the public if the government had to blatantly bail out banks; assisting the U.S. economy would be considered a problematic use of national resources

if done directly, and other solutions (e.g., opening Japan's agricultural market to boost its imports from the United States) are politically difficult; enhancing Japan's status in the international financial world would be difficult without a "deal" that would convince major powers in the IFIs to change the status quo in Japan's favor.

Chapter 5

1. Economists writing on this topic include Jeffrey Sachs (1984, 1989a, 1989b and 1989c), Benjamin Cohen (1986a, 1986b, 1992), Daniel Cohen (1991), Robert Devlin (1989), Jonathan Eaton and Mark Gersovitz (1981), Jack Guttentag and Richard Herring (1983), Suel Özler (1989), Jeremy Bulow and Kenneth Rogoff (1989), and John Williamson (1990b). Political scientists addressing it include Miles Kahler (1986b), Stephan Haggard and Robert Kaufman (1992b), Charles Lipson (1985, 1986), and sociologist Robert Wood (1986).

2. An article by Barbara Stallings (1990b) and Kinoshita 1991 are one of the two written in English on this subject. There are a few materials written in Japanese, including Tokunaga 1988; Yanagihara 1989b; and various publications from the Japan Center for International Finance (JCIF).

3. Unlike many earlier financial crises in which core countries unilaterally affected those on the periphery, this crisis was triggered by the developing countries' debts, and it pulled in major creditor countries because of these creditors' loan exposure. For a comparison of this debt crisis with early periphery financial crises, see Maddison 1985.

4. See Kraft 1984, 18–19; Volcker and Gyohten 1992, 201.

5. This $8.25 billion consists of $3.625 billion from the United States, $925 million from the BIS, and an additional $3.7 billion from the IMF (see Lustig 1996, table 1).

6. When the letter of intent for the IMF loans arrived on his desk, de Larosière insisted that there would be no IMF loans to Mexico without the commercial banks' commitment to that amount. Although his strategy received an angry response from commercial banks, it helped bring the commercial banks into the debt solution. This constituted the beginning of "concerted lending" headed by the IMF, a dominant form of rescue package operations in the 1990s as well.

7. Volcker and Gyohten 1992, 201.

8. From Latin America and the Caribbean, Argentina, Brazil, Chile, Costa Rica, Cuba, the Dominican Republic, Ecuador, Jamaica, Mexico, Nicaragua, Panama, Peru, and Uruguay concluded multilateral debt relief agreements during 1983–84 (see World Bank, *World Debt Tables,* 1994–95, 78–82).

9. See *Yomiuri Shimbun,* June 23, 1984.

10. The formal name of the Baker Plan is Program for Sustained Growth. The fifteen countries in the plan are Argentina, Bolivia, Brazil, Chile, Colombia, Ecuador, Mexico, Peru, Uruguay, Venezuela, Cote d'Ivoire, Morocco, Nigeria, the Philippines, and Yugoslavia. The coverage of the countries labeled as heavily indebted was later expanded to seventeen, including Costa Rica and Jamaica.

11. Many European banks were actually openly hostile to the plan (see *Toronto Star,* December 19, 1985).

12. See *Asahi Shimbun,* December 13, 1985. The banks emphasized that their support should be accompanied by the same effort by the debtor governments, creditor governments, international organizations, and other financial institutions.

13. Cline 1989. See also Cohen 1992, 156.

14. Nevertheless, the idea of debt reduction resonated among some policymakers (see *JEI Report* 29A [July 31, 1987]: 4–5).

15. This option exempted banks from new money obligations when they converted certain amounts of their outstanding loans to debtor countries' government bonds. This scheme was implemented to convert some debt for Argentina in August 1987.

16. For a good summary of the details of the first two programs, see Fujikawa 1988a. Some of the additional $20 billion was already committed before the announcement of the expanded program.

17. See *Washington Post,* April 23, 1987.

18. There was a discussion on the "additionality," as some people questioned how much of the money promised through this program was in addition to the amount of foreign aid and OOF that the Japanese government would provide anyway. They never reached a closure on this discussion, but many speculated that a numerical target of the recycling packages did help intensify the efforts of implementing agencies to provide more economic assistance to the countries in financial trouble, and as a result, the Recycling Program increased the amount of money given to these countries (interview with a Japanese economist, Tokyo, July 1999).

19. The idea of debt reduction was included as part of the "menu approach" of the latter half of the Baker Plan, but what was new about the Miyazawa Plan was that it also included heavy involvement of the IFIs' guarantees supported by the financial contribution of major creditor countries, especially Japan.

20. See Kinoshita 1991, 70–71. See also *JEI Report* 38B (October 7, 1988): 3–4.

21. See Cline 1989, 186.

22. See *Mainichi Shimbun,* June 14, 1988.

23. See Cline 1989, 186.

24. *Wall Street Journal,* October 14, 1988.

25. The U.S. administration was also concerned about Japan's increased influence in the IMF. See *New York Times,* September 28, 1988. In addition, there was a suspicion that the reason the Japanese were pushing for this scheme was because they wanted to arrange the deals to be more favorable to the Japanese banks (interview with an IMF official, Washington, D.C., May 1998).

26. See Rosenbluth 1991, 679–80. Jeffrey Sachs (1989b, 29) also mentions the same idea in his book.

27. Interview with a Bank of Tokyo banker, Tokyo, June 1997.

28. *Asahi Shimbun,* February 3, 1989.

29. President-elect Bush's speech on the debt problems and strategies on December 19, 1988, cited in Fujikawa 1990a, 15.

30. *Nihon Keizai Shimbun,* March 11, 1989.

31. Quote from Japanese finance minister Murayama, cited in Fujikawa 1990a, 16, my translation.

32. European banks were ready to accept some debt reduction, thanks to their large reserves and national regulatory policies that would offset the losses from debt reduction (see Lehman 1994, 209).

33. At the same IMF meeting, the United States reversed its previous position regarding an increase in Japan's IMF quota. It supported such an increase, which would move Japan's position up from the fifth largest quota (see *JEI Report* 15B [April 14, 1989]).

34. See Kinoshita 1991, 72; *JEI Report* 28B (July 14, 1989).

35. See Kinoshita 1991, 73. See also Japan Center for International Finance 1990, 16–26. Included in the $48.5 billion were $9.7 billion of Japanese commercial bank debt, but Japanese banks overwhelmingly preferred principal reduction (83 percent) and took no new money options.

36. I have divided my hypotheses into two groups, joint product and transnational linkage, for the purpose of theoretical clarity. However, this "domestic concern" component of Japan's private returns overlaps significantly with my following discussion on the transnational linkage. I here divide my discussion so that this section includes the situation under which government is actively involved in gaining such private returns (i.e., domestic stability and protection of its financial sector), while the next section includes the case of the Japanese government influenced by the pressures and demands of the private sector.

37. The MOF's role of protector of the banks is much more pertinent in Japan than in many other countries in the industrial world. Until very recently, Japanese banks had an implicit guarantee from the MOF that they would not go bankrupt (see Rosenbluth 1989, 112). Japanese policymakers and bankers call the relationship between the Japanese government and the banks a "convoy system."

38. See *Nihon Keizai Shimbun,* July 18, 1979.

39. See *Nihon Keizai Shimbun,* April 30, May 26, and December 26, 1977.

40. See *Nihon Keizai Shimbun,* December 9, 1979.

41. See *Nihon Keizai Shimbun,* January 16, 1982. The statistics are from Capital Loan Data Service, Ltd., of England, cited in the article.

42. More commission fees could offset the low profit margin of overseas lending. In 1980, a qualitative guideline introduced by the MOF favored the banks' role as leading banks in syndicated loans.

43. See Cline 1984, table 2.2.

44. This is noted by Robert Devlin (1989, 122). Andrew Spindler (1984, 201) also discusses that U.S. banks are sensitive to U.S. foreign policy and always try to guess which foreign countries carry an official "U.S. umbrella." In that sense, many Latin American countries—in particular, Mexico—do carry such an umbrella.

45. See *Nihon Keizai Shimbun,* September 19, 1982. Barbara Stallings (1990b, 7) notes: "Latin American loans were more important to Japanese banks than generally assumed. . . . Japanese exposure to Latin America was slightly *higher* than that of the United States." However, one must note that in the early 1980s, Japanese banks had a significantly lower rate of self-capitalization relative to American counterparts.

46. See *Nihon Keizai Shimbun,* November 25, 1983.

47. The total debt in Latin America is composed of about 60 percent in U.S. dollars, around 6 percent in Japanese yen, and the rest in other European currencies.

48. Part of the concern of the MOF came from the fact that it has been the Japanese banks' implicit guarantor to oversee that none of the banks would go bankrupt. However, there were real concerns regarding the Japanese banks' health, because of (1) the concentration of Latin American debt in a very few major banks, such as the Bank of Tokyo; (2) high exposure and low profitability of some of the Japanese banks' foreign operations; and (3) the thin buffer that most of major Japanese banks had against losses (again due to implicit MOF guarantee).

49. Interviews with Japanese bankers, Tokyo, April 1993. Japanese private capital flows to Latin America were fairly steady and positive until 1989 (see fig. 3.1).

50. See Kapstein 1989, 327; Rosenbluth 1989, 91.

51. See *Nihon Keizai Shimbun,* July 9, 1989.

52. Rosenbluth 1991, 684.

53. As noted by Jeffry Sachs (1989b) and mentioned in my chapter 3, 25 percent of U.S. current account deterioration was attributed to the Latin American debt crisis.

54. Jeffrey Sachs's paper on the impact of Japan's Capital Recycling Program on the improvement of the U.S. trade deficit was cited in Fujikawa 1988b. Sachs's research was said to have a noticeable impact on Japanese policymakers (interview with a Japanese economist, Tokyo, June 1996).

55. Interviews with Japanese economists, Tokyo, April 1993.

56. Senate Subcommittee on International Debt of the Committee on Finance, *Impact of the Latin American Debt Crisis on the United States,* 100th Cong., 1st sess., March 9, 1987, 114.

57. House Subcommittee on International Economic Policy and Trade of the Committee on Foreign Affairs, *The International Debt Crisis: A Review of the Brady Plan,* 101st Cong., 1st sess., April 19, 1989, 26.

58. At the congressional hearing, Treasury Department official Charles Dallara responded: "They [the Japanese] have assured us that this will be untied, and I can assure you that we will work closely with them to in the end try to avoid any inappropriate linkages here that might be developing" (House Subcommittee on International Economic Policy and Trade of the Committee on Foreign Affairs, *The International Debt Crisis: A Review of the Brady Plan,* 101st Cong., 1st sess., April 19, 1989, 26). On the Japanese side, Fujikawa (an MOF official) explains this untied nature to be an essential component of the Capital Recycling Program, so that "Japan will not lose credibility from other countries" (Fujikawa 1988a, 58, my translation).

59. The OECF has restrictions on its concessional loans to the countries whose GNP per capita is higher than an upper middle-income country as determined by the World Bank every year. In 1997, for example, the threshold for GNP per capita was $3,126.

60. See Fujikawa 1988a, 52.

61. For the details of Japan's increased FDI in the United States, see Encarnation 1992, 97–146, particularly 101, fig. 3.1. Also note table 2.3 from chapter 2 of the present book, indicating a significant increase of Japanese FDI allocation to North America (over 45 percent) in fiscal year 1985 and fiscal year 1990.

62. This voting power is set through discussions of the IMF executive board, based on the capital subscriptions of each country. See IMF, *Annual Report,* various issues, appendix 7.

63. On the point about the gap between Japan's burden sharing and its power sharing in IFIs, see Islam 1991, 221; Ogata 1989.

64. Ryokichi Hirono (1991, 178) notes that such reluctance also comes from the distrust that many of these governments had regarding Japan's ability to cooperate with them on the international financial and developmental matters in the IFI arenas.

65. Rapkin and Elston 1995, 14.

66. See Hirono 1991, 176; Rapkin and Elston 1995, 10.

67. The 45 percent increase in the overall IMF quotas after the Mexican peso crisis changed this slightly and put Japan (6.279 percent) in the second voting position, leaving Germany (6.135 percent) in the third (see *IMF Press Release* 97/63 [December 23, 1997]).

68. Interview with a banker from the Bank of Tokyo, Tokyo, June 1997.

69. See Stallings 1990b, 19.

70. Robert Devlin (1989, 122, 154) notes that well-informed American banks relied increasingly on inexperienced Japanese banks for syndicated lending during the few years before the debt crisis, while well-informed American banks stayed away from new Latin American lending before the disaster struck. Many Japanese banks increased their amount of syndicated loans in 1981 and 1982 and increasingly served as the leading bank of syndication (see *Nihon Keizai Shimbun,* January 16, 1982).

71. See Putnam 1988, 430; Schoppa 1993.

72. Frieden 1984, 153.

73. See Stallings 1990b, 20–22; *Nihon Keizai Shimbun,* November 26, 1983.

74. See Stallings 1990b; Rosenbluth 1991.

75. See Ramseyer and Rosenbluth 1993.

76. Despite the yen power of Japanese banks, the MOF was concerned about the weakness of the Japanese financial sector and believed Japan was not in a position to accrue significant losses on developing country loans (interview with a Japanese banker, Tokyo, April 1993).

77. See *Nihon Keizai Shimbun,* November 26, 1983. Information was also obtained through interviews with Japanese bankers, Tokyo, April 1993.

78. See Stallings 1990b, 20–21.

79. See *Asahi Shimbun,* March 20, 1987. The newspaper reported that the banks would continue demanding a higher rate of tax deduction for the loan-loss reserves to the government. Furthermore, a banker noted that the fact that the Japanese banks were reducing their bad loans in developing countries did not mean that they would start new loan activities there any time soon.

80. See Stallings 1990b, 20. Information was also obtained through interviews with Japanese bankers, Tokyo, April 1993. One interviewee mentioned that the system became institutionalized, and this stringent regulation on lending to developing countries discouraged Japanese banks from extending new loans to Latin America even into the 1990s. See also Latin American Information Services 1989, 61–62. Stallings (1990b, 17) also notes that the internal conflict between the Tax Bureau and the International Finance Bureau within the MOF made it difficult for the banks to achieve a tax deduction on their loan-loss reserve. The banks' demands were supported by the International Finance Bureau, which also pushed for the Capital Recycling Program discussed shortly.

81. Another book proposing debt reduction is Tokunaga 1988.

82. See Japan Bond Research Institute, *Country Risk Information,* various issues.

83. The three Brady Plan options are (1) to exchange debt for thirty-year interest reduction bonds at par (with a World Bank/IMF guarantee for repayment); (2) to swap the debt for thirty-year principal reduction bonds with 35 percent reduction in principal; and (3) to make new money commitments equal to 25 percent of the outstanding debt with no collateral.

84. Rosenbluth 1991, 682.

85. See Japan Center for International Finance 1990, 18. See also *Wall Street Journal,* February 7, 1990.

Chapter 6

1. *Wall Street Journal,* August 21, 1992.

2. "The Brady gamblers win, for now," *Economist* 326, no. 7798 (February 13, 1993): 73.

3. For a detailed analysis of the origin of the Mexican peso crisis (1994–95), see Sachs, Tornell, and Velasco 1996; Roett 1996a. For the Mexican perspective on the crisis, see Castañeda 1995.

4. See Bankers Trust Research, "Mexico Floats the Peso," *Emerging Markets,* December 23, 1994. According to the official figure from the Bank of Mexico, Mexico's foreign exchange reserve dropped to around $11 billion by December 16, 1994 (see Lustig 1996, 19).

5. The *Wall Street Journal* (February 3, 1995) reported very low currency reserve.

6. For a good summary of, evaluation of, and discussion of lessons from this Mexican Peso crisis, see Truman 1996, 199–209.

7. After the assassination of Mexican presidential candidate Colosio in March 1994, and as pressure on the peso increased due to political instability, Secretary Bentsen of the U.S. Treasury and Chairman Greenspan of the U.S. Federal Reserve set up a swap line of $6 billion. In April, the three parties of NAFTA signed an agreement to make this swap agreement permanent in the form of the North American Framework Agreement (NAFA). See Lustig 1996, 21–22.

8. *Nihon Keizai Shimbun,* January 4, 1995.

9. For a good summary of the U.S. initiative in assembling the Mexican rescue package (in both 1982 and 1995), see Lustig 1996. The United States General Accounting Office (GAO) has an official record of the U.S. assistance (1996, especially chap. 4). Consult also *IMF Press Release* 95/10 (Febuary 1, 1995).

10. The European governments were more concerned about Eastern Europe and their own economies at that time (see *Daily Telegraph,* January 30, 1995).

11. See Lustig 1996, 34.

12. A high-ranking former MOF official noted that the Japanese government was very supportive of the U.S. initiatives throughout the management of the Mexican peso crisis and that frequent phone discussions took place between the U.S. Treasury and the MOF in the early months of 1995. He noted, however, that there was not a direct request from the U.S. government for Japan to become more involved in bilateral financing for Mexico using its official resources (interview with an MOF official, Tokyo, June 1998).

13. *Kyodo News,* February 1, 1995 (via Foreign Broadcast Information Service [FBIS]).

14. See *Nihon Keizai Shimbun,* July 13, 1995.

15. See *Nihon Keizai Shimbun,* April 19, 1995.

16. In addition, Japan's MOF informed Japanese banks in January 1995 that they had removed the reserve requirement for lending to Mexico, a move completely opposite of what would be expected when considering the safety of bank lending in the country, whose risk had just increased significantly. The move also indicates an encouragement by the Japanese government to increase (or at least not decrease) Japanese lending to Mexico at the time of crisis (interview with a field representative of a Japanese bank, Mexico City, December 1997).

17. See *Export-Import Bank of Japan Press Release* 97-11 (September 1, 1997).

18. For an explanation of the Tequila Effect, see Truman 1996; Calvo and Reinhart 1996.

19. The Convertibility Plan was the key component of President Menem's economic strategy, which was launched in March 1991. This plan pegged the Argentine currency to the dollar at a rate of one Argentine peso to one U.S. dollar, and Argentine money supply was determined by the amount of its dollar reserve (otherwise called "currency

board"). This powerful policy instrument proved effective in coping with inflation, improving expectations of international investors, and enforcing fiscal discipline in the public sector. The plan did not, however, prevent the currency traders from attacking the Argentine peso, thus affecting Argentina's stock market when the financial environment became less favorable.

20. The measures included an international public relations campaign applauding the economy's good health and reiterating a strong commitment to the Convertibility Plan and provision of various safety nets to prevent bank closures.

21. See *IMF Press Release* 95/18 (April 6, 1995).

22. See *Nihon Keizai Shimbun,* April 1, 1995.

23. See *Nihon Keizai Shimbun,* April 29, 1995.

24. The sentiment among Japanese policymakers and investors was that Gurría was quite arrogant in dealing with the Japanese investors even as Mexico faced this crisis. It seemed quite clear that Gurría was confident that the United States would take care of this crisis and that Mexico would not need Japan's help in this case (interviews with people from the commercial banks and the government, Tokyo, May 1996). However, Japan's foreign minister Yohei Kono was reported to have rejected the Mexican foreign minister's request to use governmental influence over private banks to extend additional credit to Mexico (*Kyodo News,* January 9, 1995).

25. See *Financial Times,* January 12, 1995. It is important to note that the Mexican Peso crisis also shook Asian economies. On January 12 and 13, the Hong Kong dollar, the Indonesian rupiah, and the Philippine peso also came under attack.

26. Although some would disagree on this prediction, and although it is counterfactural and cannot be proven, the Japanese officials whom I interviewed in Japan (May 1995) had the sense that this Mexican crisis had a potential to become systemic.

27. See *Nihon Keizai Shimbun,* January 25, 1995.

28. The European governments' resentments were also presented when Germany, the United Kingdom, Switzerland, the Netherlands, Belgium, and Denmark abstained from supporting the IMF's Mexican rescue package of $17.8 billion on January 31 (see *Nihon Keizai Shimbun,* February 4, 1995).

29. Interview with a Japanese official, Washington, D.C., October 1995.

30. For a discussion on the impact of NAFTA on Japanese exporters and manufacturers, see Tsunekawa 1994.

31. See IMF, *Direction of Trade Statistics Yearbook,* 1995. Mexico's total trade with Japan declined from 6.6 percent in 1987 to 4.2 percent in 1994. For the United States, trade with Mexico occupied just below 6 percent in 1989, which increased to 9 percent in 1996.

32. President Bill Clinton also showed strong support for the idea of hemispheric integration and the Free Trade Area of the Americas (FTAA) during the Summit of Americas held in Miami in December 1994, just a few days before the Mexican peso devaluation.

33. United States General Accounting Office 1996.

34. In addition, Mexico's very new administration, which came into power less than a month before the crisis, had no expertise in identifying the channels and procedures to deal with Japanese public institutions (interview with a Japanese official, Washington, D.C., October 1995).

35. See Bank for International Settlements, *The Maturity Distribution of International Bank Lending.* Japanese banks arranged only two major new loans to Mexico in the early

1990s, totaling $450 million, both for Petroleo Mexicano. In addition, in 1992 there was a syndicated loan of $800 million to Petroleo Mexicano, the totality of which is covered by MITI insurance.

36. Thomas Biersteker (1995) discusses such changes in ideas influencing the economic policies of developing countries.

37. Nevertheless, if one compares the situation of the 1990s with that of the positions of the major debtors of the 1980s debt crisis, it is apparent that the option of turning to the Eastern bloc (or seriously considering such an alternative) or collectively defending the debtors' interests through collective action among the debtors seemed hardly feasible or practical even in the 1980s, as shown in chapter 5.

38. See, for example, Mochizuki 1997.

39. Some changes in the institutionalization of Asian regionalism are discussed by Donald Crone (1993) and Yoichi Funabashi (1993).

40. See Stallings and Streeck 1995. They call this arrangement "nonhegemonic interdependence."

41. David Asher (1996, 221) notes that the price-keeping operation (PKO) of the early 1990s was implemented by the MOF to support stock and land prices, which also tapped the state-controlled funds invested in the national pension, postal saving, and postal life insurance scheme.

42. The budget item for economic cooperation (ODA budget from General Account sources) steadily increased to 3.7 percent (FY 1994) and 3.6 percent (FY 1995) in yen terms. Economic cooperation was one of the few budget items that showed measurable growth during these years.

43. See Rapkin and Elston, 1995, 2–3.

44. See IMF, *International Financial Statistics,* 1995.

45. The deadline for complying with BIS capital adequacy requirements coincided with an overall decline of Japanese stock prices in the early 1990s. To meet the BIS deadline (March 1993) under its low self-capitalization ratio, banks were forced to cut back on their lending and repatriate some of their investment from abroad.

46. See *JEI Report* 31B (August 15, 1997); *Export-Import Bank of Japan Press Release* 97-11 (September 1, 1997).

47. See Purrington and A. K. 1991.

48. *Washington Post,* March 1, 1995. This debate continued well into the summer of 1995.

49. Interviews with officials from the MOF and the JEIM Bank, Tokyo, December 1997 and June 1996, respectively.

50. See Camdessus's speech "Prospect and Challenges in Our Globalized World Economy," given at the Wharton School of Business, University of Pennsylvania, Philadelphia. April 4, 1995.

51. See IMF 1997, 234–51.

52. Charles Kindleberger (1989) discusses various historical cases of this dynamic.

53. In addition, the lending rate was variable. The interest rates on loans were adjusted every three or six months according to the movement of the LIBOR. For more on new financial innovations that enabled the banks to extend long-term lending to developing countries, see Devlin 1989, 25–35.

54. Many argue that the resolution of the debt crisis and the resurgence of capital flows to Latin America are well connected via the Brady Plan. The plan allowed many major Latin American debtors to convert their bank debt to Brady bonds collaterized

with U.S. Treasury zero coupon assets (see Cline 1995a; Culpeper 1995). In addition, the stabilization and structural adjustment that many of these countries went through under the IMF and the World Bank led the Latin American governments to privatize much of their public or semipublic sectors, leading to an investment boom in their stocks and asset purchases.

55. See Goldstein and Folkerts-Landau 1994.

56. Cline 1995a, 427–28. The term *emerging market* actually came into use in the mid-1980s, when the International Finance Corporation (IFC) of the World Bank was trying to beef up support by private investors for a Third World investment fund. The first emerging market fund came out in 1986 and quickly became a boom (see *New York Times*, February 15, 1999).

57. Herzog (then Mexican ambassador to the United States), speech at the Conference on Financial Globalization and Emerging Markets: Policy Autonomy, Democratization, and Lessons from the Mexican Crisis, Brown University, November 18, 1995.

58. See, for example, Calvo, Leiderman, and Reinhart 1993; Fernandez-Arias 1996.

59. See Cline 1995a, 424–30.

60. See Ramirez de la O 1996.

61. See World Bank, *World Debt Tables*, 1994–95, 10. From the level of capital inflows, these countries include China, Mexico, Argentina, Thailand, South Korea, Brazil, Portugal, Malaysia, Turkey, Greece, India, Indonesia, Chile, Hungary, Venezuela, the Czech Republic, Poland, the Philippines, Colombia, and Peru.

62. In addition, due to the structure of some mutual funds, such as the Latin American fund, mutual fund investors hit by a major loss in Mexico had to pull out money from other places that constituted the same fund to compensate for the losses. Thus, they took capital out of such countries as Argentina regardless of the countries' creditworthiness or economic fundamentals. See Truman 1996, 202.

63. See *Nihon Keizai Shimbun*, January 7, 1995. The amount of $3 billion was discussed in informal consultations, and later the amount was reduced to $0.8 billion, when the formal request came from Mexico (see *Nihon Keizai Shimbun*, January 11, 1995).

64. Interview with a Japanese banker, Tokyo, October 1995.

65. Interview with a JCIF researcher, Tokyo, June 1995.

66. Interviews with Japanese bankers, Tokyo, April 1993. Some note that the internal structure of banks changes to accommodate the amount of business. Hence, more sections are now devoted to Asian business and very few to Latin American. Most of the bankers stress recent memory and the repeated failure of their businesses in Latin America and hold out little possibility that they will expand their operations in that region any time soon.

67. See Chuhan and Jun 1995, 92–94.

68. Japanese investors began getting into the Mexican market in late 1994, when American investors became cautious and the market was at its highest level (see *JEI Report* 2B [January 20, 1995]: 7–8).

69. For discussion on the party politics after the 1993 shift, see Kohno 1997.

70. See Mabuchi 1997, 338. However, the MOF's friends in the LDP have helped the MOF protect its core base in the reform efforts (see Hartcher 1998, 244–46).

71. See Hollerman 1988a; Pempel 1997.

72. See Yamamura 1994; Pempel 1997; Daniel Okimoto, "The Japanese Financial Crisis: A Need to Search for a New Paradigm?" (paper presented at the University of Cali-

fornia Conference on the Political Economy of the Japanese Financial Crisis, Los Angeles, February 26, 1999).

73. Pempel 1997, 348.

Chapter 7

1. By mid-2000, there seems to be a consensus that the Asian financial crisis is over (see *New York Times,* May 27, 2000; *Los Angeles Times,* June 3, 2000). However, this study, focusing on the international aspects of the Asian financial crisis, considers that the height of the Asian crisis, requiring financial crisis management, was over by the end of 1998. Nevertheless, some discussion on the future plans are still being held into the year 2001.

2. Based on the contrast between the two regions in the 1980s, several well-informed books were published. They cover regional industrial policies (Deyo 1987; Haggard 1990); economic adjustment (Nelson 1990; Haggard and Kaufman 1992b); and financial policies (Haggard, Lee, and Maxfield 1993).

3. The difference between the regions comes from the difference in the problems facing their respective economies prior to the crisis. Latin American countries faced the problem of macroeconomic fundamentals, leading to the balance-of-payments crisis. In Asia, the sudden loss of confidence by the international capital market, which was triggered by bankruptcies of banks and corporations in the region, led to the crisis. See Palma 1998, 800–802.

4. Many books have been written on the subject of economic regionalization in Asia in the 1990s, including Lincoln 1993; Funabashi 1995; Katzenstein and Shiraishi 1997; Nishijima and Smith 1996; Frankel and Kahler 1993; Hatch and Yamamura 1997.

5. Japan also appeared to pursue its narrow economic self-interest through its exports to these countries until the 1970s, which caused nonpurchase movements of Japanese goods in various countries. To improve Japan's relationship with Asia, the Fukuda Doctrine toward Southeast Asian countries was announced in 1977, stressing the equal partnership and mutual understanding between Japan and ASEAN countries. The Japanese government also dramatically increased its foreign aid to these countries from 1978. See Sudo 1988.

6. Even in the context of the Asian crisis, the presence of China as a counterweight or rival to Japan is a critical factor. See, for example, Funabashi 1995, 162–65. The decision of the Chinese government not to devalue its currency in the aftermath of the Asian crisis has been praised by the United States and other countries, making the Japanese government very nervous about China's increased positive role in Asia. In addition, although it is not extensively covered in this study, chapter 8 notes that the opposition of the Chinese government to the wider use of the yen and to the idea of a strong financial mechanism in Asia under Japan's leadership has made a regional solution of the crisis much more complex.

7. The 1994–95 Mexican currency crisis does not provide a good comparison in this sense, because the U.S. economy was quite fully recovered then, and the United States had a higher economic capacity to deal with regional crisis then than during the debt crisis.

8. The U.S. president, Bill Clinton, was cited as saying, before the APEC meeting in Vancouver, Canada: "We just want to be in a position to be supportive when we can, but

I think Japan can lead Asia out of this difficulty with the strength of its economy" (*New York Times,* November 25, 1997).

9. *Nihon Keizai Shimbun* has several articles (see, e.g., January 17, 1998; February 5, 1998) criticizing Japan's lack of initiative and active commitment in early 1998.

Chapter 8

1. There has been a debate between prominent economists regarding the costs and benefits of financial globalization for emerging market countries and the causes of the "financial crises of the twenty-first century." For a cautious view on the financial liberalization and its impact on developing countries, see Joseph Stiglitz (the World Bank's former chief economist), "Boats, Planes, and Capital Flows," *Financial Times,* March 25, 1998.

2. There are several interrelated aspects of the Asian crisis; its degree of severity depends on the country considered. Problems ranged from currency crises (immense devaluation and volatility of currencies); financial crisis, both domestic (stock market volatility and vulnerability of banking sectors, leading to credit crunches) and international (capital flight and accumulation of external debt); and other economic and social crises (bankruptcies, unemployment, social instability, political instability). In this chapter, I focus on currency and international financial crises in Asia.

3. One of the earlier publications addressing these issues is by Morris Goldstein (1998). Later came a book by Haggard (2000), edited books by Pempel (1999b) and Noble and Ravenhill (2000), as well as various special journal issues on the Asian crisis (e.g., *World Development* 26, no. 7 [1998]; *Cambridge Journal of Economics* 22 [1998]; *Brookings Review* 15, no. 3 [summer 1998]). In addition, see Krugman 1998; Wade 1998a, 1998b; Feldstein 1998; Sachs 1998; Fischer 1998; Noland, Liu, Robinson, and Wang 1998; Mallaby 1998; Kawai 1998a, 1998c; Huang and Xu 1999. Lastly, there have been numerous publications from the World Bank and the IMF, such as *International Capital Markets.*

4. For a descriptive analysis in English of the Japanese government's actions in the Asian financial crisis from the AMF to the New Miyazawa Initiative, see Hamada 1999.

5. To prevent a replay of the Mexico-type currency crisis, which also shook some currencies in Asia in 1995, the chairman of the Australian Federal Reserve Bank, Bernie Fraser, advocated an Asian version of the BIS. He envisioned a strong coordination mechanism among the Asian central bankers, with a bridge loan facility in preparation for regional financial emergencies. By November 1995, the Asian countries Thailand, Indonesia, Malaysia, Hong Kong, and Singapore (in December) joined an agreement for mutual cooperation to cross-support their currencies (see *Nihon Keizai Shimbun,* May 15, 1997).

6. See "Just what the doctor ordered?" *Economist* 344, no. 8027 (July 26, 1997), 73.

7. See *IMF Press Release* 97/33 (July 18, 1997). This EFF credit came in the form of an extension of the ongoing three-year EFF initiative of June 24, 1994, which was due to expire on July 23, 1997.

8. The Thai government was reportedly hoping to receive significant financial support from Japan without resorting to the IMF, but the Japanese government was insistent on having an agreement with the IMF as a precondition for Japan's additional financial support (*Bangkok Business Day,* July 31, 1997 [FBIS]).

9. See *Nihon Keizai Shimbun,* August 12, 1997; *IMF Press Release* 97/37 (August 20,

1997). Asian contributors to the package were Australia, Malaysia, Singapore, and Hong Kong at $1 billion each; Korea, Brunei, and Indonesia at $0.5 billion each; and later China at $1 billion.

10. *New York Times,* October 31, 1997. This point was also noted by many IMF officials whom I interviewed in Washington, D.C., in May 1998.

11. The U.S. Senate came up with a resolution preventing Washington from committing more than $1 billion in aid in any one year without congressional approval, unless the administration could prove the commitment vital to U.S. national interests. This amendment expired on September 30, 1997. See "Pacific Divide," *Far Eastern Economic Review,* November 6, 1997; *Congressional Press Releases,* August 8, 1995.

12. Quote of Japanese IMF deputy managing director Shigemitsu Sugisaki in *Bangkok the Nation,* August 12, 1997 (FBIS). Camdessus's comment in February 1997 on the possible regional arrangement to solve the regionalized financial crises reportedly helped form such an idea (interview with an MOFA official, Tokyo, June 1998).

13. *Nihon Keizai Shimbun,* August 19, 1997.

14. See *Hong Kong AFP,* September 18, 1997 (FBIS); *Nihon Keizai Shimbun,* September 23, 1997.

15. See *Nihon Keizai Shimbun,* September 22, 1997; "Rumpus in Hong Kong," *Economist* 344, no. 8036 (September 27, 1997): 15; "An Asian IMF?" *Economist* 344: 15, 84. For an analysis of the Japanese government's engagement in this unusually active and controversial initiative, see *JEI Report* 47A (December 19, 1997).

16. See *Nihon Keizai Shimbun,* September 22 and 23, 1997. Some even note that the very reason why the Japanese government pushed for the AMF scheme was to maximize its leverage in seeking more influence within the IMF. See Rowley 1997.

17. The most vocal advocate of this view is Malaysian prime minister Mahathir Mohamad (see *Nihon Keizai Shimbun,* September 14, 1997).

18. See JEI Report 47A (December 18, 1997), 8–9.

19. Actually, Tokyo gave up the idea even before this meeting (see *Kyodo News,* November 10, 1997).

20. See Rowley 1997, 1. The Manila Framework, an agreement reached during the APEC financial ministers' meeting, includes (a) establishment of a regional financial surveillance mechanism to complement global surveillance, (b) technical support to strengthen the financial sectors in each of the participating countries, (c) a call for increased IMF responsiveness in preparation for new financial crises, and (d) regional supporting mechanisms to complement the crisis management by IFIs, including the IMF. These components of the Manila Framework incorporate many of the ideas from the AMF scheme. See "Ajia tsuka kiki ni manabu," report by the Committee on Foreign Exchange and Other Transactions under the MOF, May 19, 1998, 13–14.

21. *Hong Kong AFP,* November 30, 1997 (FBIS).

22. Ever since that crisis, Thailand has been a vocal critic of the U.S. lack of interest in helping resolve economic problems in Asia. For example, see the "The Generosity of the United States, Our Great Friend, Is Even More Scarce in Time of Crisis," *Bangkok Matichon,* January 15, 1998 (FBIS). The U.S. government later became quite supportive of Thailand, because the country implemented relatively smooth economic adjustment programs and followed the IMF rules obediently, particularly in comparison to Indonesia.

23. See *Nihon Keizai Shimbun,* November 1, 1997. The *New York Times* (November 1, 1997) reported that the Clinton administration justified the U.S. financial commitment to help resolve the Indonesian crisis as follows: (a) to stop market contagion, particularly

to emerging market countries in Latin America; (b) to use this opportunity to further open the world market; and (c) to prevent market instability from turning into something more ominous. In addition, a State Department official noted that the U.S. financial contribution was "an untenable policy"; that is, "If you want to deal the cards, you have to buy some chips" (*New York Times,* October 31, 1997).

24. The "second line of defense" is a promise in which a central bank of a country in balance-of-payments difficulty could request a loan in reserve currency (usually in U.S. dollars). The central banks of the participating countries then deposit into the central bank account of the country in difficulty the amount of reserve currency committed. This idea was convenient for both the United States and Japan: the U.S. executive branch could commit a certain amount of money to the financial crisis management of Indonesia and still avoid a major fight with Congress (see *JEI Report* 42B [November 7, 1997]), and the Japanese government did not have to resort to the usual JEXIM Bank untied loans, as the JEXIM Bank's budget was depleted due to its financial commitment of $4 billion for the Thai case (interview with an MOF official, Washington, D.C., May 1998).

25. The second line of defense was constructed by bilateral funds, including contributions from Japan and Singapore ($5 billion each), the United States ($3 billion), and Australia ($1.43 billion). Other contributors included China, Malaysia, and Brunei. See *New York Times,* October 31, 1997; *IMF Press Release* 97/50 (November 5, 1997).

26. Martin Feldstein (1998) notes that the Korean financial crisis did not share the same nature as other crises of Asia during the fall of 1997.

27. The various sources of this information include *Korean Times,* November 15, 1997 (FBIS).

28. Major creditor governments, such as the United States, Canada, and Japan, were consulted for their bilateral financial support, but all of them advised the Korean government that it had to involve the IMF first (see *Nihon Keizai Shimbun,* November 21 and 23, 1997).

29. See *Asahi Shimbun,* November 22, 1997.

30. *Asahi Shimbun,* November 29, 1997; *Korean Times,* November 30, 1997 (FBIS).

31. First, the sum of the package was announced as $55 billion, but some European countries, such as Italy, joined the package later, expanding the total amount to $57 billion.

32. See *IMF Press Release* 97/55 (December 4, 1997); *Financial Times,* December 4, 1997. Some OECD countries did not specify the exact amount of their financial commitment. No Asian country participated in the financial rescue package this time. It is also worth noting that a part of the Korean rescue package represents the first time that the IMF used the Supplemental Reserve Facility (SRF) approved by the IMF board on December 17, 1997 (see *IMF Press Release* 97/59 [December 17, 1997]).

33. See *New York Times,* December 30, 1997.

34. See *Nihon Keizai Shimbun,* January 29, 1998.

35. In this system, the country fixes its exchange rate per dollar and determines the country's domestic supply of rupiah based on the amount of foreign currency it holds. This system, in effect, makes the country abandon all flexibility on its monetary policy and provides a full commitment to its fixed exchange rate.

36. See *Nihon Keizai Shimbun,* March 14, 1998. Although Washington has reportedly feared Japan's "soft" stance vis-à-vis Indonesia, one newspaper also speculated the possibility of a consultation between the United States and Japan regarding their respective

negotiation strategies with Indonesia (i.e., playing "good cop" and "bad cop" roles) while U.S. envoy Mondale made a several-hour stopover in Tokyo on his way to Jakarta (*Nihon Keizai Shimbun,* March 3, 1998). Later, the Japanese government also pledged $1 billion in JEXIM Bank untied loans to Indonesia on April 6 to entice the Indonesian government to reach an agreement with the IMF, which was realized two days later (see *Nihon Keizai Shimbun,* April 7 and 8, 1998).

37. See *JEI Report* 22B (June 12, 1998); *New York Times,* June 5, 1998.

38. Nevertheless, Indonesia continues to suffer from economic, political, and social instability, which caused concern among major powers in the realms of both economics and security into 1999.

39. For examples of domestic criticisms about the Japanese government's unresponsiveness and its banks' passive attitude and lack of initiatives, see, respectively, *Nihon Keizai Shimbun,* January 17 and February 5, 1998. On this view, see also *JEI Report* 8A and 8B (February 27, 1998). From the United States, the *New York Times* (February 22, 1998) noted, "the United States and its European allies have identified a new villain in the Asian financial crisis: not currency market speculators, not the crony capitalists of Indonesia and Korea, but the paralyzed Japanese government."

40. See *Nihon Keizai Shimbun,* February 23, 1998. Also, the United States has been frustrated by its mounting trade deficit against Japan. Commerce Secretary William Daley noted, "Japan has to understand the political reality in Washington, [in which] a soaring trade deficit and an election year are not a good mix for them" (*New York Times,* February 22, 1998).

41. See *Nihon Keizai Shimbun,* February 21, 1998.

42. See *Nihon Keizai Shimbun,* April 25, 1998; *New York Times,* April 25, 1998; *JEI Report* 17B (May 1, 1998).

43. Ministry of Foreign Affairs, "Misperception and Truth about Economies of Asia and Japan" (April 17, 1998, mimeographed).

44. Some academic discussions and publications were circulating during this time and a few months later. For example, on Japan's role in East Asia, see Kunimune 1998 and Tamaki 1998. In addition, the Japanese official position on the issue is reflected in "Ajia tsuka kiki ni manabu," report by the Committee on Foreign Exchange and Other Transactions, May 19, 1998. A whole series of publication has come out in 1999 and 2000 on the Asian crisis including Aramaki (1999), Hirata et al. (1999), Ito (1999b), Kunimune (2000), Kwan (1998), Shimazaki (1999), and Yoshitomi and Shirai (2000).

45. A publication by the newly established Asian Development Bank Institute (Yoshitomi and Ohno 1999) called for an alternative to the IMF's approach to financial crisis management. Actually, the one public figure who consistently pursued Japan's independent initiative in the Asian crisis management was then (and is now) Eisuke Sakakibara, then the MOF's vice minister of finance for international affairs.

46. In addition, massive withdrawal of Korean investment from Russia and lowering of oil prices due to the declining oil demand from Asia negatively impacted the Russian economy in 1998.

47. See *IMF Press Release* 98/31 (July 20, 1998). The Japanese government was the only bilateral financial contributor to this additional rescue package promising $1.5 billion through JEXIM Bank untied loans. The loan had already been promised to Russia in April (see *Nihon Keizai Shimbun,* July 14, 1998). See also *New York Times,* July 17, 1998; *Los Angeles Times,* August 18, 1998.

48. On July 28, 1999, the IMF approved a standby credit of $4.5 billion to support its

1999–2000 economic program (see *IMF Press Release* 99/35 [July 28, 1999]). The new loan was extended, reportedly, in order for Russia to avoid defaulting on international loans (see *Financial Times,* March 30, 1999; *New York Times,* March 30, 1999).

49. *New York Times,* October 25, 1998.

50. The IMF standby credit of $18 billion was approved on December 2, 1998. Other financial contributors included the World Bank ($4.5 billion) and the IDB ($4.5 billion). In addition, twenty or so creditor governments (including the United States and Japan), through or in coordination with the BIS, committed the total of $14.5 billion. See *New York Times,* November 13 and 14, 1998; *IMF Press Release* 98/59 (December 2, 1998); *Asahi Shimbun,* November 14, 1998).

51. See *Financial Times,* January 14, 1999; *New York Times,* January 15, 1999. The first devaluation came in the form of widening the monetary unit's band by 8 percent, and complete floating of the real came on January 18, 1999.

52. The Brazilian government and the IMF renegotiated their November package in March 1999 and agreed that $9 billion of IMF and other funds would be released (see *Financial Times,* March 9, 1999).

53. *Asahi Shimbun,* September 25, 1998. However, at the time of the Brazilian crisis, the *New York Times* (October 25, 1998) reported a comment of a U.S. official claiming that the fact that Germany and Japan were reluctant to part in its financial rescue package suggested that Latin America was becoming chiefly Washington's problem.

54. See *Nihon Keizai Shimbun,* October 1, 1998; *Washington Post,* October 1, 1998; *JEI Report* 37B (October 2, 1998). For the details and content of the initiative, see the MOF's Web page, <http://www.mof.go.jp.>. The list of countries covered in the plan was later extended to include Vietnam.

55. For example, after the U.S. Congress and Senate passed the subscription of $18 billion in capital to the IMF at the end of October 1998, the United States proposed a precautionary credit line including a capital increase of $90 billion in the IMF. The G-7 countries supported this. See *Financial Times,* October 31, 1998.

56. *Nikkei Weekly,* November 16, 1998.

57. The total amount of this AGRI fund also included contributions from the World Bank and the ADB. The U.S. money would support trade and investment in these countries, and Japan would provide at least $3 billion in addition to the already announced aid package of $30 billion through the New Miyazawa Initiative. See *New York Times,* November 18, 1998; *Nihon Keizai Shimbun,* November 17, 1998; *JEI Report* 44B (November 20, 1998).

58. See *Asahi Shimbun,* December 17, 1998. The Japanese government also stated that this financial aid would be tied to the recipient countries' procurement from Japan, to help Japan's private sector and boost its economy. Some Asian countries named as beneficiaries of the New Miyazawa Initiative had already been supported. The major financial support already indicated as of February, 2000 are to countries such as Thailand ($2.9 billion), the Philippines ($2.5 billion), Malaysia ($4.35 billion), and Korea ($8.35 billion), and Indonesia ($2.9 billion). See <http://www.mof.80.jp/english/if/e1e042a.htm> (downloaded December 5, 2000).

59. This bond guarantee package is sometimes called a "second stage" of the New Miyazawa Initiative. Japan's announcement came on May 15 at the time of the APEC finance ministers' meeting in Langkawi, Malaysia (see *Nihon Keizai Shimbun,* May 15, 1999; *Financial Times,* May 17, 1999). The JBIC was to be established on October 1, 1999, by merging the JEXIM Bank and the OECF.

60. Notable comments by the Asian leaders include one from Korean prime minister Kim Jong Pil on November 30, 1998 (see *Korean Times,* November 30, 1998), and another repeated by the Malaysian prime minister Mahathir Mohamad (see *Nihon Keizai Shimbun,* September 20, 1997). Even very recently on November 4, 2000, Thailand's finance minister supported the plan (*Asahi Shimbun,* November 5, 2000).

61. The $3 billion came from the fund that the Japanese government earmarked for the bond guarantee facility announced in May 1999.

62. See *JEI Report* 13B (March 31, 2000).

63. See Council on Foreign Exchange and Other Transactions (Gaikoku Kawase tou Shingi Kai) 2000. Appendix, 80–86 on the details of the scheme.

64. The upper house of the Japanese Diet passed the Financial Function Early Restoration Law on October 12, 1998, to help the banks get bad loans off their books and to enable the government to deal with bank failures. Although financial problems in Japan continued after the passage of this law, it set up the needed framework for the Japanese government to tackle the domestic crisis actively and systematically. See Amyx 2000 for an analysis of how financial crises in Japan are closely connected to troubles in Asia.

65. The weakened Asian currency helped Japanese companies export their goods produced in these countries to third markets. The MITI's survey indicates that 60 percent of respondents would not even rethink their Asian strategies because of the crisis, while 82 percent reported high hopes for developing production bases in these countries (ASEAN plus Korea) in the near future (MITI 1999, 165–71). Hatch and Yamamura (1997) characterize the uniqueness of Japanese FDI in Asia through a complex web of integrated vertical production networks.

66. See, for example, *Korean Times,* April 20, 1998; *Maeil Kyongje Sinmun,* February 10, 1998.

67. There have been some worrisome declines in the U.S. stockmarkets including the NASDAQ in the fall of 2000 and it is likely to lead to a major slowdown of the U.S. economy.

68. This point is illustrated by the first meeting between President Clinton and Prime Minister Obuchi, in September 1998. The key issue of their discussion was macroeconomic policy, which reflected U.S. concern about Japan's role in the Asian financial crisis (see *Journal of Commerce,* November 18, 1998).

69. Japanese direct investment in the United States (accumulated assets at the end of 1996) was $100 billion, slightly more than one-third of Japan's accumulated FDI assets abroad (see Bank of Japan, *Balance of Payments Monthly,* April 1997, 161).

70. As I noted in chapter 5, the BIS came to an agreement in December 1987 that member country banks (including Japanese banks) operating overseas would adopt a bank capital-asset ratio of 8 percent. Because the level of Japanese banks' capital was declining due to their weaker stocks, the agreement discouraged Japanese banks' loan extension.

71. The amount of bad loans (both nonperforming and extremely risky) granted by Japanese commercial banks is now reported to be between $600 billion and $1 trillion. The recuperation of these bad loans has become much more difficult due to Japan's declining and very low land prices. Most Japanese banks took land as their only collateral during the 1980s, because of its high value and the belief that prices would continue to rise. Facing these challenges, internationally weak banks like Nissaigin (Nippon Credit Bank) decided to limit their financial operations to Japan so that they could cut back on their overseas expenses, would not have to comply with the 8 percent BIS capital-asset

ratio, and thus could concentrate on regaining strength domestically. Some banks decided to weather the financial storms by either creating (or attempting to create) an alliance or by merging in part with financial institutions from the United States or Europe (e.g., Sakura Bank and Deutsche Bank, the Long-Term Credit Bank and the United Bank of Switzerland, the Industrial Bank of Japan and Travelers).

72. Even though there is still a high Japanese trade surplus against the United States, and even with Japan's financial retreat from the United States, the booming U.S. economy, with higher interest rates, created an environment of a higher dollar and a weaker yen particularly in 1997 into mid-1998. The shift from this trend came as the Russian and Brazilian crises hit the United States, and the U.S. Federal Reserve Bank (and other central banks in various European countries) lowered their interest rates between the summer and fall of 1998. The Japanese yen has appreciated significantly since the fall of 1998, raising questions about what is driving the appreciation (see *Financial Times,* January 7, 1999). The strong yen phenomenon is considered good for the Asian countries in crisis, because they can compete with Japanese goods much better in third countries and can also penetrate the Japanese market much more easily. However, it is devastating for many Japanese firms that were counting on the strategy of "exporting their way out" from severe recession.

73. Interview with an MOF official, Tokyo, June 1998.

74. Interview with an MOF official, Tokyo, June 1998. Actually, this view contradicts a comment from a former manager of the Bank of Tokyo who conveyed that he had been a part of discussion on the AMF idea from the beginning to the end. I have no way of telling who is exaggerating his point. In any case, even the Bank of Tokyo manager mentioned that due to the limited participation of the Japanese banking sector in the formulation of the scheme, the MOF could not create a framework that rallied the private sector to support and participate "on a voluntary basis" (interview with a former manager from the Bank of Tokyo, Tokyo, June 1998).

75. See Wade's debate on the Asian and IMF solutions (Wade 1998b). A particularly strong initiative was also taken by Vice Minister Eisuke Sakakibara of the MOF.

76. Interviews with a few Japanese bankers (Tokyo, June 1998) revealed that even though most of them did not publicly convey this reaction, they welcomed the possibility of having a large fund available to "bail them out" of the crisis.

77. See the interview article with a former president of Nissho Iwai, a Japanese trading company, in *Asahi Shimbun,* November 6, 1997.

78. *Asahi Shimbun,* September 20, 1997.

79. A very similar debate took place more than twenty years ago between the IMF and the OECD, on the Financial Support Fund idea presented by the OECD. See Cohen 1997, especially 14.

80. See *JEI Report* 47A (December 19, 1997), 9–10.

81. An IMF official noted that the ideas from the AMF survived within the IMF's structural change mandated in the Manila Framework and that, in a sense, it was a progressive step taken through the AMF (interview with an IMF official, Tokyo, June 1998).

82. For an analysis regarding the perspective of Japan's finance minister Kiichi Miyazawa on the need of a new and different architecture, see Yanagihara 1999.

83. See Wade 1998b, 1545–47; *Financial Times,* February 26, 1998.

84. Wade (1998b, 1540) maintains that the main and economic reason why these countries established more leveraged economies was because of their high household savings. Since the only way these ordinary people channel their savings into investment

is via banks, banks tend to have a strong incentive to lend to companies for their returns. Thus, this creates a high debt ratio of firms. World Bank researchers pointed out the possible danger of Asian financial sector weakness before the outbreak of the Asian crisis; see Claessens and Glaessner 1997.

85. However, the bank lending of the 1990s has a higher weight of project lending than do syndicate loans, which might loosen transnational linkage due to the structure of the loans.

86. Obviously, this phenomenon is nested in a larger issue of how important the financial crisis was to the international financial community overall. The more widely spread the repercussion felt among various creditor countries was, the stronger the concerns of the systemic impact were.

87. Interviews with Japanese bankers, Tokyo, June 1998.

88. See, for example, Asher 1996, 218; Mabuchi 1997, 14.

89. This is called a price-keeping operation (PKO), as noted in chapter 6, footnote 41. For details, see Asher 1996, 221–22; Wood 1994, 103–6.

90. The MOF, which wanted to be freed from the LDP's reign, gained its power by dealing with and guiding the inexperienced Morihiro Hosokawa cabinet and allying with "reformer" Ichiro Ozawa's new party in 1993. Its bet of breaking loose from the LDP in 1993 turned around to haunt it within a year, as the LDP along with the Social Democratic Party and the Sakigake Party regained coalition majority and began "revenging" the MOF for betraying the LDP during its most trying times.

91. In 1995, the collapse of Hyogo Bank, the scandal surrounding Daiwa Bank, and corruption charges against MOF officials rocked Japan's financial sector. The major case of mismanagement came at the time of the Jusen (housing loan companies) rescue, which required ¥685 billion of taxpayers' money from fiscal year 1996. See Suzuki 1996, 21; Mabuchi 1997, 6–28.

92. See Hartcher 1998, 156–57.

93. Major corruption charges in early 1998 alleged that MOF officials were "treated" by bank employees in exchange for information about the MOF's bank inspection details (*JEI Report* 9A [March 6, 1998]).

94. An official "liaison conference" was set up by Prime Minister Hashimoto in early February 1998 so that financial firms and the MOF could have a new forum in which to exchange information and opinions on financial issues on a regular basis (*JEI Report* 9A [March 6, 1998]: 9–10). However, many bankers noted that such a formal setting would not allow them to convey the frank opinions or sensitive information that they used to discuss in the after-work "drinking" setting (interviews with Japanese bankers, Tokyo, June 1998).

95. Stallings 1990b, 18–19.

96. There have been some efforts by both the Japanese government and the Bank of Tokyo-Mitsubishi to preserve such a function. For example, a new research institution, the Institute for International Monetary Affairs (IIMA), was established in December 1995, fully funded by the Bank of Tokyo, with a prominent former MOF official as the president, to analyze international monetary and financial issues (interviews with former Bank of Tokyo managers, Tokyo, June 1998; see also the IIMA website, <http://www.fastnet.ne.jp/iima>, for its prospectus).

97. See *Washington Post*, December 28, 1997.

98. See *New York Times*, December 31, 1997.

99. See *Washington Post*, December 28, 1997.

100. Interview with a former manager from the Bank of Tokyo, Tokyo, June 1998. There was a meeting of an international bank consortium at the end of January 1998, when short-term loans amounting to $24 billion from foreign banks to Korea, due in 1998, were given extensions of one to three years (see *Nihon Keizai Shimbun,* January 29, 1998).

101. Interviews with Japanese bankers (especially the ex-manager of the Bank of Tokyo), Tokyo, June 1998.

102. Interviews with a Japanese financial journalist and bankers, Tokyo, June 1998. See also *Asahi Shimbun,* December 20, 1997.

Conclusion

1. See Keohane 1984.

2. As I discussed in chapter 1, a "k-group" is an intermediate group of major powers that engages in collective action to provide public goods in the absence of a clearly dominant single hegemon. See Snidal 1985.

3. Interestingly, though not analyzed in this study, more elements of competition (e.g., trade) occur in the Japanese relationship with Asia than in U.S.–Latin American relations.

4. As I discussed in chapter 5, the U.S. Congress grew concerned that by making a large financial commitment to Latin America, Japan might threaten U.S. economic interests in the region. From this discussion, it was clear that a sense of "territory" or turf exists for the United States in Latin America.

5. As in the case of earthquake insurance, when everyone in a region gets hit by a disaster at the same time and claims their payments, the insurance system does not work (interview with an IMF official, Mexico City, December 1997).

6. The Mexican peso crisis presents a clear opposite picture from the Latin American debt crisis, in which case the Japanese government did not see much, if any, private returns from active engagement and thus was very reluctant to act.

7. Wade (1998b, 1545–47) calls the agent of such scheme "the Wall Street–Treasury–IMF complex." See also Bhagwati 1998.

8. See, for example, *New York Times,* January 17, 1998. For a critique against such arguments, see Wade 1998b.

9. *International Herald Tribune,* January 20, 1998.

10. Fukuyama 1992. On the implication of this triumph and of the Washington consensus on developing countries, see Biersteker 1995.

Bibliography

Aggarwal, Vinod K. 1987. *International Debt Threat: Bargaining among Creditors and Debtors in the 1980s.* Policy Papers in International Affairs, no. 29. Berkeley: Institute of International Studies, University of California.

———. 1993. "Building International Institutions in Asia-Pacific." *Asian Survey* 33, no. 11:1029–42.

———. 1996. *Debt Games: Strategic Interaction in International Debt Rescheduling.* Cambridge: Cambridge University Press.

Akamatsu, Kaname. 1961. "A Theory of Unbalanced Growth in the World Economy," *Weltwirtschaftliches Archiv* 86, no. 1.

Alesina, Alberto, and Geoffrey Caliner, eds. 1991. *Politics and Economics in the Eighties.* Chicago: University of Chicago Press.

Allison, Gary D., and Yasunori Sone, eds. 1993. *Political Dynamics in Contemporary Japan.* Ithaca: Cornell University Press.

Amyx, Jennifer. 2000. "Political Impediments to Far-Reaching Banking Reforms in Japan: Implications for Asia." In *The Asian Financial Crisis and the Architecture of Global Finance,* ed. Gregory W. Noble and John Ravenhill, 132–51. Cambridge: Cambridge University Press.

Andreoni, James, and Martin C. McGuire. 1993. "Identifying the Free Riders: A Simple Algorithm for Determining Who Will Contribute to a Public Good." *Journal of Public Economics* 51:447–54.

Andrews, David. 1994. "Capital Mobility and State Autonomy: Toward a Structural Theory of International Monetary Relations." *International Studies Quarterly* 38, no. 2:193–218.

Aoki, Akira. 1989. "New Directions for Japan's Economic and Financial Cooperation with Latin America." Background paper presented at the Fourth Latin America–Japan Business and Financial Cooperation Symposium, Nagoya, Japan, November 12–14.

Aramaki, Kenji. 1999. *Ajia Suka kiki to IMF: Gurobaraizeshon no Hikari to Kage* (The Asian Currency Crisis and the IMF: The Light and Shadow of Globalization). Tokyo: Nihon Keizai Hyoron sha.

Arase, David. 1995. *Buying Power: The Political Economy of Japan's Foreign Aid.* Boulder: Lynne Rienner.

Arndt, Sven W., and J. David Richardson, eds. 1987. *Real Financial Linkages among Open Economies.* Cambridge: MIT Press.

Aron, Raymond. 1967. "What Is a Theory of International Relations?" *Journal of International Affairs* 21, no. 2:185–206.

Aronson, Jonathan David. *Money and Power: Banks and the World Monetary System.* Beverly Hills: Sage, 1977.

Arredonado, Maria Luisa. 1989. "Aumenta la Influencia de Japón en América Latina." *Visión,* March 6, pp. 6–15.

Asher, David L. 1996. "What Became of the Japanese 'Miracle.'" *Orbis* 40, no. 2:215–34.

Aspe, Pedro, Andres Bianchi, and Domingo Cavallo. 1992. *Sea Changes in Latin America.* New York: Group of Thirty.

Axelrod, Robert. 1981. "The Emergence of Cooperation among Egoists." *American Political Science Review* 75, no. 2:306–18.

Axelrod, Robert, and Robert O. Keohane. 1985. "Achieving Cooperation under Anarchy: Strategies and Institutions." *World Politics* 38, no. 1:226–54.

Ayakawa, Masako. 1990. *Soren, Touou, Chunanbei no Saimu to Kinyuu.* Tokyo: Touyou Keizai shinpo sha.

Balassa, Bela, and Marcus Noland. 1988. *Japan in the World Economy.* Washington, D.C.: Institute for International Economics.

Baldwin, David A. 1985. *Economic Statecraft.* Princeton: Princeton University Press, 1985.

Barbone, Luca. 1988. "Import Barriers: An Analysis of Time-Series Cross-Section Data." *OECD Economic Studies* 11 (autumn): 155–68.

Beck, Nathaniel, and Jonathan N. Katz. 1995. "What to Do (and Not to Do) with Time-Series Cross-Section Data." *American Political Science Review* 89, no. 3:634–47.

Berger, Suzanne, and Ronald Dore, eds. 1996. *National Diversity and Global Capitalism.* Ithaca: Cornell University Press.

Bergsten, C. Fred, and William R. Cline. 1987. *The United States–Japan Economic Problem.* 2d Rev. ed. Washington, D.C.: Institute for International Economics.

Bergsten, C. Fred, and Randall C. Henning. 1996. *Global Economic Leadership and the Group of Seven.* Washington, D.C.: Institute for International Economics.

Bergsten, C. Fred, Robert O. Keohane, and Joseph S. Nye Jr. 1975. "International Economics and International Politics: A Framework for Analysis." *International Organization* 29, no. 1:3–36.

Bergsten, C. Fred, and Marcus Noland. 1993a. *Reconcilable Differences? United States–Japan Economic Conflict.* Washington, D.C.: Institute for International Economics.

———, eds. 1993b. *Pacific Dynamism and the International Economic System.* Washington, D.C.: Institute for International Economics.

Bernard, Mitchell, and John Ravenhill. 1995. "Beyond Product Cycles and Flying Geese: Regionalization, Hierarchy, and the Industrialization of East Asia." *World Politics* 47, no. 2:171–209.

Bhagwati, Jagdish. 1998. "The Capital Myth: The Difference between Trade in Widgets and Dollars." *Foreign Affairs* 77, no. 3: 7–12.

Bienen, Henry, ed. 1992. *Power, Economics, and Security: The United States and Japan in Focus.* Boulder: Westview.

Biersteker, Thomas J. 1995. "The 'Triumph' of Liberal Economic Ideas in the Developing World." In *Global Change, Regional Response: The New International Context of Development,* ed. Barbara Stallings, 174–96. Cambridge: Cambridge University Press.

Bird, Graham. 1987. *International Financial Policy and Economic Development: A Disaggregated Approach.* New York: MacMillan.

———. 1989. *Commercial Bank Lending and Third World Debt.* New York: St. Martin's.

Bloodgood, Laura S. 1993. "The Politics of Sovereign Debt Rescheduling: A Comparative Analysis of the Brazilian and Mexican Negotiations." Paper presented at the annual meeting of the American Political Science Association, Washington, D.C., September 2–5.

Borden, William S. 1984. *The Pacific Alliance: United States Foreign Economic Policy and Japanese Trade Recovery, 1947–1955.* Madison: University of Wisconsin Press.

Borrow, Davis B., and Stephen R. Hill. 1991. "Non-Military Determinants of Military Budgets: The Japanese Case." *International Studies Quarterly* 35, no. 1:39–61.

Boughton, James. 1994. "The IMF and the Latin American Debt Crisis: Seven Common Criticisms." IMF Paper on Policy Analysis and Assessment 94/23, Washington, D.C., October.

———. 1997. "From Suez to Tequila: The IMF as Crisis Manager." IMF Working Paper 97/90, Washington, D.C., July.

Bouzas, Roberto. 1996. "The Mexican Peso Crisis and Argentina's Convertibility Plan: Monetary Virtue or Monetary Impotence?" In *The Mexican Peso Crisis: International Perspectives,* ed. Riordan Roett, 71–92. Boulder: Lynne Rienner.

Boyer, Robert. 1996. "The Convergence Hypothesis Revisited: Globalization but Still the Century of Nations?" In *National Diversity and Global Capitalism,* ed. Suzanne Berger and Ronald Dore, 29–59. Ithaca: Cornell University Press.

Bronte, Stephen. 1982. *Japanese Finance: Markets and Institutions.* London: Euromoney Publications.

Brook, William L., and Robert M. Orr Jr. 1985. "Japan's Foreign Economic Assistance." *Asian Survey* 25, no. 3:322–40.

Broz, J. Lawrence. 1997. *The International Origins of the Federal Reserve.* Ithaca: Cornell University Press.

———. 1998. "The Origins of Central Banking: Solutions to the Free-Rider Problem." *International Organization* 52, no. 2:231–68.

———. 1999. "Origins of the Federal Reserve System." *International Organization* 53, no. 1:39–70.

Bruce, Neil. 1990. "Defense Expenditures by Countries in Allied and Adversarial Relationships." *Defense Economics* 1 (May): 179–95.

Bueno, Gerardo M. 1989. "México y Japón en el Comercio International." *Comercio Exterior* 39, no. 8:710–14.

Buira, Ariel. 1996. "Reflections on the Mexican Crisis of 1994." In *Private Capital Flows to Emerging Markets after the Mexican Crisis,* ed. Guillermo A. Calvo, Morris Goldstein, and Eduard Hochreiter, 307–20. Washington, D.C.: Institute for International Economics.

Bulow, Jeremy, and Kenneth Rogoff. 1989. "Multilateral Negotiations for Rescheduling Developing Country Debt: A Bargaining-Theoretic Framework." In *Analytical Issues in Debt,* ed. Jacob A. Frankel, Michael P. Dooley, and Peter Wickhan, 194–207. Washington, D.C.: International Monetary Fund.

Burstein, Daniel. 1988. *Yen: Japan's New Financial Empire and Its Threat to America.* New York: Simon and Schuster.

Burton, F. N., and H. Inoue. 1985. "The Influence of Country Risk Factors on Interest Rate Differentials on International Bank Lending to Sovereign Borrowers." *Applied Economics* 17, no. 3:491–507.

Calder, Kent E. 1985. "The Emerging Politics of the Trans-Pacific Economy: A Stable U.S.-Japanese Foundation?" *World Policy Journal* 2, no. 4:593–624.

———. 1988. "Japanese Foreign Economic Policy Formation: Explaining the Reactive State." *World Politics* 40, no. 4:517–41.

———. 1993. *Strategic Capitalism: Private Business and Public Purpose in Japanese Industrial Finance.* Princeton: Princeton University Press.

———. 1997. "Assault on the Bankers' Kingdom: Politics, Markets, and the Liberalization of Japanese Industrial Finance." In *Capital Ungoverned: Liberalizing Finance in Interventionist States,* ed. Michael Loriaux, Meredith Woo-Cumings, Kent E. Calder, Sylvia Maxfield, and Sofia Perez, 17–56. Ithaca: Cornell University Press.

———. 1998. "Japan's Crucial Role in Asia's Financial Crisis." *Japan Quarterly* 45, no. 2:4–9.

Caldwell, J. Alexander. 1972. "The Evolution of Japanese Economic Cooperation, 1950–1970." In *Pacific Basin Development: The American Interests,* ed. Harold B. Malmgren, 23–60. Lexington, Mass: Lexington.

Calvo, Guillermo A., Leonardo Leiderman, and Carmen M. Reinhart. 1993. "Capital Inflows and Real Exchange Rate Appreciation in Latin America." *IMF Staff Papers* 40, no. 1 (March): 108–51.

Calvo, Sara, and Carmen M. Reinhart. 1996. "Capital Flows to Latin America: Is There Evidence of Contagion Effects?" In *Private Capital Flows to Emerging Markets after the Mexican Crisis,* ed. Guillermo A. Calvo, Morris Goldstein, and Eduard Hochreiter, 151–71. Washington, D.C.: Institute for International Economics.

Cassen, Robert. 1994. *Does Aid Work? Report to an Intergovernmental Task Force.* Oxford: Oxford University Press.

Castañeda, Jorge G. 1995. *The Mexican Shock: Its Meaning for the United States.* New York: New Press.

Cerny, Philip G., ed. 1993. *Finance and World Politics: Markets, Regimes, and States in the Post-hegemonic Era.* Vermont: Edward Elgar.

Chan, Steve. 1993. *East Asian Dynamism: Growth, Order, and Security in the Pacific Region.* New York: Westview.

Chenery, Hollis B., and Alan M. Strout. 1966. "Foreign Assistance and Economic Development." *American Economic Review* 56, no. 4:679–733.

Chow, Gregory C. 1960. "Tests of Equality between Sets of Coefficients in Two Linear Regressions." *Econometrica* 28, no. 3:591–605.

Chuhan, Punam, Stijn Claessens, and Nlander Mamingi, 1993. "Equity and Bond Flows to Latin America and Asia: The Role of External and Domestic Factors." Washington, D.C., World Bank, World Bank Policy Research Working Paper, no. 1160.

Chuhan, Punam, and Kwang W. Jun. 1995. "Latin American Financing in Japan's Capital Markets." In *Coping with Capital Surges: The Return of Finance to Latin America,* ed. Ricardo Ffrench-Davis and Stephany Griffith-Jones, 75–98. Boulder: Lynne Rienner.

Claessens, Stijn, and Thomas Glaessner. 1997. *Are Financial Sector Weaknesses Undermining the East Asian Miracle?* Washington, D.C.: World Bank.

Cline, William R. 1983. *International Debt and the Stability of the World Economy.* Washington, D.C.: Institute for International Economics.

———. 1984. *International Debt: Systemic Risk and Policy Response.* Washington, D.C.: Institute for International Economics.

———. 1987. *Mobilizing Bank Lending to Debtor Countries.* Washington, D.C.: Institute for International Economics.

———. 1989. "The Baker Plan and Brady Plan Reformulation: An Evaluation." In *Dealing with the Debt Crisis,* ed. Ishrat Husai and Ishac Diwan, 176–92. Washington, D.C.: World Bank.

———. 1995a. *International Debt Reexamined.* Washington, D.C.: Institute for International Economics.

———. 1995b. *Predicting External Imbalances for the United States and Japan.* Washington, D.C.: Institute for International Economics.

Cohen, Benjamin J. 1977. *Organizing the World's Money: The Political Economy of International Monetary Relations.* New York: Basic.

———. 1985. "International Debt and Linkage Strategies: Some Foreign-Policy Implications for the United States." *International Organization* 39, no. 4:699–727.

———. 1986a. "International Debt and Linkage Strategies: Some Foreign-Policy Implications for the United States." In *The Politics of International Debt*, ed. Miles Kahler, 127–55. Ithaca: Cornell University Press.

———. 1986b. *In Whose Interest? International Banking and American Foreign Policy.* New Haven: Yale University Press.

———. 1992. "U.S. Debt Policy in Latin America: The Melody Lingers On." In *In the Shadow of the Debt: Emerging Issues in Latin America*, ed. Richard C. Leone, 153–72. New York: Twentieth Century Fund Press.

———. 1993. "The Triad and the Unholy Trinity: Lessons for the Pacific Region." In *Pacific Economic Relations in the 1990s: Cooperation or Conflict?* ed. Richard Higgott, Richard Leaver, and John Ravenhill, 133–58. Boulder: Lynne Rienner.

———. 1996. "Phoenix Risen: The Resurrection of Global Finance." *World Politics* 48, no. 2:268–96.

———. 1997. *The Financial Support Fund of the OECD: A Failed Initiative.* Essays in International Finance, no. 204. Princeton: Princeton University.

Cohen, Daniel. 1991. *Private Lending to Sovereign States: A Theoretical Autopsy.* Cambridge: MIT Press.

Conybeare, John A. C. 1984. "Public Goods, Prisoners' Dilemmas, and the International Political Economy." *International Studies Quarterly* 28, no. 1:5–22.

Crone, Donald. 1993. "Does Hegemony Matter? The Reorganization of the Pacific Political Economy." *World Politics* 45, no. 4:501–25.

Culpeper, Roy. 1995. "Resurgence of Private Flows to Latin America: The Role of North American Investors." In *Coping with Capital Surges: The Return of Finance to Latin America*, ed. Ricardo Ffrench-Davis and Stephany Griffith-Jones, 1–40. Boulder: Lynne Rienner.

Curtis, Gerald L. 1981. "Japanese Security Policies and the United States." *Foreign Affairs* 59, no. 4:852–74.

———. 1988. *The Japanese Way of Politics.* New York: Columbia University Press.

Cusack, Thomas R., and Joyce P. Kaufman. 1994. "The Evolution of Western Foreign Aid Programs." FS III 94-206. Berlin. Mimeographed.

Cypher, James M. 1990. *State and Capital in Mexico: Development Policy since 1940.* Boulder: Westview.

Dennis, Geoffrey E. J. 1983. "The Growth of International Bank Lending, 1972–1982: Concepts, Measurement, and Causes." *Aussenwirtschaft* 38 (September): 263–83.

Dermiguc-Kunt, Asli, and Eduardo Fernandez-Arias. 1992. "Burden-Sharing among Official and Private Creditors." World Bank Working Papers, no. 943, Washington, D.C., August.

Desmond, Edward. 1997. "Japan: A Model for What Not to Do." *Fortune* 136, no. (November 24): 98.

Destler, I. M., Hideo Sato, Priscilla Clapp, and Hamo Fukui. 1976. *Managing Alliance: The Politics of US-Japanese Relations.* Washington, D.C.: Brookings Institution.

Destler, I. M., and Hideo Sato. 1982. *Coping with US-Japanese Economic Conflicts.* Lexington, MA: Lexington Books.

Devlin, Robert. 1989. *Debt and Crisis in Latin America: The Supply Side of the Story.* Princeton: Princeton University Press.

Devlin, Robert, Ricardo Ffrench-Davis, and Stephany Griffith-Jones. 1995. "Surges in

Capital Flows and Development: An Overview of Policy Issues." In *Coping with Capital Surges: The Return of Finance to Latin America,* ed. Ricardo Ffrench-Davis and Stephany Griffith-Jones, 225–60. Boulder: Lynne Rienner.

Deyo, Frederic C., ed. 1987. *The Political Economy of the New Asian Industrialism.* Ithaca: Cornell University Press.

Diaz-Alejandro, Carlos. 1985. "Good-Bye Financial Repression, Hello Financial Crash." *Journal of Development Economics* 19, nos. 1 and 2:1–24.

Dickey, David A., and Wayne A. Fuller. 1981. "Likelihood Ratio Statistics for Autoregressive Time Series with a Unit Root." *Econometrica* 49, no. 4:1057–72.

Dittmer, Lowell. 1981. "The Strategic Triangle: An Elementary Game-Theoretical Analysis." *World Politics* 32, no. 4:485–515.

Doherty, Eileen Marie. 1987. "Japan's Expanding Foreign Aid Program." *Asian Affairs: An American Review* 14, no. 3:129–49.

Dollar, David. 1992. "Outward-Orientated Developing Economies Really Do Grow More Rapidly: Evidence from 95 LDCs, 1976–1985." *Economic Development and Cultural Change* 40, no. 3:523–44.

Doner, Richard F. 1993. "Japanese Foreign Investment and the Creation of a Pacific Asian Region." In *Regionalism and Rivalry: Japan and the United States in Pacific Asia,* ed. Jeffrey A. Frankel and Miles Kahler, 159–216. Chicago: University of Chicago Press.

Dooley, Michael P. 1996. "A Survey of Literature on Controls over International Capital Transactions." *IMF Staff Papers* 43, no. 4:639–87.

Dooley, Michael P., and Peter Isard. 1991. "A Note on Fiscal Policy, Investment Location Decisions, and Exchange Rates." *Journal of International Money and Finance* 10, no. 1:161–68.

Drucker, Peter E. 1993a. "The End of Japan, Inc.?" *Foreign Affairs* 72, no. 2:10–15.

———. 1993b. "Japan, Inc.'s Shaky Future." *Harper's* 287, no. 1718:14–17.

———. 1998. "In Defense of Japanese Bureaucracy." *Foreign Affairs* 77, no. 5:68–80.

Dudley, Leonard, and Claude Montmarquette. 1976. "A Model of the Supply of Bilateral Foreign Aid." *American Economic Review* 66, no. 1:132–42.

Eaton, Jonathan, and Mark Gersovitz. 1981. "Debt with Potential Repudiation: Theoretical and Empirical Analysis." *Review of Economic Studies* 48, no. 152:289–309.

Eckstein, Harry. 1975. "Case Study and Theory in Political Science." In *Handbook of Political Science,* vol. 7, *Strategy of Inquiry,* ed. Fred I. Greenstein and Nelson W. Polsby, 79–137. Reading, Mass.: Addison-Wesley.

Edelman, John A., and Hollis B. Chenery. 1977. "Aid and Income Distribution." In *The New International Economic Order: The North-South Debate,* ed. Jagdish N. Bhagwati, 27–49. Cambridge: MIT Press.

Eichengreen, Barry. 1994. *International Monetary Arrangements for the Twenty-First Century.* Washington, D.C.: Brookings Institution.

———. 1997. "The Tyranny of the Financial Markets." *Current History* 96, no. 613:377–82.

———. 1999. *Toward a New International Financial Architecture: A Practical Post-Asia Agenda.* Washington, D.C.: Institute for International Economics.

Eichengreen, Barry, and Albert Fishlow. 1998. "Contending with Capital Flows: What Is Different about the 1990s." In *Capital Flows and Financial Crises,* ed. Miles Kahler, 23–68. Ithaca: Cornell University Press.

Encarnation, Dennis J. 1992. *Rivals beyond Trade: America versus Japan in Global Competition.* Ithaca: Cornell University Press.

Encarnation, Dennis J., and Mark Mason. 1990. "Neither MITI nor America: The Political Economy of Capital Liberalization in Japan." *International Organization* 44, no. 1:25–54.

Engle, Robert F., and C. W. J. Granger. 1987. "Co-Integration and Error Correction: Representation, Estimation, and Testing." *Econometrica* 55, no. 2:251–76.

Ensign, Margee. 1992. *Doing Good or Doing Well? Japan's Foreign Aid Program.* New York: Columbia University Press.

Evans, Peter. 1992. "The State as Problem and Solution: Predation, Embedded Autonomy, and Structural Change." In *The Politics of Economic Adjustment: International Constraints, Distributive Conflicts, and the State,* ed. Stephan Haggard and Robert R. Kaufman, 139–81. Princeton: Princeton University Press.

Faber, Mike. 1990. "The Next Plan after Brady?" *World Development* 18, no. 12:1703–10.

Fallows, James M. 1989. "Containing Japan." *The Atlantic* 63, no. 5 (May): 40–52.

———. 1994. *Looking at the Sun: The Rise of the New East Asian Economic and Political System.* New York: Pantheon.

Feinberg, Richard E., and Valeriana Kallab, eds. 1984. *Uncertain Future: Commercial Banks and the Third World.* New Burnswick, N.J.: Transaction.

Feldstein, Martin. 1998. "Refocusing the IMF." *Foreign Affairs* 77, no. 2:20–33.

Felix, David, ed. 1990. *Debt and Transfiguration? Prospects for Latin America's Economic Revival,* Armonk, N.Y.: M. E. Sharpe.

Fernandez-Arias, Eduardo. 1996. "The New Wave of Private Capital Inflows: Push or Pull?" *Journal of Development Economics* 48, no. 2:389–418.

Ffrench-Davis, Ricardo. 1984. "International Private Lending and Borrowing Strategies of Developing Countries." *Journal of Development Planning: World Recovery and Monetary Reform* 14:119–64.

———. 1987. "Latin American Debt: Debtor-Creditor Relations." *Third World Quarterly* 9, no. 4:1167–83.

Ffrench-Davis, Ricardo, and Stephany Griffith-Jones, eds. 1995. *Coping with Capital Surges: The Return of Finance to Latin America.* Boulder: Lynne Rienner.

Fischer, Stanley. 1998. "In Defense of the IMF: Specialized Tolls for a Specialized Task." *Foreign Affairs* 77, no. 4:103–6.

Fishlow, Albert. 1986. "Lessons from the Past: Capital Markets during the Nineteenth Century and the Interwar Period." In *The Politics of International Debt,* ed. Miles Kahler, 37–93. Ithaca: Cornell University Press.

Frankel, Jeffrey A. 1984. *The Yen/Dollar Agreement: Liberalizing Japanese Capital Markets.* Policy Analysis in International Economics, no. 9. Washington, D.C.: Institute for International Economics.

———. 1993. "Is Japan Creating a Yen Bloc in East Asia and the Pacific?" In *Regionalism and Rivalry: Japan and the United States in Pacific Asia,* ed. Jeffrey A. Frankel and Miles Kahler, 53–88. Chicago: University of Chicago Press.

Frankel, Jeffrey, and Miles Kahler, eds. 1993. *Regionalism and Rivalry: Japan and the United States in Pacific Asia.* Chicago: University of Chicago Press.

Freeman, John R. 1983. "Granger Causality and the Time Series Analysis of Political Relationships." *American Journal of Political Science* 27, no. 2:327–58.

Frieden, Jeffry. 1981. "Third World Indebted Industrialization: International Finance and State Capitalism in Mexico, Brazil, Algeria, and South Korea." *International Organization* 35, no. 3:407–31.

———. 1984. "Studies in International Finance: Private Interest and Public Policy in the International Political Economy." Ph.D. diss., Columbia University.

———. 1987. *Banking on the World: The Politics of American International Finance.* New York: Harper and Row.

———. 1991a. *Debt, Development, and Democracy: Modern Political Economy and Latin America, 1965–1985.* Princeton: Princeton University Press.

———. 1991b. "Invested Interests: The Politics of National Economic Policies in a World of Global Finance." *International Organization* 45, no. 4:425–51.

———. 1993. "Domestic Politics and Regional Cooperation: The United States, Japan, and Pacific Money and Finance." In *Regionalism and Rivalry: Japan and the United States in Pacific Asia,* ed. Jeffrey A. Frankel and Miles Kahler, 423–48. Chicago: University of Chicago Press.

———. 1994. "International Investment and Colonial Control: A New Interpretation." *International Organization* 48, no. 4:559–93.

Frieden, Jeffry A., and Ronald Rogowski. 1996. "The Impact of the International Economy on National Policies: An Analytical Overview." In *Internationalization and Domestic Politics,* ed. Robert O. Keohane and Helen V. Milner, 25–47. Cambridge: Cambridge University Press.

Friscia, A. Blake. 1992. "Japanese Economic Relations with Latin America: An Overview." In *Japan and Latin America in the New Global Order,* ed. Susan Kaufman Purcell and Robert M. Immerman, 5–68. Boulder: Lynne Rienner.

Fujikawa, Tesuma. 1987. "Kaesu Kaesanai, Kaesenai Kaesubeki: Kaihatsu Tojokoku no Ruiseki Saimu Mondai." *Finance* 23, no. 9 (December): 22–27.

———. 1988a. "Maware Maaware Okaneha Tennkanoo Mawarimono: 300 okudoru no Shikinn Kanryusochi." *Finance* 23, no. 12 (March): 48–58.

———. 1988b. "Doryoku Shinbou Nintai, Dekireba Kibouno Ruiseki Saimu Mondai." *Finance* 24, no. 5 (August): 29–47.

———. 1988c. "Aa Intanashonaru Wareraga Kikann: Ruiseki Saimu Mondai ni okeru Kokusai Kikan no Yakuwari." *Finance* 24, no. 6 (September): 21–35.

———. 1989a. "Shuyaku, Imada Tojosezu." *Raten Amerika Jiho,* July, 9–17.

———. 1989b. "Ruiseki Saimu Mondai ha Dareno Mondaika." *Raten Amerika Jiho,* October, 5–18.

———. 1989c. "Binbounin ga Shikin wo Dasu." *Raten Amerika Jiho,* November, 13–19.

———. 1990a. "Ruiseki Saimu Mondai no Aratana Tenkai." *Raten Amerika Jiho,* March, 5–24.

———. 1990b. "Aratana Saimu Senryaku no Dai ippo." *Raten Amerika Jiho,* May, 23–35.

Fujioka, Masao. 1979. *Japan's International Finance: Today and Tomorrow.* Tokyo: Japan Times.

Fukuchi, Takao, and Mitsuhiro Kagami, eds. 1990. *Perspectives on the Pacific Basin Economy: A Comparison of Asia and Latin America.* I.D.E. Symposium Proceedings no. 10. Tokyo: Institute of Developing Economies and The Asian Club Foundation.

Fukushima, Mitsuo, and Takii Mitsuo, eds. 1998. *97 nen Ajia Tsuuka kiki: Higashi Ajia 9 kakoku, Chiiki niokeru Haikei to Eikyou wo Bunseki suru.* Ajiken Toppiku Reports, no. 28. Tokyo: Ajia Keizai Kenkyujo.

Fukuyama, Francis. 1992. *The End of History and the Last Man.* New York: Free Press.

Funabashi, Yoichi. 1993. "The Asianization of Asia." *Foreign Affairs* 72, no. 5:75–85.

———. 1995. *Asia Pacific Fusion: Japan's Role in APEC.* Washington, D.C.: Institute for International Economics.

———. 1998. "Tokyo's Depression Diplomacy." *Foreign Affairs* 77, no. 6:26–36.

Galbraith, John Kenneth. 1994. *A Short History of Financial Euphoria.* New York: Whittle.

Gardner, Richard N. 1980. *Sterling-Dollar Diplomacy in Current Perspective: The Origins and the Prospects of Our International Economic Order.* New York: Columbia University Press.

Garrett, Geoffrey, and Peter Lange. 1996. "Internationalization, Institutions, and Political Change." In *Internationalization and Domestic Politics,* ed. Robert O. Keohane and Helen V. Milner, 48–75. Cambridge: Cambridge University Press.

Garten, Jeffrey. 1999. "Lessons for the Next Financial Crisis." *Foreign Affairs* 78, no. 2: 76–92.

Gasiorowski, Mark J. 1986. "Dependency and Cliency in Latin America." *Journal of Interamerican Studies and World Affairs* 28, no. 3:47–65.

George, Alexander L. 1979. "Case Studies and Theory Development: The Method of Structured, Focused Comparison." In *Diplomacy: New Approaches in History, Theory, and Policy,* ed. Paul Gordon Lauren, 43–67. New York: Free.

George, Alexander L., and Timothy J. McKeown. 1985. "Case Studies and Theories of Organizational Decision Making." *Advances in Information Processing in Organizations* 2:21–58.

Gereffi, Gary. 1989. "Rethinking Development Theory: Insights from East Asia and Latin America." *Sociological Forum* 4, no. 4:505–33.

Gereffi, Gary, and Don Wyman, eds. 1990. *Manufacturing Miracles: Paths of Industrialization in Latin America and East Asia.* Princeton: Princeton University Press.

Gersovitz, Mark. 1985. "Banks' International Lending Decisions: What We Know and Implications for Future Research." In *International Debt and the Developing Countries: World Bank Symposium, 1985,* ed. Gordon W. Smith and John T. Cuddington, 61–77. Washington, D.C.: World Bank.

Gilpin, Robert. 1987. *The Political Economy of International Relations.* Princeton: Princeton University Press.

Giovannini, Alberto. 1996. "Borrowing in International Capital Markets: Lessons from Experience." In *Private Capital Flows to Emerging Markets after the Mexican Crisis,* ed. Guillermo A. Calvo, Morris Goldstein, and Eduard Hochreiter, 99–107. Washington, D.C.: Institute for International Economics.

Goldstein, Joshua S., and John R. Freeman. 1990. *Three-Way Street: Strategic Reciprocity in World Politics.* Chicago: University of Chicago Press.

Goldstein, Morris. 1998. *The Asian Financial Crises: Causes, Cures, and Systemic Implications.* Washington, D.C.: Institute for International Economics.

Goldstein, Morris, and Guillermo A. Calvo. 1996. "What Role for the Official Sector?" In *Private Capital Flows to Emerging Markets after the Mexican Crisis,* ed. Guillermo A. Calvo, Morris Goldstein, and Eduard Hochreiter, 233–82. Washington, D.C.: Institute for International Economics.

Goldstein, Morris, and David Folkerts-Landau. 1994. *International Capital Markets Systemic Issues in International Finance.* Washington, D.C.: IMF, 1994.

Gonzales, Sergio Galves, and Victor Kerber Palma. 1990. "Una Década en la Relación México-Japón." *Foro Internacional* 30, no. 3:536–54.

Goodman, Laurie S. 1983. "Syndicated Eurolending: Pricing and Practice" In *Interna-*

tional Finance Handbook, ed. Abraham M. George and Ian H. Giddy, 1:3–29. New York: Wiley-Interscience.

Gordon, Bernard K. 1978. "Japan, the United States, and Southeast Asia." *Foreign Affairs* 56, no. 3:579–600.

Goto, Kazumi. 1995. "Japan's Aid Administration: Its Challenges for the Future." *Journal of International Development* 7, no. 2:253–60.

Gourevitch, Peter. 1978. "The Second Image Reversed: The International Sources of Domestic Politics." *International Organization* 32, no. 4:881–912.

Gowa, Joanne. 1987. "Rational Hegemons, Excludable Goods, and Small Groups: An Epitaph for Hegemonic Stability Theory?" *World Politics* 41, no. 3:307–24.

Grabendorff, Wolf. 1996. "Repercussions of the Mexican Monetary Crisis across the Atlantic: Ripples, Breakers, or a Sea Change in European Perspectives?" In *The Mexican Peso Crisis: International Perspectives,* ed. Riordan Roett, 93–112. Boulder: Lynne Rienner.

Grabendorff, Wolf, and Riordan Roett, eds. 1985. *Latin America, Western Europe, and the United States: Reevaluating the Atlantic Triangle.* New York: Praeger.

Greene, James. 1983. "Bank Lending to Third World Countries in the 1980's." *Journal of Banking and Finance* 7, no. 4:553–58.

Greene, William H. 1990. *Econometric Analysis.* New York: MacMillan.

———. 1992. *LIMDEP: User's Manual and Reference Guide.* Version 6.0. New York: Econometric Software.

Grieco, Joseph M. 1988. "Anarchy and the Limits of Cooperation: A Realist Critique of the Newest Liberal Institutionalism." *International Organization* 42, no. 3:485–507.

———. 1990. *Cooperation among Nations: Europe, America, and Non-Tariff Barriers to Trade.* Ithaca: Cornell University Press.

Griffith-Jones, Stephany. 1984. *International Finance and Latin America.* New York: St. Martins.

———. 1987. *Managing Third World Debt: Report of the Second Working Party established by the All Party Parliamentary Group on Overseas Development.* London: Overseas Development Institute.

———. 1991. "International Financial Markets: A Case of Market Failure." In *States or Markets? Neo-Liberalism and the Development Policy Debate,* ed. Cristopher Colclough and James Manor, 101–20. New York: Clarendon.

———. 1995. "How Can Future Currency Crises Be Prevented or Better Managed?" Paper presented at a seminar organized by Fondad and De Nederlandsche Bank, September 18.

Griffith-Jones, Stephany, and Barbara Stallings. 1995. "New Global Financial Trends: Implications for Development." In *Global Change, Regional Response: The New International Context of Development,* ed. Barbara Stallings, 143–73. Cambridge: Cambridge University Press.

Guttentag, Jack, and Richard Herring. 1983. *The Lender-of-Last-Resort Function in an International Context.* Essays in International Finance, no. 151. Princeton: Princeton University.

———. 1985. "Commercial Bank Lending to Developing Countries: From Overlending to Underlending to Structural Reform." In *International Debt and the Developing Countries: World Bank Symposium, 1985,* ed. Gordon W. Smith and John T. Cuddington, 129–50. Washington, D.C.: World Bank.

Haas, Peter. 1990. *Saving the Mediterranean.* New York: Columbia University Press.

Haggard, Stephan. 1985. "The Politics of Adjustment: Lessons from the IMF's Extended Fund Facility." *International Organization* 39, no. 3:505–34.

———. 1990. *Pathways from the Periphery: The Politics of Growth in the Newly Industrializing Countries.* Ithaca: Cornell University Press.

———. 2000. *The Political Economy of the Asian Financial Crisis.* Washington, D.C.: Institute for International Economics.

Haggard, Stephan, and Robert R. Kaufman. 1992a. "Introduction: Institutions and Economic Adjustment." In *The Politics of Economic Adjustment: International Constraints, Distributive Conflicts, and the State,* ed. Stephan Haggard and Robert R. Kaufman, 3–37. Princeton: Princeton University Press.

———, eds. 1992b. *The Politics of Economic Adjustment: International Constraints, Distributive Conflicts, and the State.* Princeton: Princeton University Press.

Haggard, Stephan, Chung H. Lee, and Sylvia Maxfield, eds. 1993. *The Politics of Finance in Developing Countries.* Ithaca: Cornell University Press.

Haggard, Stephan, and Sylvia Maxfield. 1996. "The Political Economy of Financial Internationalism in the Developing World." In *Internationalization and Domestic Politics,* ed. Robert O. Keohane and Helen V. Milner, 209–39. Cambridge: Cambridge University Press.

Haggard, Stephan, and Beth A. Simmons. 1987. "Theories of International Regimes." *International Organization* 41, no. 3:491–517.

Hale, David D. 1990. "Global Finance and the Retreat to Managed Trade." *Harvard Business Review,* January–February, 150–62.

Hallerberg, Mark, and William Roberts Clark. 1997. "How Should Political Scientists Measure Capital Mobility? A Review." Paper presented at the annual meeting of the American Political Science Association, Washington, D.C., August 28–31.

Hamada, Koichi. 1985. *The Political Economy of International Monetary Interdependence.* Trans. Charles Yuji Horioka and Chi-Hung Kwan. Cambridge: MIT Press.

———. 1999. "From the AMF to the Miyazawa Initiative: Observations on Japan's Currency Diplomacy." *Journal of East Asian Affairs* 13, no. 1 (spring/summer): 33–50.

Hamada, Koichi, and Akiyoshi Horiuchi. 1987. "The Political Economy of the Financial Market." In *The Political Economy of Japan,* vol. 1, *The Domestic Transformation,* ed. Kozo Yamamura and Yasukichi Yasuba, 223–60. Stanford: Stanford University Press.

Hanabusa, Masamichi. 1991. "A Japanese Perspective on Aid and Development." In *Yen for Development: Japanese Foreign Aid and the Politics of Burden-Sharing,* ed. Shafiqul Islam, 88–104. New York: Council on Foreign Relations Press.

Hardin, Russell. 1982. *Collective Action.* Baltimore: Johns Hopkins University Press.

Hart, Jeffrey. 1976. "Three Approaches to the Measurement of Power in International Relations." *International Organization* 30, no. 2:289–305.

Hartcher, Peter. 1998. *The Ministry: How Japan's Most Powerful Institution Endangers World Markets.* Boston: Harvard Business School Press.

Harvey, A. C. 1990. *The Econometric Analysis of Time Series.* 2d ed. Cambridge: MIT Press.

Hasegawa, Sukehiro. 1975. *Japanese Foreign Aid: Policy and Practice.* New York: Praeger.

Hatch, Walter, and Kozo Yamamura. 1997. *Asia in Japan's Embrace: Building a Regional Production Alliance.* Cambridge: Cambridge University Press.

Haynes, Stephen E., Michael M. Hutchison, and Raymond F. Mikesell. 1986. *Japanese Financial Policies and the U.S. Trade Deficit.* Essays in International Finance, no. 162. Princeton: Princeton University.

Healey, Derek. 1991. *Japanese Capital Exports and Asian Economic Development.* Paris: Organization for Economic Cooperation and Development.

Helleiner, Eric. 1989. "Money and Influence: Japanese Power in the International Monetary and Financial System." *Millennium: Journal of International Studies* 18, no. 3:343–58.

———. 1994. *States and the Reemergence of Global Finance: From Bretton Woods to the 1990s.* Ithaca: Cornell University Press.

———. 1995. "Explaining the Globalization of Financial Markets: Bringing States Back In." *Review of International Political Economy* 2, no. 2:315–41.

Heller, H. Robert. 1987. "The Debt Crisis and the Future of International Bank Lending." *American Economic Review* 77, no. 2:171–75.

Helweg, M. Diana. 2000. "Japan: A Rising Sun?" *Foreign Affairs* 79, no. 4 (July/August): 26–39.

Henning, C. Randall. 1994. *Currencies and Politics in the United States, Germany, and Japan.* Washington, D.C.: Institute for International Economics.

———. 1998. "Systemic Conflict and Regional Monetary Integration: The Case of Europe." *International Organization* 52, no. 3:537–73.

Herring, Richard J., ed. 1983. *Managing International Risk: Essays Commissioned in Honor of the Centenary of the Wharton School, Univ. of Pennsylvania.* Cambridge: Cambridge University Press.

Higgott, Richard, Richard Leaver, and John Ravenhill, eds. 1993. *Pacific Economic Relations in the 1990s: Cooperation or Conflict?* Boulder: Lynne Rienner.

Hirata, Akira. 1995. "An Integrated Economic Policy towards Developing Countries? The Case of Japan." *Journal of International Development* 7, no. 2:261–80.

Hirata, Jun, Shigeru Kodama, Hirokazu Hiratuka, and Matoo Shigenami. 1999. *Nijuiseiki gata Kinyuukiki to IMF* (The 21st Century Type Financial Crisis and the IMF). Tokyo: Toyo Keizai Shimpo Sha.

Hiratsuka, Daiyu. 1998. "Bunseki Repoto: 21 seikigata no Ajia Tsuka kiki, Ajia Keizai no Fukkou to Nihon no Yakuwari." *Ajiken Warudo Torendo* 35 (June): 38–42.

Hirono, Ryokichi. 1991. "Japan's Leadership Role in the Multilateral Development Institutions." In *Yen for Development: Japanese Foreign Aid and the Politics of Burden-Sharing,* ed. Shafiqul Islam, 171–81. New York: Council on Foreign Relations Press.

Hollerman, Leon. 1988a. *Japan, Disincorporated: The Economic Liberalization Process.* Stanford, Calif.: Hoover Institution Press.

———. 1988b. *Japan's Economic Strategy in Brazil: Challenge for the United States.* New York: Lexington.

Hook, Steven, ed. 1996. *Foreign Aid toward the Millennium.* Boulder: Lynne Rienner.

Horisaka, Kotaro. 1991. "Japan and Latin America: Changes of Paradigm." Tokyo. Mimeographed.

———. 1993. "Japan's Economic Relations with Latin America." In *Japan, the United States, and Latin America: Toward a Trilateral Relationship in the Western Hemisphere,* ed. Barbara Stallings and Gabriel Székely, 49–76. Baltimore: Johns Hopkins University Press.

Horne, James. 1985. *Japan's Financial Markets: Conflicts and Consensus in Policymaking.* Boston: Allen and Unwin.

Hosono, Akio. 1985. "Japan and Latin America." In *Japan's Foreign Relations: A Global Search for Economic Security,* ed. Robert S. Ozaki and Walter Arnold, 187–99. Boulder: Westview.

Hosono, Akio, and Keiko Hata, eds. 1993. *Raten Amerika no Kokusai Kankei.* Serie de América Latina, no. 3. Tokyo: Shin hyoron.

Hsiao, Cheng. 1986. *Analysis of Panel Data.* Cambridge: Cambridge University Press.

Huang, Haizhou, and Chenggang Xu. 1999. "East Asia: Miracle or Bubble? Financial Institutions and the Financial Crisis in East Asia." *European Economic Review* 42:903–14.

Huizinga, Harry. 1989. "The Commercial Bank Claims on Developing Countries: How Have Banks Been Affected?" In *Dealing with the Debt Crisis: A World Bank Symposium,* ed. Ishrat Husai and Ishac Diwan, 129–45. Washington, D.C.: World Bank.

Hurrell, Andrew. 1995. "Explaining the Resurgence of Regionalism in World Politics." *Review of International Studies* 21, no. 4:331–58.

Iida, Keisuke. 1993a. "Analytic Uncertainty and International Cooperation: Theory and Application to International Economic Policy Coordination." *International Studies Quarterly* 37, no. 4:431–57.

Iida, Keisuke. 1993b. "The Political Economy of Exchange-Rate Policy: U.S. and Japanese Intervention Policies, 1977–90." *Journal of Public Policy* 13, no. 4:327–49.

Ikenberry, G. John, David Lake, and Michael Mastanduno. 1988. "Introduction: Approaches to Explaining American Foreign Economic Policy." *International Organization* 42, no. 1:1–32.

Inada, Ju-ichi. 1989. "Japan's Aid Diplomacy: Economic, Political, or Strategic?" *Millennium: Journal of International Studies* 18, no. 3:399–414.

———. 1993. "Democratization, Marketization, and Japan's Emerging Role as a Foreign Aid Donor." Program on U.S.-Japan Relations Occasional Paper 93-03, Cambridge, MA.

Inoguchi, Takashi. 1988. "The Ideas and Structures of Foreign Policy: Looking Ahead with Caution." In *The Political Economy of Japan,* vol. 2, *The Changing International Context,* ed. Takashi Inoguchi and Daniel I. Okimoto, 23–63. Stanford: Stanford University Press.

———. 1991. "Japan's Global Role in a Multipolar World." In *Yen for Development: Japanese Foreign Aid and the Politics of Burden-Sharing,* ed. Shafiqul Islam, 11–26. New York: Council on Foreign Relations Press.

Inoguchi, Takashi, and Daniel I. Okimoto, eds. 1988. *The Political Economy of Japan.* Vol. 2, *The Changing International Context.* Stanford: Stanford University Press.

Inter-American Development Bank and Export-Import Bank of Japan, eds. 1989. *The Final Report of the Fourth Symposium on Financial and Business Cooperation between Latin America and Japan.* Tokyo: Export-Import Bank of Japan and Inter-American Development Bank.

Islam, Shafiqul, ed. 1991. *Yen for Development: Japanese Foreign Aid and the Politics of Burden-Sharing,* New York: Council on Foreign Relations Press.

Ito, Takatoshi. 1993. "U.S. Political Pressure and Economic Liberalization in East Asia." In *Regionalism and Rivalry: Japan and the United States in Pacific Asia,* ed. Jeffrey A. Frankel and Miles Kahler, 391–422. Chicago: University of Chicago Press.

———. 1998. "The Development of the Thailand Currency Crisis: A Chronological Review." *Kaigai Toushi Kenkyu jo Ho* 24, no. 9 (Sept.–Oct.): 66–93.

———. 1999a. "Ajia Tuka Kiki to IMF (The Asian Currency Crisis and the IMF)." *Keizai Kenjyu* 50, no. 1 (January) 68–93.

———. 1999b. "Ajia Keizai Kiki to Wagakuni no Yakuwari (The Asian Economic Crisis and the Role of Japan)," *Gaiko Forum* (February 1999): 26–31.

James, Harold. *International Monetary Cooperation since Bretton Woods.* New York: Oxford University Press.

Janow, Merit E. 1994. "Trading with an Ally: Progress and Discontent in U.S.-Japan Trade Relations." In *The United States, Japan, and Asia: Challenges for U.S. Policy,* ed. Gerald L. Curtis, 53–95. New York: Norton.

Johnson, Chalmers. 1982. *MITI and the Japanese Miracle: The Growth of Industrial Policy, 1925–1975.* Stanford: Stanford University Press.

———. 1995. "Trade, Revisionism, and the Future of Japanese-American Relations." In *Japan: Who Governs?* 69–95. New York: Norton.

Johnson, Chalmers, and Barry Keehn. 1994. "A Disaster in the Making." *National Interest* 36 (summer): 14–22.

———. 1995. "The Pentagon's Ossified Strategy." *Foreign Affairs* 74, no. 4:103–14.

Jun, Kwang W., Frank Sader, Haruo Horaguchi, and Hyuntai Kwak. 1993. "Japanese Foreign Direct Investment: Recent Trends, Determinants, and Prospects." Policy Research Working Paper 1213, World Bank, Washington, D.C., November.

Kahler, Miles. 1986a. "Politics and International Debt: Explaining the Crisis." In *The Politics of International Debt,* ed. Miles Kahler, 11–36. Ithaca: Cornell University Press.

———, ed. 1986b. *The Politics of International Debt.* Ithaca: Cornell University Press.

———. 1998. *Capital Flows and Financial Crises.* Ithaca: Cornell University Press.

Kahn, Mohsin S., and Carmen M. Reinhart, eds. 1993. "Capital Flows in the APEC Region." IMF Occasional Paper 122, Washington, D.C., March.

Kaneko, Masaru, Kazuo Konishi, Naohiko Jin-no, and Masayoshi, Turumi. 1999. "Keizai Saisei he no Taikou Tei-an (An Alternative Proposal for Economic Revival)." *Sekai* (January): 35–62.

Kapstein, Ethan B. 1989. "Resolving the Regulator's Dilemma: International Coordination of Banking Regulations." *International Organization* 43, no. 2:323–47.

———. 1996. "Shockproof: The End of the Financial Crisis." *Foreign Affairs* 75, no. 1:2–8.

Kasamatsu, Felix S. 1989. "An Overview of the Latin American Economy: Global Context, Recent Trends, and Outlook." Background paper presented at the Fourth Latin America–Japan Business and Financial Cooperation Symposium, Nagoya, Japan, November 12–14.

Katada, Saori N. 1997. "Two Aid Hegemons: Japanese-American Interactions and Aid Allocations to Latin America and the Caribbean." *World Development* 25, no. 6:931–45.

———. 1998. "The Japanese Government in Two Mexican Crises: An Emerging Lender-of-Last-Resort?" *Pacific Affairs* 71, no. 1:61–79.

Katada, Saori N., and Timothy J. McKeown. 1998. "Aid Politics and Electoral Politics: Japan, 1970–1992." *International Studies Quarterly* 42, no. 3:591–600.

Kato, Kozo. 1996. "Kaihatsu Kyotyoku Seisaku omeguru Nihon to Doitsu no Taisho sei: 'Gaikyou kokka' Nihon, 'naiko kokka' Doitsu?" *Leviathan* 18:96–118.

——— 1998. *Tsusho Kokka no Kaihatsu Kyoryoku Seisaku: Nichi Doku no Kokusai teki Ichi to Kokunai Seido to no Kanren.* Tokyo: Bokutaku sha.

Kato, Kozo, Yuichiro Miwa, Tsutomu Shibata, Yoshikaz Miwa, Koichiro Fukui, Nobuhiko Ichikawa, Aiichiro Mogi, and Masahiro Furuta. 1994. *Policy-Based Finance: The Experience of Postwar Japan.* World Bank Discussion Papers, no. 211. Washington, D.C.: World Bank.

Kato, Masakatsu. 1969. "A Model of U.S. Foreign Aid Allocation: An Approach of a Decision-Making Scheme." In *Approaches to Measurement in International Relations:*

A Non-evangelical Survey, ed. Jo]hn E. Mueller, 198–215. New York: Appleton-Century-Crofts.

Katzenstein, Peter J. 1978. "Introduction: Domestic and International Forces and Strategies of Foreign Economic Policy." In *Between Power and Plenty: Foreign Economic Policies of Advanced Industrial States,* ed. Peter J. Katzenstein, 3–22. Madison: University of Wisconsin Press.

Katzenstein, Peter J., and Martin Rouse. 1993. "Japan as a Regional Power in Asia." In *Regionalism and Rivalry: Japan and the United States in Pacific Asia,* ed. Jeffrey A. Frankel and Miles Kahler, 217–48. Chicago: University of Chicago Press.

Katzenstein, Peter J., and Takashi Shiraishi, eds. 1997. *Network Power: Japan and Asia.* Ithaca: Cornell University Press.

Katzenstein, Peter J., and Yutaka Tsujinaka. 1995. "'Bullying,' 'Buying,' and 'Binding': US-Japanese Transnational Relations and Domestic Structures." In *Bringing Transnational Relations Back In: Non-state Actors, Domestic Structures, and International Institutions,* ed. Thomas Risse-Kappen, 79–111. Cambridge: Cambridge University Press.

Kawai, Masahiro. 1995. "Accumulation of Net External Assets in Japan." In *Japan, Europe, and International Financial Markets: Analytical and Empirical Perspectives,* ed. Ryuzo Sato, Richard M. Levich, and Rama V. Ramachandran, 73–123. Cambridge: Cambridge University Press.

———. 1998a. "The East Asian Currency Crisis: Causes and Lessons." *Contemporary Economic Policy* 16 (April): 157–72.

———. 1998b. "Higashi Ajia no Tsuka, Kinyuu Kiki to Nihon." *Sekai,* March, 81–88.

———. 1998c. "Tsuka Kiki Hakyu no Mekanizumu to Kyoukun." *Keizai Seminar* 521 (June): 24–31.

Kennedy, Peter. 1992. *A Guide to Econometrics.* 3d ed. Cambridge: MIT Press.

Keohane, Robert O. 1971. "The Big Influence of Small Allies." *Foreign Policy* 2:161–82.

———. 1984. *After Hegemony.* Princeton: Princeton University Press.

Keohane, Robert O., and Helen V. Milner, eds. 1996. *Internationalization and Domestic Politics.* Cambridge: Cambridge University Press.

Keohane, Robert O., and Joseph S. Nye Jr. 1977. *Power and Interdependence.* Boston: Little, Brown.

———. 1987. "Power and Interdependence Revisited." *International Organization* 41, no. 4:724–53.

Kerber, Victor Palma. 1989. "La Utopia del Pacífico." Mexico City. Mimeographed.

Kernell, Samuel, ed. 1991. *Parallel Politics: Economic Policymaking in Japan and the United States.* Tokyo: Japan Center for International Exchange and Brookings Institution.

Kindleberger, Charles P. 1970. *Power and Money: The Economics of International Politics and the Politics of International Economy.* New York: Basic.

———. 1981. "Dominance and Leadership in the International Economy: Exploitation, Public Goods, and Free Rides." *International Studies Quarterly* 25, no. 2:242–54.

———. 1986a. "International Public Goods without International Government." *American Economic Review* 76, no. 1:1–13.

———. 1986b. *The World in Depression, 1929–1939.* Berkeley: University of California Press.

———. 1989. *Manias, Panics, and Crashes: A History of Financial Crises.* Rev. ed. New York: Basic.

King, Gary, Robert O. Keohane, and Sidney Verba. 1994. *Designing Social Inquiry: Scientific Inference in Qualitative Research.* Princeton: Princeton University Press.

Kinoshita, Toshihiko. 1991. "Developments in the International Debt Strategy and Japan's Response." *EXIM Review* 10, no. 2:62–80.

———. 1998. "Higashi Ajia: Taigai Shihon Izongata Keizai Hatten no Zeijakusei no Kokufuku ni mukete." *Kokusai Mondai* 457 (April): 26–44.

Knorr, Klaus. 1975. *The Power of Nations: The Political Economy of International Relations.* New York: Basic.

Knorr, Klaus, and Frank N. Trager, eds. 1977. *Economic Issues and National Security.* New York: National Security Education Program of New York University.

Kohama, Hirohisa. 1998. "IMF Kyusai Pakkeiji wo Dou Hyoka suruka." *Keizai Seminar* 521 (June): 38–45.

———. 1999. "Higashi Ajia Keizai Kiki to Nihon no Yakuwari (The East Asian Economic Crisis and the Role of Japan)." *Sekai Keizai Hyoron* (March): 49–57.

Kohno, Masaru. 1997. *Japan's Postwar Party Politics.* Princeton: Princeton University Press.

Kojima, Kiyoshi. 1978a. *Direct Foreign Investment: A Japanese Model of Multinational Business Operations.* New York: Praeger.

———. 1978b. "Direct Foreign Investment to Developing Countries: The Issue of Over-presence." *Hitotsubashi Journal of Economics* 19, no. 1–2, December, 1–15.

———. 1986. "Japanese-Style Direct Foreign Investment." *Japanese Economic Studies* 14, no. 3:52–82.

Komiya, Ryutaro. 1996. "Guarded Optimism about the Economy." *Japan Echo* 24, no. 1:10–16.

Koppel, Bruce M., and Robert M. Orr Jr., eds. 1993. *Japan's Foreign Aid: Power and Policy in a New Era.* Boulder: Westview.

Kraft, Joseph. 1984. *The Mexican Rescue.* New York: Group of Thirty.

Krasner, Stephen D. 1976. "State Power and the Structure of International Trade." *World Politics* 27, no. 3:317–47.

———. 1984. "Approaches to the State: Alternative Conceptions and Historical Dynamics." *Comparative Politics* 16, no. 2:223–46.

———. 1985. "Structural Causes and Regime Consequences: Regimes as Intervening Variables." In *International Regimes,* ed. Stephen D. Krasner, 1–22. Ithaca: Cornell University Press.

Krause, Lawrence B., and Sueo Sekiguchi. 1976. "Japan and the World Economy." In *Asia's New Giant: How the Japanese Economy Works,* ed. Hugh Patrick and Henry Rosovsky, 383–458. Washington, D.C.: Brookings Institution.

Krugman, Paul. 1998. "Saving Asia: It's Time to Get Radical." *Fortune* 138, no. 5 (September 7): 75–80.

Kubota, Akira. 1985. "Foreign Aid: Giving with One Hand?" *Japan Quarterly* 32, no. 2:140–44.

Kuczynski, Pedro-Pablo. 1982/83. "Latin American Debt." *Foreign Affairs* 61, no. 2:344–64.

———. 1988. *Latin American Debt.* Baltimore: Johns Hopkins University Press.

Kunimoto, Iyo. 1993. "Japanese Migration to Latin America." In *Japan, the United States, and Latin America: Toward a Trilateral Relationship in the Western Hemisphere,* ed. Barbara Stallings and Gabriel Székely, 99–121. Baltimore: Johns Hopkins University Press.

Kunimune, Kozo. 1998. "Higashi Ajia de Nihon go Hatasubeki Yakuwariwa Nanika." *Keizai Seminar* 521 (June): 16–23.

Kunimune, Kozo, ed. 2000. *Ajia Tuka Kiki: Sono Gen-in to Taiou no Mondaiten* (The Asian Currency Crisis: The Cause and the Problems in Prescription). IDE Research Series No. 501. Chiba: Institute of Developing Economies.

Kurosawa, Sei-ichi. 1999. "Higashi Ajia Tuka Kinyuu Kiki to IMF Puroguramu no Mondai ten (The East Asian Currency and Financial Crisis and the Problems of the IMF Programs)." *Sekai Keizai Hyoron* (April) 27–35.

Kwan, C. H. 1998a. "A Japanese Perspective of Asia's Currency Crisis." Tokyo. Mimeographed.

———. 1998b. *En to Gen karamiru Ajia Tuka Kiki* (The Asian Currency Crisis Viewed from the Yen and the Yuan). Tokyo: Iwanami Shoten.

Landau, George, Julio Feo, and Akio Hosono. 1990. *Latin America at a Crossroads: The Challenge to the Trilateral Countries.* Report to the Trilateral Commission. New York, Paris, and Tokyo: The Triangle Paper 39.

Latin American Information Services. 1989. *Japan Inc. in Latin America: Status Report on Aid, Trade, Investment, and Debt.* Washington, D.C.

Lehman, Howard P. 1994. "International Creditors and the Third World: Strategies and Policies from Baker to Brady." *Journal of Developing Areas* 28 (January): 191–218.

Lehman, Howard P., and Jennifer L. McCoy. 1992. "The Dynamics of the Two-Level Bargaining Game: The 1988 Brazilian Debt Negotiations." *World Politics* 44, no. 4:600–644.

Leiderman, Leonardo, and Alfredo E. Thorne. 1996. "The 1994 Mexican Crisis and Its Aftermath: What Are the Main Lessons?" In *Private Capital Flows to Emerging Markets after the Mexican Crisis,* ed. Guillermo A. Calvo, Morris Goldstein, and Eduard Hochreiter, 1–43. Washington, D.C.: Institute for International Economics.

Lim, Linda Y. C. 1995. "Southeast Asia: Success through International Openness." In *Global Change, Regional Response: The New International Context of Development,* ed. Barbara Stallings, 238–71. Cambridge: Cambridge University Press.

Lincoln, Edward J. 1988. *Japan: Facing Economic Maturity.* Washington, D.C.: Brookings Institution.

———. 1990. *Japan's Unequal Trade.* Washington, D.C.: Brookings Institution.

———. 1993. *Japan's New Global Role.* Washington, D.C.: Brookings Institution.

———. 1998. "Japan's Financial Mess." *Foreign Affairs* 77, no. 3:57–66.

Lipson, Charles. 1981. "The International Organization and Third World Debt." *International Organization* 35, no. 4:603–31.

———. 1985. "Bankers' Dilemmas: Private Cooperation in Rescheduling Sovereign Debts." *World Politics* 38, no. 1:200–225.

———. 1986. "International Debt and International Institutions." In *The Politics of International Debt,* ed. Miles Kahler, 219–44. Ithaca: Cornell University Press.

Loriaux, Michael. 1997. "The End of Credit Activism in International States." In *Capital Ungoverned: Liberalizing Finance in Interventionist States,* by Michael Loriaux, Meredith Woo-Cumings, Kent E. Calder, Sylvia Maxfield, and Sofia Perez, 1–16. Ithaca: Cornell University Press.

Loser, Claudio, and Eliot Kalter, eds. 1992. "Mexico: The Strategy to Achieve Sustained Economic Growth." IMF Occasional Paper 99, Washington, D.C., September.

Lowenthal, Abraham F. 1990. *Partners in Conflict: The United States and Latin America in the 1990s.* Baltimore: Johns Hopkins University Press.

Lumsdaine, David Halloran. 1993. *Moral Vision in International Politics: The Foreign Aid Regime, 1949–1989.* Princeton: Princeton University Press.

Lustig, Nora. 1995. "The Mexican Peso Crisis: The Foreseeable and the Surprise." Brookings Discussion Papers in International Economics, no. 114, Washington, D.C., June.

———. 1996. "Mexico in Crisis, the U.S. to the Rescue: The Financial Assistance Packages of 1982 and 1995." Brookings Discussion Papers, Washington, D.C., June.

Mabuchi, Masaru. 1997. *Okurasho wa Naza Oitsumerareta noka.* Chuko Shinsho 1359, Tokyo: Chuo Koron Shinsha.

MacEachron, David. 1982/83. "The United States and Japan: The Bilateral Potential." *Foreign Affairs* 61, no. 2:400–415.

Maddison, Angus. 1985. *Two Crisis: Latin America and Asia, 1929–1938 and 1973–1983.* Paris: Development Centre of the Organisation for Economic Co-operation and Development.

Maeda, Masahiro, and Akio Hosono, eds. 1988. *Raten Amerika no Ruiseki saimu Monidai to Nihon no Taio.* Tokyo: Raten Amerika Kyokai.

Maeda, Masahiro, Hajime Mizuno, and Akio Hosono, eds. 1987. *Ruiseki saimu wo Kakaeru Raten Amerika to Nihon.* Tokyo: Raten Amerika Kyokai.

Maizels, Alfred, and Machiko K. Nissanke. 1984. "Motivations for Aid to Developing Countries." *World Development* 12, no. 9:879–900.

Mallaby, Sebastian. 1998. "America in Asia's Mirror: From Commodore Perry to the IMF." *National Interest* 52 (summer): 13–21.

Mansfield, Edward D., and Helen V. Milner. 1997. "The Political Economy of Regionalism: An Overview." In *The Political Economy of Regionalism,* ed. Edward D. Mansfield and Helen V. Milner, 1–19. New York: Columbia University Press.

Mansfield, Mike. 1989. "The U.S. and Japan: Sharing Our Destinies." *Foreign Affairs* 68, no. 2:3–15.

Martin, Lisa L. 1992. *Coercive Cooperation: Explaining Multilateral Economic Sanctions.* Princeton: Princeton University Press.

———. 1993. "Credibility, Costs, and Institutions: Cooperation on Economic Sanctions." *World Politics* 45, no. 3:406–32.

Maruya, Yoshio, ed. 1988. *Raten America no Keizai kiki to Gaikoku Toshi.* Kekyu sosho 376. Tokyo: Ajia Keizai Kenkyujo.

Mathis, John F., ed. 1981. *Offshore Lending by U.S. Commercial Banks.* Washington, D.C.: Bankers' Association for Foreign Trade.

Matsukawa, Michiya. 1987. *The Japanese Trade Surplus and Capital Outflow.* Occasional Papers, no. 22. New York: Group of Thirty.

Maxfield, Sylvia. 1997. "Capital Mobility and Mexican Financial Liberalization." In *Capital Ungoverned: Liberalizing Finance in Interventionist States,* by Michael Loriaux, Meredith Woo-Cumings, Kent E. Calder, Sylvia Maxfield, and Sofia Perez, 92–119. Ithaca: Cornell University Press.

———. 1998. "Effects of International Portfolio Flows on Government Policy Choices." In *Capital Flows and Financial Crises,* ed. Miles Kahler, 69–92. Ithaca: Cornell University Press.

McDonald, Donogh C. 1982. "Debt Capacity and Developing Country Borrowing: A Survey of the Literature." *IMF Staff Papers* 29, no. 4:603–46.

McKenzie, George, and Stephan Thomas. 1992. *Financial Instability and the International Debt Problem.* New York: St. Martin's.

McKibbin, Warwick J., and Jeffrey D. Sachs. 1991. *Global Linkages: Macroeconomic Inter-*

dependence and Cooperation in the World Economy. Washington, D.C.: Brookings Institution.
McKinnon, Ronald I. 1973. *Money and Capital in Economic Development.* Washington, D.C.: Brookings Institution.
McLeod, Ross H., and Ross Garnaut, eds. 1998. *East Asia in Crisis: From Being a Miracle to Needing One?* New York: Routledge.
Mendelsohn, M. S. 1980. *Money on the Move: The Modern International Capital Market.* New York: McGraw-Hill.
———. 1981. *The Outlook for International Banking: A Survey of Opinion among Leading International Bankers.* New York: Group of Thirty.
Milner, Helen. 1992. "International Theories of Cooperation among Nations: Strengths and Weaknesses." *World Politics* 44, no. 3:466–96.
———. 1997. *Interests, Institutions, and Information: Domestic Politics and International Relations.* Princeton: Princeton University Press.
Milner, Helen V., and Robert O. Keohane. 1996a. "Internationalization and Domestic Politics: An Introduction." In *Internationalization and Domestic Politics,* ed. Robert O. Keohane and Helen V. Milner, 3–24. Cambridge: Cambridge University Press.
———. 1996b. "Internationalization and Domestic Politics: A Conclusion." In *Internationalization and Domestic Politics,* ed. Robert O. Keohane and Helen V. Milner, 243–58. Cambridge: Cambridge University Press.
Minor, Michael. 1985. "Decision Models and Japanese Foreign Policy Decision Making." *Asian Survey* 25, no. 12:1229–41.
Mishan, E. J. 1969. "The Relationship between Joint Products, Collective Goods, and External Effects." *Journal of Political Economy* 77, no. 3:329–48.
Mishkin, Frederic S. 1992. *The Economics of Money, Banking, and Financial Markets.* 3d ed. Boston: Mishikin Economics.
———. 1996. *Understanding Financial Crises: A Developing Country Perspective.* Working Paper Series, no. 5600, Cambridge, MA, National Bureau of Economic Research.
Miyashita, Akitoshi. 1999. "Gaiatsu and Japan's Foreign Aid: Rethinking the Reactive-Proactive Debate." *International Studies Quarterly* 43 no. 4:695–731.
Mochizuki, Mike, ed. 1997. *Toward a True Alliance: Restructuring U.S.-Japan Security Relations.* Washington, D.C.: Brookings Institution.
Montiel, Peter J. 1996. "Policy Responses to Surges in Capital Inflows: Issues and Lessons." In *Private Capital Flows to Emerging Markets after the Mexican Crisis,* ed. Guillermo A. Calvo, Morris Goldstein, and Eduard Hochreiter, 189–218. Washington, D.C.: Institute for International Economics.
Morita, Akio, and Shintaro Ishihara. 1989. *"No" to Ieru Nihon: Shin Nichi-Bei Kankei no kado.* Tokyo: Kobunsha.
Mosley, Paul. 1985. "The Political Economy of Foreign Aid: A Model of the Market for a Public Good." *Economic Development and Cultural Change* 33, no. 2:373–93.
Mulgan, Aurelia George. 2000. "Japan: A Setting Sun?" *Foreign Affairs* 79, no. 4 (July/August): 40–52.
Muramatsu, Michio, and Ellis S. Kraus. 1987. "The Conservative Policy Line and the Development of Patterned Pluralism." In *The Political Economy of Japan,* vol. 1, *The Domestic Transformation,* ed. Kozo Yamamura and Yasukichi Yasuba, 516–54. Stanford: Stanford University Press.
Murphy, R. Taggart. 1989. "Power without Purpose: The Crisis of Japan's Global Financial Dominance." *Harvard Business Review,* March–April, 71–83.

———. 1996. *The Weight of the Yen: How Denial Imperils American's Future and Ruins an Alliance.* New York: Norton.

Nakai, Saori. 1989. "Japan's Foreign Aid, 1970–1987: The Underlying Forces of Change." Master's thesis, University of North Carolina at Chapel Hill.

Nakakita, Toru. 1998. "Sekai Hyojun to Ajia Kinyuu Kiki." *Kokusai Mondai* 457 (April): 2–14.

Nakane, Chie. 1967. *Tate Shakai no Ningen Kankei: Tan-itsu Shakai no Riron.* Tokyo: Koudansha Gendai Shinsho.

Nakao, Shigeo. 1995. *The Political Economy of Japan Money.* Tokyo: University of Tokyo Press.

Nau, Henry R. 1990. *The Myth of America's Decline: Leading the World Economy into the 1990's.* New York: Oxford University Press.

Naya, Seiji. 1990. "Economic Performance: NIEs and Beyond." In *Perspectives on the Pacific Basin Economy: A Comparison of Asia and Latin America,* ed. Takao Fukuchi and Mitsuhiro Kagami, 153–92. Tokyo.

Nelson, Joan M., ed. 1990. *Economic Crisis and Policy Choice: The Politics of Adjustment in the Third World.* Princeton: Princeton University Press.

Nester, William R. 1992. *Japan and the Third World: Patterns, Power, Prospects.* New York: St. Martin's.

Nihon Ginko [Bank of Japan]. 1995. *Wagakuni no Kinyuu Seido.* New ed. Tokyo: Nihon Shinyou chosa.

Nishijima, Shoji, and Peter H. Smith, eds. 1996. *Cooperation or Rivalry: Regional Integration in the Americas and the Pacific Rim.* Boulder: Westview.

Noble, Gregory W., and John Ravenhill. 2000. "Causes and Consequences of the Asian Financial Crisis." In *The Asian Financial Crisis and the Architecture of Global Finance,* ed., Noble, Gregory W. and John Ravenhill. Cambridge: Cambridge University Press. 1–35.

Noble, Gregory W., and John Ravenhill, eds. 2000. *The Asian Financial Crisis and the Architecture of Global Finance.* Cambridge: Cambridge University Press.

Noguchi, Yukio. 1996. "Macroeconomic Policies and Asset Price Inflation: A Political-Economic Analysis of the 'Bubble' Economy." In *U.S.-Japan Macroeconomic Relations: Interaction and Interdependence in the 1980s,* ed. Yukio Noguchi and Kozo Yamamura, 52–78. Seattle: University of Washington Press.

Noland, Marcus, Li-Gang Liu, Sherman Robinson, and Zhi Wang. 1998. *Global Economic Effects of the Asian Currency Devaluations.* Policy Analysis in International Economics, no. 56. Washington, D.C.: Institute for International Economics.

Nunnenkamp, Peter. 1985. "Bank Lending to Developing Countries and Possible Solutions to International Debt Problems." *Kyklos* 38, no. 4:555–77.

———. 1986. "Bank Lending and Government Intervention in Capital Markets: Has Recycling Gone Too Far?" In Herbert Giersch, (ed.), *The International Debt Problem: Lessons for the Future,* ed. Herbert Giersch, 42–65. Kiel: Institut für Weltwirtschaft an der Universität Kiel.

———. 1990. "Determinants of Voluntary and Involuntary Bank Lending to Developing Countries in the 1980s." *Kyklos* 43, no. 4:555–77.

Nye, Joseph S., Jr. 1995. "The Case for Deep Engagement." *Foreign Affairs* 74, no. 4:90–102.

Ochi, Shoji. 1991. "Japanese Banks and Third World Debt." In *Yen for Development: Japanese Foreign Aid and the Politics of Burden-Sharing,* ed. Shafiqul Islam, 152–60, with comments by Barbara Stallings on 161–68. New York: Council on Foreign Relations Press.

Ogata, Sadako. 1989. "Shifting Power Relations in Multilateral Development Banks." *Journal of International Studies* 22:1–25.

Ohmae, Ken-ichi. 1991. *The Borderless World: Power and Strategy in the Interlinked Economy.* New York: Harper Perennial.

Okamoto, Yumiko, and Kazuhiko Yokota. 1992. "Nihon no Enjo seisaku no Suryou Bunseki." *Journal of International Development Studies* 1, no. 2:1–13.

Okimoto, Daniel I., ed. 1982. *Japan's Economy: Coping with Change in the International Environment.* Boulder: Westview.

Okita, Saburo. 1989. "Japan's Quiet Strength." *Foreign Policy* 75:128–45.

Olson, Mancur. 1971. *The Logic of Collective Action: Public Goods and the Theory of Groups.* Cambridge: Harvard University Press.

Organski, A. F. K. 1958. *World Politics.* New York: Knopf.

Orr, Robert M., Jr. 1988. "The Aid Factor in U.S.-Japan Relations." *Asian Survey* 28, no. 7:740–56.

———. 1990. *The Emergence of Japan's Foreign Aid Power.* New York: Columbia University Press.

Osugi, K. 1990. *Japan's Experience of Financial Deregulation since 1984 in an International Perspective.* BIS Economic Papers, no. 26. Basel: Bank for International Settlements.

Oye, Kenneth A. 1992. *Economic Discrimination and Political Exchange: World Political Economy in the 1930s and 1980s.* Princeton: Princeton University Press.

———, ed. 1986. *Cooperation under Anarchy.* Princeton: Princeton University Press.

Ozawa, Terumoto. 1979. *Multinationalism, Japanese Style: The Political Economy of Outward Dependency.* Princeton: Princeton University Press.

———. 1980. "Japan's New Resource Diplomacy: Government-Backed Group Investment." *Journal of World Trade Law* 14, no. 1:3–13.

———. 1989. *Recycling Japan's Surplus for Developing Countries.* Paris: Development Centre of the Organisation for Economic Cooperation and Development.

Özler, Sule. 1989. "Commercial Bank Lending to Developing Countries: The Expansion of the Market." *Contemporary Policy Issues* 7, no. 3:1–10.

———. 1992. "The Evolution of Credit Terms: An Empirical Study of Commercial Bank Lending to Developing Countries." *Journal of Development Economics* 38, no. 1:79–97.

Padoan, Pier Carlo. 1990. "The Debt Crisis: From Declining Hegemony to Multilateralism." In *Debt and Transfiguration? Prospects for Latin America's Economic Revival,* ed. David Felix, 199–217. Armonk, N.Y.: M. E. Sharpe.

———. 1997. "Regional Agreements as Clubs: The European Case." In *The Political Economy of Regionalism,* ed. Edward D. Mansfield and Helen V. Milner, 105–33. New York: Columbia University Press.

Palma, Gabriel. 1998. "Three and a Half Cycles of 'Mania, Panic, and [Asymmetric] Crash': East Asia and Latin America Compared." *Cambridge Journal of Economics* 22:789–808.

Patrick, Hugh, and Henry Rosovsky 1976. "Japan's Economic Performance: An Overview." In *Asia's New Giant: How the Japanese Economy Works,* ed. Hugh Patrick and Henry Rosovsky, 1–62. Washington, D.C.: Brookings Institution.

Pauly, Louis W. 1987. *Regulatory Politics in Japan: The Case of Foreign Banking.* Ithaca: China-Japan Program, Cornell University.

———. 1988. *Opening Financial Markets: Banking Politics on the Pacific Rim.* Ithaca: Cornell University Press.

———. 1990. "Institutionalizing a Stalemate: National Financial Policies and the International Debt Crisis." *Journal of Public Policy* 10, no. 1:23–43.

———. 1997. *Who Elected the Bankers? Surveillance and Control in the World Economy.* Ithaca: Cornell University Press.

Pempel, T. J. 1978. "Japanese Foreign Economic Policy: The Domestic Bases for International Behavior." In *Between Power and Plenty: Foreign Economic Policies of Advanced Industrial States,* ed. Peter J. Katzenstein, 139–90. Madison: University of Wisconsin Press.

———. 1987. "The Unbundling of 'Japan, Inc.': The Changing Dynamics of Japanese Policy Formation." *Journal of Japanese Studies* 13, no. 2:271–306.

———. 1992. "Of Dragons and Development." *Journal of Public Policy* 12, no. 1:79–95.

———. 1997. "Regime Shift: Japanese Politics in a Changing World Economy." *Journal of Japanese Studies* 23, no. 2:333–61.

———. 1998. *Regime Shift: Comparative Dynamics of the Japanese Political Economy.* Ithaca: Cornell University Press.

———. 1999a. "Structural Gaiatsu: International Finance and Political Change in Japan." *Comparative Political Studies* 32, no. 8 (December): 908–32.

———, ed. 1999b. *The Politics of the Asian Economic Crisis.* Ithaca: Cornell University Press.

Perry, Guillermo, and Daniel Lederman. 1998. "Financial Vulnerability, Spillover Effects, and Contagion: Lessons from the Asian Crisis for Latin America." World Bank, Washington, D.C. Mimeographed.

Petri, Peter A. 1993. "The East Asian Trading Bloc: An Analytical History." In *Regionalism and Rivalry: Japan and the United States in Pacific Asia,* ed. Jeffrey A. Frankel and Miles Kahler, 21–52. Chicago: University of Chicago Press.

Pincus, John. 1965. *Economic Aid and International Cost Sharing.* Baltimore: Johns Hopkins University Press.

Polanyi, Karl. 1944. *The Great Transformation.* 1975. Reprint, New York: Octagon.

Posen, Adam S. 1998. *Restoring Japan's Economic Growth.* Washington, D.C.: Institute for International Economics.

Prestowitz, Clyde. 1988. *Trading Places: How We Are Giving Our Future to Japan and How to Reclaim It.* New York: Basic.

Purcell, Susan Kaufman, and Robert M. Immerman. 1992. *Japan and Latin America in the New Global Order.* Boulder: Lynne Rienner.

Purrington, Courtney, and A. K. 1991. "Tokyo's Policy Responses during the Gulf Crisis." *Asian Survey* 31, no. 4:307–23.

Putnam, Robert D. 1988. "Diplomacy and Domestic Politics: The Logic of Two-Level Games." *International Organization* 42, no. 3:427–60.

Pyle, Kenneth J. 1992. "Can Japan Lead? The New Internationalism and the Burdens of History." In *Power, Economics, and Security: The United States and Japan in Focus,* ed. Henry Bienen, 189–225. Boulder: Westview.

Ragin, Charles C. 1987. *The Comparative Method: Moving beyond Qualitative and Quantitative Strategies.* Berkeley: University of California Press.

Ragin, Charles C., and Howard S. Becker, eds. 1992. *What Is a Case? Exploring the Foundations of Social Inquiry.* Cambridge: Cambridge University Press.

Ramirez de la O, Rogelio. 1996. "The Mexican Peso Crisis and Recession of 1994–1995:

Preventable Then, Avoidable in the Future?" In *The Mexican Peso Crisis: International Perspectives,* ed. Riordan Roett, 11–32. Boulder: Lynne Rienner.

Ramseyer, J. Mark, and Frances McCall Rosenbluth. 1993. *Japan's Political Marketplace.* Cambridge: Harvard University Press.

Rapkin, David P., and John U. Elston. 1995. "Institutional Adjustment to Changed Power Distributions: Japan and the United States in the IMF." Paper presented at the annual meeting of the International Studies Association, Chicago, Ill., February 21–25.

Richardson, J. David. 1990. "The Political Economy of Strategic Trade Policy." *International Organization* 44, no. 1:107–35.

Rieffel, Alexis. 1985. *The Role of the Paris Club in Managing Debt Problems.* Essays in International Finance, no. 161. Princeton: Princeton University.

Risse-Kappen, Thomas. 1995. "Bringing Transnational Relations Back In: Introduction." In *Bringing Transnational Relations Back In: Non-State Actors, Domestic Structures, and International Institutions,* ed. Thomas Risse-Kappen, 3–33. Cambridge: Cambridge University Press.

Rix, Alan. 1980. *Japan's Economic Aid: Policy-Making and Politics.* New York: St.Martin's.

———. 1984. "National Power and Japanese Foreign Policy." In *Japan's Impact on the World,* ed. Alan Rix and Ross Mouer, 87–101. Canberra: Japanese Studies Associations of Australia.

Roett, Riordan. 1996a. "The Mexican Devaluation and the U.S. Response: Potomac Politics, 1995-Style." In *The Mexican Peso Crisis: International Perspectives,* ed. Riordan Roett, 33–48. Boulder: Lynne Rienner.

———. 1996b. "Lessons and Conclusions." In *The Mexican Peso Crisis: International Perspectives,* ed. Riordan Roett, 113–20. Boulder: Lynne Rienner.

Roosa, Robert V. 1986. *The United States and Japan in the International Monetary System, 1946–1985.* Occasional Papers, no. 21. New York: Group of Thirty.

Rosecrance, Richard, and Jennifer Taw. 1990. "Japan and the Theory of International Leadership." *World Politics* 42, no. 2:184–209.

Rosenbluth, Frances McCall. 1989. *Financial Politics in Contemporary Japan.* Ithaca: Cornell University Press.

———. 1991. "Japanese Banks in Mexico: The Role of Government in Private Decisions." *International Journal* 46, no. 4:668–86.

———. 1996. "Internationalization and Electoral Politics in Japan." In *Internationalization and Domestic Politics,* ed. Robert O. Keohane and Helen V. Milner, 137–56. Cambridge: Cambridge University Press.

Rosenthal, Robert W. 1991. "On the Incentives Associated with Sovereign Debt." *Journal of International Economics* 30, no. 112:167–76.

Rowley, Anthony. 1997. "International Finance: Asian Fund, Rest in Peace." *Capital Trends* 2, no. 1 (December): 1–3.

Ruggie, John Gerard. 1983. "International Regime, Transactions, and Change: Embedded Liberalism in the Postwar Economic Order." In *International Regimes,* ed. Stephen D. Krasner, 195–231. Ithaca: Cornell University Press.

Sachs, Jeffrey. 1984. *Theoretical Issues in International Borrowing.* Princeton Studies in International Finance, no. 54. Princeton: Princeton University.

———. 1989a. "Efficient Debt Reduction." In *Dealing with the Debt Crisis,* ed. Ishrat Husai and Ishac Diwan, 176–92. Washington, D.C.: World Bank.

———. 1989b. *New Approaches to the Latin American Debt Crisis.* Essays in International Finance, no. 174. Princeton: Princeton University.

———. 1998. "The IMF and the Asian Flu." *American Prospect* 37 (March/April): 16–21.

———, ed. 1989c. *Developing Country Debt and Economic Performance.* Vol. 1, *The International Financial System.* Washington, D.C.: National Bureau of Economic Research.

Sachs, Jeffrey, and Harry Huizinga. 1987. "U.S. Commercial Banks and the Developing-Country Debt Crisis." *Brookings Papers on Economic Activity* 2:555–606.

Sachs, Jeffrey, Aaron Tornell, and Andres Velasco. 1996. *Financial Crises in Emerging Markets: The Lessons from 1995.* Working Paper Series, no. 5576, Cambridge, MA: National Bureau of Economic Research.

Sakakibara, Eisuke. 1997. "The Once and Future Boom." *Economist* 342 (March 22): 89–90.

Samejima, Shinsuke. 1982. "Can Japan Steer Its Foreign Aid Policy Clear of Militarism?" *Japan Quarterly* 29, no. 1:30–38.

Sandler, Todd. 1992. *Collective Action: Theory and Application.* Ann Arbor: University of Michigan Press.

Sandler, Todd, and John T. Tschirhart. 1980. "The Economic Theory of Clubs: An Evaluative Survey." *Journal of Economic Literature* 18 (December): 1481–521.

Sato, Hideo. 1996. "Global Leadership Sharing: A Framework of Analysis." In *Leadership Sharing in the New International System: Japan and the United States,* ed. Hideo Sato and I. M. Destler, 1–29. Ibaraki, Japan: University of Tsukuba.

Sato, Hideo, and I. M. Destler, eds. 1996. *Leadership Sharing in the New International System: Japan and the United States.* Ibaraki, Japan: University of Tsukuba.

Schadler, Susan, Maria Carkovic, Adam Bennett, and Robert Kahn. 1993. "Recent Experiences with Surges in Capital Inflows." IMF Occasional Paper 108, Washington, D.C., December.

Schaller, Michael. 1997. *Altered States: The United States and Japan since the Occupation.* Oxford: Oxford University Press.

Schmiegelow, Henrik. 1986. "Global Dimensions in U.S.-Japan Relations." *Aussenpolitik* 37, no. 3:222–38.

———. 1990. "The Mexican Debt Agreement: A Model for Solving the International Debt Problem?" *Aussenpolitik* 41, no. 3:291–96.

Schmiegelow, Henrik, and Michele Schmiegelow. 1986. "How Japan Affects the International System." *International Organization* 44, no. 4:553–88.

Schmiegelow, Michele, ed. 1986. *Japan's Response to Crisis and Change in the World Economy.* Armonk, N.Y.: M. E. Sharpe.

Schoppa, Leonard J. 1993. "Two-Level Games and Bargaining Outcomes: Why Gaiatsu Succeeds in Japan in Some Cases but Not Others." *International Organization* 47, no. 3:353–86.

———. 1997. *Bargaining with Japan: What American Pressure Can and Cannot Do.* New York: Columbia University Press.

Schwenninger, Sherle R. 1995. "America's New Solvency Crisis." *World Policy Journal* 12, no. 2:1–24.

Shilling, John D., ed. 1992. *Beyond Syndicated Loans: Sources of Credit for Developing Countries.* World Bank Technical Paper 163. Washington, D.C.: World Bank.

Shimazaki, Kyuya. 1999. *Tuka Kiki to Yen no Kokusaika* (Currency Crisis and Internationalization of the Yen). Tokyo: Taga Shuppan.

Silverman, David, ed. 1997. *Qualitative Research: Theory, Method, and Practice.* London: Sage.

Simmons, Beth A. 1994. *Who Adjusts? Domestic Sources of Foreign Economic Policy during the Interwar Years.* Princeton: Princeton University Press.

Simons, Herbert A. 1953. "Notes on the Observation and Measurement of Political Power." *Journal of Politics* 15, no. 4:500–516.

Sims, Christopher A. 1980. "Macroeconomics and Reality." *Econometrica* 48, no. 1:1–35.

Smith, Clint E. 1996. "International Perspectives on the Mexican Peso Crisis: An Introduction." In *The Mexican Peso Crisis: International Perspectives,* ed. Riordan Roett, 1–10. Boulder: Lynne Rienner.

Smith, Peter H. 1990. "Japan, Latin America, and the New International Order." Visiting Research Fellow Monograph Series, no. 179. Tokyo: Institute of Developing Economies.

———. 1996. *Talons of the Eagle: Dynamics of U.S.-Latin American Relations.* New York: Oxford University Press.

Smith, Roy C. 1989. *The Global Bankers.* New York: Truman Tally.

Smith, Roy C., and Ingo Walter, 1997. *Global Banking.* New York: Oxford University Press.

Smith, Tony. 1990. "The Underdevelopment of Development Literature: The Case of Dependency Theory." *World Politics* 31, no. 2:247–88.

Snidal, Duncan. 1985. "The Limits of Hegemonic Stability Theory." *International Organization* 39, no. 4:579–614.

Solberg, Ronald L. 1988. *Sovereign Rescheduling: Risk and Portfolio Management.* London and Boston: Unwin Hyman.

Spindler, Andrew. 1984. *The Politics of International Credit: Private Finance and Foreign Policy in Germany and Japan.* Washington, D.C.: Brookings Institution.

Stallings, Barbara. 1987. *Banker to the Third World: U.S. Portfolio Investment in Latin America, 1990–1986.* Berkeley: University of California Press.

———. 1990a. "Debtor versus Creditors: Power Relations and Policy Response to the 1980s Crisis." In *Debt and Transfiguration? Prospects for Latin America's Economic Revival,* ed. David Felix, 83–103. Armonk, N.Y.: M. E. Sharpe, 1990.

———. 1990b. "The Reluctant Giant: Japan and the Latin American Debt Crisis." *Journal of Latin American Studies* 22, (February): pt. 1, 1–30.

———. 1990c. "The Role of Foreign Capital in Economic Development: A Comparison of Latin America and East Asia." In *Manufacturing Miracles: Paths of Industrialization in Latin America and East Asia,* ed. Gray Gereffi and Don Wyman, 55–89. Princeton: Princeton University Press.

———. 1992. "International Influence on Economic Policy: Debt, Stabilization, and Structural Reform." In *The Politics of Economic Adjustment: International Constraints, Distributive Conflicts, and the State,* ed. Stephan Haggard and Robert R. Kaufman, 41–88. Princeton: Princeton University Press.

———. 1995. "Introduction: Global Change, Regional Response." In *Global Change, Regional Response: The New International Context of Development,* ed. Barbara Stallings, 1–30. Cambridge: Cambridge University Press.

Stallings, Barbara, and Wolfgang Streeck. 1995. "Capitalism in Conflict? The United States, Europe, and Japan in the Post–Cold War World." In *Global Change, Regional Response: The New International Context of Development,* ed. Barbara Stallings, 67–99. Cambridge: Cambridge University Press.

Stallings, Barbara, and Gabriel Székely. 1993a. "The New Trilateralism: The United States,

Japan, and Latin America." In *Japan, the United States, and Latin America: Toward a Trilateral Relationship in the Western Hemisphere,* ed. Barbara Stallings and Gabriel Székely, 3–45. Baltimore: Johns Hopkins University Press.

———, eds. 1993b. *Japan, the United States, and Latin America: Toward a Trilateral Relationship in the Western Hemisphere.* Baltimore: Johns Hopkins University Press.

Stimson, James A. 1985. "Regression in Space and Time: A Statistical Essay." *American Journal of Political Science* 29, no. 4:914–47.

Strange, Susan. 1983. "Cave! Hic Dragons: A Critique of Regime Analysis." In *International Regimes,* ed. Stephen D. Krasner, 337–54. Ithaca: Cornell University Press.

———. 1987. "The Persistent Myth of Lost Hegemony." *International Organization* 41, no. 4:551–74.

———. 1994. *States and Market.* 2d ed. London: Pinter.

———. 1998. *Mad Money: When Markets Outgrow Governments.* Ann Arbor: University of Michigan Press.

Sudo, Sueo. 1988. "Japan-ASEAN Relations: New Dimensions in Japanese Foreign Policy." *Asian Survey* 28, no. 5:509–25.

Summers, Robert, and Alan Heston. 1991. "The Penn World Table (Mark 5): An Expanded Set of International Comparisons, 1950–1987." *Quarterly Journal of Economics,* May, 1–41.

Suzuki, Yoshio. 1980. *Money and Banking in Contemporary Japan: The Theoretical Setting and Its Application.* New Haven: Yale University Press.

———. 1996. "Reviving Financial Markets with a New Regulatory System." *Japan Echo* 28, no. 1:21–24.

Takeda, Yasuhiro. 1991. "Aid Strategy in the Post–Cold War Era." USJP Occasional Paper 91-15, Program on U.S.-Japan Relations, Center for International Affairs and Reischauer Institute of Japanese Studies, Harvard University.

Tamaki, Rintaro. 1998. "Ajia Tsuka Kiki to IMF no Taio." *Keizai Seminar* 521 (June): 10–14.

Teranishi, Juro. 1983. "Wagakuni no Seifu Kaihatsu Enjo (ODA) Seisaku ni tsuite." *Keizai Kenkyu* 34, no. 2:121–29.

———. 1986. "The "Catch-up" Process, Financial System, and Japan's Rise as a Capital Exporter." *Hitotsubashi Journal of Economics* 27, special issue: 133–46.

Tokunaga, Yoshiro. 1988. *Ruiseki Saimu mondai to Nihon Keizai: Nihon Shudo no Saimu menjo wo Teian suru.* Tokyo: Touyou Keizai shinpo sha.

Truman, Edwin M. 1996. "The Risks and Implications of External Financial Shocks: Lessons from Mexico." International Finance Discussion Papers, no. 535, Board of Governors of the Federal Reserve System, Washington, D.C., January.

Tsunekawa, Keiichi. 1994. "NAFTA's Impact on Japan." Occasional Paper 58, Woodrow Wilson Center Asian Program, Washington, D.C.

Tussie, Diana, ed. 1982. *Latin America in the World Economy: New Perspectives.* New York: St. Martin's.

Tyson, Laura D'Andrea. 1992. *Who's Bashing Whom? Trade Conflict in High-Technology Industries.* Washington, D.C.: Institute for International Economics.

Ueda, Hideaki. 1995. "Japan's Aid Policies and Institutions." *Journal of International Development* 7, no. 2:245–51.

Uriu, Robert. 2000. "The Impact of Policy Ideas: Revisionism and the Clinton Administration's Trade Policy toward Japan." In *New Perspectives on U.S.-Japan Relations,* ed. Gerald L. Curtis, 213–40. Tokyo: Japan Center for International Exchange.

Usui, Mikoto. 1979. "Enjo Kyo kyusha no Kodo—Shiron." *Annual of Japan Economic Policy Association* 27:64–69.

———. 1987. "Nikoku kan Kaihatsu Enjo Kyouyo Kodo no Bunseki." *Annual of Japan Economic Policy Association* 35:145–51.

Van Wolferen, Karl. 1989. *The Enigma of Japanese Power: People and Politics in a Stateless Nation.* New York: Knopf.

Varas, Augusto. 1995. "Latin America: Toward a New Reliance on the Market." In *Global Change, Regional Response: The New International Context of Development,* ed. Barbara Stallings, 272–308. Cambridge: Cambridge University Press.

Vincent, Jack E. 1983. "WEIS vs. COPDAB: Correspondence Problems." *International Studies Quarterly* 27, no. 2:161–68.

Viner, Jacob. 1948. "Power versus Plenty as Objectives of Foreign Policy in the Seventeenth and Eighteenth Centuries." *World Politics* 1, no. 1:1–29.

Vogel, Ezra F. 1979. *Japan as Number One: Lessons for America.* Cambridge: Harvard University Press.

———. 1986. "Pax Nipponica?" *Foreign Affairs* 64, no. 4:752–67.

———. 1994. "Japan as Number One in Asia." In *The United States, Japan, and Asia: Challenges for U.S. Policy,* ed. Gerald L. Curtis, 159–83. New York: Norton.

Volcker, Paul A., and Toyoo Gyohten. 1992. *Changing Fortunes: The World's Money and the Threat to American Leadership.* New York: Times.

Wade, Robert. 1996a. "Globalization and Its Limits: Reports of the Death of the National Economy Are Greatly Exaggerated." In *National Diversity and Global Capitalism,* ed. Suzanne Berger and Ronald Dore, 60–87. Ithaca: Cornell University Press.

———. 1996b. "Japan, the World Bank, and the Art of Paradigm Maintenance: The East Asian Miracle in Political Perspective." *New Left Review* 217 (May/June): 3–36.

———. 1998a. "The Asian Crisis and the Global Economy: Causes, Consequences, and Cure." *Current History* 97, no. 622:361–73.

———. 1998b. "The Asian Debt-and-Development Crisis of 1997–?: Causes and Consequences." *World Development* 26, no. 8:1535–53.

Wadhwani, Sushil. 1996. "Explaining the Crisis and Preventing Future Crisis." In *Private Capital Flows to Emerging Markets After the Mexican Crisis,* ed. Guillermo A. Calvo, Morris Goldstein, and Eduard Hochreiter, 301–6. Washington, D.C.: Institute for International Economics.

Wallich, Henry C. 1984. *Insurance of Bank Lending to Developing Countries.* Occasional Papers, no. 15. New York: Group of Thirty.

Wan, Ming. 1993. "Spending Strategies in World Politics: How Japan Used Its Economic Power, 1952–1992." Ph.D. diss., Harvard University.

———. 1995. "Spending Strategies in World Politics: How Japan Has Used Its Economic Power in the Past Decade." *International Studies Quarterly* 39, no. 1:85–108.

Webb, Michael C. 1991. "International Economic Structures, Government Interests, and International Coordination of Macroeconomic Adjustment Policies." *International Organization* 45, no. 3:309–42.

Wellons, Philip A. 1982. "Economic Nationalism and International Banking: The Implications for U.S. Policy." Working paper, Cambridge, MA.

———. 1985. "International Debt: The Behavior of Banks in a Politicized Environment." *International Organization* 39, no. 3:441–71.

———. 1987. *Passing the Buck: Banks, Governments, and Third World Debt.* Cambridge: Harvard Business School Press.

Wellons, Philip A., et. al. 1986. *Banks and Specialized Financial Intermediaries in Development.* Paris: Development Centre of the Organization for Economic Co-operation and Development.

Wertman, Patricia A. 1995. "The Mexican Support Package: A Survey and Analysis." Congressional Reporting Service Report for Congress, Report No. 95-1006E, September 19.

Williamson, John. 1988. *Voluntary Approaches to Debt Relief.* Policy Analysis in International Economics, no. 25. Washington, D.C.: Institute for International Economics.

———. 1990a. "The Progress of Policy Reform in Latin America." In *Latin American Adjustment: How Much Has Happened?* ed. John Williamson, 353–420. Washington, D.C.: Institute for International Economics.

———, ed. 1990b. *Latin American Adjustment: How Much Has Happened?* Washington, D.C.: Institute for International Economics.

Wionczek, Miguel S., Serrato Marcela, Toshiaki Yuasa, and Yoshio Maruya. 1981. *The Economic Relations between Japan and Mexico, with Special Reference to the Influences of Mexican Petroleum Development.* Joint Research Programs Series, no. 27. Washington, D.C.: Institute of Developing Economies.

Wionczek, Miguel S., and Miyokei Shinohara, eds. 1982. *Las Relaciones Económicas Entre México y Japón: Influencia del Desarrollo Petrolero Mexicano.* Mexico City: El Colegio de México.

Wood, Christopher. 1994. *The End of Japan Inc.: And How the New Japan Will Look.* New York: Simon and Schuster.

Wood, Robert E. 1986. *From Marshall Plan to Debt Crisis: Foreign Aid and Development Choices in the World Economy.* Berkeley: University of California Press.

Yamamura, Kozo. 1994. "The Deliberate Emergence of a Free Trader: The Japanese Political Economy in Transition." In *Japan: A New Kind of Superpower?* ed. Craig Garby and Mary Brown Bullock, 35–52. Baltimore: Johns Hopkins University Press.

———. 1996. "The Legacies of a Bargain: The Reagan Deficits and Japan's 'Bubble.'" In *U.S.-Japan Macroeconomic Relations: Interaction and Interdependence in the 1980s,* ed. Yukio Noguchi and Kozo Yamamura, 13–52. Seattle: University of Washington Press.

Yamamura, Kozo, and Yasukichi Yasuba, eds. 1987. *The Political Economy of Japan.* Vol. 1, *The Domestic Transformation.* Stanford: Stanford University Press.

Yanaga, Chitoshi. 1968. *Big Business in Japanese Politics,* New Haven: Yale University Press.

Yanagihara, Toru. 1989a. "Financial Flows in the Pacific Basin." In *Perspectives on the Pacific Basin Economy: A Comparison of Asia and Latin America,* ed. Takao Fukuchi and Mitsuhiro Kagami, 107–142. Tokyo.

———, ed. 1989b. *Keizai Kaihatsu Shien to shiteno Shikin Kanryu.* Kenkyu sosho 387. Tokyo: Ajia Keizai Kenkyu jo.

Yarbrough, Beth V., and Robert M. Yarbrough. 1987. "Cooperation in the Liberalization of International Trade: After Hegemony, What?" *International Organization* 41, no. 1:1–26.

———. 1994. "Regionalism and Layered Governance: The Choice of Trade Institutions." *Journal of International Affairs* 48, no. 1:95–117.

Yasutomo, Dennis T. 1983. *Japan and the Asian Development Bank.* New York: Praeger.

———. 1986. *The Manner of Giving: Strategic Aid and Japanese Foreign Policy.* New York: Lexington.

———. 1989/90. "Why Aid? Japan as an 'Aid Great Power.'" *Pacific Affairs* 62, no. 4:490–503.

———. 1995. *The New Multilateralism in Japan's Foreign Policy.* New York: St. Martin's.

Yoon, Young-Kwan. 1990. "The Political Economy of Transition: Japanese Foreign Direct Investments in the 1980s." *World Politics* 43, no. 1:1–27.

Yoshitomi, Masaru. 1989. *Japan's Savings and External Surplus in the World Economy.* Occasional Papers, no. 26. New York: Group of Thirty.

Yoshitomi, Masaru, and Kenich Ohno. 1999. "Capital-Account Crisis and Credit Contraction: The New Nature of Crisis Requires New Policy Responses." ADB Institute Working Paper Series, no. 2, Tokyo, May.

Yoshitomi, Masaru, and Sayuri Shirai. 2000. *Technical Background Paper for Policy Recommendations for Preventing Another Capital Account Crisis.* Tokyo: Asian Development Bank Institute.

Young, Oran R. 1991. "Political Leadership and Regime Formation: On the Development of Institutions in International Society." *International Organization* 45, no. 3:281–308.

Zellner, Arnold. 1962. "An Efficient Method of Estimating Seemingly Unrelated Regressions and Tests for Aggregation Bias." *Journal of the American Statistical Association* 57:348–68.

Zysman, John. 1983. *Governments, Markets, and Growth: Financial Systems and the Politics of Industrial Change.* Ithaca: Cornell University Press.

Index

Page numbers in italics refer to tables and figures.

ADB (Asian Development Bank), 127; in Asian crisis, 174, 178, 179, 197, 260n. 57; Asian Currency Crisis Support Facility, 186, 261n. 61; U.S. and Japanese voting positions in, 240n. 57

AGRI (Asia Growth Recovery Initiative), 185, 260n. 57

aid-doubling plans, 44, 238n. 17

AMF (Asian Monetary Fund), 4–5, 7, 232n. 12; controversy over, 170, 179, 185, 186, 195–98, 262nn. 74, 75, 76, 81; controversy over and Thai crisis, 175–77, 257nn. 12, 16, 17

anarchy, 234n. 20

APEC (Asia Pacific Economic Cooperation): and the AMF, 176; establishment of, 25; on Korean crisis, 178; Manila Framework, 176–77, 257n. 20

Argentina: Convertibility Plan, 150, 251–52n. 19, 252n. 20; IDB loan to, 150; Japanese OOF to, 83, *83;* in Latin American debt crisis, 123, 130, 247n. 15; loans to, 150; Mexican peso crisis effects on, 117, 148, 149–51, 156, 161, 251–52n. 19, 252n. 20, 254n. 62; World Bank loan to, 150

ASEAN (Association of Southeast Asian Nations), 44, 168–69, 186, 197, 232n. 12, 255n. 5

ASEAN+3, 186, 197

Asia: economies of, 216–17, 262–63n. 84, 264n. 7; emerging markets in, 52–53. *See also* Asian crisis; Asian crisis, Japan and U.S. in

ASIAD (Japanese foreign aid to Asia), 91

Asia Growth Recovery Initiative. *See* AGRI

Asian crisis: end of, 255n. 1; IMF-led solutions as threatening Asian economic autonomy, 5, 167–71; and international stability, 5, 232n. 17; vs. Latin American debt crisis, 167–70, 214–16, 255n. 3; vs. Mexican peso crisis, 233n. 5, 255n. 7; U.S. stability during, 232n. 17. *See also* Thai crisis

Asian crisis, Japan and U.S. in, 3, 172–207, 210, 256n. 2; and the ADB, 178, 179, 197, 260n. 57; AGRI, 185, 260n. 57; AMF controversy, 170, 175–77, 179, 185, 186, 195–98, 262nn. 74, 75, 76, 81; and ASEAN+3, 186, 197; Asian Currency Crisis Support Facility, 186, 261n. 61; and Asian economies, 262–63n. 84; and Bank of Japan, 206; Chiang Mai Initiative, 186, 232n. 12; and Clinton administration, 179, 255–56n. 8; and FILP, 181–82; and the IMF, 177–79, 182, 197–98, 199, 205, 258nn. 28, 31, 32, 259n. 45; Indonesian crisis, 177–78, 179–81, 199, 257–58n. 23, 258nn. 24, 25, 258–59n. 36; Japanese interests in Asia, 186–90, *189–90,* 194, 261nn. 64, 65; Japanese private returns, 9, 195, 214; Japanese vs. U.S. involvement, 177–82, 185, 186, 217–18, 257–58n. 23, 258–59n. 36, 259nn. 39, 44, 45; Japan's domestic politics, 199, *200–202,* 203–4, 263nn. 89, 90, 91, 92, 93, 94, 96; Japan's motivation, 171; and JBIC, 185, 260n. 59; and JEXIM Bank, 181–82; Korean crisis, 178–82, 190, 199, 204–7, 258nn. 26, 28, 31, 32, 264n. 100; vs. Latin American debt crisis, 188, 198; Manila Framework, 176–77, 179, 197, 257n. 20, 262n. 81; New Miyazawa Initiative, 5, 6, 183–86, 188, 197, 232n. 12, 256n. 4, 260nn. 57, 58, 59, 261n. 60; OECD support, 179, 258n. 32; secondary/financier role of, 4–5; transnational institutional linkages, 198–99, 263nn. 85, 86; U.S. interest in Japan's recovery, 12; and the U.S.

Asian crisis (*continued*)
Treasury Department, 177; vs. U.S. behavior, 5; U.S.-Japanese relations and U.S. presence, 9, 191–95, *193–94*, 197, 261nn. 68, 69, 262n. 72; and the World Bank, 178, 179, 260n. 57
Asian Currency Crisis Support Facility, 186, 261n. 61
Asian Development Bank. *See* ADB
Asian Monetary Fund. *See* AMF
Asia Pacific Economic Cooperation. *See* APEC
Association of Southeast Asian Nations. *See* ASEAN
Australia, 257n. 9

BACs (bank advisory committees), 10, 31, 110, 140, 141, 212–13
bailouts/rescue packages: concerted lending, 246n. 6; and motivation to cooperate, lead, and follow, 19, 20, 29, 233nn. 3, 5. *See also* Asian crisis, Japan and U.S. in; Latin American debt crisis; Latin American debt crisis, Japan in; Mexican peso crisis; Mexican peso crisis, Japan in; Thai crisis
Baker, James, 125, 126–27
Baker Plan (Program for Sustained Growth), 125, 126–27, 129, 141, 246nn. 10, 11, 12, 247n. 19
Baldwin, David, 233n. 3
bank advisory committees. *See* BACs
Bank for International Settlements. *See* BIS
Bank of America, 124
Bank of England, 124
Bank of Japan, 124, 132, 148–49, 203, 206, 242n. 93
Bank of Thailand, 173–74
Bank of Tokyo, 11, 132, 133, 140, 141, 148n. 48, 204, 263n. 96
Bank of Tokyo-Mitsubishi, 204, 263n. 96
banks: follow-the-leader psychology among, 81; Japanese, bad loans granted by, 261–62n. 71; Japanese, follow-the-customer mentality of, 244n. 25; Japanese, leadership of, 132; Japanese, overseas activities of, 132; and the "Japan Premium," 206; lending by, Japanese, 50–51, 52, 72, 239n. 45, 240n. 50, 242n. 91; project lending of, 263n. 85; rankings of, 60, *64*, 241n. 74; U.S., foreign policy expertise of, 133, 248n. 44. *See also* syndicated loans; *specific banks by name*
Bentsen, Lloyd, 251n. 7
Bidaya, Thanong, 174
BIS (Bank for International Settlements): Brazilian rescue package, 260n. 50; capital adequacy standard of, 72, 161, 192, 242n. 91, 253n. 45, 261n. 70, 261–62n. 71; and Latin American debt crisis, 124, 246n. 5; and Latin American debt crisis, Japan in, 133, 135
Black Monday stock market crash, 69, 231n. 3
bloc economies, exclusive, 1
Bolivia, 123–25
borderlessness in financial world, 30, 235–36n. 42
Boughton, James, 232n. 2
Bradley, Bill, 125
Brady, Nicholas, 129
Brady Plan, 4, 52, 129–30, *131*, 139, 247n. 32, 250n. 83; conversion of debt to bonds, 253–54n. 54; and Japanese banks, 143, 144; Japanese government's contributions to, 145; and resurgence of capital flows to Latin America, 253–54n. 54
Brazil: crisis in, 184, 260nn. 50, 51, 52, 53, 262n. 72; Japanese OOF to, 83, *83;* in Latin American debt crisis, 123, 126, 127, 141, 142; in Mexican peso crisis, 148; migration of Japanese farmers to, 78
Bretton Woods system, 21
Brunei, 257n. 9
bubble economy, 71–72, 241n. 77
BUDGET (overall Japanese central budget), 91, 111
Burma, 237n. 12
Bush, George, 128–29

Cambodia, 237n. 12
Camdessus, Michel, 157, 257n. 12

capital mobility, 236n. 42
Capital Recycling Program, 3; initiation of, 46, 76, 81, 83, 127; Japanese contributions to, 127, 130, 135, 247n. 16; and Japanese foreign aid and OOF, 81, 83, 247n. 18; and Japanese-U.S. relations, 136–37, 249n. 58; and JEXIM Bank, 46, 127, 137; and the MOF, 137; and the OECF, 137, 249n. 59; U.S. firms' involvement in, 137
Carter administration, 65
CASURUS (trade surplus vis-à-vis U.S.), 92, 94, 108
"catch-up process," 41
Cavallo, Domingo, 150, 156
Cayman Islands, 142
Chase Manhattan, 124
Chiang Mai Initiative, 186, 232n. 12
Chile, 102–3
China: and the AMF, 195; and Japan, 42, 44, 168, 169, 255n. 6; and the Thai crisis, 257n. 9
CitiCorp, 124, 126, 149, 161
Cline, William R., 158
Clinton, Bill, 148, 184, 252n. 32, 261n. 68
Clinton administration: and Asian crisis, 179, 255–56n. 8; and Indonesian crisis, 257–58n. 23; and Mexican peso crisis, 7, 122, 145, 148, 151–52, 156, 175, 232n. 13; and Russian crisis, 183
cold war, end of, 154
collective action, 2, 19–34; hegemonic stability theory of k-group formation, 7, 23–24, 211–12, 264n. 2. *See also* motivation to cooperate, lead, and follow
Colombo Plan, 42
Colossio, Donald, 160, 251n. 7
Commercial Bank of Mexico (Bancomext), 149
complex interdependence, 23, 234n. 14
comprehensive security, 44–45, 238n. 22
convoy system, 203, 236n. 50, 248n. 37
Cooke Committee (BIS), 133
cooperation, definition of, 232n. 10
Costa Rica, 83
crisis management, 1–14, 209–19; collective action in (*see* collective action); forms of, 19; and Japanese domestic politics, 10–13; Japan in, 2–5, 232n. 12; and macroeconomic policies, 231n. 1; motivation for, based on private returns for creditor governments, 8–9, 12–13, 119–20; need for external intervention as constant, 232n. 15; as public good, 12, 19; recent crises, 231n. 3; stability as aim of, 2; and transnational linkages among creditor countries, 9–10, 11–13. *See also* Asian crisis; Black Monday stock market crash; crisis management as a joint product; EMS crises; international cooperation and crisis management; Latin American debt crisis; Mexican peso crisis; Third World debt crisis
crisis management as a joint product, 217; and Japanese interests in Asia, 186–90, *189–90,* 194, 261nn. 64, 65; in Latin American debt crisis, 119–20, 131–39, *134,* 248n. 36; in Mexican peso crisis, 119–20, 151–56; and U.S.-Japanese relations in Asian crisis, 9, 191–95, *193–94,* 197, 261nn. 68, 69, 262n. 72
currency-board system, 180, 258n. 35

DAC (Development Assistance Committee), 237–38n. 15
Daiwa Bank, 192, 242n. 93, 263n. 91
Dallara, Charles, 129, 249n. 58
D'Amato, Alfonse, 156
data sources, 223–24, 227–30
debt reduction negotiations, 130, 248n. 35
debt relief, menu approach to, 127, 247nn. 15, 19
de Larosière, Jacques, 124, 246n. 6
developing countries: capital flows to, 52–53, *54–55,* 240nn. 53, 55; dependence on IFIs and OECD members, 154, 253n. 37; and Japan's economic integration, 52–53, *54–55,* 240nn. 53, 55. *See also* "emerging market" countries
development, Japanese model of, 154, 242nn. 88, 89
Development Assistance Committee. *See* DAC

Development Co-operation (OECD), 237–38n. 15
Development Initiative Program, 130
Devlin, Robert, 31, 81, 243nn. 7, 11, 250n. 70
DIFEX (difference in world market share), 91, 107, 245nn. 40, 41
DIFINRT (interest rate differentials between Japan and LIBOR), 95, 112
discipline of debtors, 21
domestic dynamics/politics, 10–13; in Asian crisis, 199, *200–202,* 203–4, 263nn. 88, 89, 90, 91, 92, 93, 94, 96; in Latin American debt crisis, 110–11, 120–21, 139–43, 144, 250nn. 70, 76, 79, 80; in Mexican peso crisis, 120–21, 161–63, 254nn. 66, 68, 70

earthquake insurance, 264n. 5
East Asia. *See* Asia; Asian crisis; Asian crisis, Japan and U.S. in
Economic Planning Agency, 237n. 7
economic structural change, 102–3, 245n. 36
Ecuador, 123–25
EFF (Extended Fund Facility), 130
Egypt, 45
El Salvador, 83
"emerging market" countries, 160, 254n. 56. *See also* developing countries
EMS (European Monetary System) crises, 231n. 3
epistemic communities, 23, 234n. 15
ESF (Exchange Stabilization Fund), 124, 156, 175, 257n. 11
European Community, 25
Euroyen bond market, 51–52
exchange rates: and appreciation of the yen, 50, 57–58, 133, 241n. 68; Bretton Woods fixed system of, 50, 69; yen-dollar fluctuations, 51–52, 69, *70,* 192, 194–95, 241n. 68, 262n. 72. *See also* Mexican peso crisis; Mexican peso crisis, Japan in
Exchange Stabilization Fund. *See* ESF
Export-Import Bank of Japan. *See* JEXIM Bank
Extended Fund Facility. *See* EFF
FDI (foreign direct investment): definition of, 100; Japanese activities, 78–79, 244n. 25; Japanese allocation to North America, 137–38, 249n. 61; and Japan's economic integration, 48–50, *49,* 65, *67,* 68, 239nn. 35, 36, 42, 45
FILP (Fiscal Investment and Loan Program): in Asian crisis, 181–82; and MOF, 239n. 31; OOF as funded by, 88–89, 243nn. 14, 19
Financial Function Early Restoration Law, 261n. 64
Fiscal Investment and Loan Program. *See* FILP
Fischer, Stanley, 197
"flying geese pattern" of industrialization, 50, 239n. 38
foreign aid: vs. economic cooperation, 237n. 7; GNP thresholds for, 46, 238–39n. 30; and Japan's economic integration, 41–42, *43,* 44–46, 237nn. 10, 14, 237–38n. 15, 238nn. 18, 26, 28. *See also specific programs and institutions by name*
foreign direct investment. *See* FDI
Foreign Exchange and Trade Control Law (1980), 51
Fraser, Bernie, 256n. 5
free-rider problem, 6, 19, 56–57, 235n. 37, 240–41n. 64
FTAA (Free Trade Area for the Americas), 252n. 32
Fujikawa, Tesuma, 249n. 58
Fujimori, Alberto, 100, 244n. 30
Fujioka, Masao, 51
Fukuda, Takeo, 44
Fukuda Doctrine, 255n. 5
Fukushima Bank, 241n. 74
functionalism, 234n. 25
fungibility of economic resources/goods, 19, 29–30, 233n. 3

G-5 (Group of Five), 233n. 8
G-7 (Group of Seven), 21, 69, 127–28, 130, 176, 181, 185, 233n. 8, 260n. 55
G-10 (Group of Ten), 72, 233n. 8, 234–35n. 28

G-77 (Group of Seventy-Seven), 42. *See also* UNCTAD
GAB (General Arrangements to Borrow), 233n. 8, 234–35n. 28
General Electric Co., 137
General Motions Interamerica Corp., 137
GGNPPC (GNP per capita of the country), 100, 102, 112
Greenspan, Alan, 251n. 7
Group of Five. *See* G-5
Group of Seven. *See* G-7
Group of Seventy-Seven. *See* G-77
Group of Ten. *See* G-10
Group on the Yen-Dollar Exchange Rate, 51–52
Gurría, José Angel, 151, 156, 252n. 24
GVBOND (Japanese claims to U.S. government bonds), 94, 109

Haas, Peter, 234n. 15
Habibie, B. J., 181
Hashimoto, Ryutaro, 178, 181, 263n. 94
hegemonic stability, theory of, 22–24, 234n. 11
hegemonistic threat of Japan, 65, 71, 241n. 75, 242n. 85
Hokkaido Takushoku Bank, 187–88
Honduras, 83
Hong Kong, 173–74, 177, 252n. 25, 256n. 5, 257n. 9
Hosokawa, Morihiro, 162, 263n. 90
"hot money," 158
HRI Inc., 137
Hungary, 52–53
Hyogo Bank, 263n. 91

IBRD (International Bank for Reconstruction and Development). *See* World Bank
IDA (International Development Association), 127, 139
IDB (Inter-American Development Bank), 132, 155, 260n. 50
IFC (International Finance Corporation), 254n. 56
IFIs (international financial institutions): capital contributions to, 20; developing countries' dependence on, 154, 253n. 37; Japanese contribution allocated among, 127; and Japan in Latin American debt crisis, 138–39, 144, 249nn. 62, 64, 67; and Japan's economic integration, 69; Japan's status/involvement in, 138–39, 153, 154, 155, 249n. 64; rescue packages by, 2
IIMA (Institute for International Monetary Affairs), 263n. 96
IMF (International Monetary Fund), 2, 21; ability to manage crises, 19, 232n. 2; vs. AMF, 175–76, 196–97, 257n. 16; in Asian crisis, 177–79, 182, 197–98, 199, 205, 258nn. 28, 31, 32, 259n. 45; in Asian crisis and Asian economic autonomy, 5, 167–71; Brazilian rescue package, 184, 260nn. 50, 52; capital contributions to, 20; concerted lending by, 246n. 6; EEF credit, 174, 256n. 7; Emergency Financing Mechanism, 174; and Indonesia, 4, 179–81, 258–59n. 36; Interim Committee, 127–28, 135; Japan's contribution to, 127, 247n. 33; Japan's influence in, 247n. 25; Korean rescue packages, 4; and Latin American debt crisis, 124, 126, 128, 130, 246nn. 5, 6, 247n. 33; and motivation to cooperate, lead, and follow, 21–22; vs. OECD, 262n. 79; Philippines supported by, 174, 256n. 7; in Russian crisis, 183, 259–60n. 48; SAF/ESAF, 245n. 36; SRF of, 179, 258n. 32; Thai rescue package, 4, 173, 174, 176–77, 179, 256nn. 7, 8; voting positions in, 138–39, 155, 240n. 57, 249nn. 62, 67. *See also* World Bank/IMF annual meeting
IMMIG (number of Japanese immigrants), 100, 105
indebted industrialization, 51
Indonesia: crisis in, 177–78, 179–81, 199, 257–58n. 23, 258nn. 24, 25, 258–59n. 36; currency, 175, 176, 252n. 25; and IMF, tensions with, 179–81, 258–59n. 36; instability of, continuing, 259n. 38; reparations agreement with Japan, 237n. 12; and Thai crisis, 256n. 5
industrialization, 50, 51, 57, 239n. 38

initiative, lack of, 1
Institute for International Monetary Affairs. *See* IIMA
institutionalization, 21–22, 233n. 8
institutional linkages. *See* transnational institutional linkages
Inter-American Development Bank. *See* IDB
International Bank for Reconstruction and Development (IBRD). *See* World Bank
international cooperation and crisis management, 209–19; forms of, 23, 234n. 13; future prospects of, 218–19; outside-in view of unit-level foreign policy formation, 213–14; regional contrasts in, 214–18; and regionalism, 212–13, 264nn. 3, 4, 5; systemic explanation of, 211–12. *See also* crisis management; motivation to cooperate, lead, and follow
International Development Association. *See* IDA
International Finance Corporation. *See* IFC
international financial institutions. *See* IFIs
International Monetary Fund. *See* IMF
international stability: and Asian crisis, 5, 232n. 17; and Latin American debt crisis, 5, 131; and Mexican peso crisis, 5; as a public good, 209
International Trade Administration (U.S. Dept. of Commerce), 137
interviews and contacts, 225–26

Japan: and Asia/ASEAN countries, 168–69, 255n. 5; autonomy of the state, 32–33; and China, 168, 169, 255n. 6; concern over U.S. economy, 135–38, 249nn. 58, 61; defeat in World War II, 36, 56; domestic economic stability in, 131–35, *134*, 248n. 36; economic-cooperation budget of, 253n. 42; financial/private sectors, political influence of, 10–11, 33, 100–101, 139, 141, 143, 236n. 54; foreign policy behavior of, interpretations of, 6–13; foreign policy of, pillars of, 237n. 7; *gaiatsu* (external pressure), 27, 33, 140; governmental involvement in domestic/international economic activity, 32, 236nn. 49, 50; interest in Asia vs. other developing regions, 6–7; interest rates in, 52, *73*, 138; internationalization of private financial institutions of, 27, 140; Japanese–Latin American relations, in general, 78–81, *82–83*, 83, *84–86;* and Korea, 168; ministries of, 237n. 7; as a nonhegemonic power, 2, 3, 231n. 7; passive/reactive foreign policy of, 6, 26–27, 71, 214; power balance with U.S., 6, 8, 169–70, 191, 240n. 61, 243n. 18; as pursuing selfish economic interests, 6; recession in, 6, *59–61, 70,* 71–74, *73,* 154, 242nn. 88, 89, 91; reconstruction/recovery following World War II, 56; "second image reversed" view in foreign policy of, 27; sovereignty regained by, 56, 168; and United Nations, contributions to, 155; and Vietnam, 168; in World War II, 168–69. *See also* Asian crisis, Japan and U.S. in; Japan's economic integration; Latin American debt crisis, Japan in; Mexican peso crisis, Japan in
Japan Bank for International Cooperation. *See* JBIC
Japanese Foreign Aid Program (International Trade Administration), 137
Japanese-U.S. economic linkages, 8, 11–12
Japanese-U.S. trade balance, 135–36, 191–92, 249n. 53, 259n. 40, 262n. 72
Japan International Cooperation Agency. *See* JICA
Japan Plant Kyokai, 137
Japan's economic integration, 14, 35–75; appreciation of the yen, 50, 57–58, 241n. 68; bank lending, 50–51, 52, 72, 239n. 45, 240n. 50, 242n. 91; banks, ranking of, 60, *64,* 241n. 74; bubble economy, 71–72, 241n. 77; and China, 42, 44; Colombo Plan, 42; and developing countries, 52–53, *54–55,* 240nn. 53, 55; and economic competitiveness,

49; FDI, 48–50, *49,* 65, *67,* 68, 239nn. 35, 36, 42, 45; foreign aid by, 41–42, *43,* 44–46, 237nn. 10, 14, 237–38n. 15, 238nn. 18, 26, 28; free-rider problem, 6, 56–57, 240–41n. 64; hegemonistic threat of Japan, 65, 71, 241n. 75, 242n. 85; and IFIs, 69; industrialization, 57; interest rates, 52, *73;* Japan as source of development finance in general, 36, *37–38,* 39; Japanese importing of manufactured goods, 35, 39, 41, 236n. 1; and Japanese model of development, 242nn. 88, 89; and Japan's foreign policy, 41–42, 44–45, 238n. 22; JEXIM Bank financing of national projects, 49; JEXIM Bank lending policies, 51; JEXIM Bank loans, 46, *47,* 239n. 31; and liberalization of Japanese finance, 50, 51–53, 138; national projects, 48–49, 51, 239n. 36; and natural resources, 48–49; and oil crisis of 1973, 39, 42, 50; OOF, 46–48, *47,* 239n. 31 (*see also* Latin American debt crisis, Japan in); and power asymmetry between Japan and U.S., 240n. 61, 243n. 18; public-private sector interaction, 53; recession in the 1990s, *59–61, 70,* 71–74, *73,* 242nn. 88, 89, 91; reparation agreements, 42, 168, 237n. 12; "rich country" status, 42; and Taiwan, 42; trade, 36, *37–38,* 39, *40,* 41, 237n. 5; trade practices as "unfair," 58, 59–60; U.S.-Japanese relations in general, 53–54, 56, 74–75, 240nn. 56, 57; U.S.-Japanese relations, 1945–70s, 56–57, 241n. 67; U.S.-Japanese relations, 1980s, 57–71, *59–64, 66–68, 70,* 74–75, 241nn. 70, 71, 73, 77, 242n. 83; U.S.-Japanese relations, 1990s, *59–61, 68, 70,* 71–75, *73,* 242nn. 88, 89, 91, 93
JBA Investment, 142
JBIC (Japan Bank for International Cooperation), 185, 237n. 14, 260n. 59
JEXIM Bank (Export-Import Bank of Japan), 4; in Asian crisis, 181–82; and the Brady Plan, 130, *131;* and Capital Recycling Program, 46, 127, 137; commercial orientation of, 42; foreign aid implemented by, 237n. 14; in Indonesian crisis, 185, 259n. 36; and Japan's economic integration, 46, *47,* 49, 51, 239n. 31; and Latin American debt crisis, Japan in, 127, 130, *131;* in Mexican peso crisis, 149, 150, 232n. 11; OOF implemented by, 88–89; in Russian crisis, 259n. 47; in Thai crisis, 174, 258n. 24. *See also* JBIC
JICA (Japan International Cooperation Agency), 88
JLOANO (outstanding Japanese bank loans), 100, 101, 103, 105, 111, 245n. 42
JOFF (Japanese official flows to Latin America), 95, 111
joint product of public/private goods, 19, 28, 29–30, 34, 235nn. 40, 41
JOUT (Japanese bank exposure to Latin American debt), 94, 95
JPRV (Japanese private capital flows to Latin America), 95, 110
Jusen rescue, 263n. 91

k-group formation, 23–24, 211–12, 264n. 2
Kim Dae Jung, 205
Kim Jong Pil, 261n. 60
Kim Yong-sam, 178
Kindleberger, Charles, 57
Kono, Yohei, 252n. 24
Korea, 11; crisis in, 178–82, 190, 199, 204–7, 258nn. 26, 28, 31, 32, 264n. 100; currency of, 176; IMF rescue packages for, 4; indebtedness of, *202,* 205; reparations agreement with Japan, 237n. 12; and the Thai crisis, 257n. 9

laissez-faire policy vs. public intervention, 231n. 2
Laos, 237n. 12
Latin America: emerging markets in, 52–53; Japanese immigrants in, 78, 100, 105; Japanese–Latin American relations in general, 78–81, *82–83,* 83, *84–86*
Latin American debt crisis, 117–22; Argentina in, 123, 130, 247n. 15; vs. Asian

Latin American debt crisis (*continued*) crisis, 167–70, 188, 198, 214–16, 255n. 3; background/causes of, 123–25, 246n. 3; Baker Plan, 125, 126–27, 129, 141, 246nn. 10, 11, 12, 247n. 19; and the BIS, 124, 246n. 5; Bolivia in, 123–25; Brady Plan, 4, 52, 129–30, *131,* 139, 247n. 32, 250n. 83, 253–54n. 54; Brazil in, 123, 126, 127, 141, 142; and Citi-Corp, 124, 126; crisis management as a joint product, 119–20; and decline of U.S. leadership, 1; Ecuador in, 123–25; and the IMF, 124, 126, 128, 130, 246nn. 5, 6, 247n. 33; and international stability, 5, 131; liquidity vs. insolvency, 126; menu approach to debt relief, 127, 247nn. 15, 19; methodology of case study, 118–19; vs. Mexican peso crisis, 157–58, *159,* 160–61, 162–63, 253n. 53, 253–54n. 54, 264n. 6; Mexican rescue packages in, 124, 126, 246nn. 5, 6; Mexico in, 123–24, 126, 130, 141, 246nn. 5, 6; and Morgan Guarantee, 126; Peru in, 124–25; Philippines in, 130; recovery prospects, 145; transnational linkages and domestic dynamics, 120–21; Venezuela in, 130. *See also* Latin American debt crisis, Japan in

Latin American debt crisis, Japan in, 1, 2, 14–15, 74–113, 123–44, 210, 245–46n. 3; bank lending, 79–81, 89, 100–101, 243nn. 7, 8, 15, 244n. 25; and BIS standard, 133, 135; Brady Plan and Japanese banks, 143, 144; controlling variables, 111–12, 245n. 43; crisis management as a joint product, 131–39, *134,* 248n. 36; debt reduction negotiations, 130, 248n. 35; domestic economic stability in Japan, 131–35, *134,* 248n. 36; factors increasing Japanese commitment, 77–78; FDI activities by Japan, 78–79, 244n. 25; Japan and the IFIs, 138–39, 144, 249nn. 62, 64, 67; Japanese–Latin American relations, in general, 78–81, *82–83,* 83, *84–86;* Japanese private capital flows to Latin America, 248n. 49; Japanese-U.S. economic linkages, 8, 11–12; Japanese-U.S. trade balance, 135–36, 249n. 53; Japan's concern over U.S. economy, 135–38, 249nn. 58, 61; Japan's debt exposure, 133, *134,* 140–41, 148nn. 45, 47, 48; Japan's economic interests as limited, 6; Japan's financial sector in Latin America, 8; Japan's involvement, 123–30; Japan's nonpresence in Latin America, 6–7; and JBA Investment, 142; and JEXIM Bank, 127, 130, *131;* methodology of analysis of, 77, 87–88, 242n. 2; Miyazawa Plan, 3, 4, 6, 123, 127–29, 135, 143, 184, 247nn. 19, 25; models, regression, operationalization of variables, and results from time series, 89–98, *90, 93, 95, 97,* 243nn. 16, 19, 244nn. 24, 25; models, regression, operationalization of variables, and results from time-series cross-section data, 98–105, *104,* 244nn. 28, 29, 32, 245nn. 36, 39; models with financial flows disaggregated by ODA, OOF, and private flows, 88–89; ODA and OOF allocation over time, 81, *82–86,* 83; ODA vs. OOF, 77, 88, 242–43n. 4, 243n. 13 (*see also specific models by name*); and OECF, 127; and organizing variables, 87–88; and population, 103; private/public benefits constructing a joint product, 87, 105, *106,* 107–10, 245nn. 39, 40, 41; transnational linkages, 87, 113, 121; transnational linkages and domestic dynamics, 110–11, 139–43, 144, 250nn. 70, 76, 79, 80; U.S. debt exposure, 135, 140–41; and U.S.-Japanese relations, 81, 87, 92, 113, 121–22, 244n. 21; and variables of interests, 87; and the World Bank, 130. *See also* Capital Recycling Program; Mexican peso crisis

LDC (less developed countries) tied loans, 238n. 26

LDP (Liberal Democratic Party), 236n. 54; and the financial bureaucracy/sector, 146, 215; level of support for, 91–92, 112; loss of majority position, 146, 162, 203; and MOF, 162, 254n. 70, 263n. 90

LDPSP (public support to LDP), 91–92, 112
leadership, definition of, 240n. 61
lender-of-last-resort arrangements, 25, 142, 231n. 5, 234–35n. 28, 235n. 29
Liberal Democratic Party. *See* LDP
LIBOR (London Interbank Offered Rate), 244n. 24
London Club, 31
London Interbank Offered Rate. *See* LIBOR
Long-Term Credit Bank of Japan, 132, 133
LTFLW (Japanese claims to U.S. long-term securities), 92, 94, 109

Maekawa, Haruo, 124
Mahathir, Mohamad, 257n. 17, 261n. 60
major nonhegemonic power, definition of, 3, 231n. 9
Malaysia, 173–74, 256n. 5, 257n. 9
Manila Framework, 176–77, 179, 197, 257n. 20, 262n. 81
Mansfield, Mike, 240n. 56
Marakanond, Rerngchai, 174
maturity transformation, 52, 240n. 50
Menem, Carlos, 150, 251–52n. 19
Mercosur, 25
methodology, 13–14, 118–19, 232nn. 19, 21
Mexican peso crisis, 231n. 3; Argentina affected by, 117, 148, 149–51, 156, 161, 251–52n. 19, 252n. 20, 254n. 62; vs. Asian crisis, 233n. 5, 255n. 7; Asian economies affected by, 252n. 25; BIS rescue package, 151–52, 252n. 28; Brazil in, 148; and Clinton administration, 122, 151–52, 156, 175; crisis management as a joint product, 119–20; Europe's limited involvement in, 148, 151, 251n. 10, 252n. 28; IMF loan to Argentina, 150; and Indonesian crisis, 252n. 25; and international stability, 5; vs. Latin American debt crisis, 157–58, *159,* 160–61, 162–63, 253n. 53, 253–54n. 54, 264n. 6; methodology of case study, 118–19; Mexican stock market drop, 147, 148; Mexico's recovery from, 149; the Philippines in, 148; as systemic, 151, 232n. 13, 252n. 26; transnational linkages and domestic dynamics, 120–21; U.S. engagement in, 151–53, 156, 163, 252n. 31. *See also* Mexican peso crisis, Japan in
Mexican peso crisis, Japan in, 2–3, 145–63; bank lending, 153, 252–53n. 35; and Bank of Japan, 148–49; and Bank of Tokyo, 149, 151; BIS rescue package, 147–49, 161, 254n. 63; and CitiCorp, 149, 161; and Clinton administration, 145, 148; crisis management as joint product, 151–56; domestic dynamics, 161–63, 254nn. 66, 68, 70; and Fuji Bank, 149; IDB loans, 148; and the IMF, 145, 148; and Industrial Bank of Japan, 149; international/domestic change and Japan's motivation, 154–56, 253nn. 37, 45, 253nn. 40, 41; and international financial environment, changes in, 145–46; and Japan's economic/political conditions, changes in, 146; Japan's financial-sector exposure, 10–11; Japan's initial support, 148–49, 251n. 11; Japan's limited involvement, 4, 11, 117, 147–51, 152, 163, 251nn. 12, 16, 252nn. 24, 34; Japan's private returns, 8–9, 153; Japan's stake in supporting U.S., 12; and JEXIM Bank, 149, 150, 232n. 11; Mexican foreign exchange reserve, 147, 251n. 4; and MOF encouragement of Japanese lending to Mexico, 251n. 16; and Morgan Guarantee, 149, 161; rescue package, 147–48; and Sumitomo Bank, 149; swap agreement, 148, 251n. 7; Tequila Effect, 150; Tesobonos, 147; transnational institutional linkages among financial sectors, 157–61, *159,* 253n. 53, 253–54n. 54; and U.S. vs. Japanese economic growth, *59,* 153; U.S.-IMF rescue package, 149; World Bank loans, 148
Mexico: emerging markets of, 145; Japanese FDI in, 239n. 35; Japanese OOF to, 83, *83;* in Latin American debt crisis, 123–24, 126, 130, 141, 246nn. 5, 6;

Mexico: emerging markets of (*continued*) migration of Japanese farmers to, 78; rescue packages for, 124, 126, 246nn. 5, 6. *See also* Latin American debt crisis; Mexican peso crisis
Ministry of Finance. *See* MOF
Ministry of Foreign Affairs. *See* MOFA
Ministry of International Trade and Industry. *See* MITI
"Misperception and Truth about the Economies of Asia and Japan" (MOFA), 182
MITI (Ministry of International Trade and Industry), 44, 46, 51, 149, 237n. 7
Mitsubishi Bank, 11, 204. *See also* Bank of Tokyo-Mitsubishi
Mitsui Bank, 133
Mitsuzuka, Hiroshi, 174, 175–76
Miyazawa, Kiichi, 184, 197
Miyazawa Plan, 3, 4, 6, 123, 127–29, 135, 143, 184, 247nn. 19, 25. *See also* New Miyazawa Initiative
Mobilizing International Surpluses for World Development, 142–43
MOF (Ministry of Finance), 11, 237n. 7; and the AMF, 195–96, 262n. 74; banking deregulation by, 79; on bank lending, 51, 239n. 45; convoy system of, 203, 236n. 50, 248n. 37; corruption in/status of, 203–4, 263nn. 91, 93; and Daiwa Bank, 192, 263n. 91; and FILP, 239n. 31; Foreign Exchange Fund Special Account, 206; International Finance Bureau, 195, 197; and JBA Investment, 142; and the Korean crisis, 206; and LDP, 162, 254n. 70, 263n. 90; and loan-loss reserves, 141–42, 250nn. 76, 79, 80; price-keeping operation of, 203, 253n. 41, 263n. 89; as protector of Japanese banks, 133, 135, 142, 203–4, 248nn. 37, 48; reaction to Black Monday, 69; syndicated lending encouraged by, 80, 132, 243n. 8, 248n. 42
MOFA (Ministry of Foreign Affairs), 237n. 7; on Mexican rescue package, 124; "Misperception and Truth about the Economies of Asia and Japan," 182
Mondale, Walter, 181, 258–59n. 36
Morgan, J. P., 120, 161
Morgan Guarantee, 126
MOSS (Market-Oriented Sector Selective) talks, 58
motivation to cooperate, lead, and follow, 14, 19–34; and bailouts/rescue packages, 19, 20, 29, 233nn. 3, 5; and complex interdependence, 23, 234n. 14; and costs of public goods, 19; and discipline of debtors, 21; and epistemic communities, 23, 234n. 15; and financial flows as public goods, 235n. 36; and free riding, 19, 235n. 37; and fungibility of economic resources/goods, 19, 29–30, 233n. 3; and the IMF, 21–22; and institutionalization, 21–22, 233n. 8; international cooperation, forms of, 23, 234n. 13; and joint product of public/private goods, 19, 28, 29–30, 34, 235nn. 40, 41; and k-group formation, 23–24, 211–12, 264n. 2; and lender-of-last-resort arrangements, 25, 234–35nn. 28, 29; and nonregional arrangements, 234–35n. 28; and power asymmetry, 24, 32, 236n. 46; and prisoner's dilemma, 21; and regionalism, 20, 24–26, 234n. 25; "second image reversed" view, 27, 32; and sources of Japan's actions in crisis management, 27–28; systemic explanation of, 22–24, 234nn. 11, 13, 15; and taxpayer resistance, 20; and transnational linkages, 23, 28, 30–34, 235–36n. 42, 235n. 35, 236n. 46; unit-level factors in, 26–27. *See also* international cooperation and crisis management
Mulford, David, 145
Murayama, Tatsuo, 129–30
mutual funds, 161, 254n. 62

NAB (New Arrangements to Borrow), 174, 235n. 28
NAFA (North American Framework Agreement), 25, 251n. 7
NAFTA (North American Free Trade Agreement), 25, 145, 152, 251n. 7
Nakao, Shigeo, 52, 65, 241n. 75
Nakasone, Yasuhiro, 127

national projects, 48–49, 51, 78–79, 239n. 36
natural resources, 48–49
neofunctionalism, 234n. 25
New Arrangements to Borrow. *See* NAB
New Japan Party (Nihon Shinto), 162
New Miyazawa Initiative, 5, 6, 183–86, 188, 197, 232n. 12, 256n. 4, 260nn. 57, 58, 59, 261n. 60
news data, 228–30
Nihon Keizai Shimbun, 124
Nippon Credit Bank (Nissaigin), 242n. 91, 261–62n. 71
nonhegemonic interdependence, 154, 253n. 40
North American Framework Agreement. *See* NAFA
North American Free Trade Agreement. *See* NAFTA
North-North debt crisis, 74–75
North-South debt crisis, 74

Obuchi, Keizo, 184, 185, 261n. 68
ODA (official development assistance) donors, *38,* 42, 44–46, 238nn. 16, 18, 27, 28; allocation over time, 81, *82–86,* 83; ASIAD, 91; definition of, 242–43n. 4; five-year Japanese plan, 128; implementing agencies of, 88; Japan's contributions, 155, 253n. 42; and Latin American debt crisis, 76, 81, *82–86,* 83, 88–89; vs. OOF, 77, 88, 242–43n. 4, 243n. 13; to Paraguay, 83; to Peru, 83, 244n. 30. *See also* foreign aid
OECD (Organization for Economic Cooperation and Development), 42, 46, 237–38n. 15; in Asian crisis, 179, 258n. 32; developing countries' dependence on, 154, 253n. 37; on Financial Support Fund, 262n. 79; vs. IMF, 262n. 79; Mexican membership in, 145
OECF (Overseas Economic Cooperation Fund), 42, 45, 46, 49, 51, 88, 127, 237n. 14, 238–39n. 30. *See also* JBIC
official development assistance donors. *See* ODA donors
Ohira, Masayoshi, 238n. 22
oil crisis (1973), 39, 42, 50
OMAs (orderly marketing agreements), 58
Omnibus Trade and Competitiveness Act (1988), 58–59
OOF (other official flows), 46–48, *47,* 239n. 31; allocation over time, 81, *82–86,* 83; definition of, 242–43n. 4; funding of, 88–89, 243n. 14; vs. ODA, 77, 88, 242–43n. 4, 243n. 13. *See also* Latin American debt crisis, Japan in
OPEC (Organization of Petroleum Exporting Countries), 80
OPEN (debtor country's openness to world trade), 102–3, 110
orderly marketing agreements. *See* OMAs
Organization for Economic Cooperation and Development. *See* OECD
Organization of Petroleum Exporting Countries. *See* OPEC
Overseas Economic Cooperation Fund. *See* OECF
Ozawa, Ichiro, 263n. 90

Pakistan, Japanese foreign aid to, 45
Panama, 239n. 35
Paraguay, 78, 83
PBL (policy-based lending), 45, 137
Persian Gulf crisis (1990–91), 155, 240–41n. 64
Peru, 78, 83, 124–25, 244n. 30
Petroleo Mexicano, 252–53n. 35
Philippines: currency affected by Mexican peso crisis, 252n. 25; in Latin American debt crisis, 130; reparations agreement with Japan, 237n. 12; and the Thai crisis, 174, 256n. 7
Plaza Accord (1985), 57–58, 69, 136
policy-based lending. *See* PBL
POP (country's population), 100, 112
population, 103
power asymmetry: Japan-U.S., 6, 8, 169–70, 191, 240n. 61, 243n. 18; and motivation to cooperate, lead, and follow, 24, 32, 236n. 46
prisoner's dilemma, 21
private/public benefits constructing a joint product, 87, 105, *106,* 107–10, 245nn. 39, 40, 41

private returns: definition of, 8; Japanese and Asian crisis, 9, 195, 214; Japanese and Mexican peso crisis, 8–9, 153; as motivation for crisis management, 8–9, 12–13, 119–20
Program for Sustained Growth. *See* Baker Plan
public good/goods: costs of, 19; definition of, 231n. 4; financial flows as, 235n. 36; international crisis management as, 1; joint product of public/private goods, 19, 28, 29–30, 34, 235nn. 40, 41; as nonexclusionary, 19; vs. private good, 8, 232n. 16
public-private sector interaction, 53

Ragin, Charles, 118
Reagan administration, inflation stabilization under, 65
Reaganomics, 65
regime theory, 211
regionalism: and functionalism, 234n. 25; and international cooperation, 212–13, 264nn. 3, 4, 5; and motivation to cooperate, lead, and follow, 20, 24–26, 234n. 25
reparations agreements, 42, 237n. 12
rescue packages. *See* bailouts/rescue packages
Risse-Kappen, Thomas, 26
Rosecrance, Richard, 71, 243n. 18
Rubin, Robert, 184, 205
Russian crisis, 183, 259–60nn. 46, 47, 48, 262n. 72

Sachs, Jeffrey, 135–36, 243n. 20, 249nn. 53, 54
SAF/ESAF (Structural Adjustment Facility and Enhanced Structural Adjustment Facility by the IMF), 245n. 36
Sakakibara, Eisuke, 176, 242n. 88, 259n. 45, 262n. 75
Sakigake Party, 263n. 90
SAL (Structural Adjustment Loan by the World Bank), 245n. 36
Schoppa, Leonard J., 27
SECALs (Sector Adjustment Loans), 130
"second image reversed" view, 27, 32
"second line of defense," 258n. 24
Sector Adjustment Loans. *See* SECALs
Security Supporting Assistance (U.S.), 45
semiconductors, 59, 241n. 73
SII (Structural Impediments Initiative), 27, 58
Silva Herzog, Jesús, 123, 158
Singapore, 173–74, 256n. 5, 257n. 9
Sino-Japanese Peace and Friendship Treaty (1978), 44
Snidal, Duncan, 23
Social Democratic Party, 263n. 90
Southeast Asia. *See* Asia; Asian crisis; Asian crisis, Japan and U.S. in
South Korea. *See* Korea
South Vietnam, 237n. 12
Soviet Union, 56, 154
Spindler, Andrew, 80
SRF (Supplemental Reserve Facility), 179, 258n. 32
statistical sources, 227–28
strategic aid, 45. *See also* foreign aid
Structural Adjustment Facility and Enhanced Structural Adjustment Facility by the IMF. *See* SAF/ESAF
Structural Adjustment Loan by the World Bank. *See* SAL
Structural Impediments Initiative. *See* SII
Sudan, 45
Suharto, 180–81
Sumitomo Bank, 132
Summit of Americas (1994), 252n. 32
Supplemental Reserve Facility. *See* SRF
syndicated loans, 10, 79, 81, 243nn. 6, 11; cross-default clauses of, 140, 158; Japanese banks' leadership in, 140, 250n. 70; MOF encouragement of, 80, 132, 243n. 8, 248n. 42; and project lending, 263n. 85; U.S. banks' reliance on Japanese banks' expertise on, 250n. 70

Takeshita, Noburu, 45, 128–29
Taw, Jennifer, 71, 243n. 18

Thai crisis, 4, 6, 9, 11, 155–56; and the ADB, 174; AMF controversy, 175–77, 257nn. 12, 16, 17; Asian support in, 174, 257n. 9; currency, 173–74, 256n. 5; IMF rescue package, 173, 174, 176–77, 179, 256nn. 7, 8; and Indonesian crisis, 256n. 5; U.S. limited involvement, 174–75, 177; U.S. relations with, 257n. 22
Thailand's reparations agreement with Japan, 237n. 12
Third World debt crisis, 52, 74, 231n. 3, 242n. 3
tied loans, 45, 238n. 26
Tokyo Stock Exchange, 203
Toronto Summit (1988), 45, 127–28
trade: and financial flows, 80; Japanese-U.S. trade balance, 135–36, 191–92, 249n. 53, 259n. 40, 262n. 72; minilateral arrangements, 25. *See also* Japan's economic integration
TRADE (Japanese trade with the country), 100, 101, 103
transnational institutional linkages, 9–10, 13, 210, 217; in Asian crisis, 198–99, 263nn. 85, 86; and domestic dynamics, 110–11, 139–43, 144, 250nn. 70, 76, 79, 80; and domestic dynamics in Latin American debt crisis, 120–21; institutional vs. economic, 31–32, 235n. 35, 236n. 46; Japanese-U.S. economic linkages, 8, 11–12; in Latin American debt crisis, 87, 113, 121; in Latin American debt crisis and Japanese domestic dynamics, 110–11, 120–21, 139–43, 144, 250nn. 70, 76, 79, 80; in Mexican peso crisis, 120–21, 157–61, *159,* 253n. 53, 253–54n. 54; and motivation to cooperate, lead, and follow, 23, 28, 30–34, 235–36n. 42, 235n. 35, 236n. 46; in Thai crisis, 199
Turkey, 52–53

UNCTAD (United Nations Conference on Trade and Development), 42. *See also* G-77
UN General Assembly, 245n. 38
United Nations Conference on Trade and Development. *See* UNCTAD
United Nations University. *See* UNU
United States: budget/trade deficits of, 65, 259n. 40; and cold war security, 56; debt exposure in Latin America, 135, 140–41; economic stagnation of, 58, *59–61,* 65; foreign aid by, 45, 238n. 27; hegemony of, 56, 57, 91, 169–70; interest rates in, 52, 73, *73;* investments in Mexico, 242n. 92; leadership of, decline of, 1; opposition to Japan's crisis management, 7; prosperity in 1990s, *59–61, 70,* 71–74, *73;* relations with Japan (*see* Japan's economic integration); savings and loan problems of, 191; Security Supporting Assistance from, 45; stock market growth/declines in, 191, 261n. 67; trade balance deterioration of, 92, 243n. 20
UN Security Council, 103, 245n. 38
UNU (United Nations University), 142–43
U.S. Federal Reserve Bank, 272n. 72
U.S. Federal Reserve Board, 124
U.S. Senate Committee on Finance, 136
U.S. Treasury Department, 177
USAID (U.S. aid to Latin America), 92–93, 101, 109
USOUT (U.S. bank exposure to Latin American debt), 95, 110
USPRV (lagged residuals from cointegrating regression), 95
USTRD (U.S. trade with a country), 102, 105, 109

Venezuela, 83, 130
Venice Summit (1987), 127, 247n. 18
VERs (voluntary export restraints), 58
Vogel, Ezra F., 241n. 67
Volcker, Paul, 65
voluntary export restraints. *See* VERs

Wall Street–Treasury–IMF complex, 264n. 7
Wells Fargo, 243n. 11

WIDER (World Institute for Development Economics Research), 142–43
World Bank, 21, 132; in Asian crisis, 178, 179, 260n. 57; Brazilian rescue package, 260n. 50; capital contributions to, 20; *The East Asian Miracle,* 69; Japan's contributions to/voting position in, 139, 155; Japan Special Fund, 127; and Latin American debt crisis, Japan in, 130; in Mexican peso crisis, 148, 150; and Russian crisis, 183; SAL, 245n. 36; in Thai crisis, 174; U.S. and Japanese voting positions in, 240n. 57
World Bank/IMF annual meeting, 125, 126–27, 128, 173, 175–76, 183, 185
World Institute for Development Economics Research. *See* WIDER

Yamaichi Securities, 187–88
Yamamura, Kozo, 65, 241n. 77
Yeltsin, Boris, 183
yen: appreciation of, 50, 57–58, 241n. 68; internationalization of, 51–52. *See also* exchange rate
Yen-Dollar Agreement (1984), 69
Yim Chang-yol, 178
Yoshida Doctrine, 41, 237n. 7
YVSUSD (value of yen vs. U.S. dollar), 107, 245n. 41

Zedillo, Ernesto, 149